NORAGAMI
STRAY GOD

ADACHITOKA

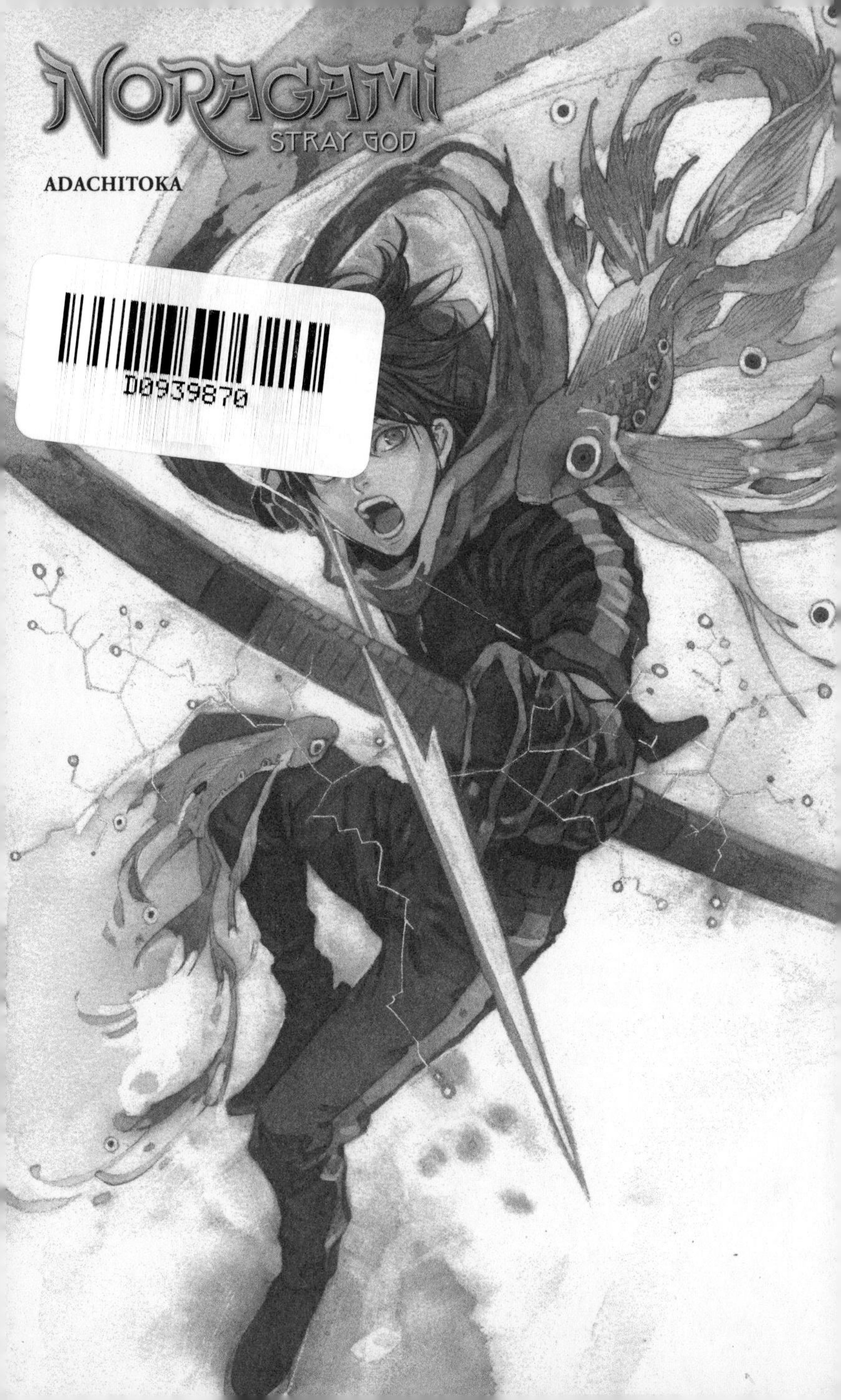

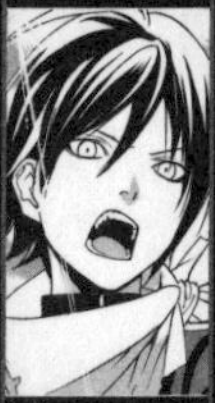

YATO
A minor deity who always wears a sweatsuit.

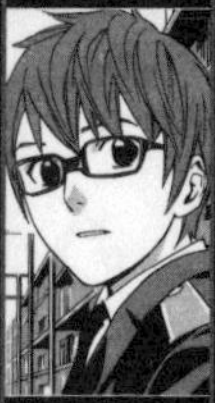

KAZUMA/ KAZUNÉ
Bishamon's shinki who now works for Yato.

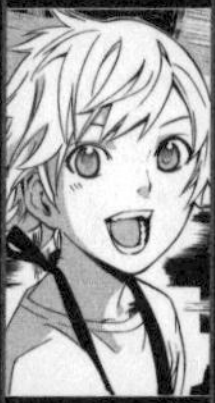

YUKINÉ
Yato's shinki who turns into swords.

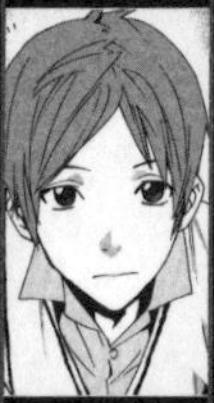

KÔTO FUJISAKI
The crafter who disrupts the world order. Yato's father.

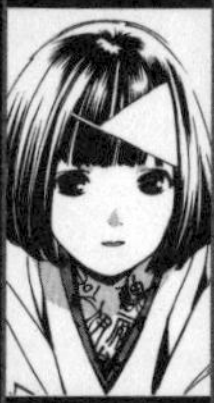

STRAY
A shinki who serves an unspecified number of deities.

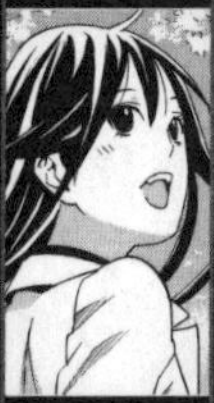

HIYORI IKI
A high school student who has become half ayakashi.

characters

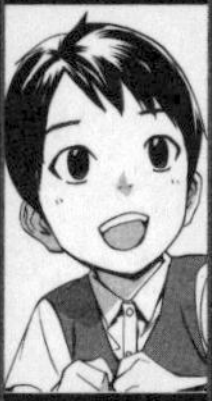

EBISU
A business-god in the making, one of the Seven Gods of Fortune.

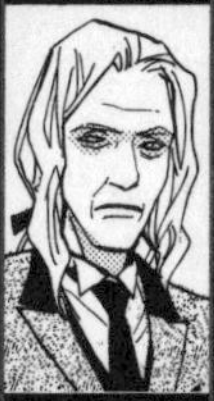

IWAMI
A shinki who knows Ebisu's history.

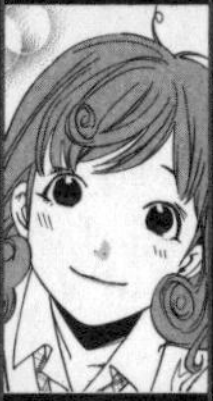

KOFUKU
A goddess of poverty who calls herself Ebisu after the god of fortune.

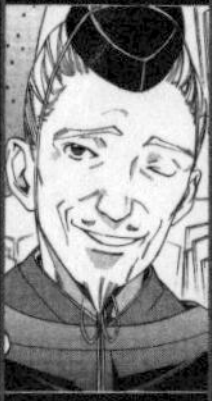

TENJIN
The god of learning, Sugawara no Michizane.

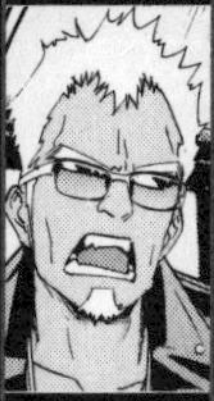

ÔKUNI-NUSHI (DAIKOKU-TEN)
Number one of the Seven Gods of Fortune.

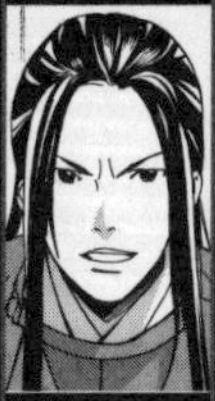

TAKE-MIKAZUCHI
A warrior god who causes Brave Lightning to strike the earth.

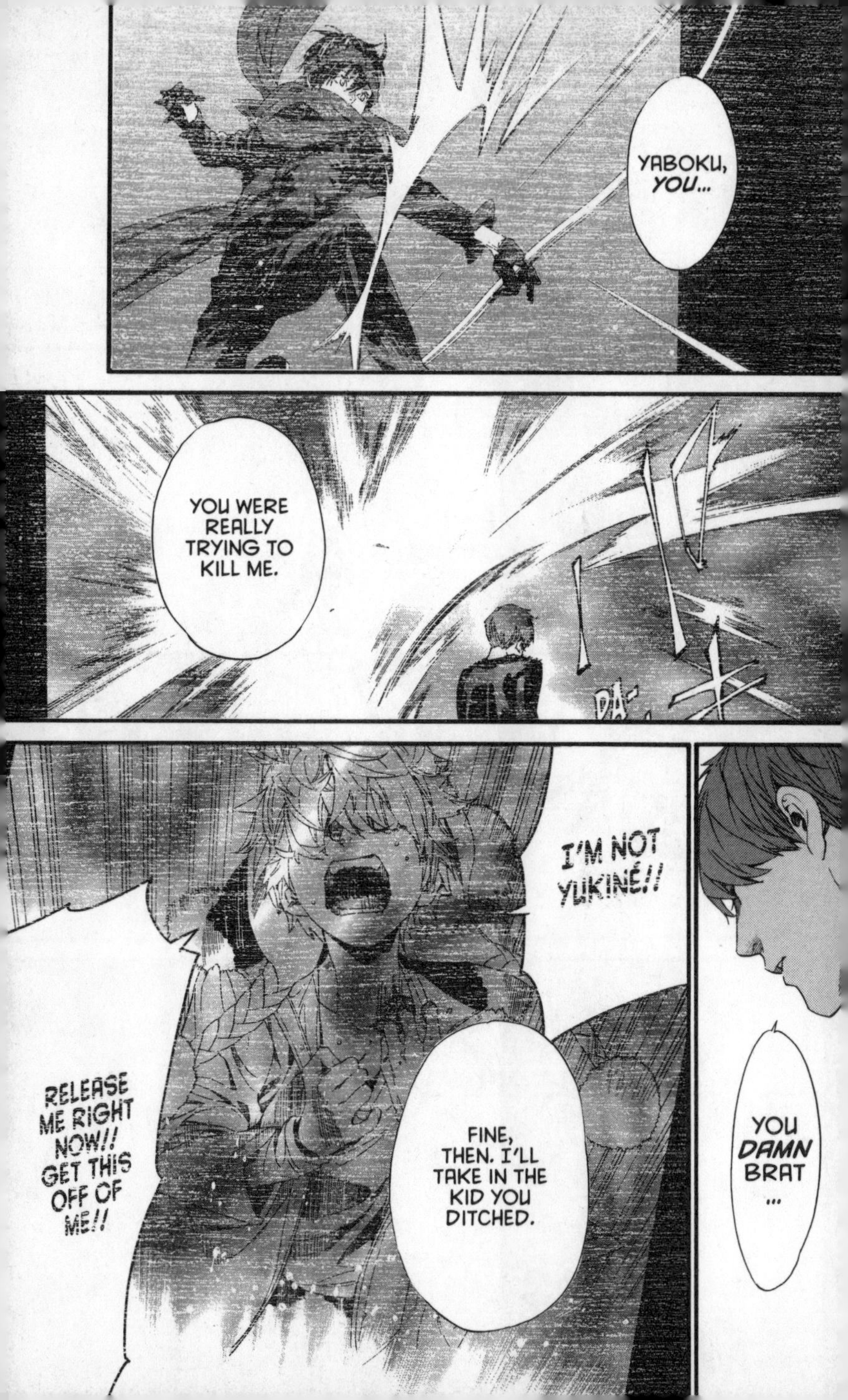
YABOKU, YOU...
YOU WERE REALLY TRYING TO KILL ME.
DA-
YOU DAMN BRAT ...
I'M NOT YUKINÉ!!
FINE, THEN. I'LL TAKE IN THE KID YOU DITCHED.
RELEASE ME RIGHT NOW!! GET THIS OFF OF ME!!

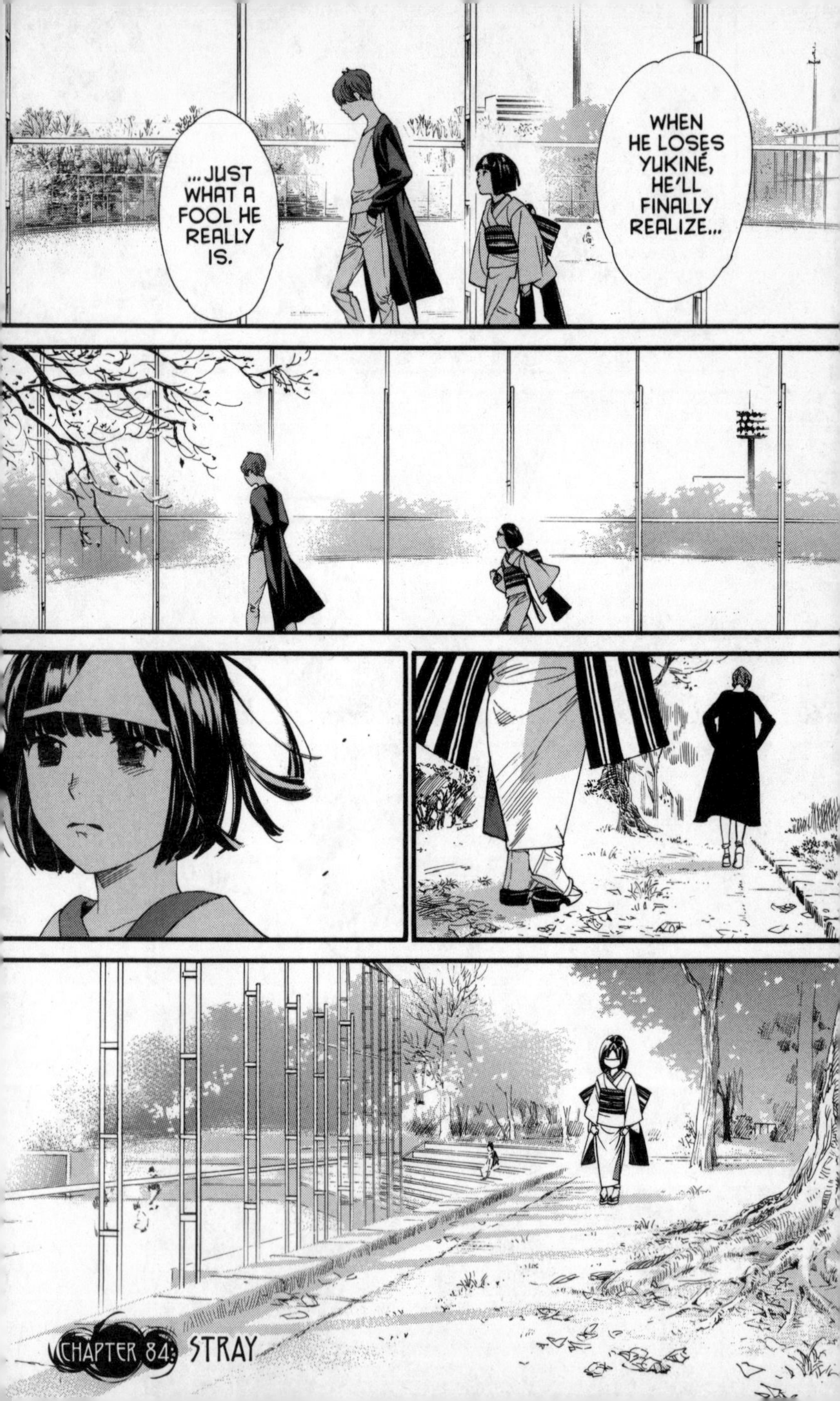
WHEN HE LOSES YUKINÉ, HE'LL FINALLY REALIZE...
...JUST WHAT A FOOL HE REALLY IS.
CHAPTER 84: STRAY

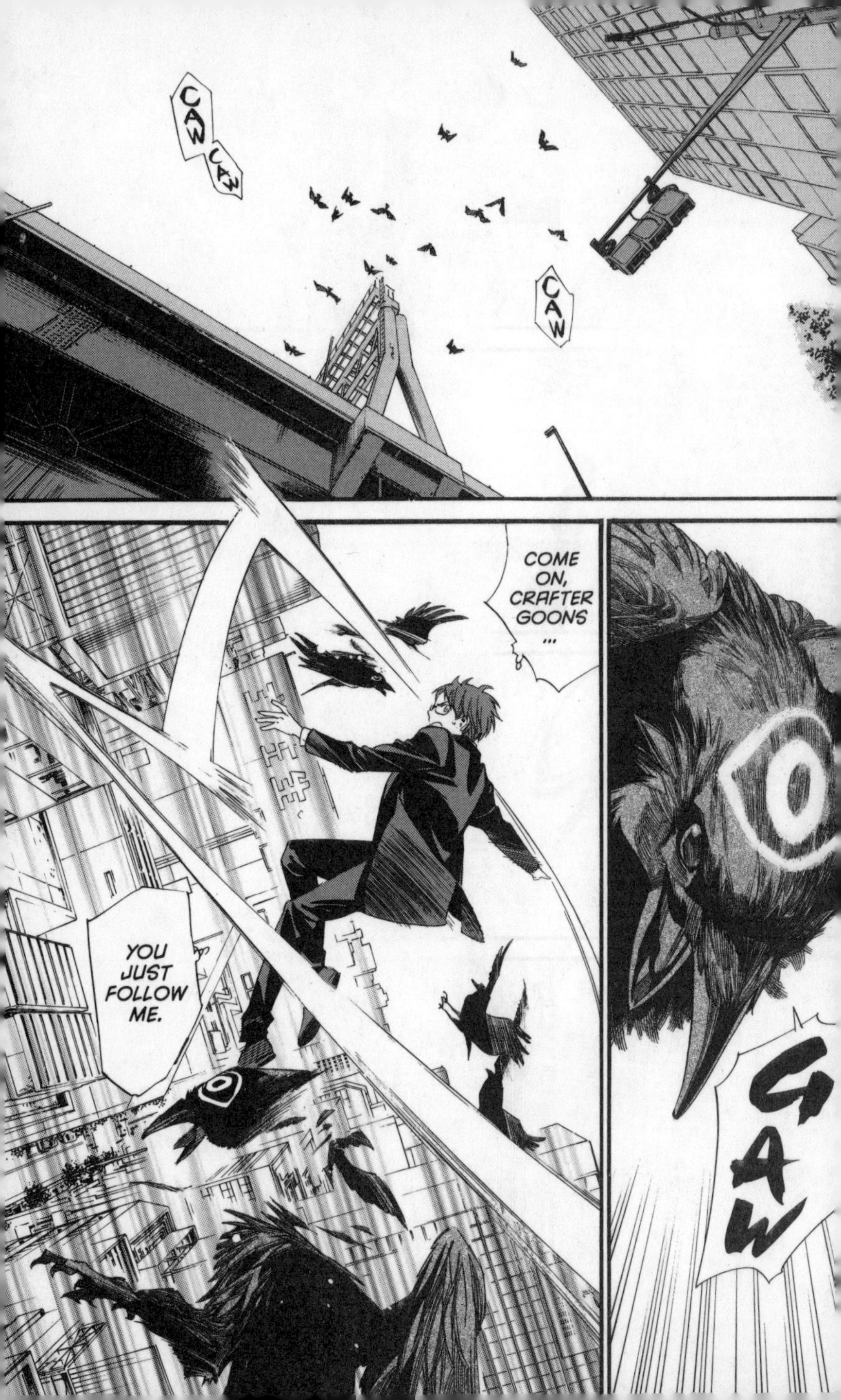
CAW CAW
CAW
GAW
COME ON, CRAFTER GOONS ...
YOU JUST FOLLOW ME.

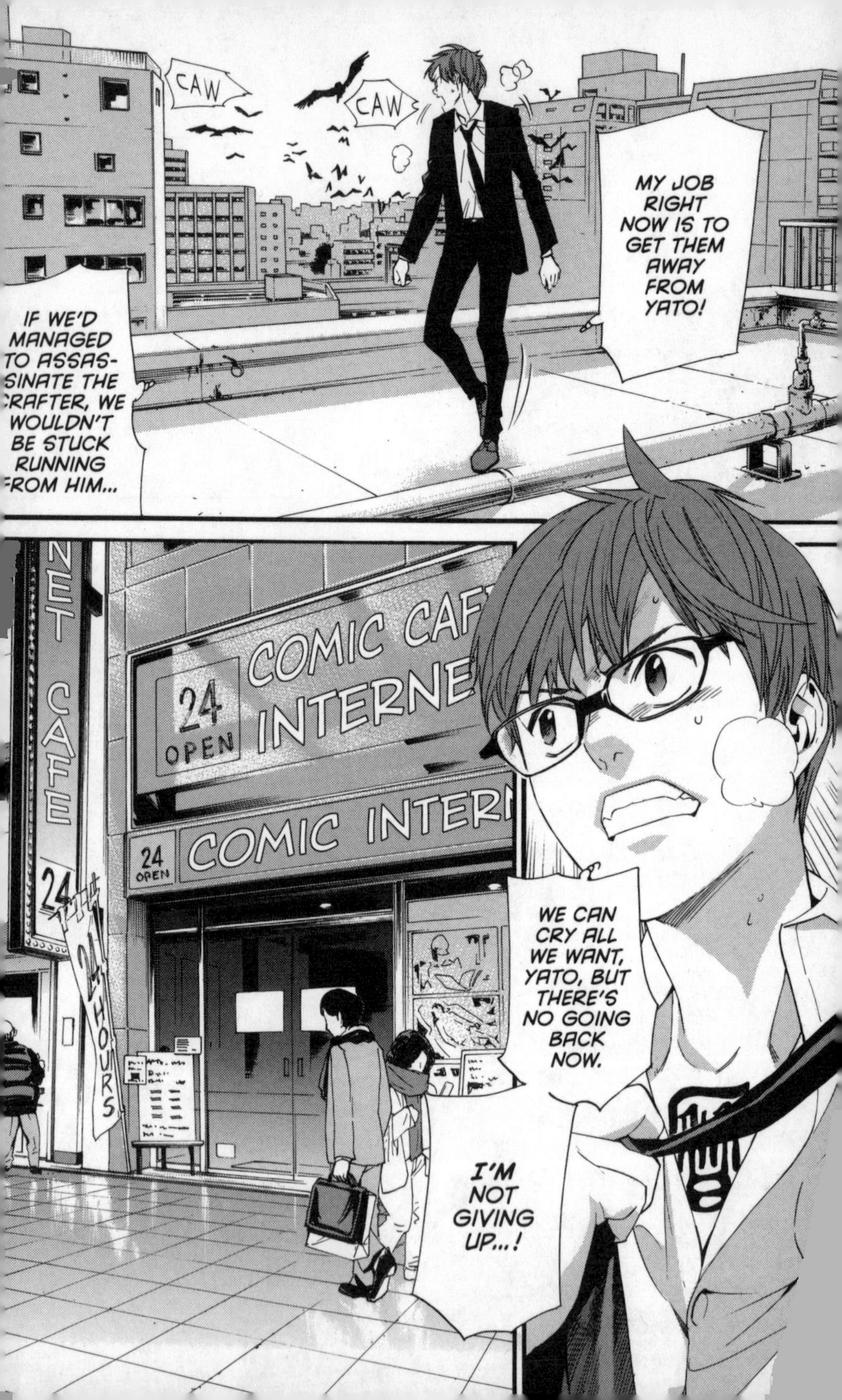
CAW
CAW
MY JOB RIGHT NOW IS TO GET THEM AWAY FROM YATO!
IF WE'D MANAGED TO ASSAS-SINATE THE CRAFTER, WE WOULDN'T BE STUCK RUNNING FROM HIM...
COMIC CAF
INTERNE
24 OPEN
COMIC INTER
24 OPEN
NET CAFE
24
24 HOURS
WE CAN CRY ALL WE WANT, YATO, BUT THERE'S NO GOING BACK NOW.
I'M NOT GIVING UP...!

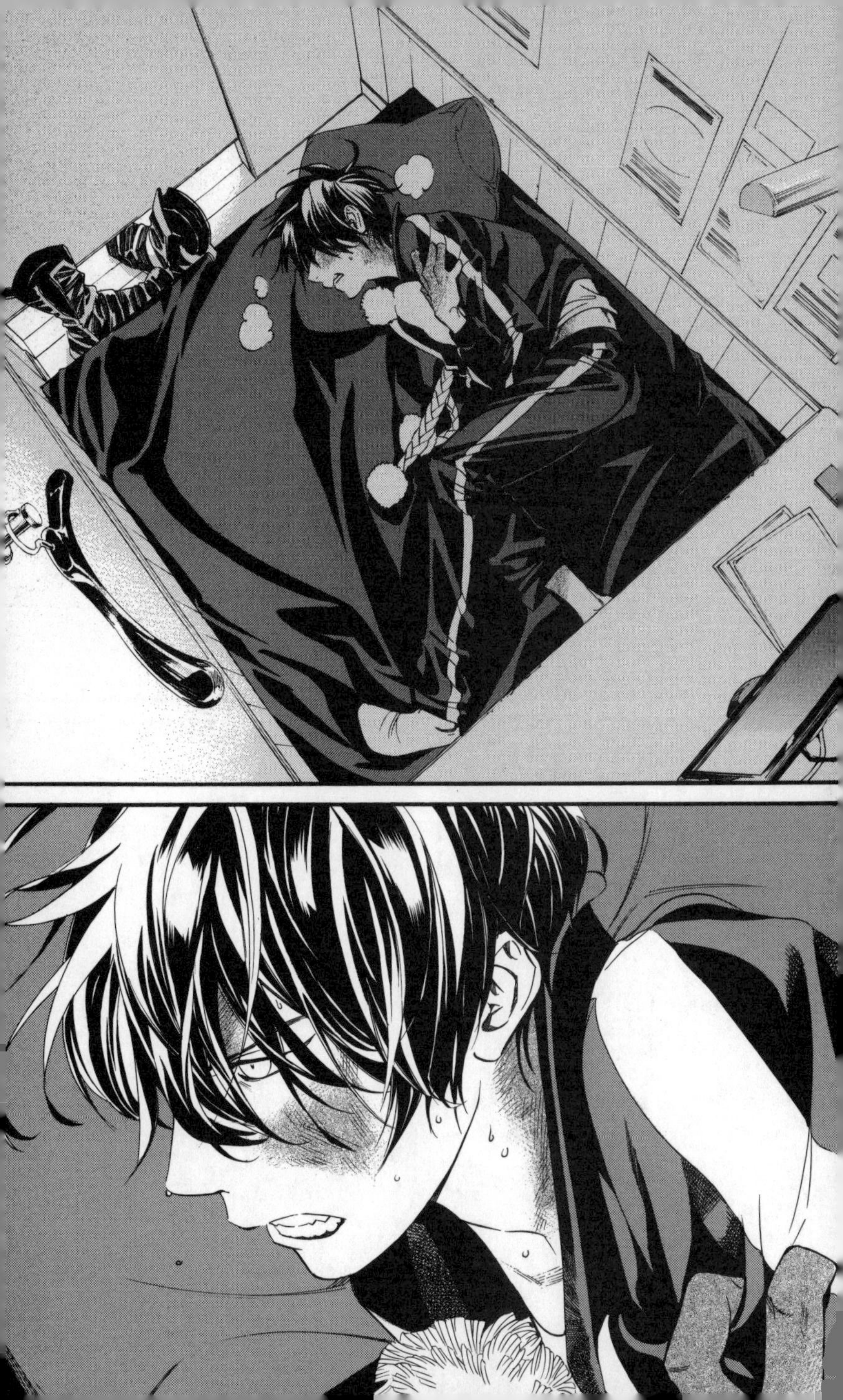

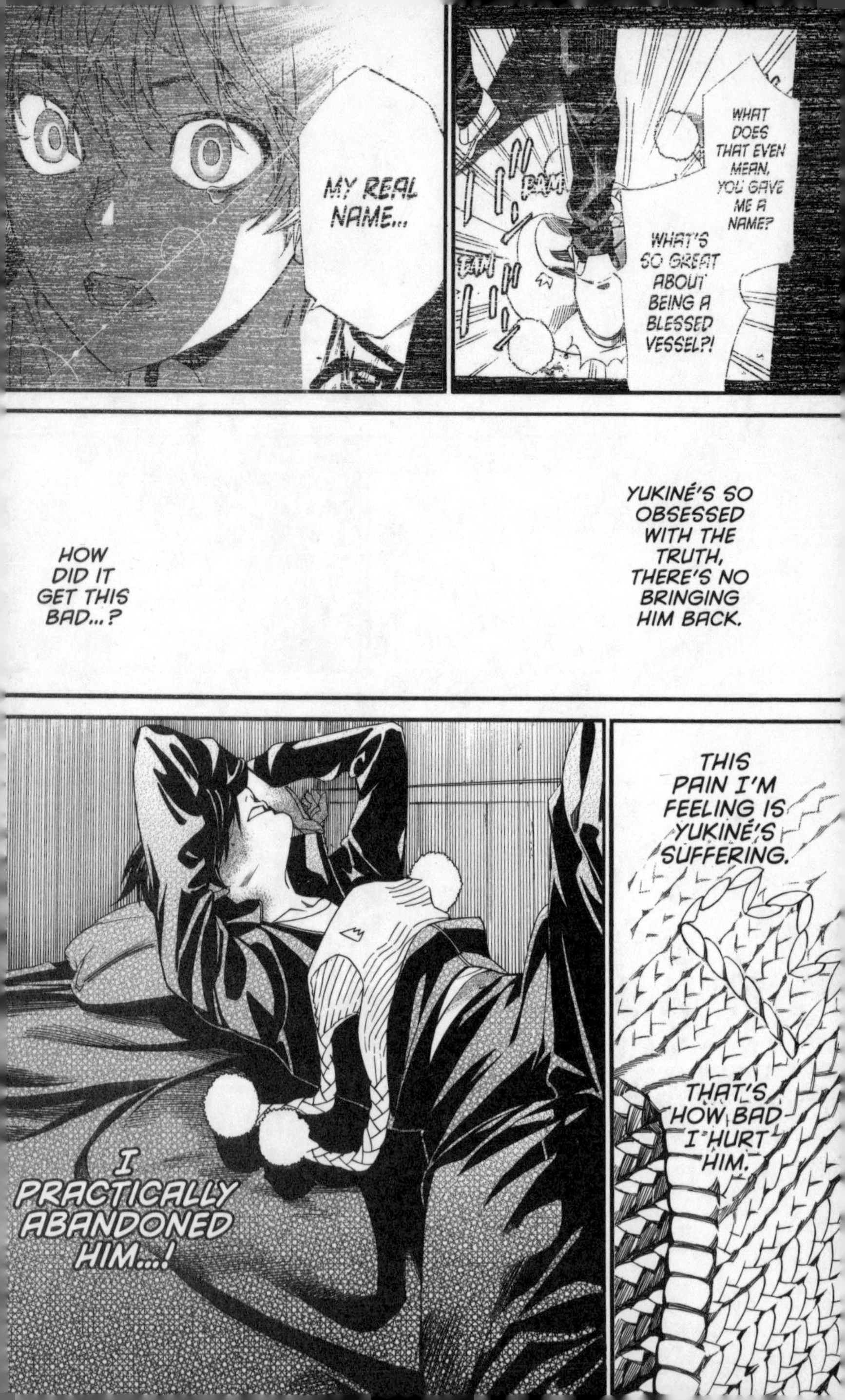
WHAT DOES THAT EVEN MEAN, YOU GAVE ME A NAME?
WHAT'S SO GREAT ABOUT BEING A BLESSED VESSEL?!
BAM
MY REAL NAME...
YUKINÉ'S SO OBSESSED WITH THE TRUTH, THERE'S NO BRINGING HIM BACK.
HOW DID IT GET THIS BAD...?
THIS PAIN I'M FEELING IS YUKINÉ'S SUFFERING.
THAT'S HOW BAD I HURT HIM.
I PRACTICALLY ABANDONED HIM...!

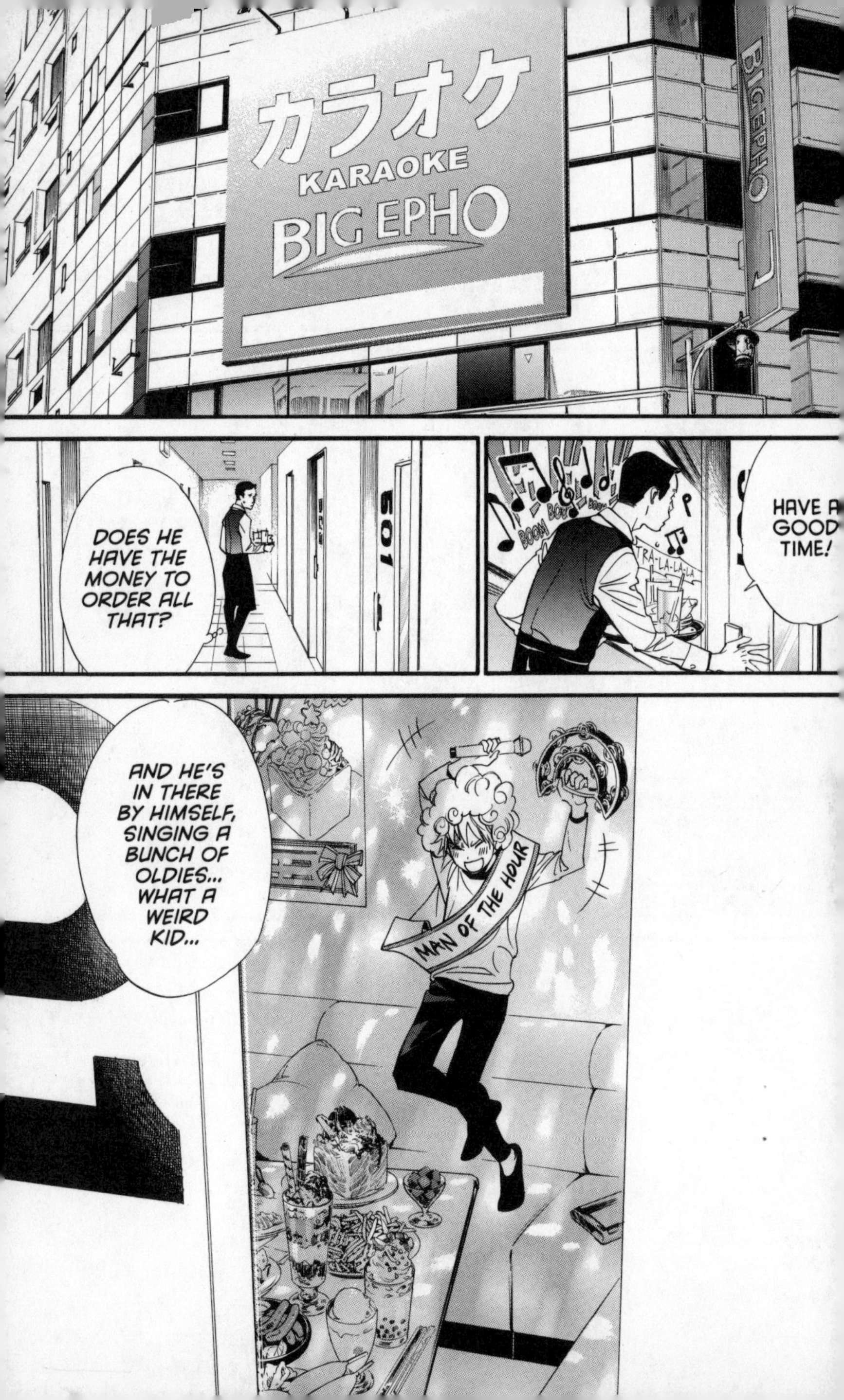

カラオケ
KARAOKE
BIG EPHO
BIG EPHO
HAVE A GOOD TIME!
BOOM BOOM BOOM
TRA-LA-LA-LA
501
DOES HE HAVE THE MONEY TO ORDER ALL THAT?
AND HE'S IN THERE BY HIMSELF, SINGING A BUNCH OF OLDIES... WHAT A WEIRD KID...
MAN OF THE HOUR

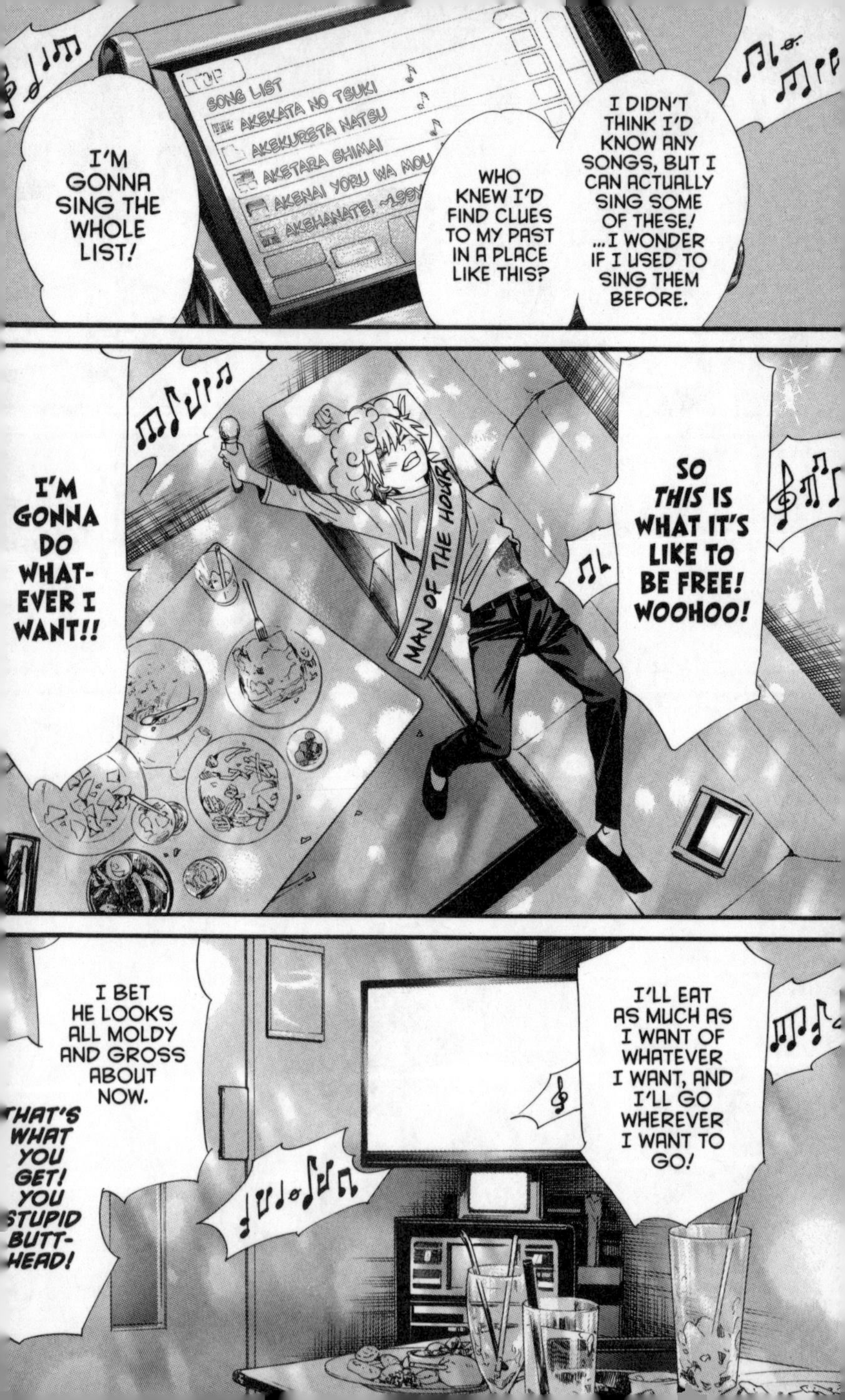
TOP
SONG LIST
AKEKATA NO TSUKI
AKEKURETA NATSU
AKETARA SHIMAI
AKENAI YORU WA MOU
I DIDN'T THINK I'D KNOW ANY SONGS, BUT I CAN ACTUALLY SING SOME OF THESE! ...I WONDER IF I USED TO SING THEM BEFORE.
WHO KNEW I'D FIND CLUES TO MY PAST IN A PLACE LIKE THIS?
I'M GONNA SING THE WHOLE LIST!
SO *THIS* IS WHAT IT'S LIKE TO BE FREE! WOOHOO!
MAN OF THE HOUR
I'M GONNA DO WHAT-EVER I WANT!!
I'LL EAT AS MUCH AS I WANT OF WHATEVER I WANT, AND I'LL GO WHEREVER I WANT TO GO!
I BET HE LOOKS ALL MOLDY AND GROSS ABOUT NOW.
THAT'S WHAT YOU GET! YOU STUPID BUTT-HEAD!

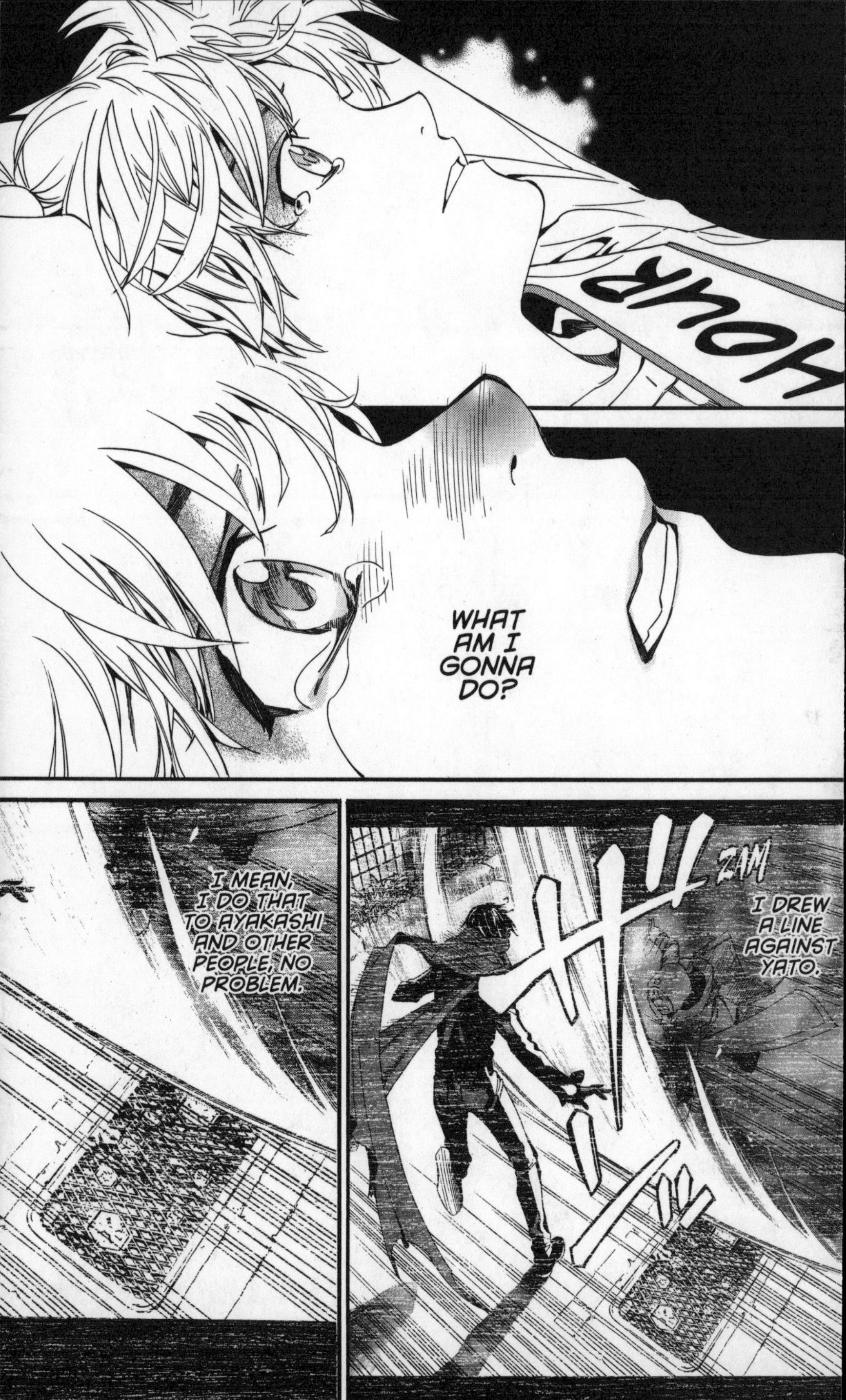
WHAT AM I GONNA DO?
ZAM
I DREW A LINE AGAINST YATO.
I MEAN, I DO THAT TO AYAKASHI AND OTHER PEOPLE, NO PROBLEM.

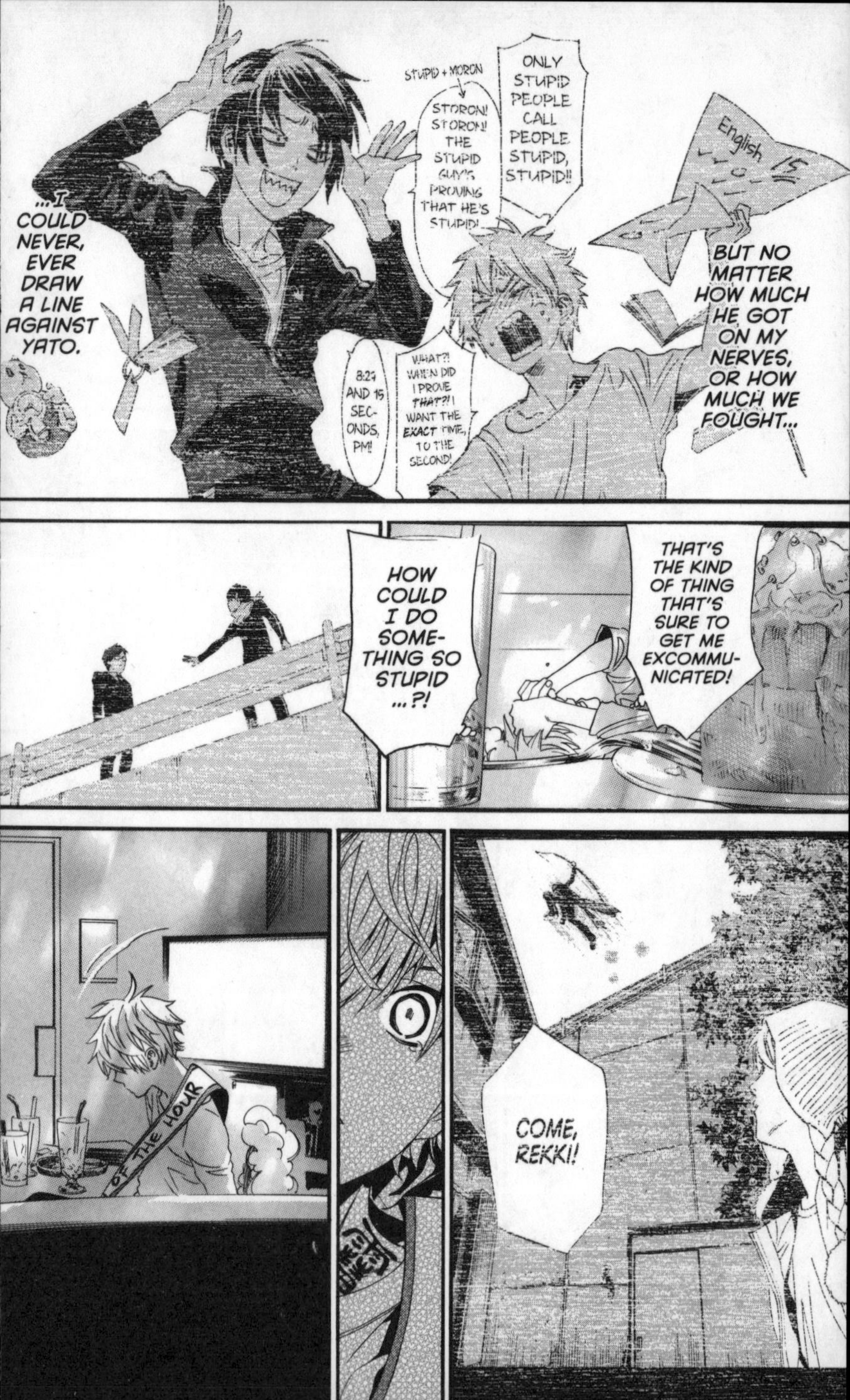
ONLY STUPID PEOPLE CALL PEOPLE STUPID, STUPID!!
STUPID + MORON
STORON! STORON! THE STUPID GUY'S PROVING THAT HE'S STUPID!
English 15
BUT NO MATTER HOW MUCH HE GOT ON MY NERVES, OR HOW MUCH WE FOUGHT...
WHAT?! WHEN DID I PROVE THAT?! I WANT THE EXACT TIME, TO THE SECOND!
8:27 AND 15 SECONDS, PM!
...I COULD NEVER, EVER DRAW A LINE AGAINST YATO.
THAT'S THE KIND OF THING THAT'S SURE TO GET ME EXCOMMUNICATED!
HOW COULD I DO SOMETHING SO STUPID ...?!
COME, REKKI!
OF THE HOUR

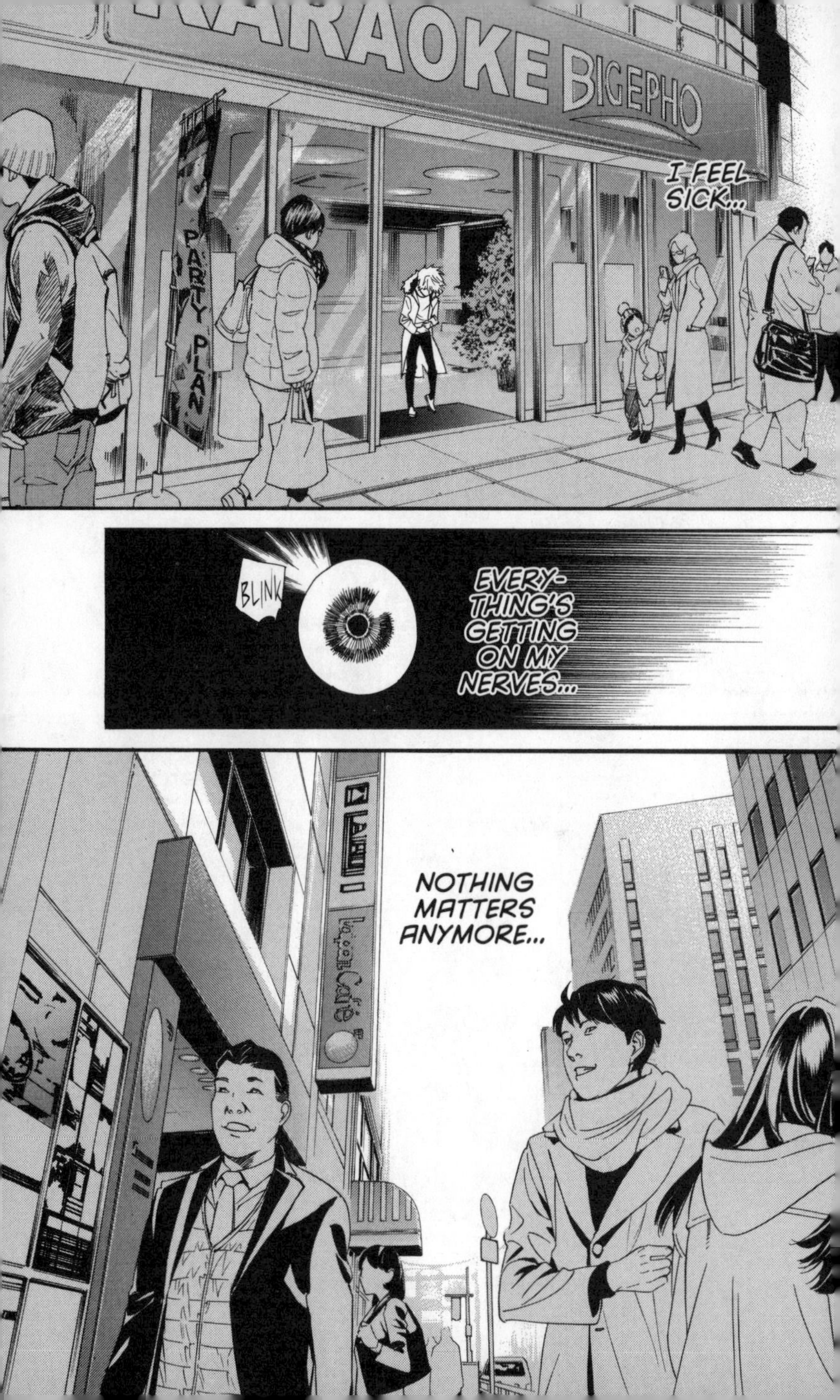
KARAOKE BIGEPHO
I FEEL SICK...
PARTY PLAN
EVERY-THING'S GETTING ON MY NERVES...
BLINK
NOTHING MATTERS ANYMORE...

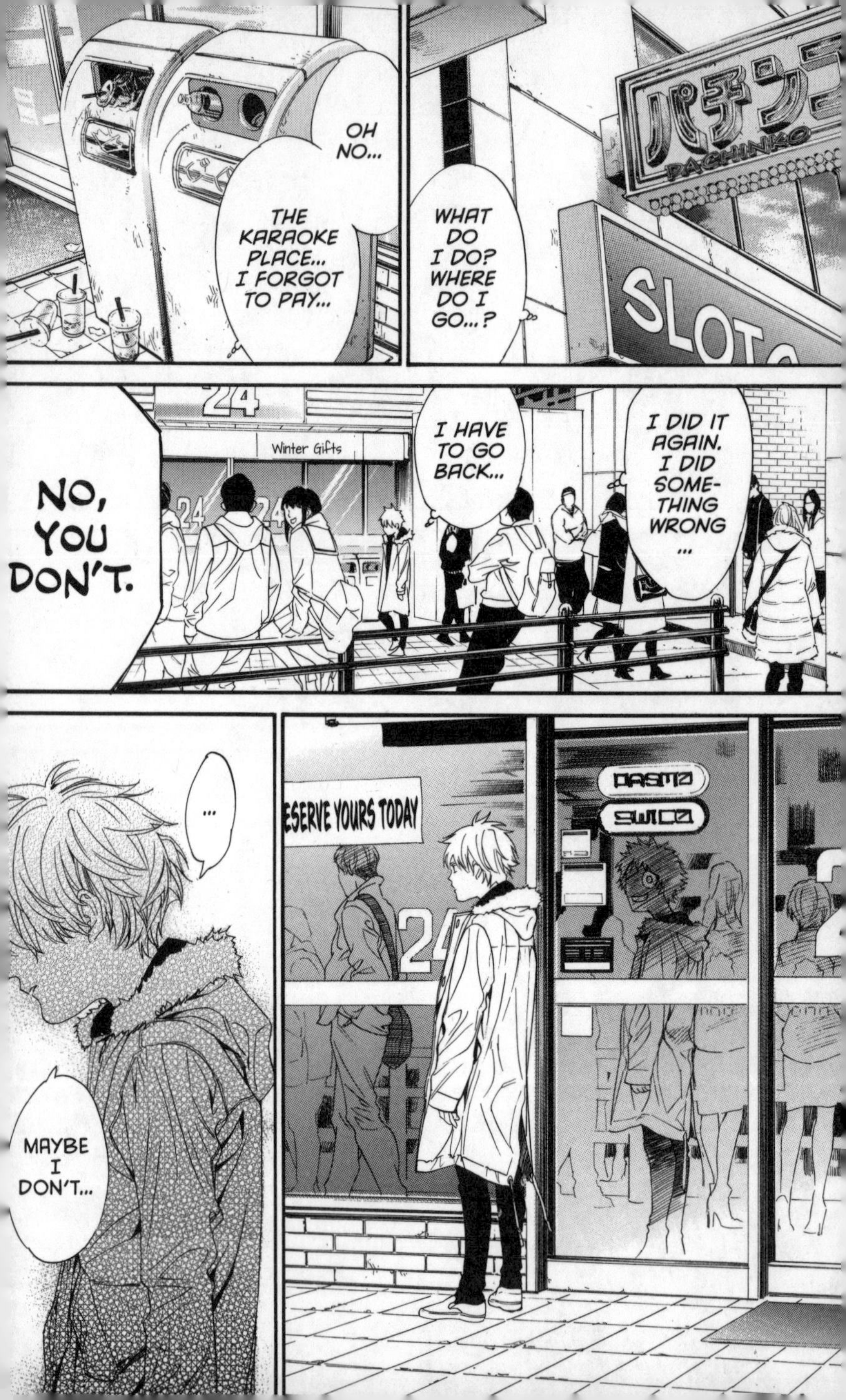
PACHINKO
WHAT DO I DO? WHERE DO I GO...?
OH NO...
THE KARAOKE PLACE... I FORGOT TO PAY...
I DID IT AGAIN. I DID SOME-THING WRONG...
I HAVE TO GO BACK...
Winter Gifts
NO, YOU DON'T.
ESERVE YOURS TODAY
...
MAYBE I DON'T...

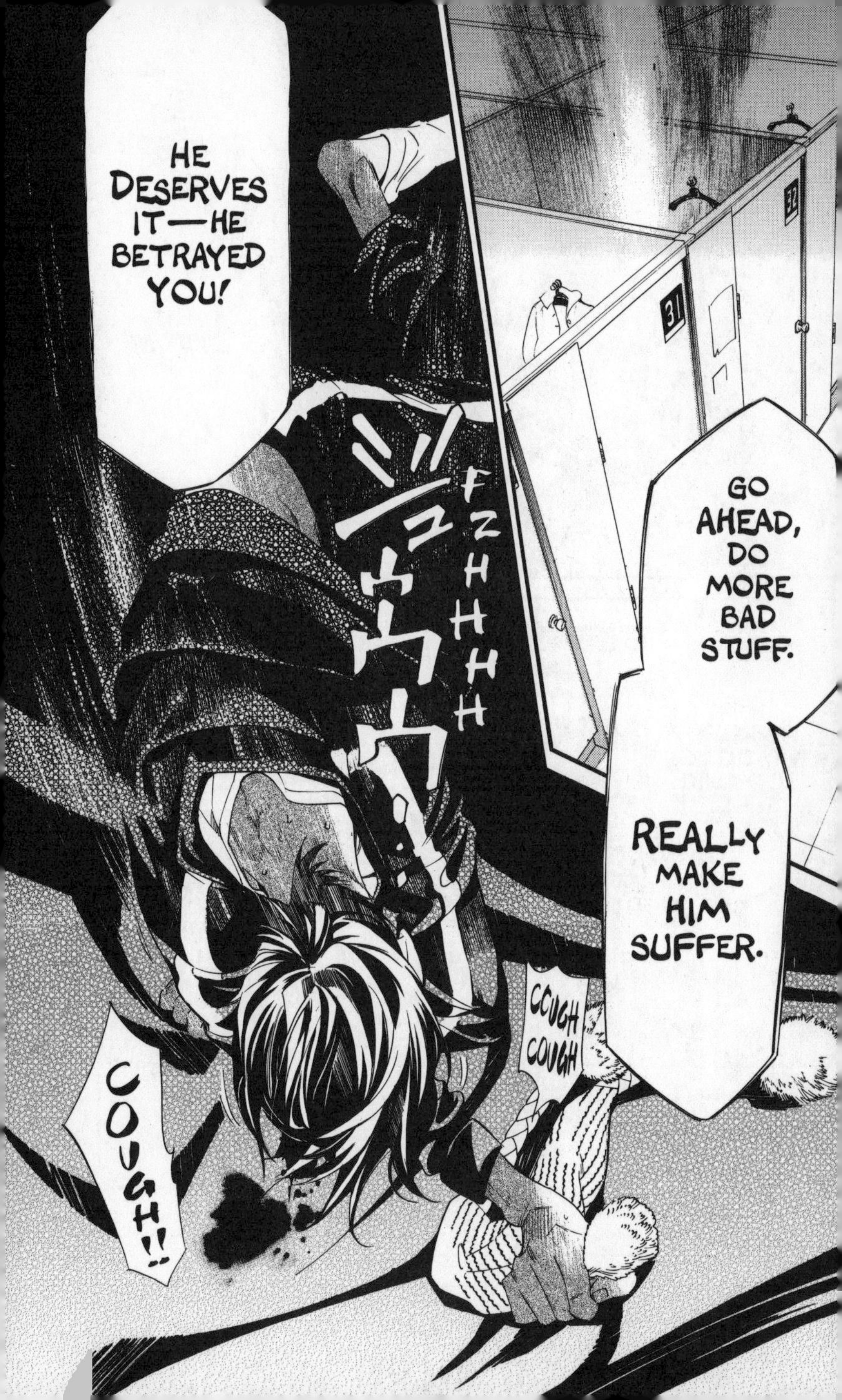
HE DESERVES IT—HE BETRAYED YOU!
GO AHEAD, DO MORE BAD STUFF.
REALLY MAKE HIM SUFFER.
ジュウウ
FZHHHH
COUGH COUGH
COUGH!!

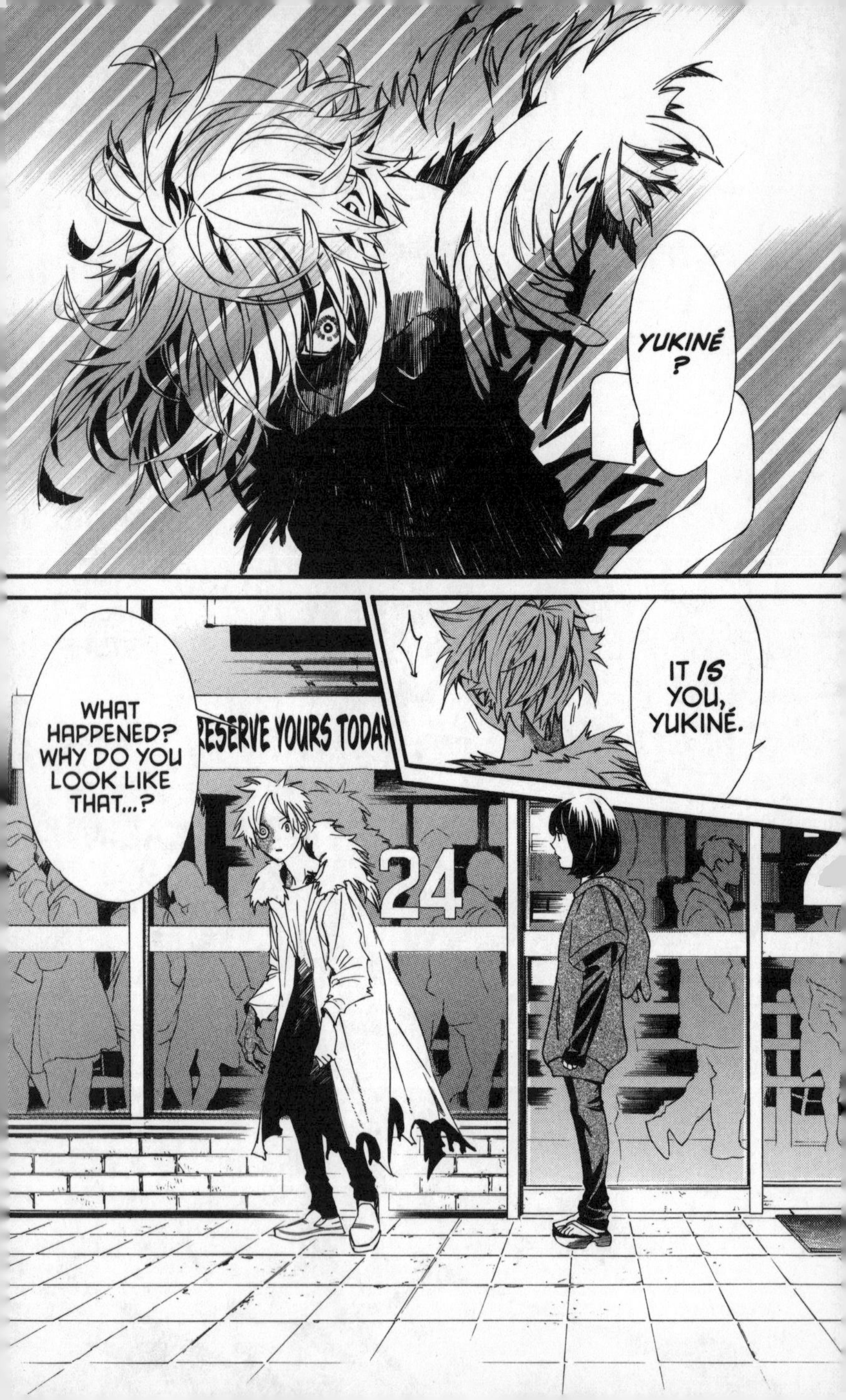
YUKINÉ ?
IT IS YOU, YUKINÉ.
WHAT HAPPENED? WHY DO YOU LOOK LIKE THAT...?
RESERVE YOURS TODAY
24

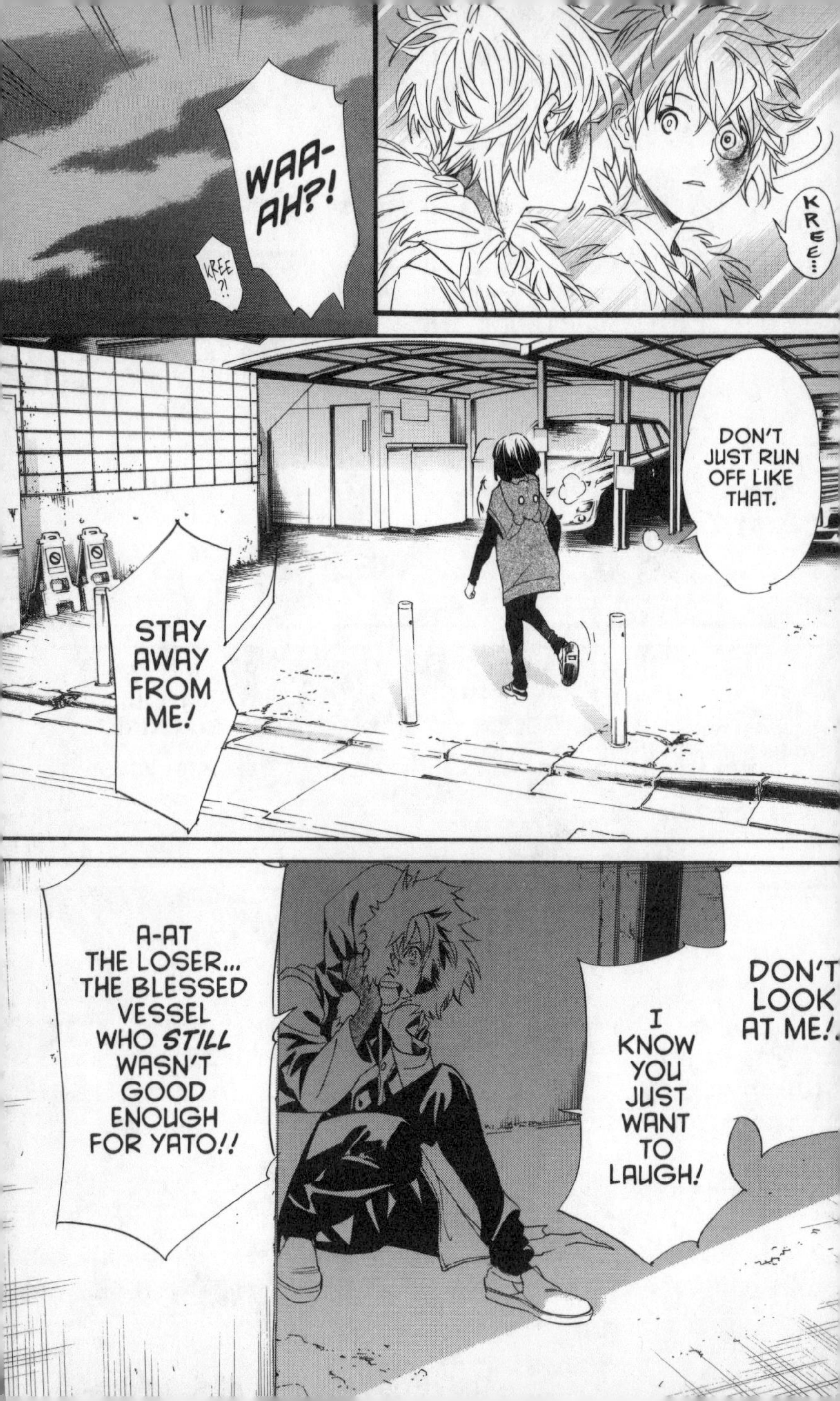
KREE...
WAA-AH?!
KREE?!
DON'T JUST RUN OFF LIKE THAT.
STAY AWAY FROM ME!
DON'T LOOK AT ME!
I KNOW YOU JUST WANT TO LAUGH!
A-AT THE LOSER... THE BLESSED VESSEL WHO *STILL* WASN'T GOOD ENOUGH FOR YATO!!

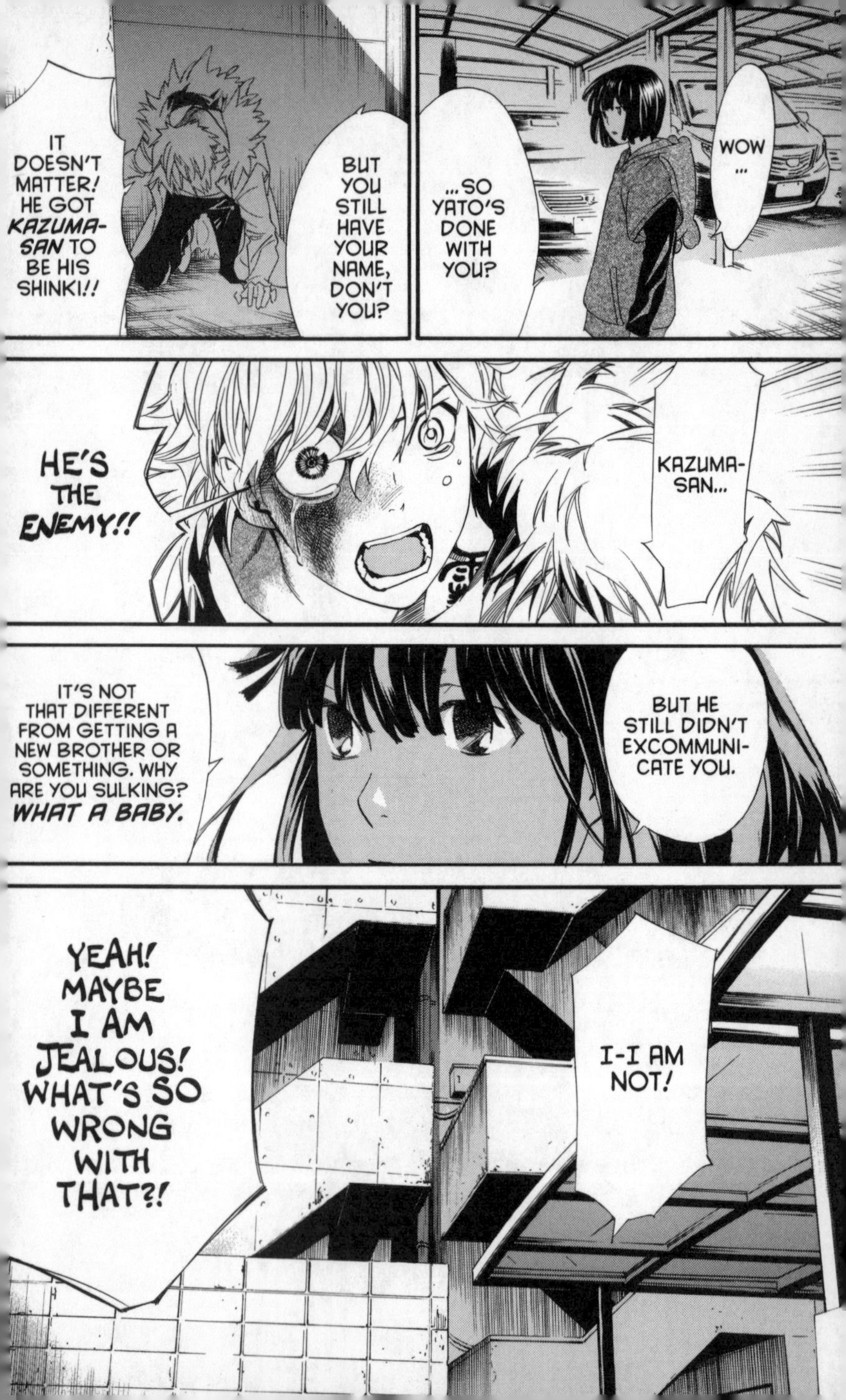
WOW ...
...SO YATO'S DONE WITH YOU?
BUT YOU STILL HAVE YOUR NAME, DON'T YOU?
IT DOESN'T MATTER! HE GOT KAZUMA-SAN TO BE HIS SHINKI!!
KAZUMA-SAN...
HE'S THE ENEMY!!
BUT HE STILL DIDN'T EXCOMMUNICATE YOU.
IT'S NOT THAT DIFFERENT FROM GETTING A NEW BROTHER OR SOMETHING. WHY ARE YOU SULKING? WHAT A BABY.
I-I AM NOT!
YEAH! MAYBE I AM JEALOUS! WHAT'S SO WRONG WITH THAT?!

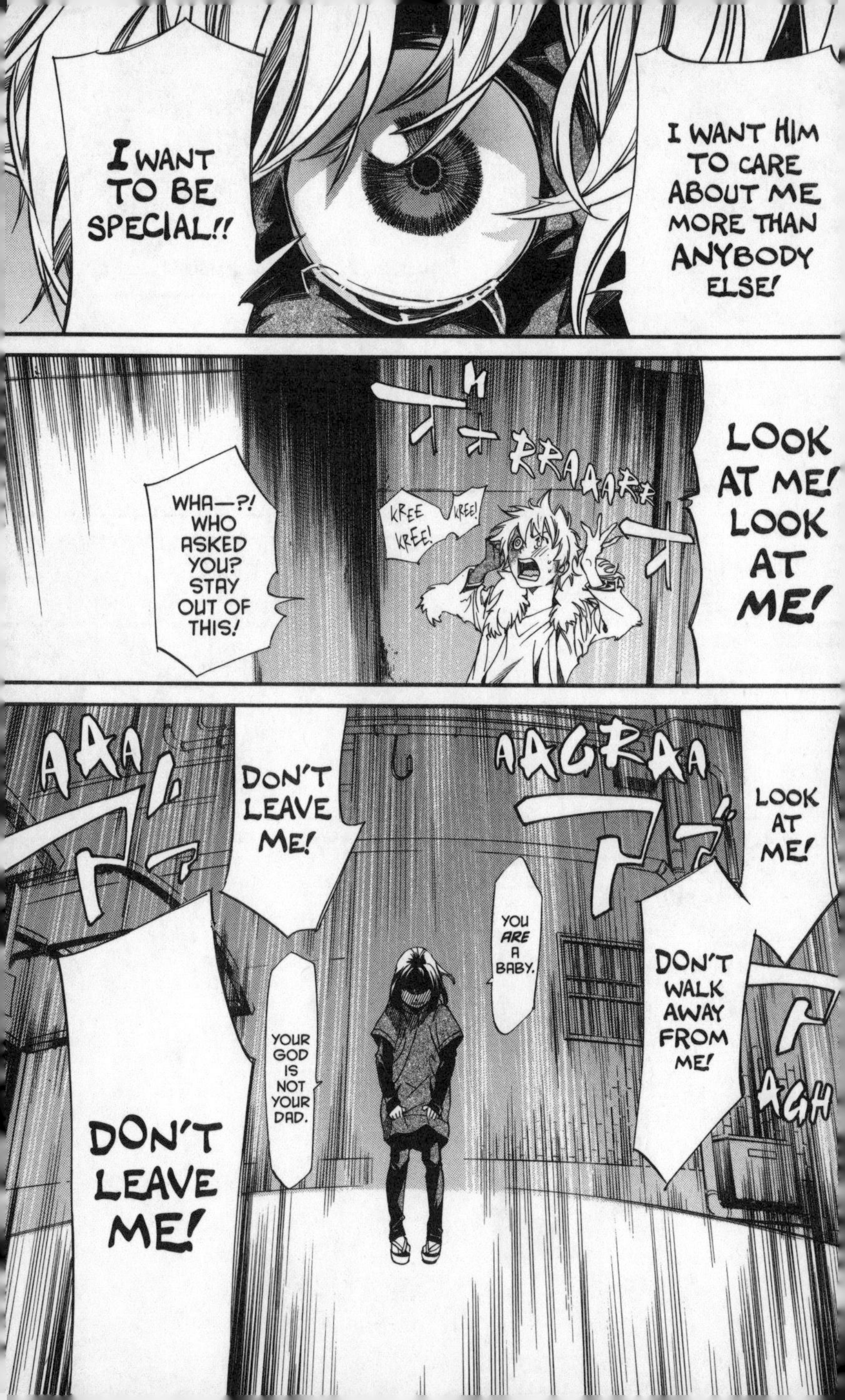
I WANT HIM TO CARE ABOUT ME MORE THAN ANYBODY ELSE!
I WANT TO BE SPECIAL!!
LOOK AT ME! LOOK AT ME!
HRRAAAARR
KREE!
KREE KREE!
WHA—?! WHO ASKED YOU? STAY OUT OF THIS!
LOOK AT ME!
AAGRAA
DON'T WALK AWAY FROM ME!
AGH
YOU ARE A BABY.
DON'T LEAVE ME!
AAA
YOUR GOD IS NOT YOUR DAD.
DON'T LEAVE ME!

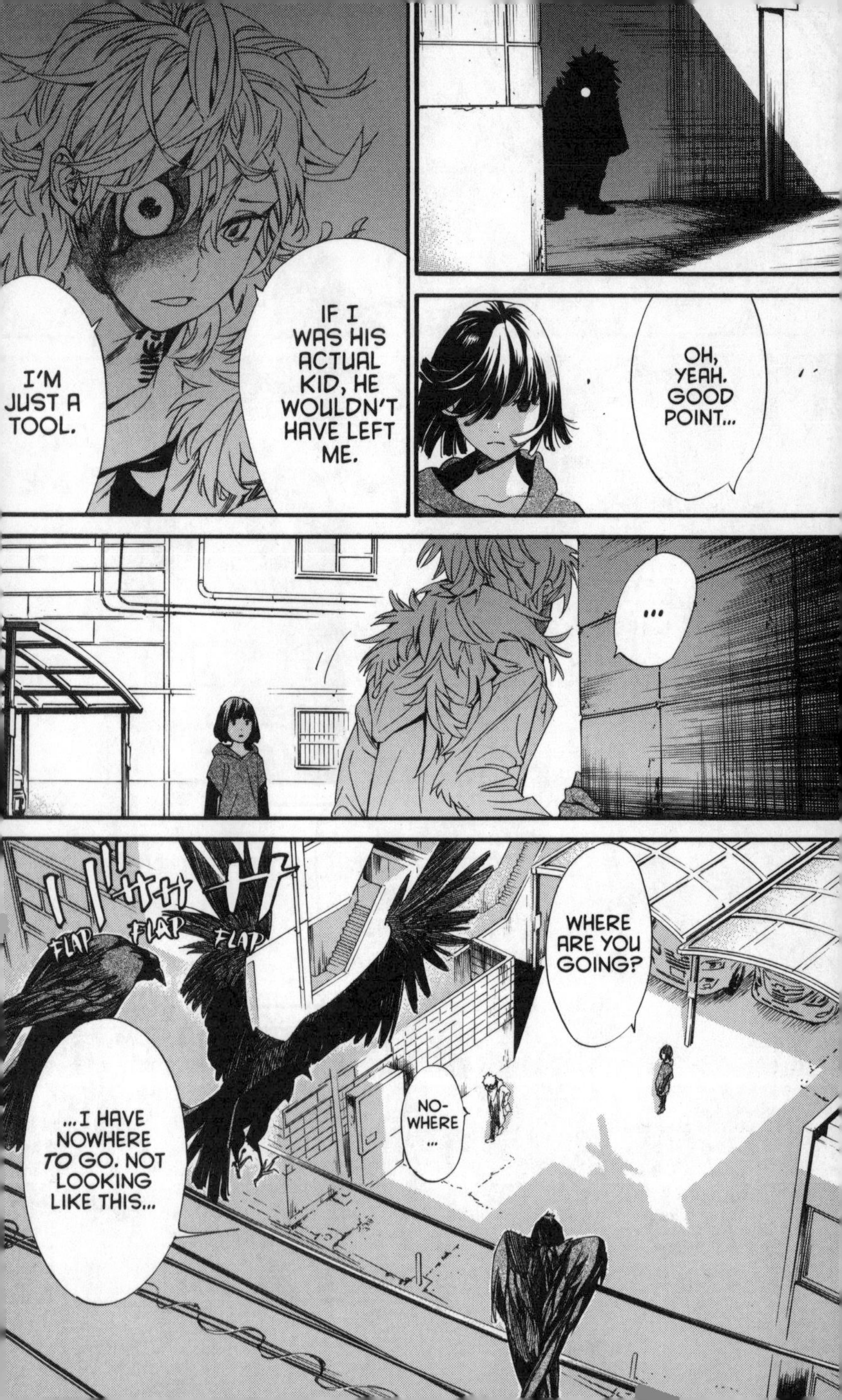
OH, YEAH. GOOD POINT...
IF I WAS HIS ACTUAL KID, HE WOULDN'T HAVE LEFT ME.
I'M JUST A TOOL.
...
WHERE ARE YOU GOING?
NO-WHERE ...
...I HAVE NOWHERE *TO* GO. NOT LOOKING LIKE THIS...
FLAP
FLAP
FLAP

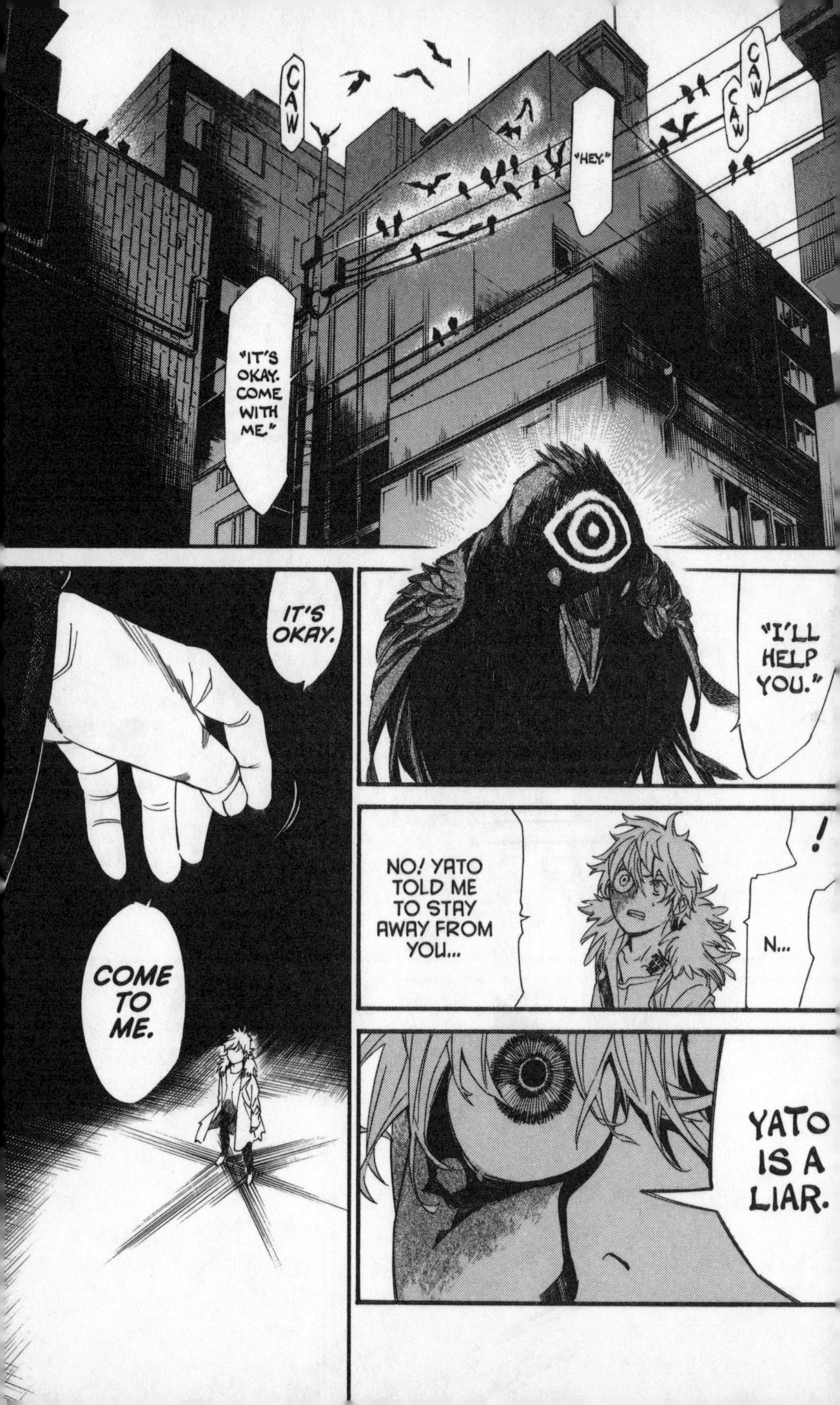
CAW
CAW
"HEY."
CAW
"IT'S OKAY. COME WITH ME."
"I'LL HELP YOU."
!
N...
NO! YATO TOLD ME TO STAY AWAY FROM YOU...
YATO IS A LIAR.
IT'S OKAY.
COME TO ME.

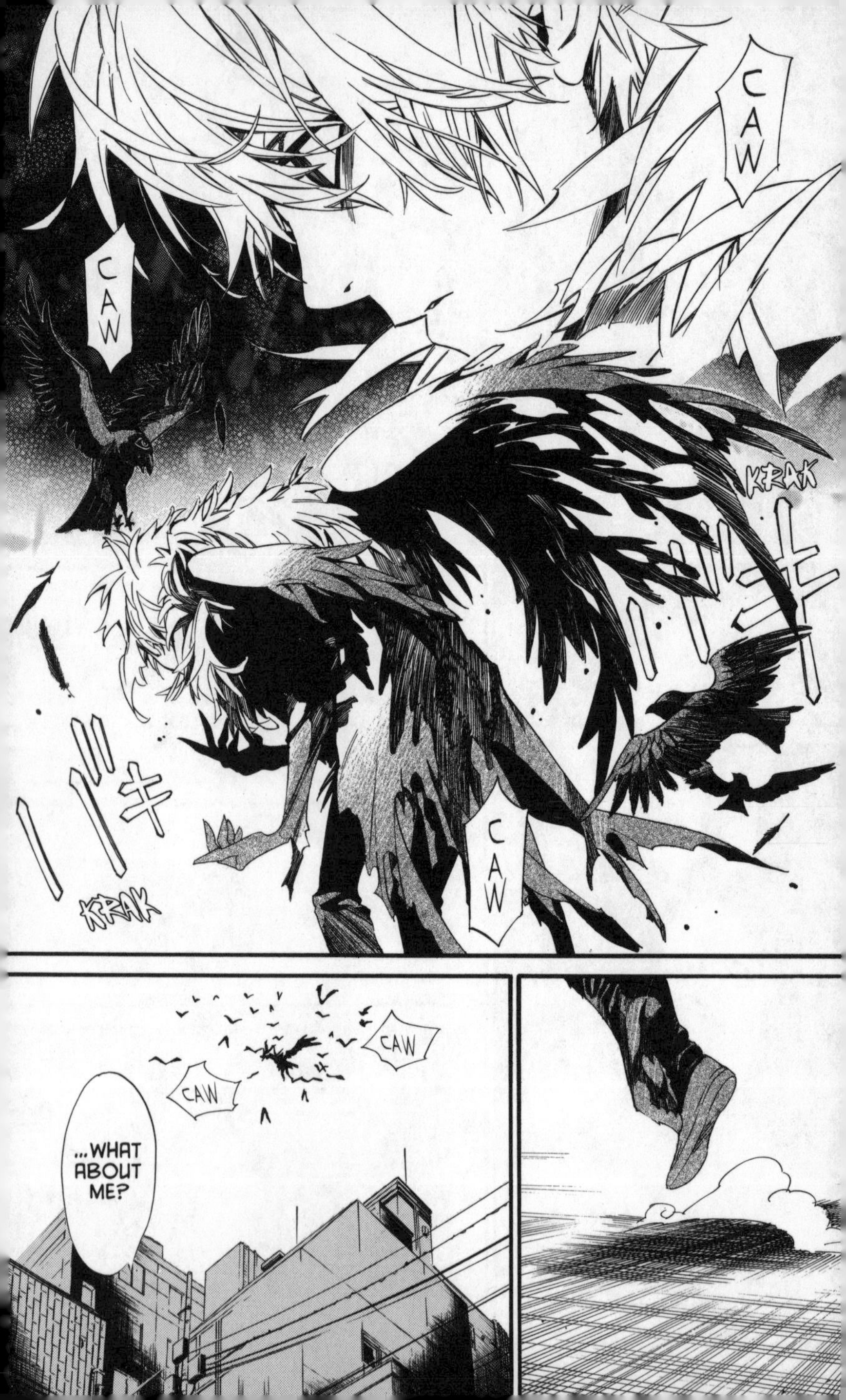
CAW
CAW
KRAK
CAW
KRAK
CAW
CAW
...WHAT ABOUT ME?

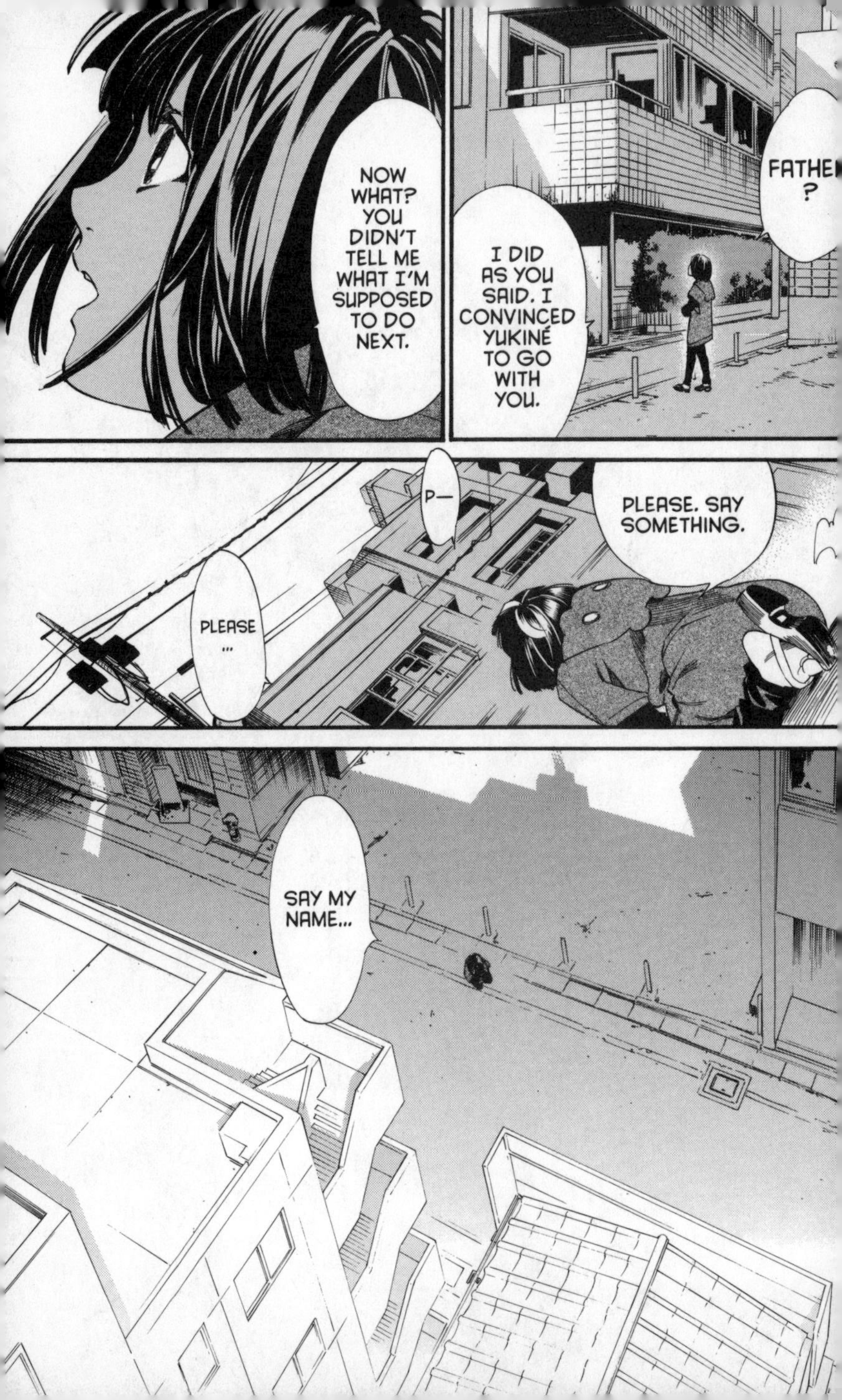

FATHE ?
I DID AS YOU SAID. I CONVINCED YUKINÉ TO GO WITH YOU.
NOW WHAT? YOU DIDN'T TELL ME WHAT I'M SUPPOSED TO DO NEXT.
PLEASE. SAY SOMETHING.
P—
PLEASE...
SAY MY NAME...

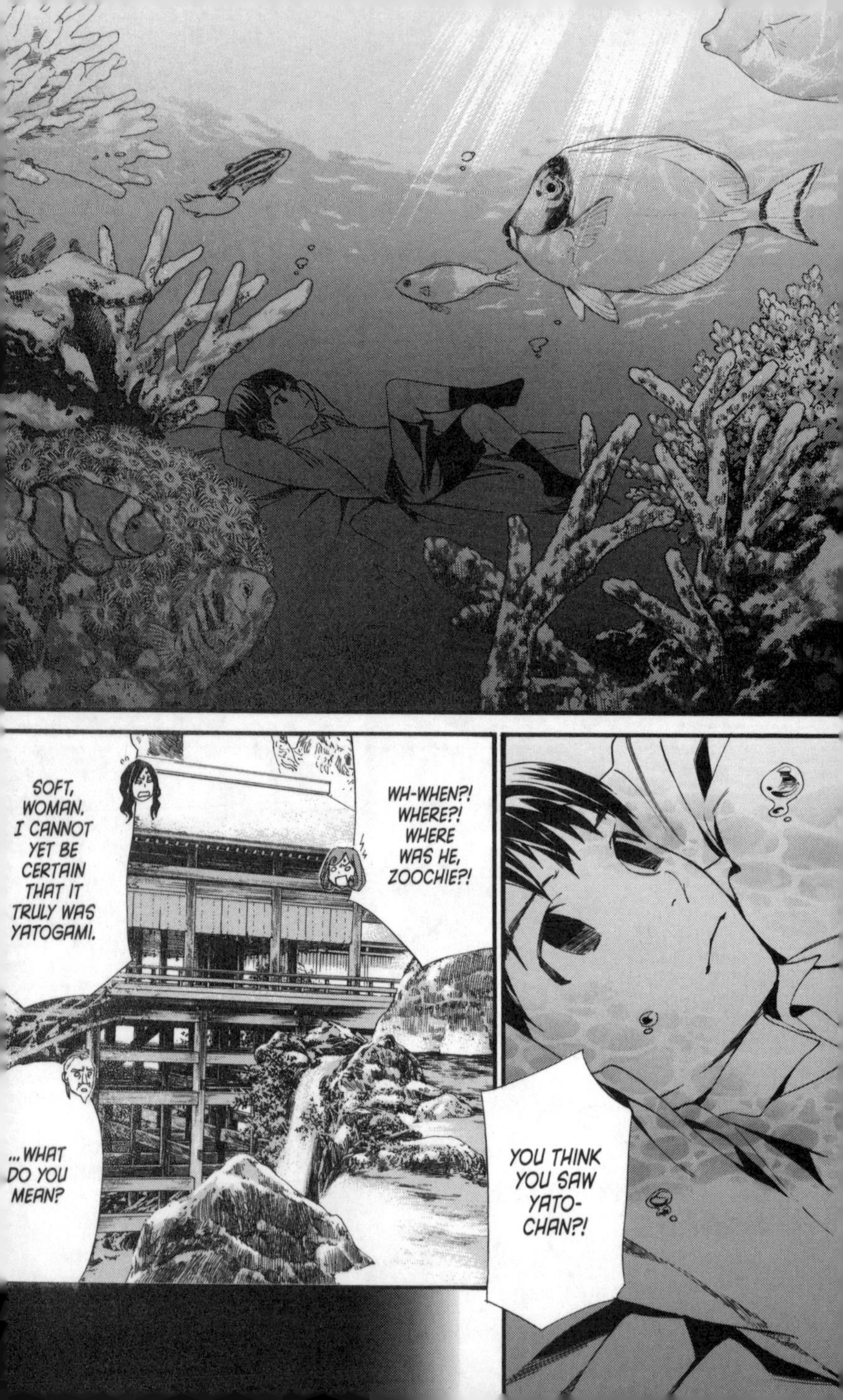
YOU THINK YOU SAW YATO-CHAN?!
WH-WHEN?! WHERE?! WHERE WAS HE, ZOOCHIE?!
SOFT, WOMAN. I CANNOT YET BE CERTAIN THAT IT TRULY WAS YATOGAMI.
...WHAT DO YOU MEAN?

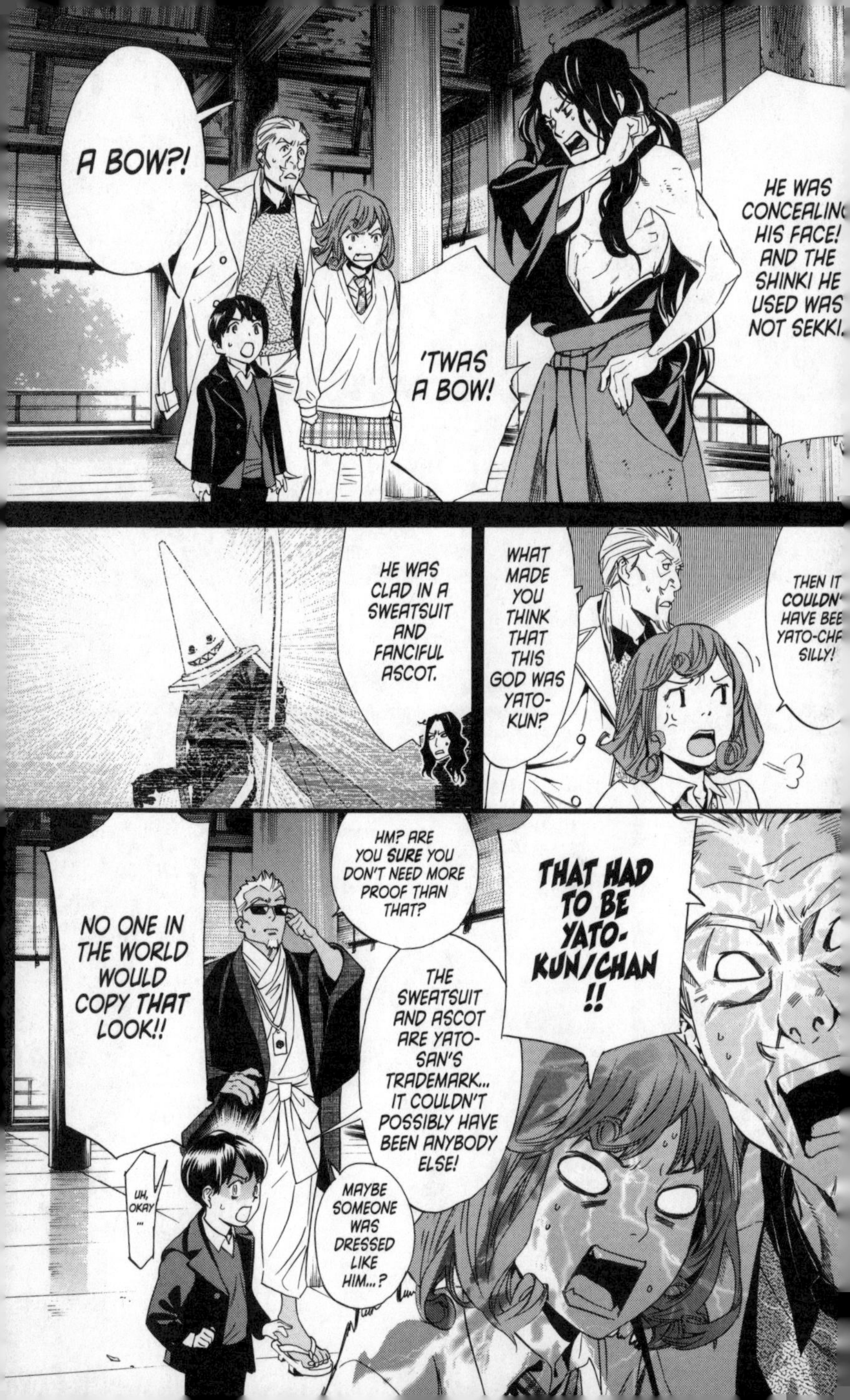

HE WAS CONCEALING HIS FACE! AND THE SHINKI HE USED WAS NOT SEKKI.
'TWAS A BOW!
A BOW?!
THEN IT COULDN' HAVE BEE YATO-CHA SILLY!
WHAT MADE YOU THINK THAT THIS GOD WAS YATO-KUN?
HE WAS CLAD IN A SWEATSUIT AND FANCIFUL ASCOT.
THAT HAD TO BE YATO-KUN/CHAN!!
HM? ARE YOU SURE YOU DON'T NEED MORE PROOF THAN THAT?
THE SWEATSUIT AND ASCOT ARE YATO-SAN'S TRADEMARK... IT COULDN'T POSSIBLY HAVE BEEN ANYBODY ELSE!
MAYBE SOMEONE WAS DRESSED LIKE HIM...?
NO ONE IN THE WORLD WOULD COPY THAT LOOK!!
UH, OKAY...

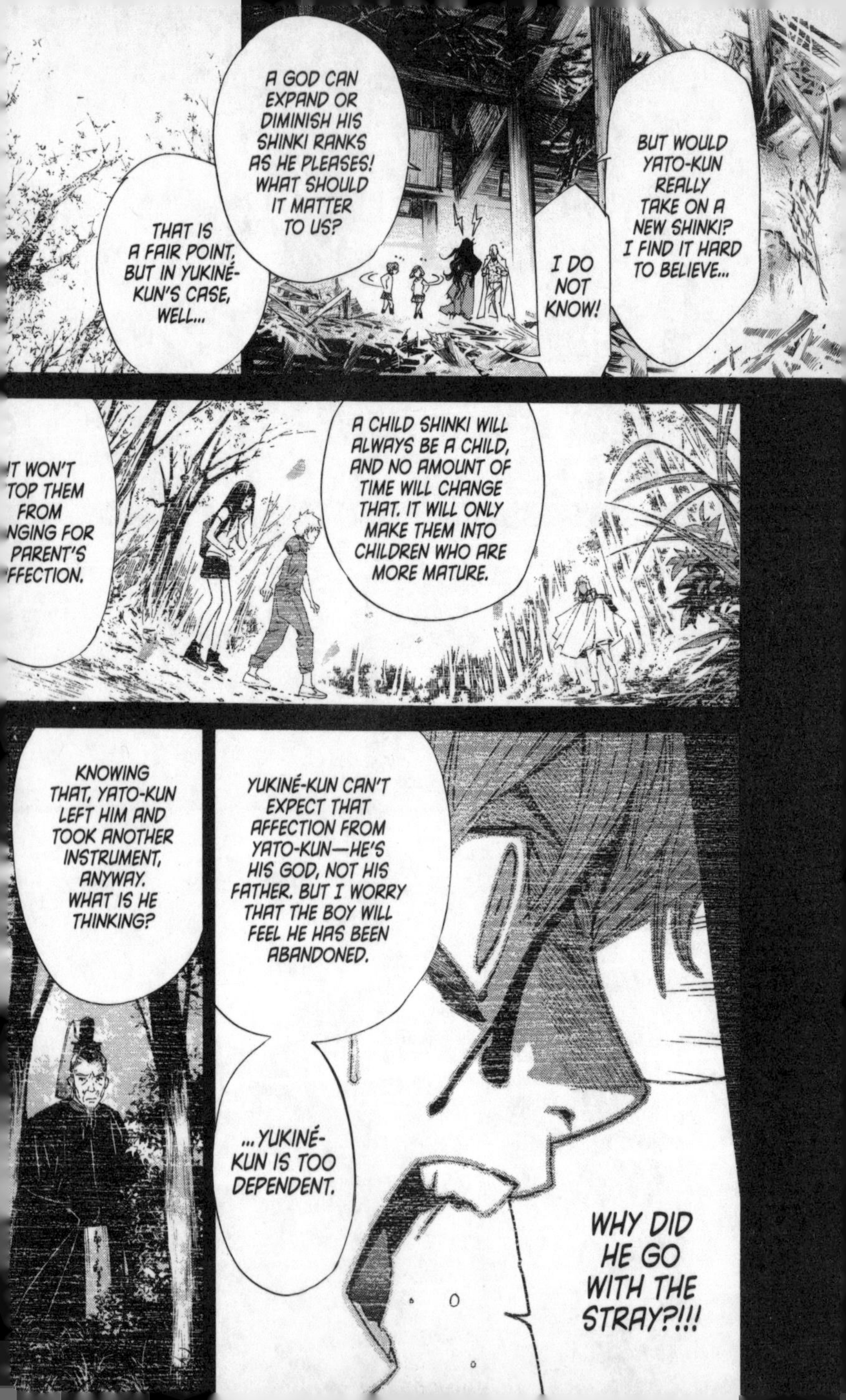
BUT WOULD YATO-KUN REALLY TAKE ON A NEW SHINKI? I FIND IT HARD TO BELIEVE...
I DO NOT KNOW!
A GOD CAN EXPAND OR DIMINISH HIS SHINKI RANKS AS HE PLEASES! WHAT SHOULD IT MATTER TO US?
THAT IS A FAIR POINT, BUT IN YUKINÉ-KUN'S CASE, WELL...
A CHILD SHINKI WILL ALWAYS BE A CHILD, AND NO AMOUNT OF TIME WILL CHANGE THAT. IT WILL ONLY MAKE THEM INTO CHILDREN WHO ARE MORE MATURE.
IT WON'T TOP THEM FROM NGING FOR PARENT'S FFECTION.
YUKINÉ-KUN CAN'T EXPECT THAT AFFECTION FROM YATO-KUN—HE'S HIS GOD, NOT HIS FATHER. BUT I WORRY THAT THE BOY WILL FEEL HE HAS BEEN ABANDONED.
...YUKINÉ-KUN IS TOO DEPENDENT.
WHY DID HE GO WITH THE STRAY?!!!
KNOWING THAT, YATO-KUN LEFT HIM AND TOOK ANOTHER INSTRUMENT, ANYWAY. WHAT IS HE THINKING?

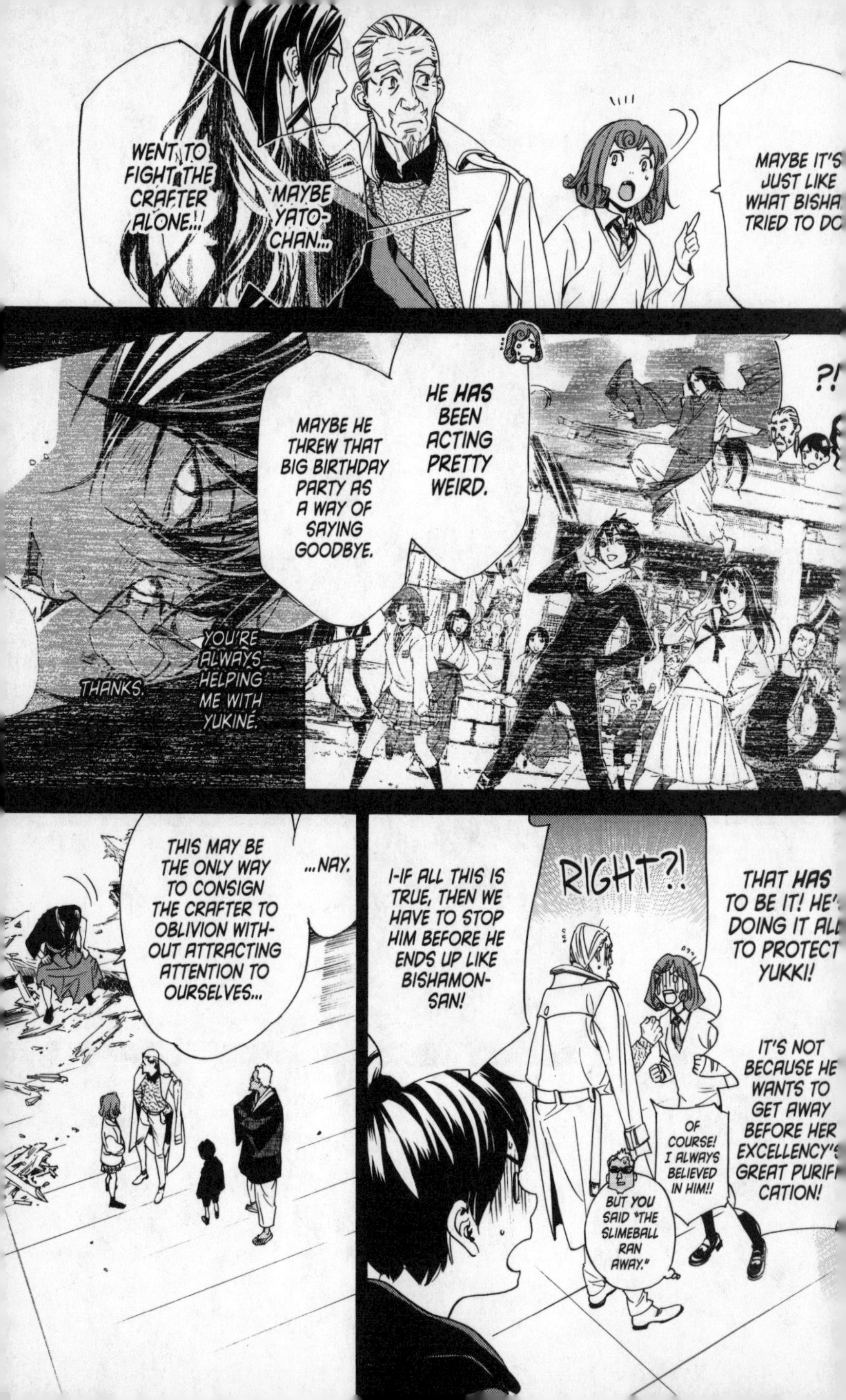
MAYBE IT'S JUST LIKE WHAT BISHA TRIED TO DO
MAYBE YATO-CHAN...
WENT TO FIGHT THE CRAFTER ALONE...!
?!
HE HAS BEEN ACTING PRETTY WEIRD.
MAYBE HE THREW THAT BIG BIRTHDAY PARTY AS A WAY OF SAYING GOODBYE.
YOU'RE ALWAYS HELPING ME WITH YUKINE.
THANKS.
THAT HAS TO BE IT! HE' DOING IT AL TO PROTECT YUKKI!
RIGHT?!
IT'S NOT BECAUSE HE WANTS TO GET AWAY BEFORE HER EXCELLENCY'S GREAT PURIFI CATION!
OF COURSE! I ALWAYS BELIEVED IN HIM!!
BUT YOU SAID "THE SLIMEBALL RAN AWAY."
I-IF ALL THIS IS TRUE, THEN WE HAVE TO STOP HIM BEFORE HE ENDS UP LIKE BISHAMON-SAN!
...NAY.
THIS MAY BE THE ONLY WAY TO CONSIGN THE CRAFTER TO OBLIVION WITHOUT ATTRACTING ATTENTION TO OURSELVES...

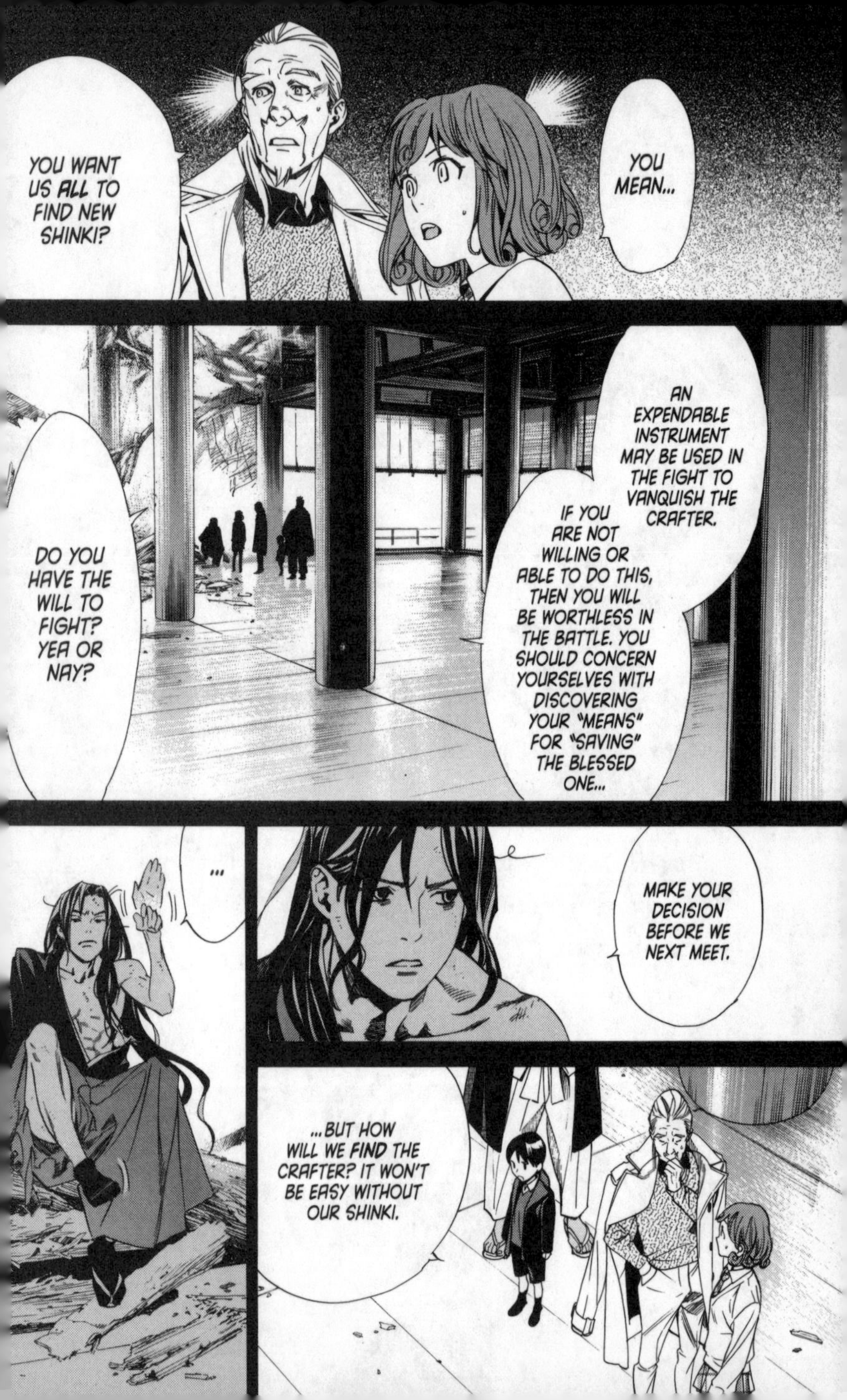
YOU MEAN...
YOU WANT US ALL TO FIND NEW SHINKI?
AN EXPENDABLE INSTRUMENT MAY BE USED IN THE FIGHT TO VANQUISH THE CRAFTER.
IF YOU ARE NOT WILLING OR ABLE TO DO THIS, THEN YOU WILL BE WORTHLESS IN THE BATTLE. YOU SHOULD CONCERN YOURSELVES WITH DISCOVERING YOUR "MEANS" FOR "SAVING" THE BLESSED ONE...
DO YOU HAVE THE WILL TO FIGHT? YEA OR NAY?
MAKE YOUR DECISION BEFORE WE NEXT MEET.
...BUT HOW WILL WE FIND THE CRAFTER? IT WON'T BE EASY WITHOUT OUR SHINKI.
...

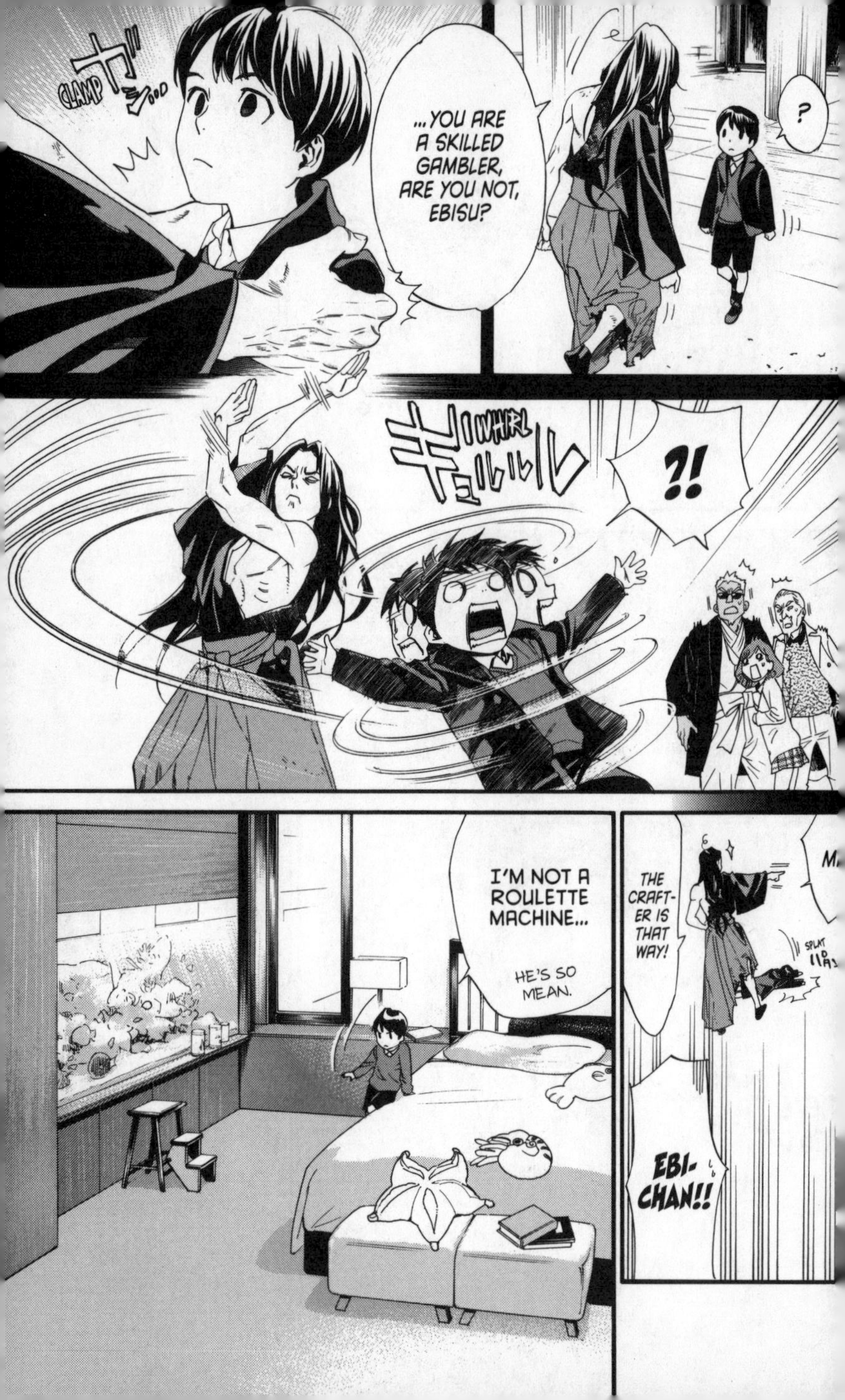
?
CLAMP
...YOU ARE A SKILLED GAMBLER, ARE YOU NOT, EBISU?
WHIRL
?!
THE CRAFTER IS THAT WAY!
SPLAT
EBI-CHAN!!
I'M NOT A ROULETTE MACHINE...
HE'S SO MEAN.

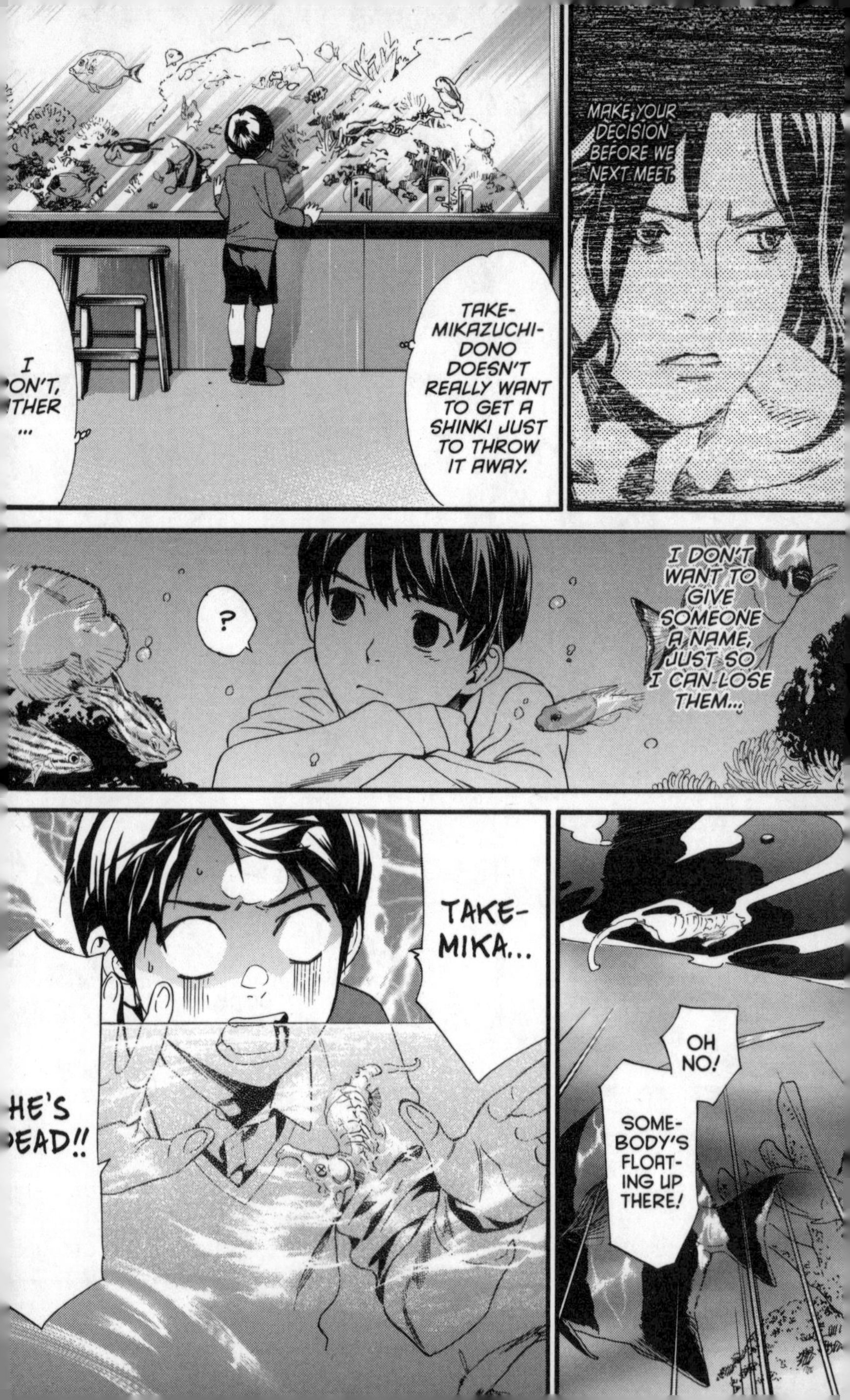
MAKE YOUR DECISION BEFORE WE NEXT MEET.
TAKE-MIKAZUCHI-DONO DOESN'T REALLY WANT TO GET A SHINKI JUST TO THROW IT AWAY.
I ON'T, THER ...
I DON'T WANT TO GIVE SOMEONE A NAME, JUST SO I CAN LOSE THEM...
?
OH NO!
SOMEBODY'S FLOATING UP THERE!
TAKE-MIKA...
HE'S EAD!!

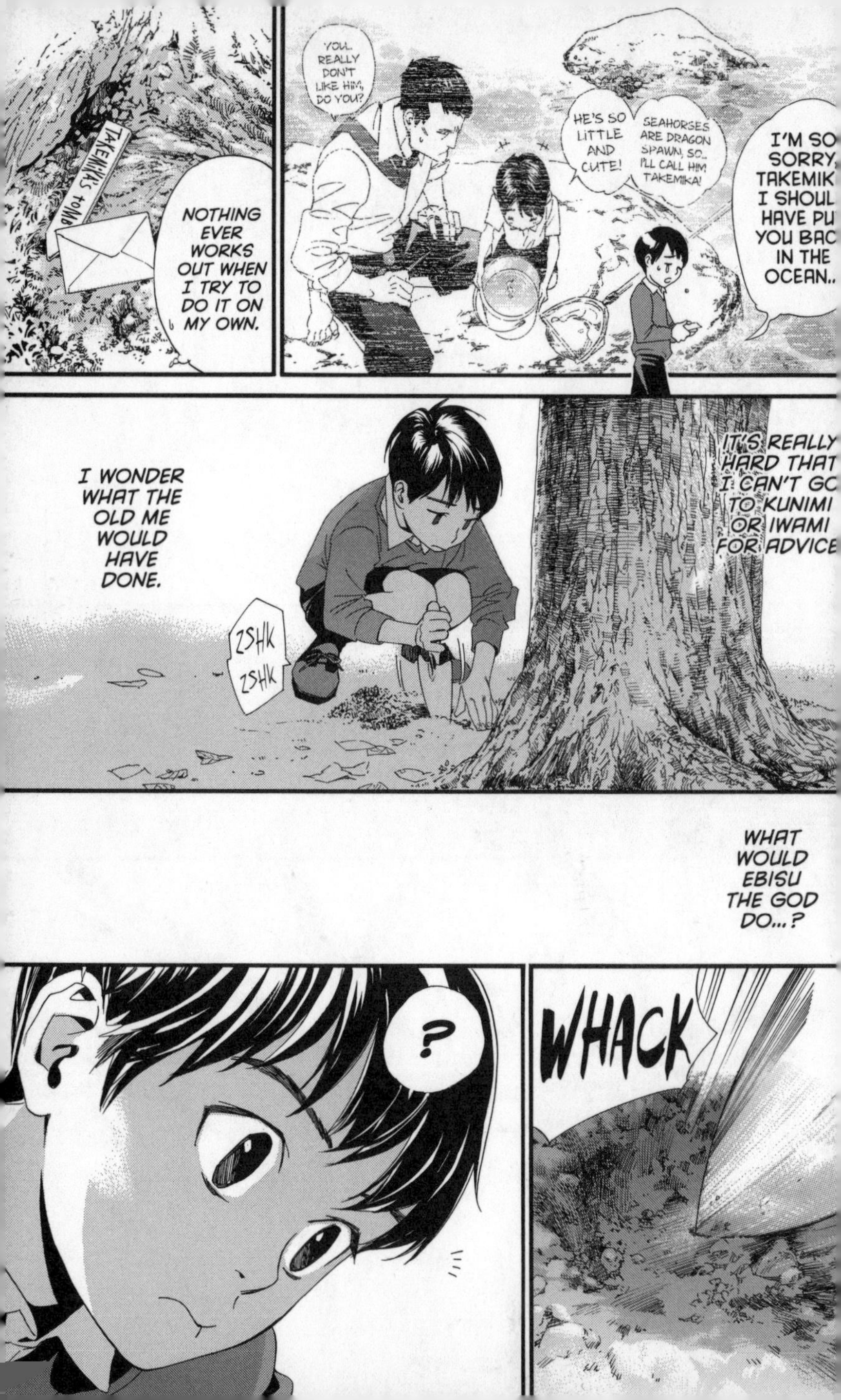
I'M SO SORRY, TAKEMIK I SHOUL HAVE PU YOU BAC IN THE OCEAN..
SEAHORSES ARE DRAGON SPAWN, SO... I'LL CALL HIM TAKEMIKA!
HE'S SO LITTLE AND CUTE!
YOU... REALLY DON'T LIKE HIM, DO YOU?
TAKEMIKA'S tomb
NOTHING EVER WORKS OUT WHEN I TRY TO DO IT ON MY OWN.
IT'S REALLY HARD THAT I CAN'T GO TO KUNIMI OR IWAMI FOR ADVICE
I WONDER WHAT THE OLD ME WOULD HAVE DONE.
ZSHK
ZSHK
WHAT WOULD EBISU THE GOD DO...?
WHACK
?

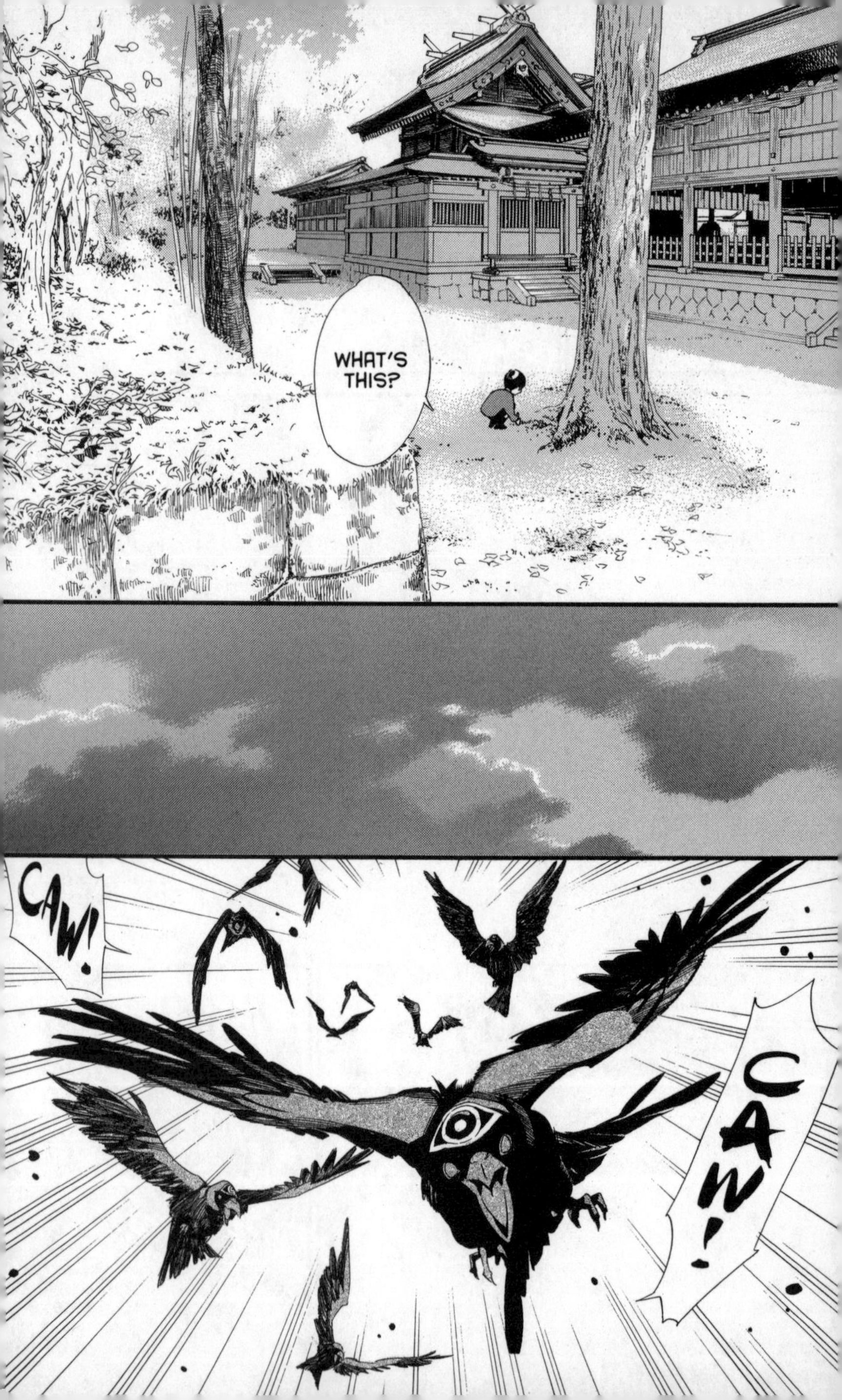
WHAT'S THIS?
CAW!
CAW!

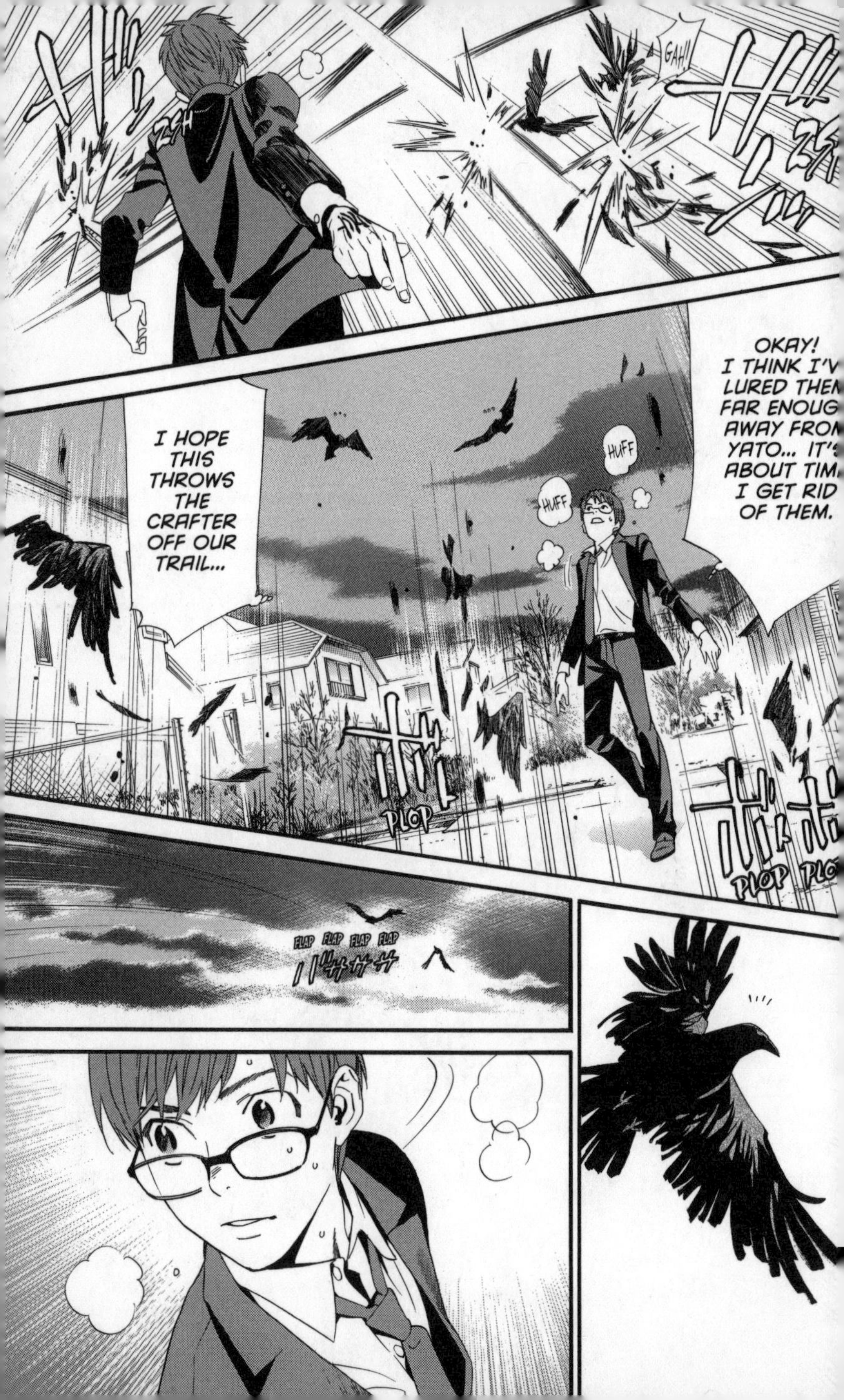
GAH!
ZSH
OKAY! I THINK I'V LURED THEM FAR ENOUG AWAY FROM YATO... IT'S ABOUT TIM I GET RID OF THEM.
HUFF
HUFF
PLOP PLOP
PLOP
I HOPE THIS THROWS THE CRAFTER OFF OUR TRAIL...
FLAP FLAP FLAP FLAP

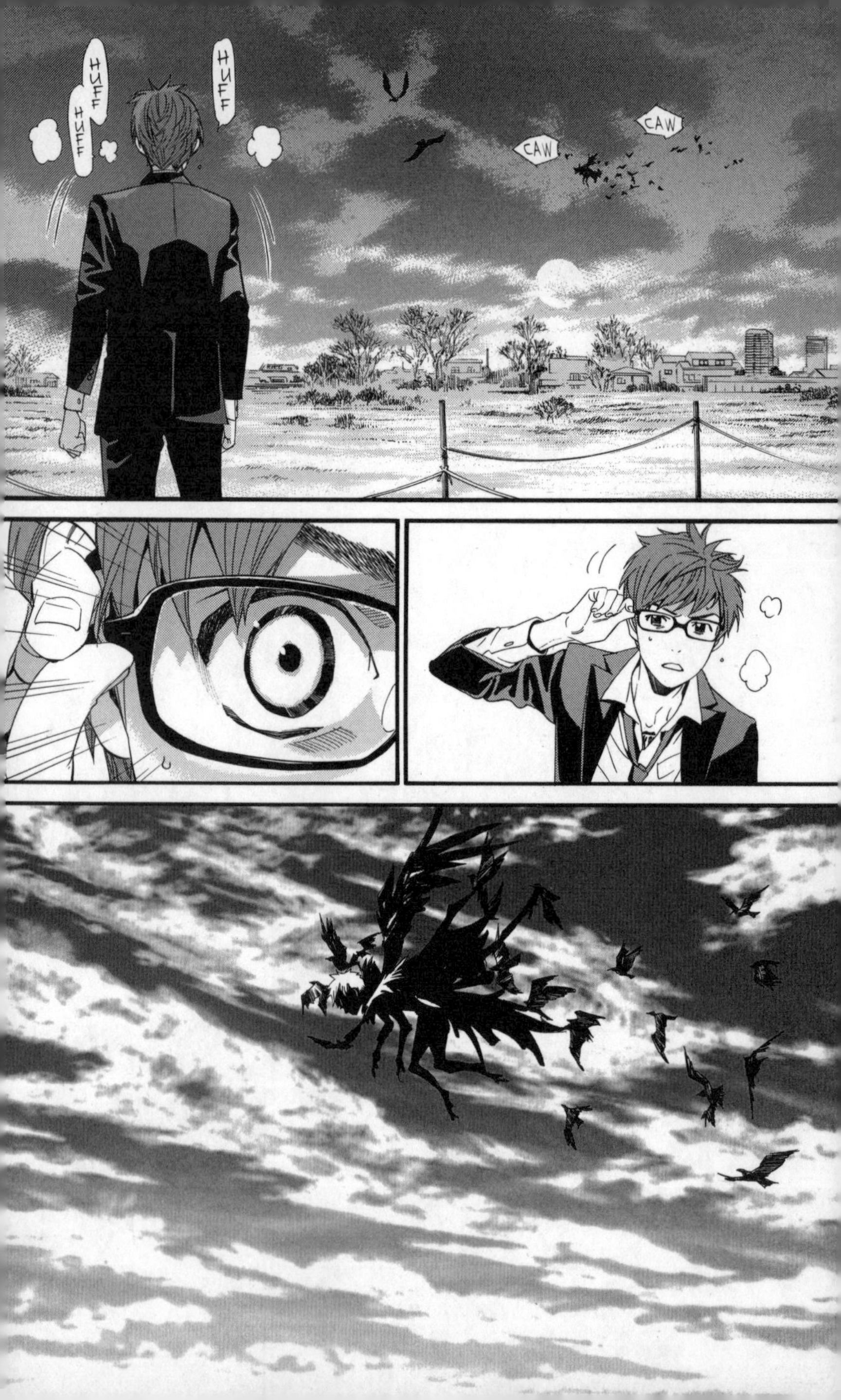
CAW
CAW
HUFF
HUFF HUFF

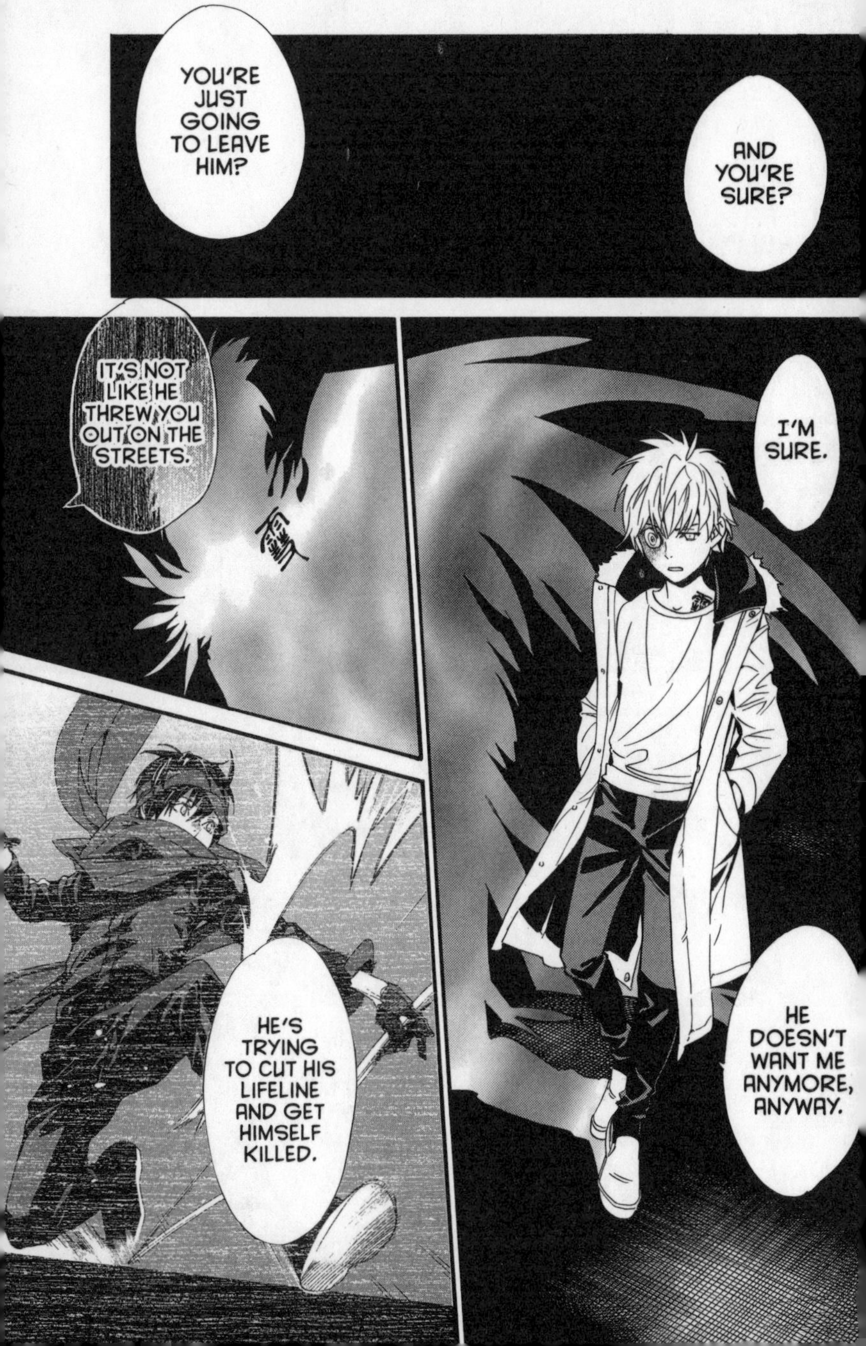
YOU'RE JUST GOING TO LEAVE HIM?
AND YOU'RE SURE?
I'M SURE.
HE DOESN'T WANT ME ANYMORE, ANYWAY.
IT'S NOT LIKE HE THREW YOU OUT ON THE STREETS.
HE'S TRYING TO CUT HIS LIFELINE AND GET HIMSELF KILLED.

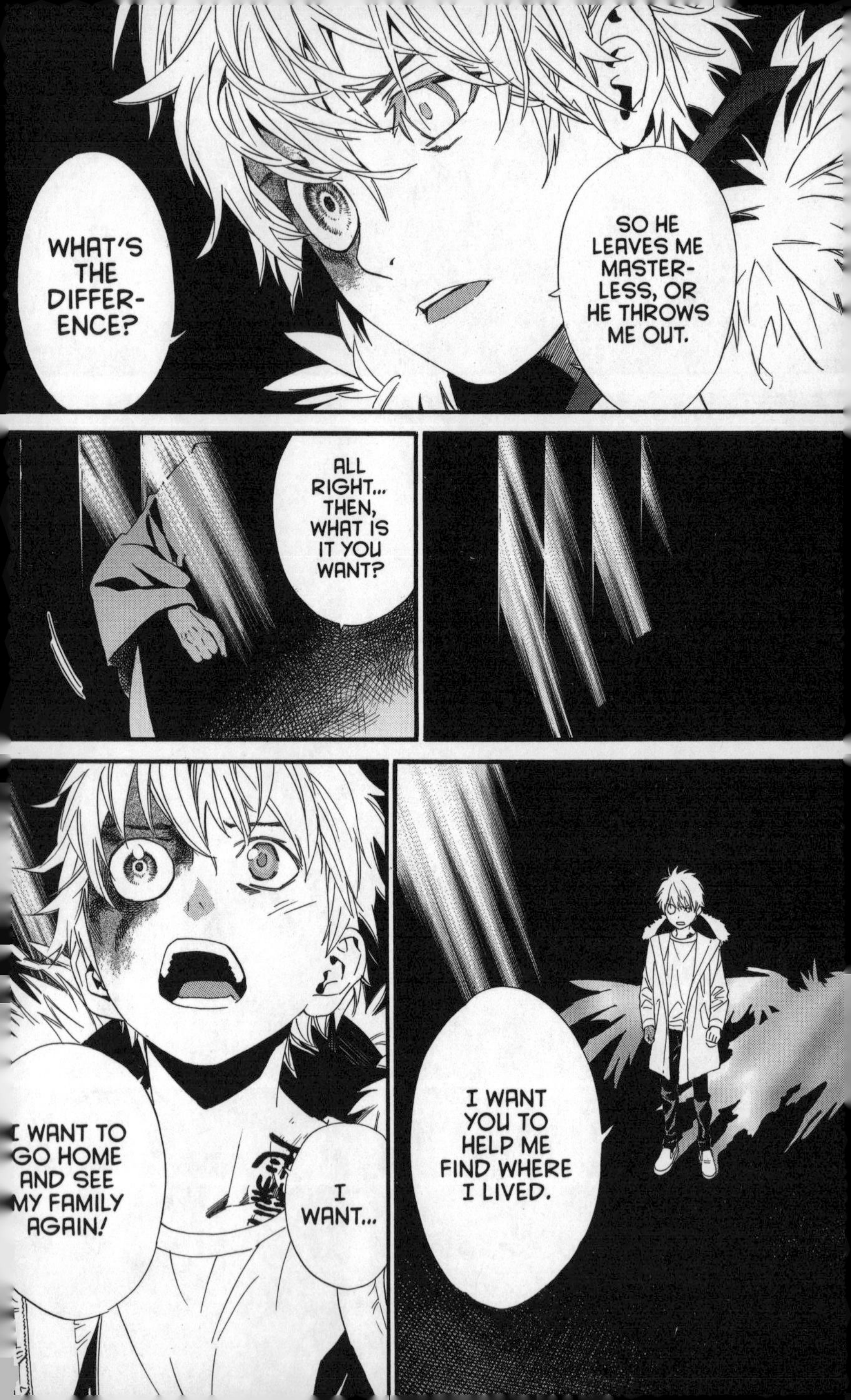
SO HE LEAVES ME MASTER-LESS, OR HE THROWS ME OUT.
WHAT'S THE DIFFER-ENCE?
ALL RIGHT... THEN, WHAT IS IT YOU WANT?
I WANT YOU TO HELP ME FIND WHERE I LIVED.
I WANT...
I WANT TO GO HOME AND SEE MY FAMILY AGAIN!

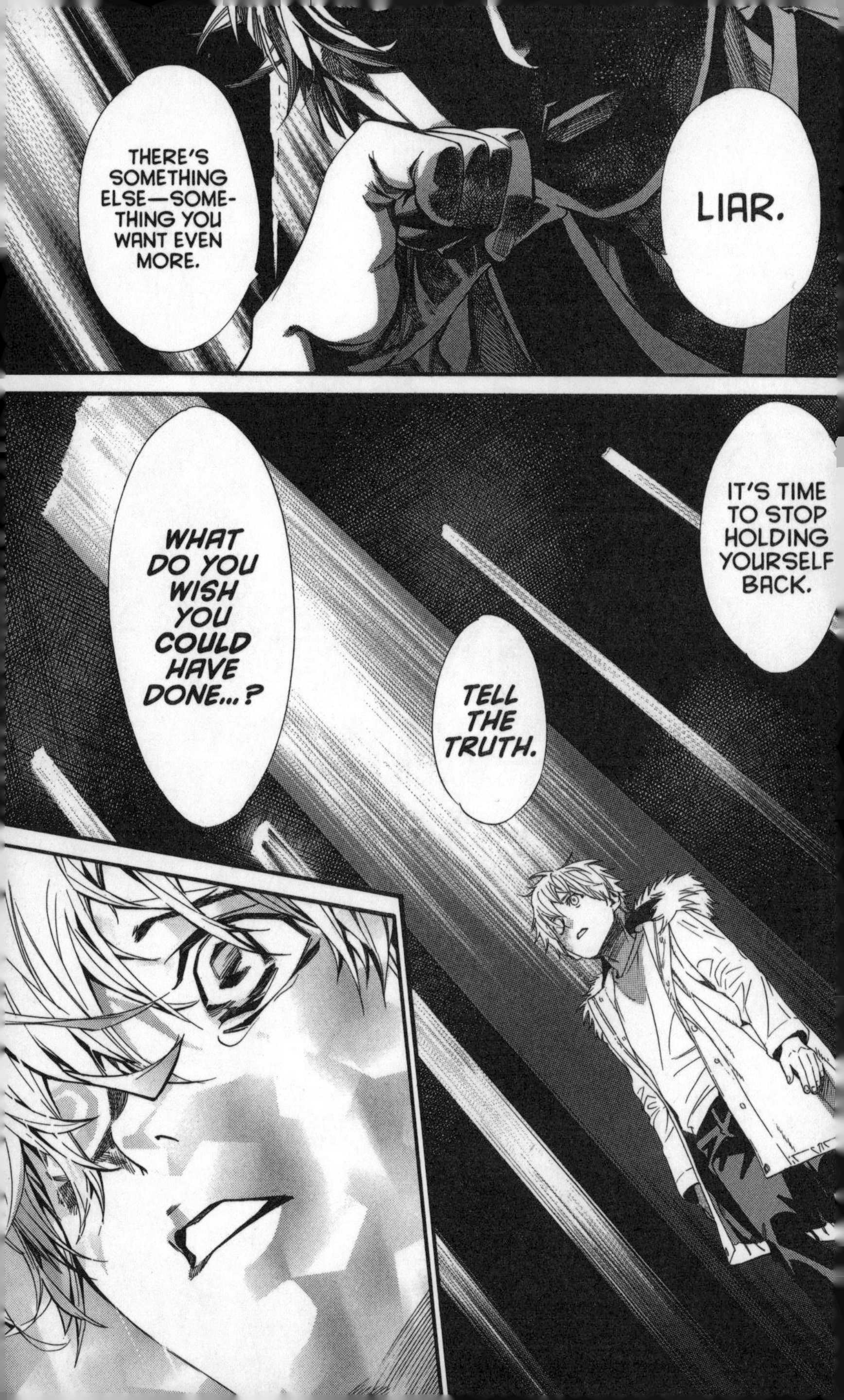
LIAR.
THERE'S SOMETHING ELSE—SOMETHING YOU WANT EVEN MORE.
IT'S TIME TO STOP HOLDING YOURSELF BACK.
TELL THE TRUTH.
WHAT DO YOU WISH YOU COULD HAVE DONE...?

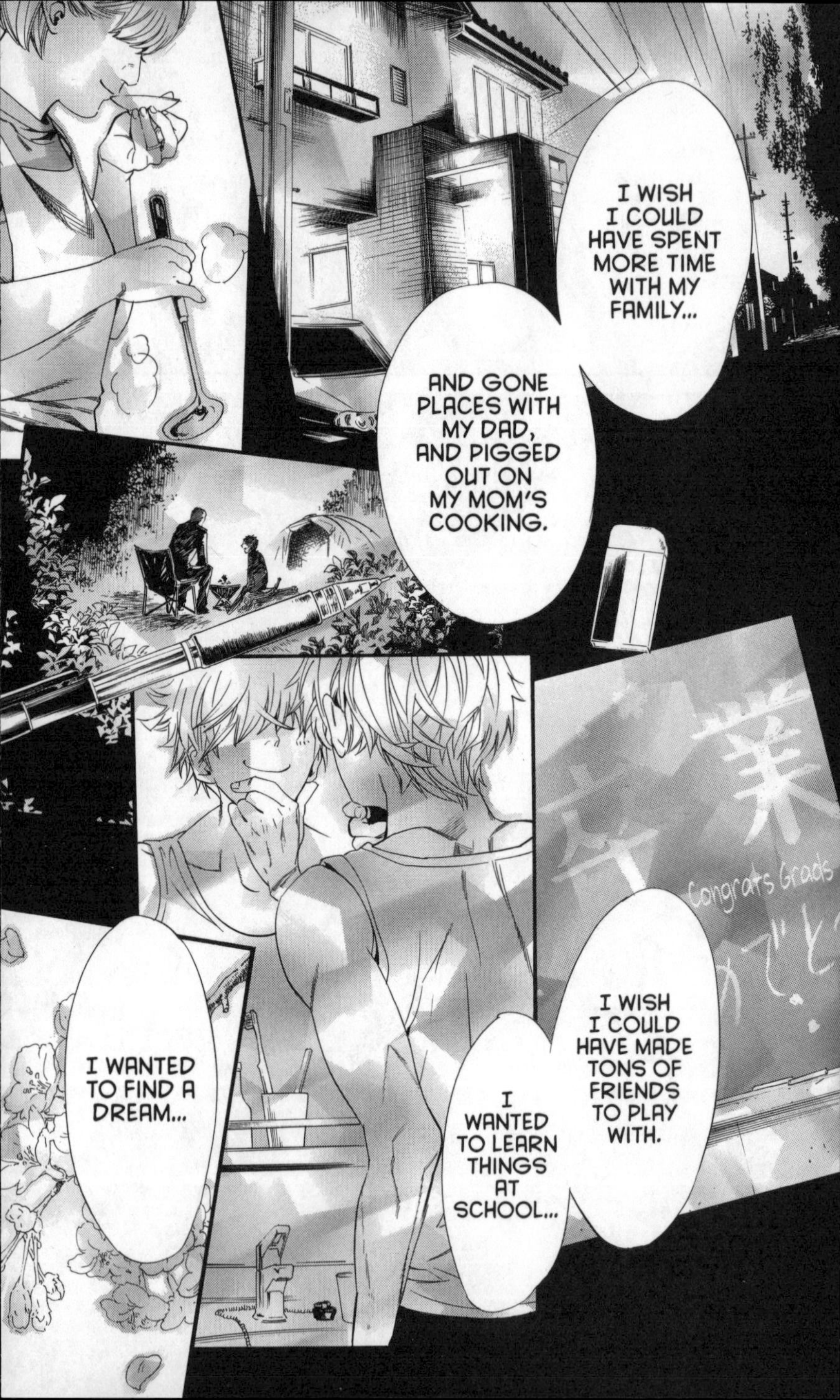
I WISH I COULD HAVE SPENT MORE TIME WITH MY FAMILY...
AND GONE PLACES WITH MY DAD, AND PIGGED OUT ON MY MOM'S COOKING.
Congrats Grads
I WISH I COULD HAVE MADE TONS OF FRIENDS TO PLAY WITH.
I WANTED TO LEARN THINGS AT SCHOOL...
I WANTED TO FIND A DREAM...

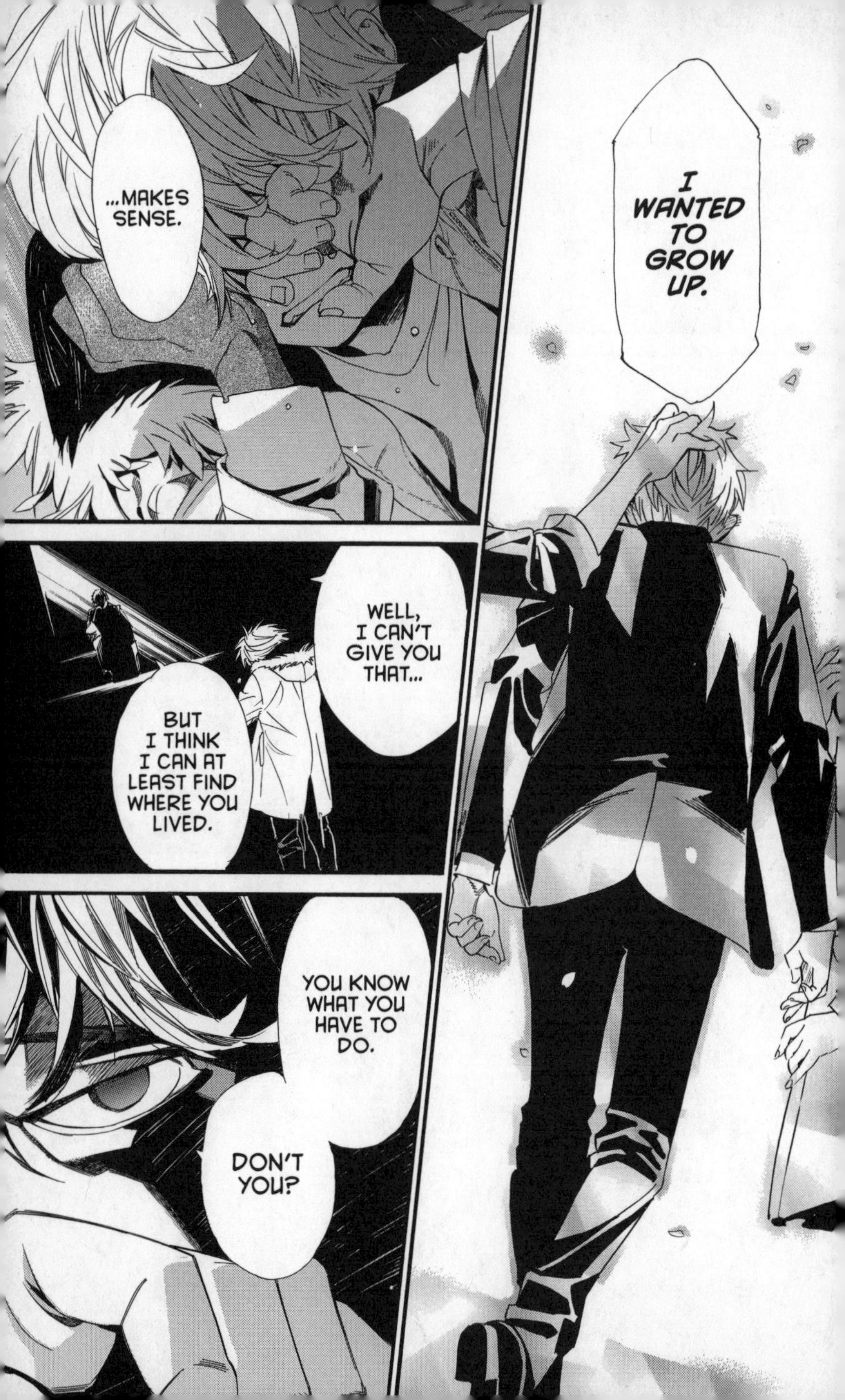
I WANTED TO GROW UP.
...MAKES SENSE.
WELL, I CAN'T GIVE YOU THAT...
BUT I THINK I CAN AT LEAST FIND WHERE YOU LIVED.
YOU KNOW WHAT YOU HAVE TO DO.
DON'T YOU?

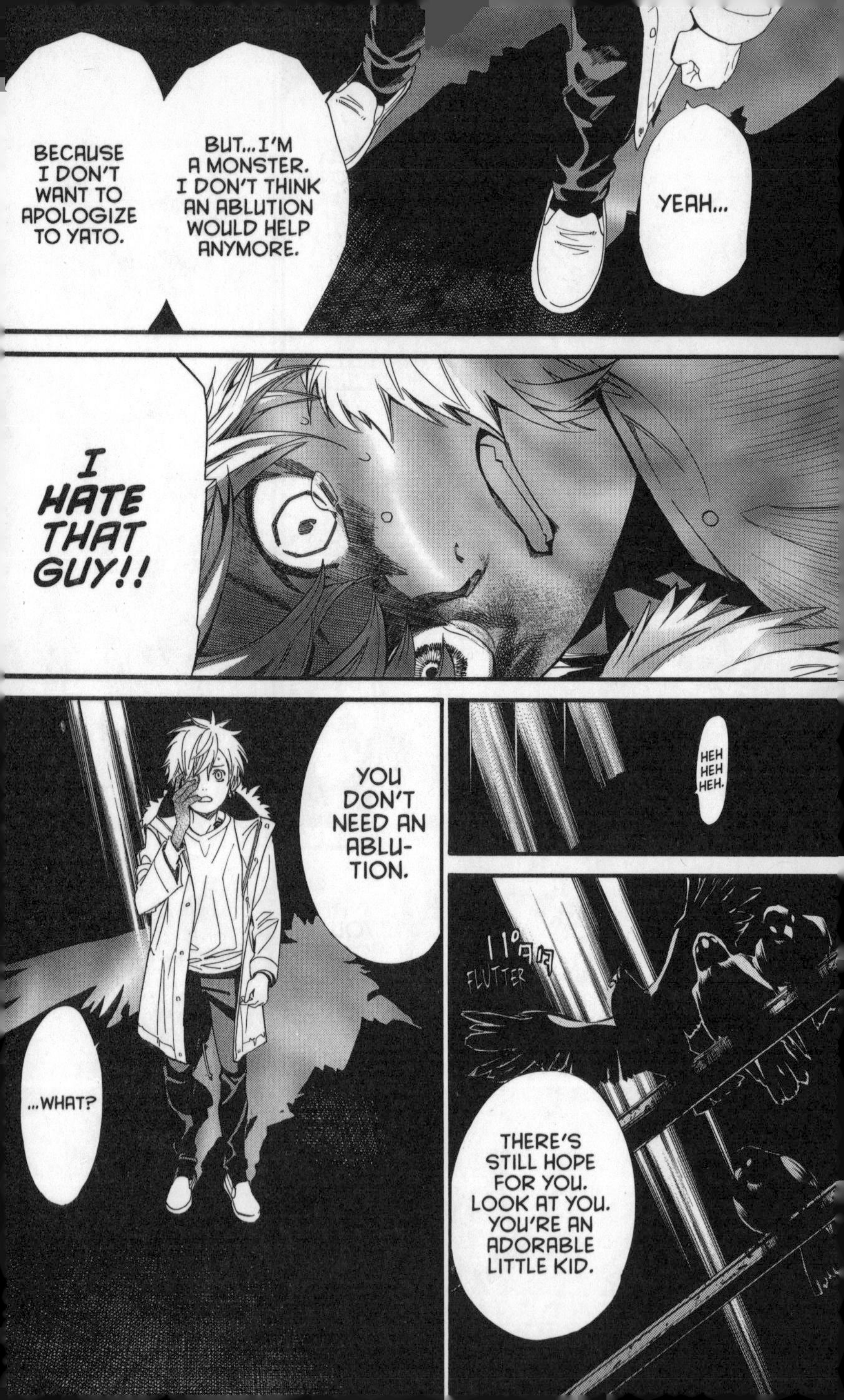
YEAH...
BUT...I'M A MONSTER. I DON'T THINK AN ABLUTION WOULD HELP ANYMORE.
BECAUSE I DON'T WANT TO APOLOGIZE TO YATO.
I HATE THAT GUY!!
HEH HEH HEH.
FLUTTER
THERE'S STILL HOPE FOR YOU. LOOK AT YOU. YOU'RE AN ADORABLE LITTLE KID.
YOU DON'T NEED AN ABLU-TION.
...WHAT?

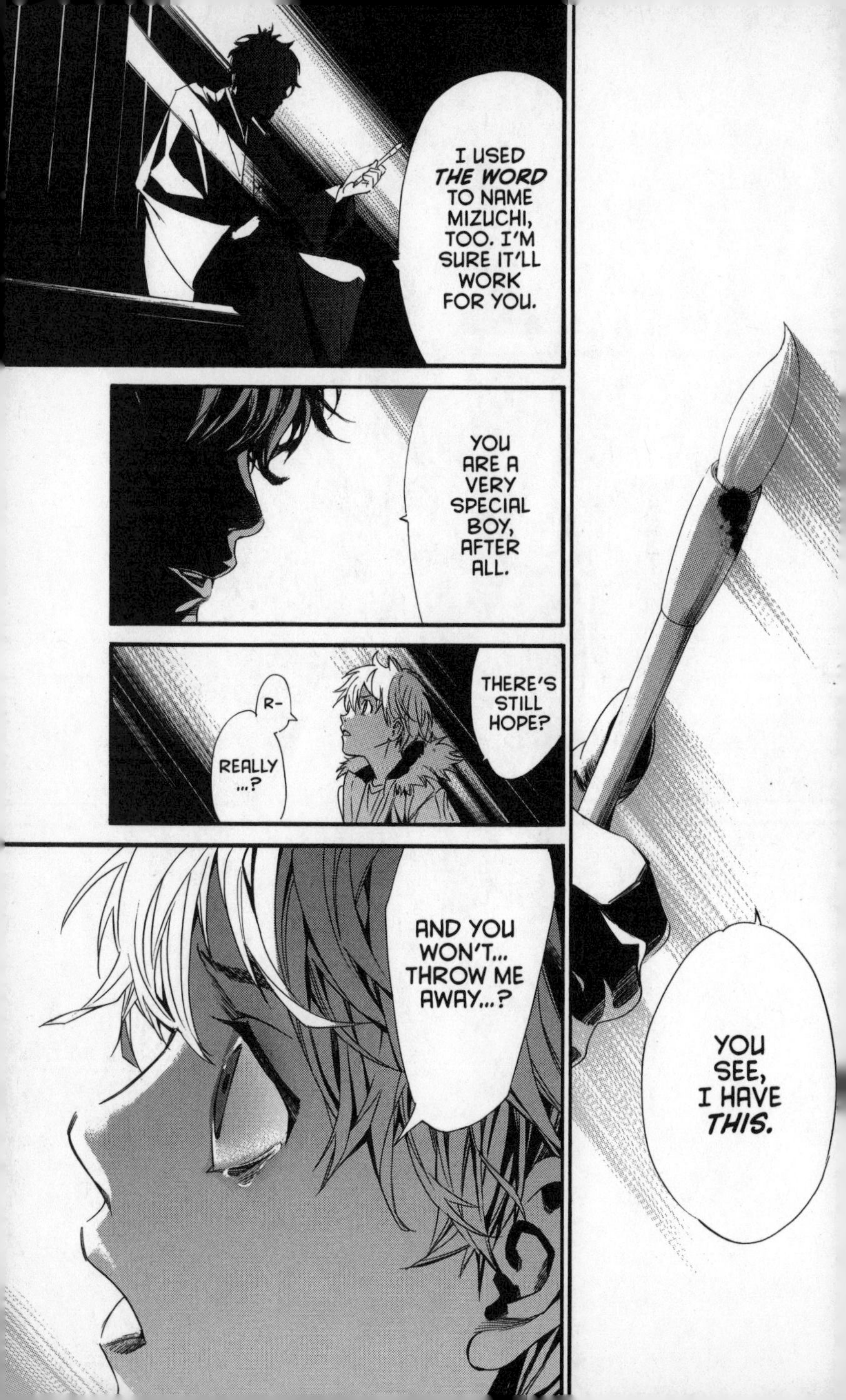
YOU SEE, I HAVE *THIS.*
I USED *THE WORD* TO NAME MIZUCHI, TOO. I'M SURE IT'LL WORK FOR YOU.
YOU ARE A VERY SPECIAL BOY, AFTER ALL.
THERE'S STILL HOPE?
R-
REALLY ...?
AND YOU WON'T... THROW ME AWAY...?

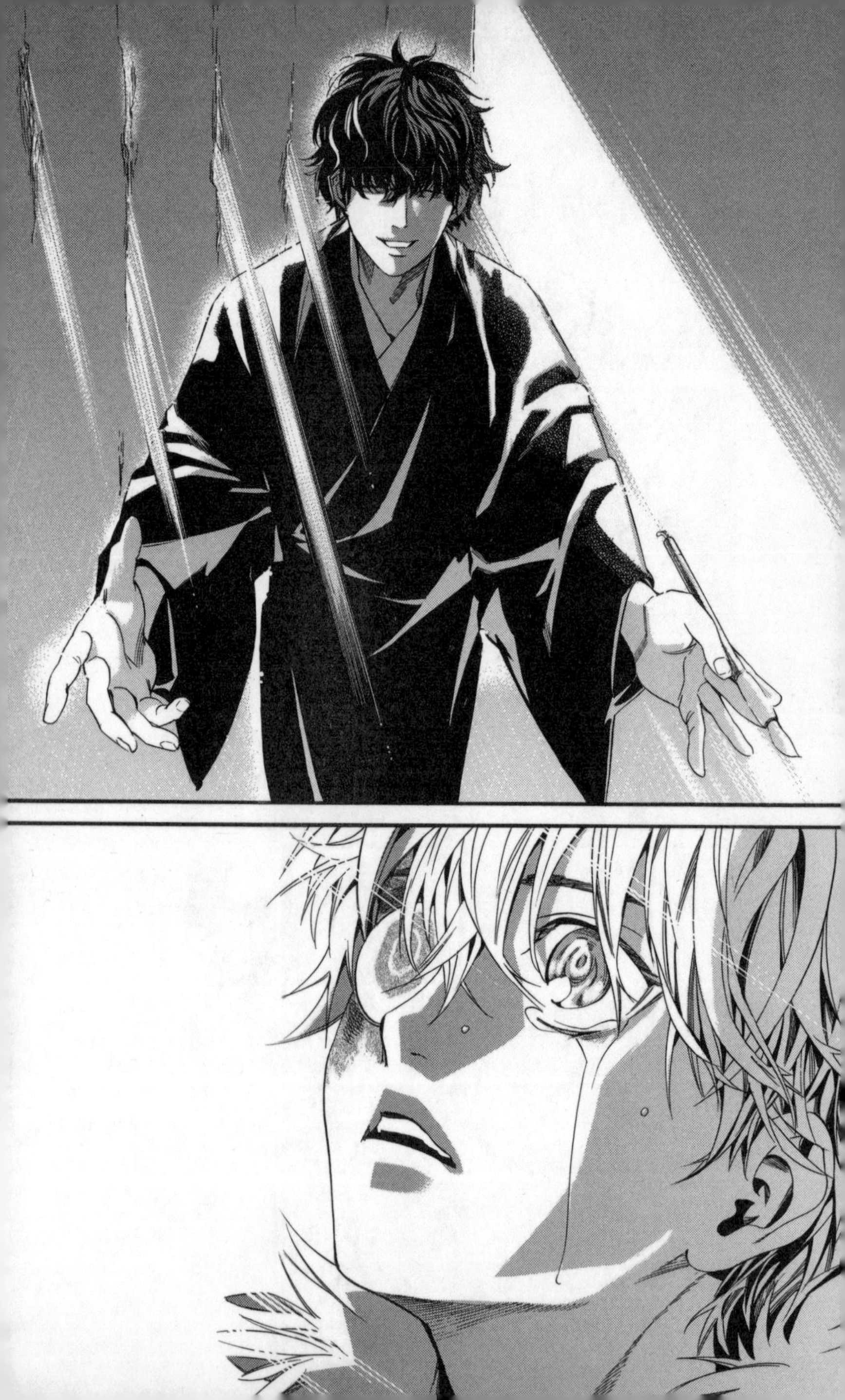

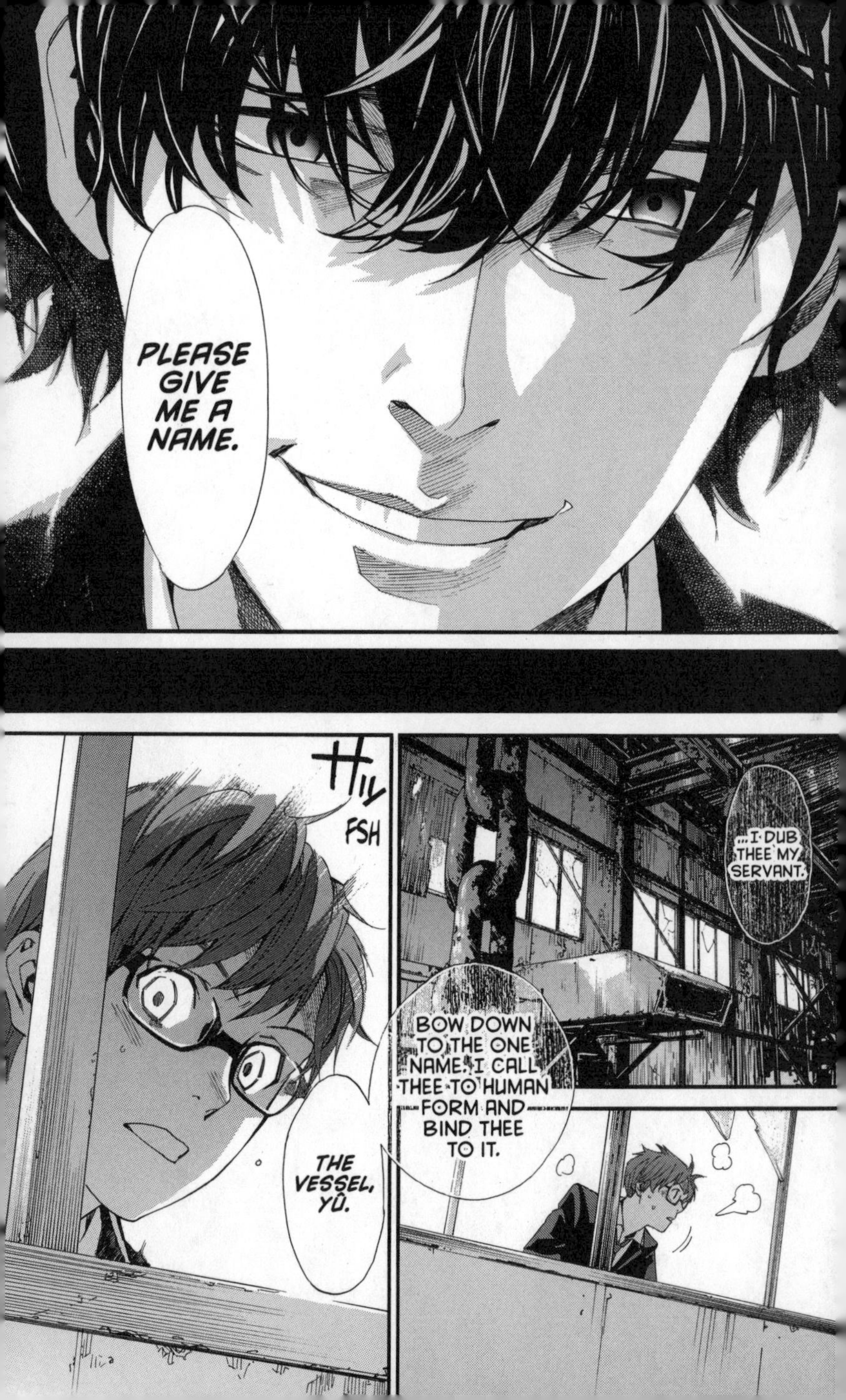
PLEASE GIVE ME A NAME.
...I DUB THEE MY SERVANT.
BOW DOWN TO THE ONE NAME. I CALL THEE TO HUMAN FORM AND BIND THEE TO IT.
FSH
THE VESSEL, YÛ.

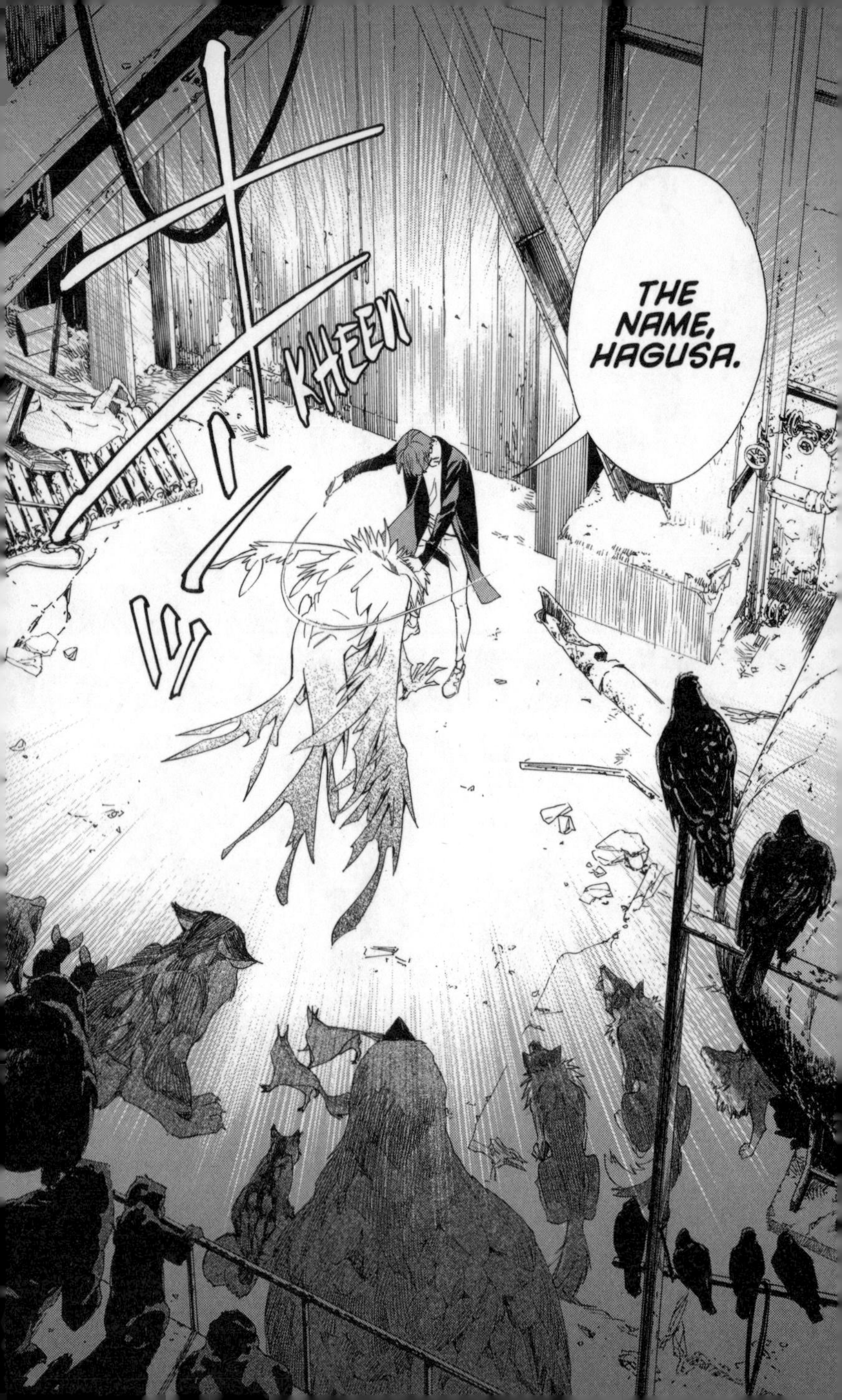
THE NAME, HAGUSA.
KHEEN

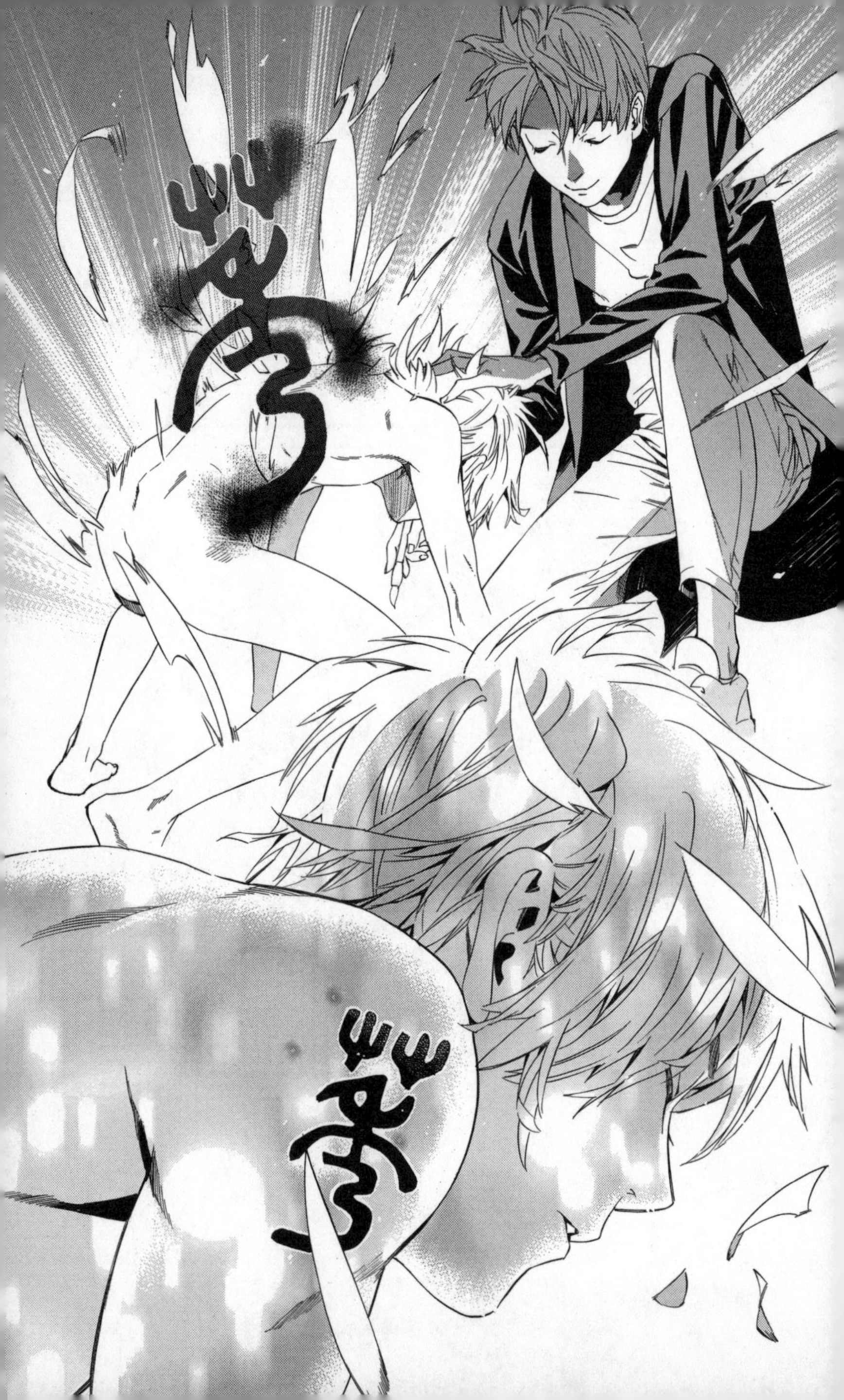

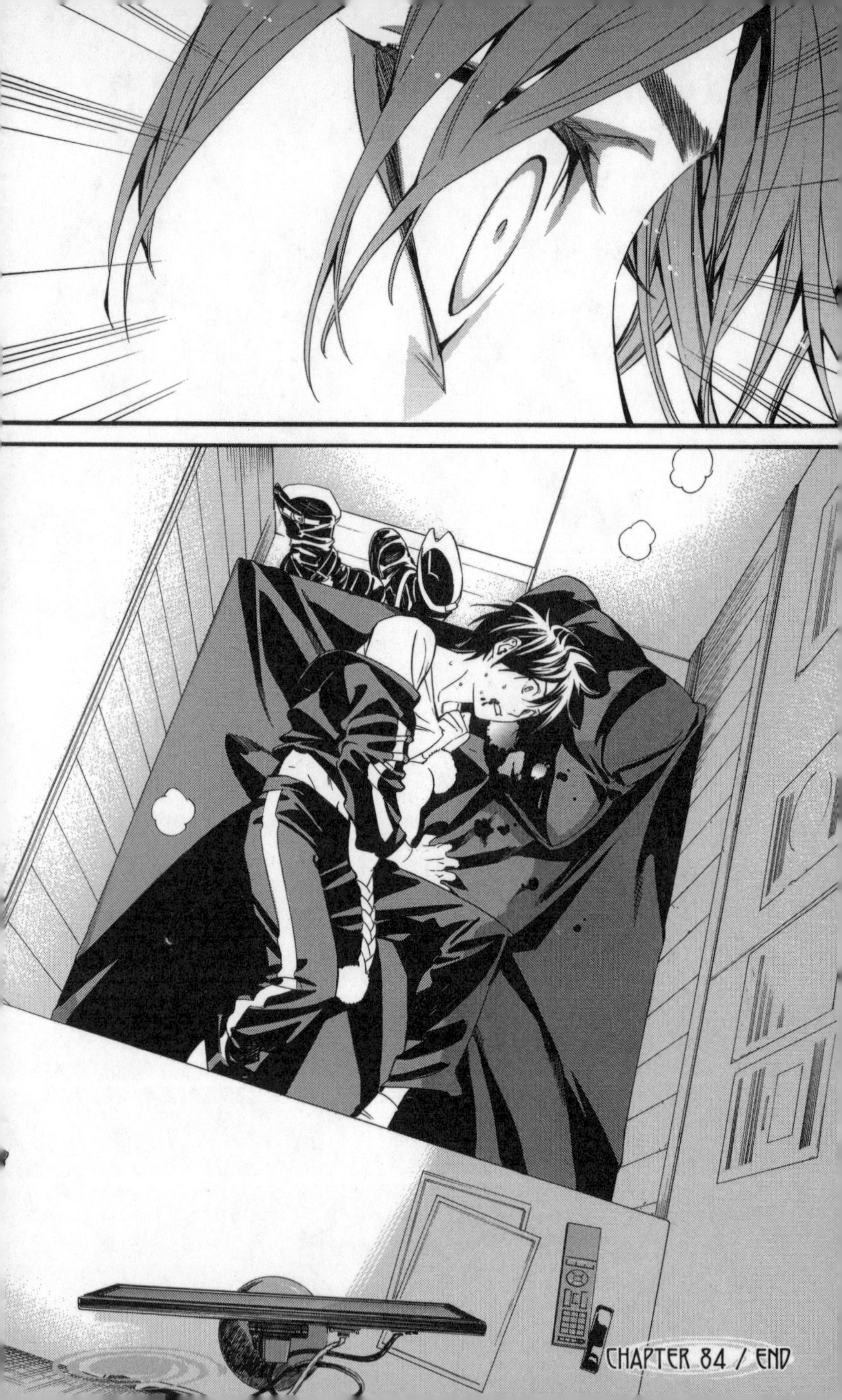
CHAPTER 84 / END

野

皀

神

師

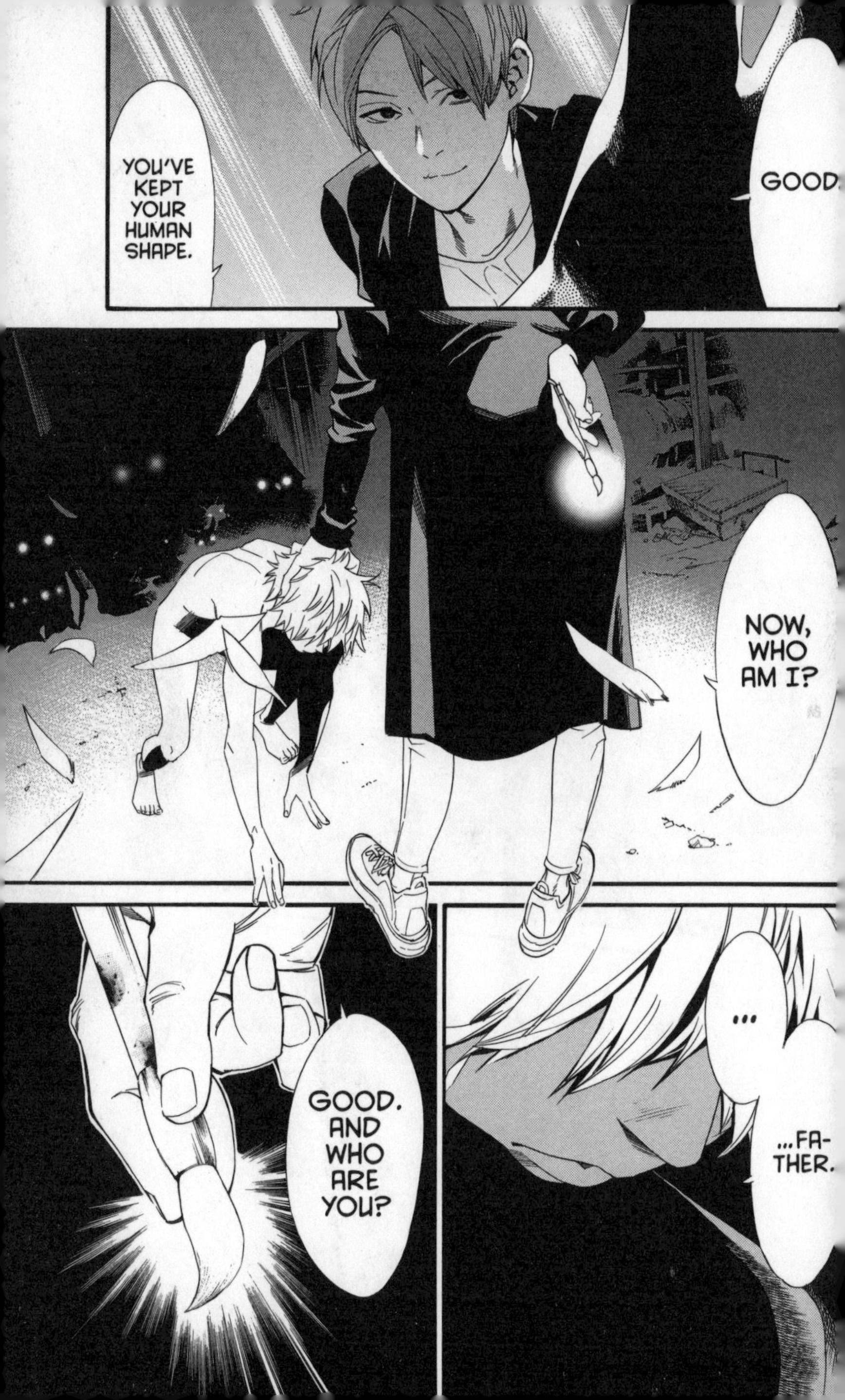
GOOD.
YOU'VE KEPT YOUR HUMAN SHAPE.
NOW, WHO AM I?
...
...FA-THER.
GOOD. AND WHO ARE YOU?

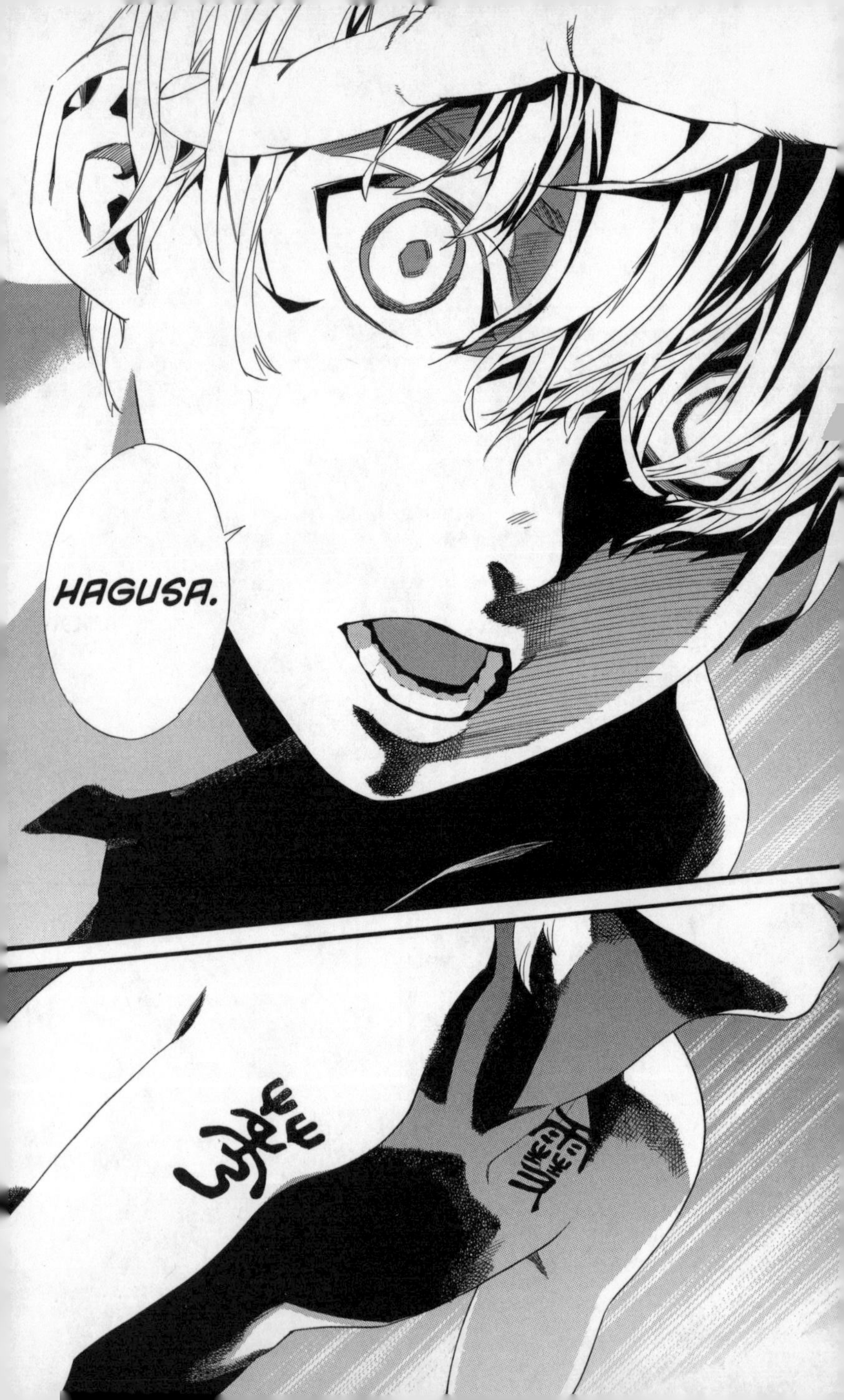
HAGUSA.

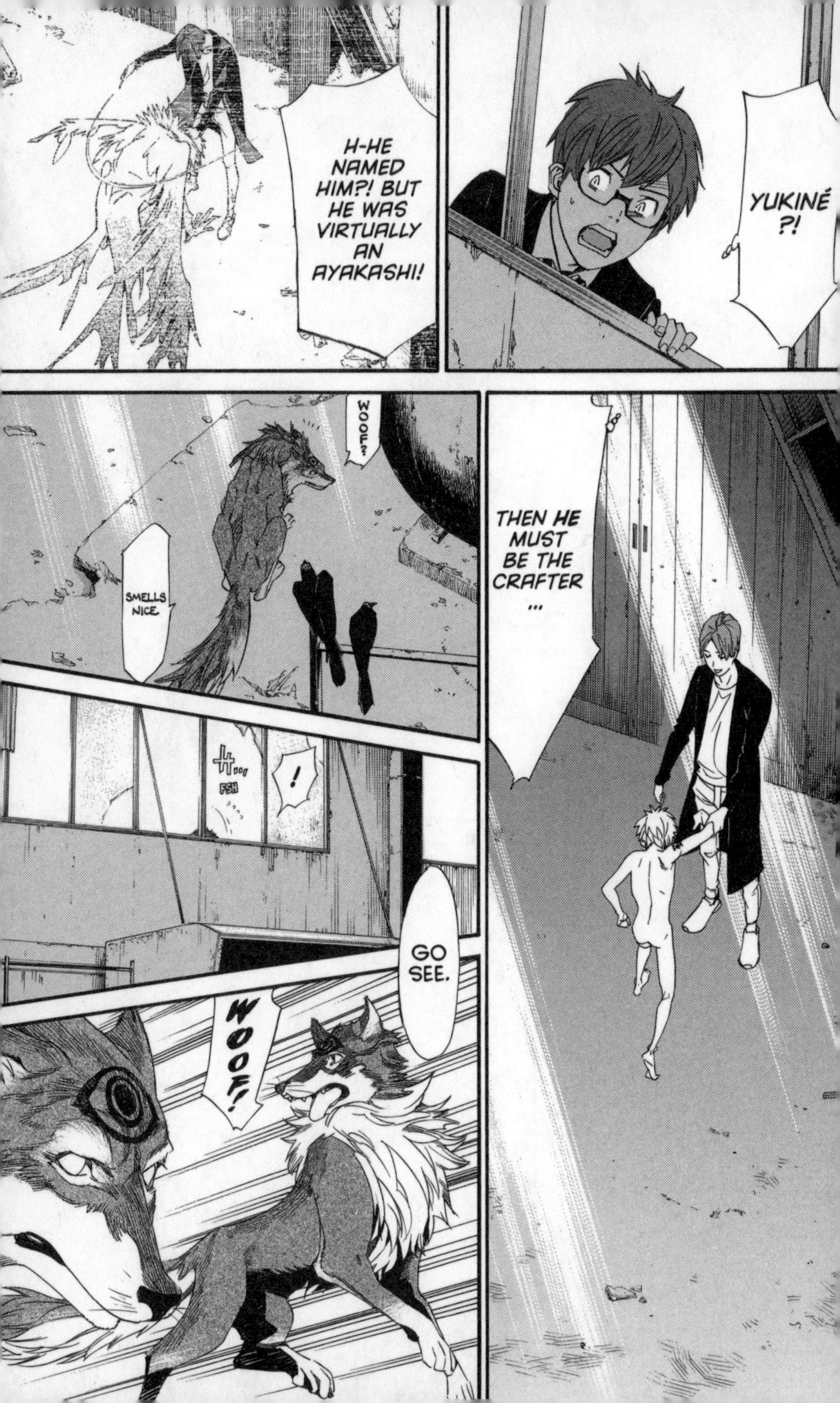
YUKINÉ ?!
H-HE NAMED HIM?! BUT HE WAS VIRTUALLY AN AYAKASHI!
THEN HE MUST BE THE CRAFTER ...
WOOF?
SMELLS NICE
FSH...
!
GO SEE.
WOOF!

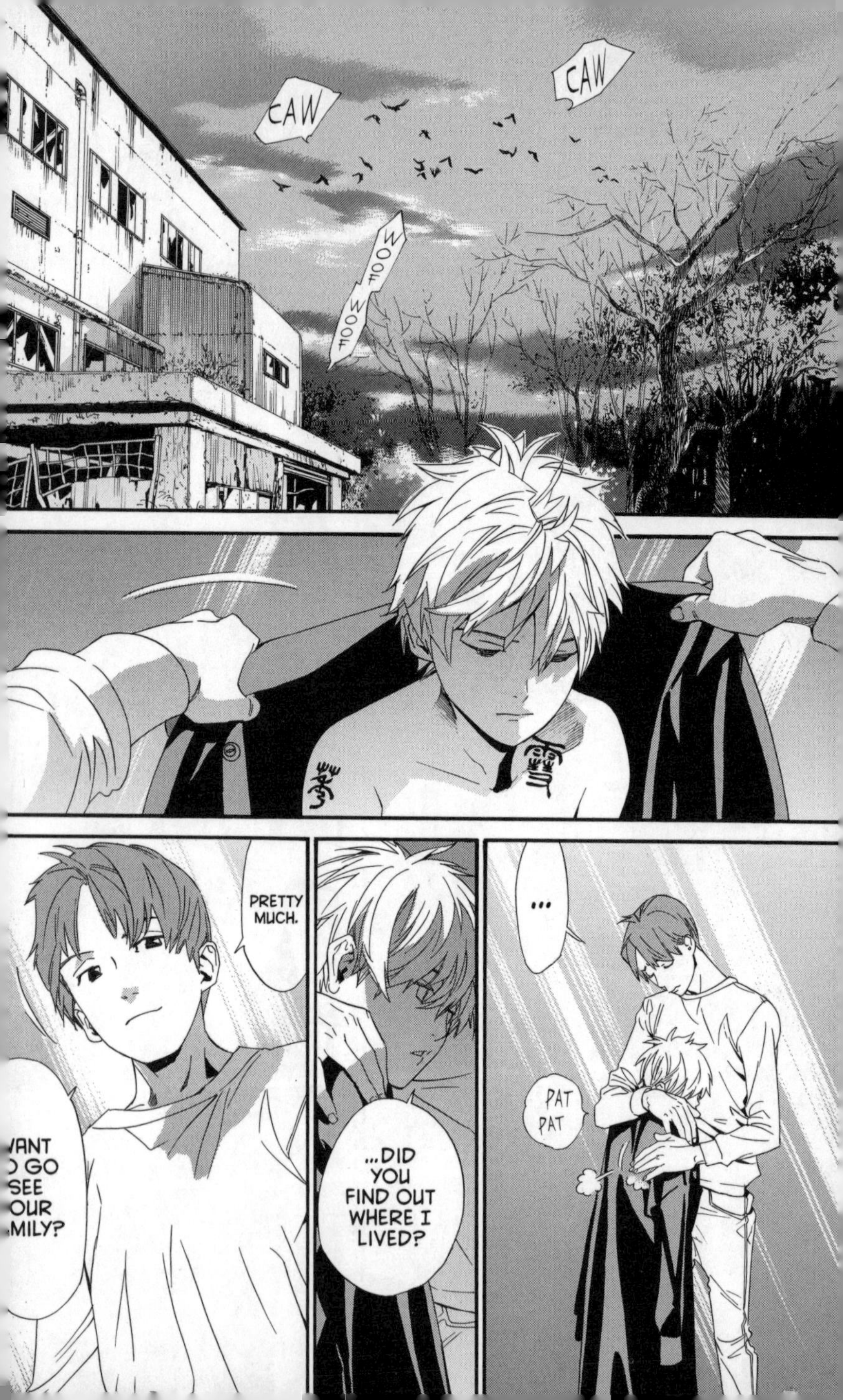
CAW
CAW
WOOF WOOF
...
PAT PAT
...DID YOU FIND OUT WHERE I LIVED?
PRETTY MUCH.
WANT O GO SEE OUR MILY?

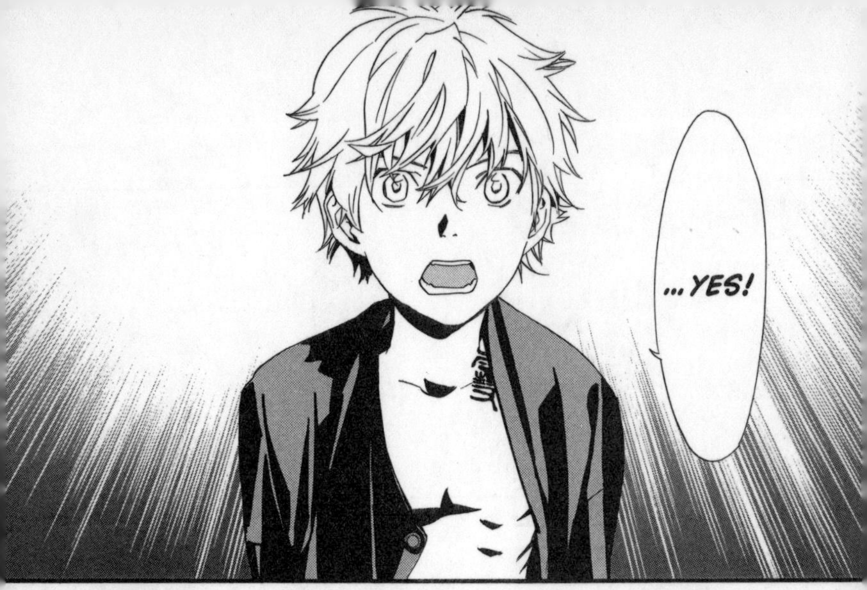
...YES!

CHAPTER 85: MISSING YOU

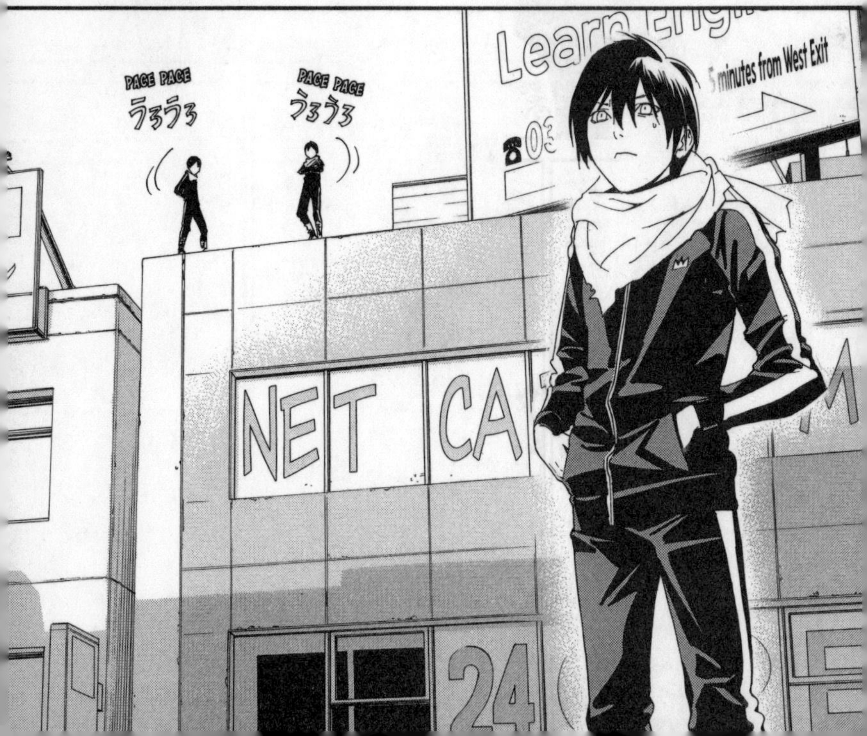
5 minutes from West Exit
PACE PACE
うろうろ
PACE PACE
うろうろ
NET CA
24

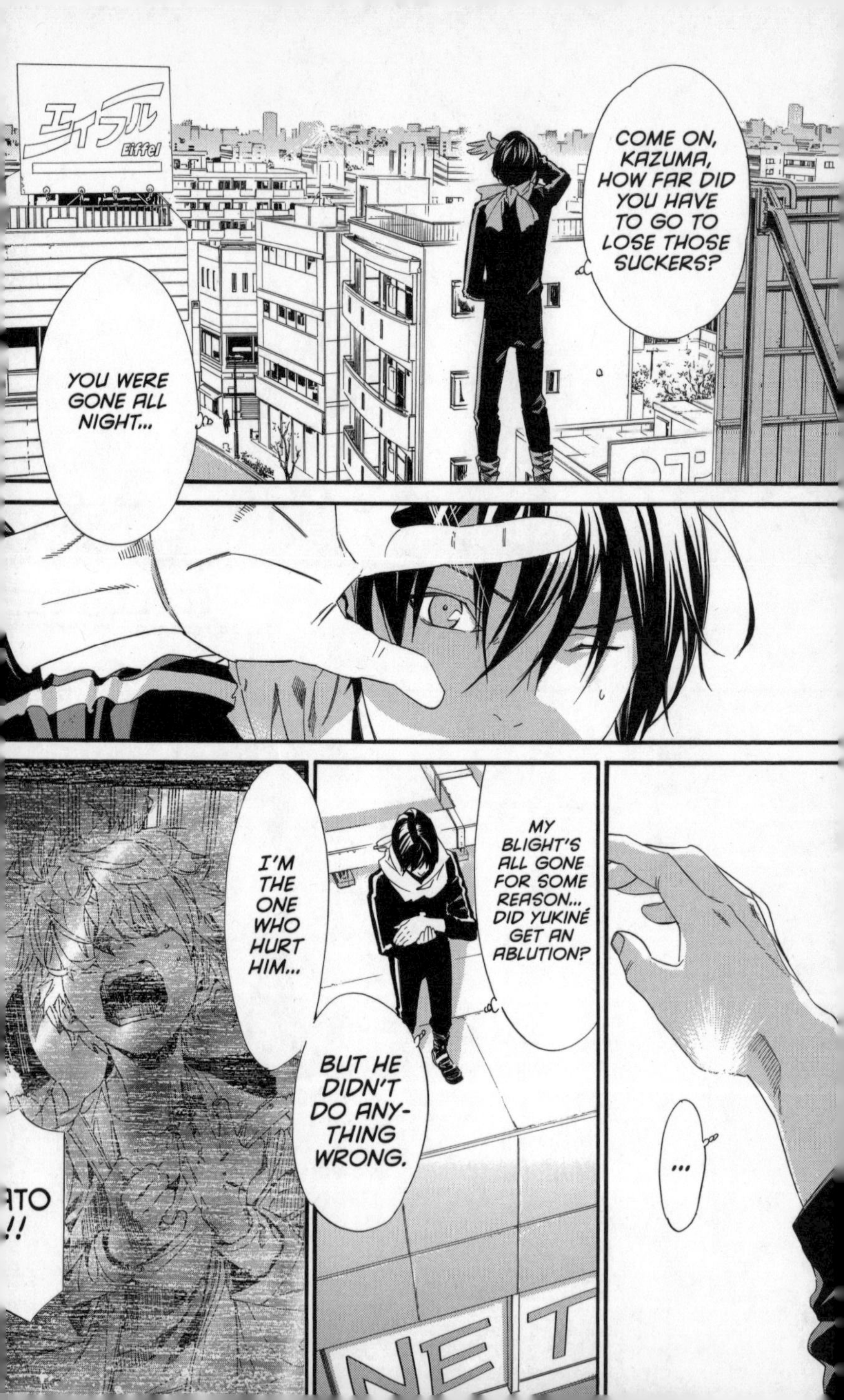
COME ON, KAZUMA, HOW FAR DID YOU HAVE TO GO TO LOSE THOSE SUCKERS?
エイフル Eiffel
YOU WERE GONE ALL NIGHT...
...
MY BLIGHT'S ALL GONE FOR SOME REASON... DID YUKINÉ GET AN ABLUTION?
I'M THE ONE WHO HURT HIM...
BUT HE DIDN'T DO ANY-THING WRONG.

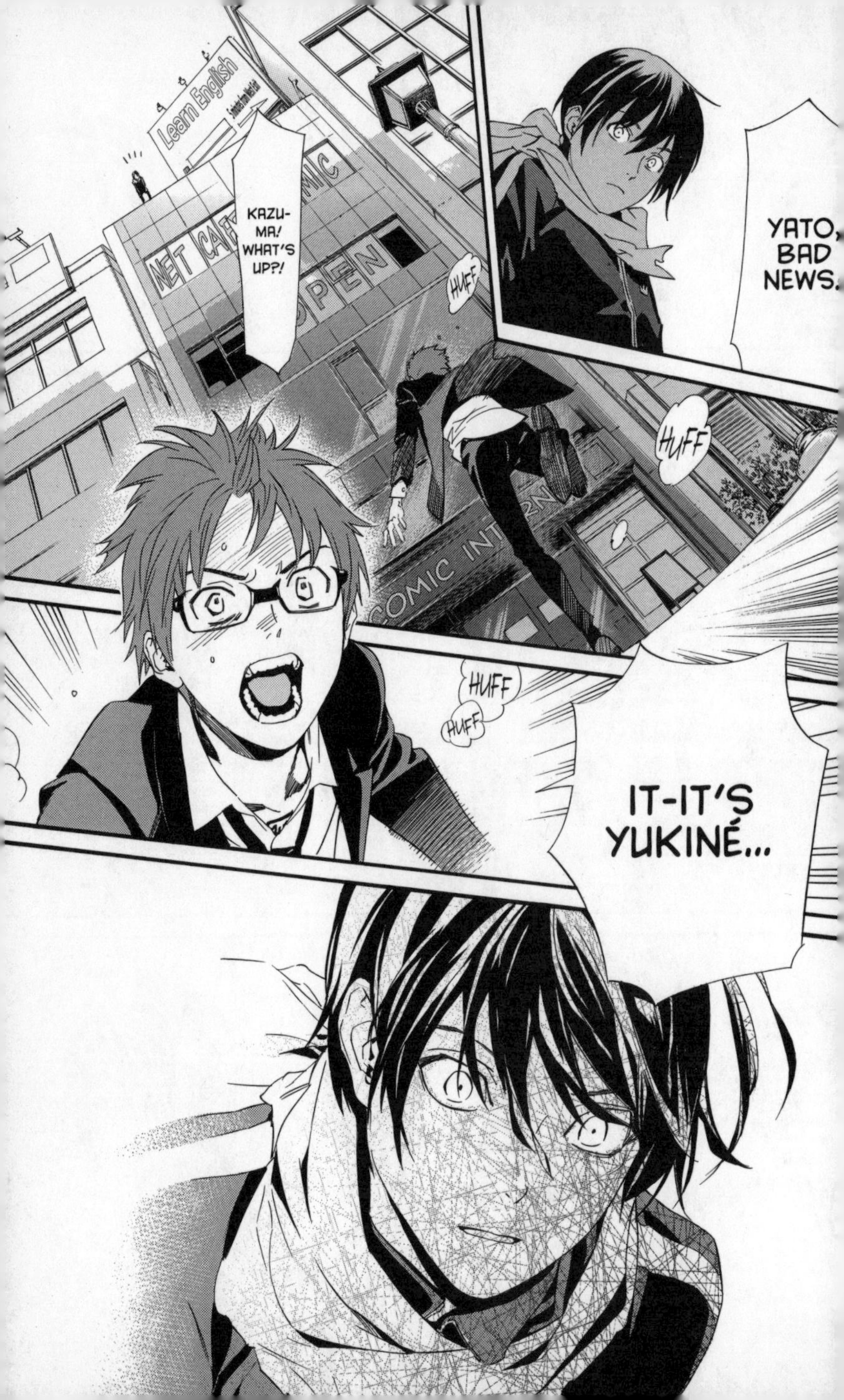

Learn English
OPEN
KAZUMA! WHAT'S UP?!
HUFF
YATO, BAD NEWS.
HUFF
HUFF
HUFF
IT-IT'S YUKINÉ...

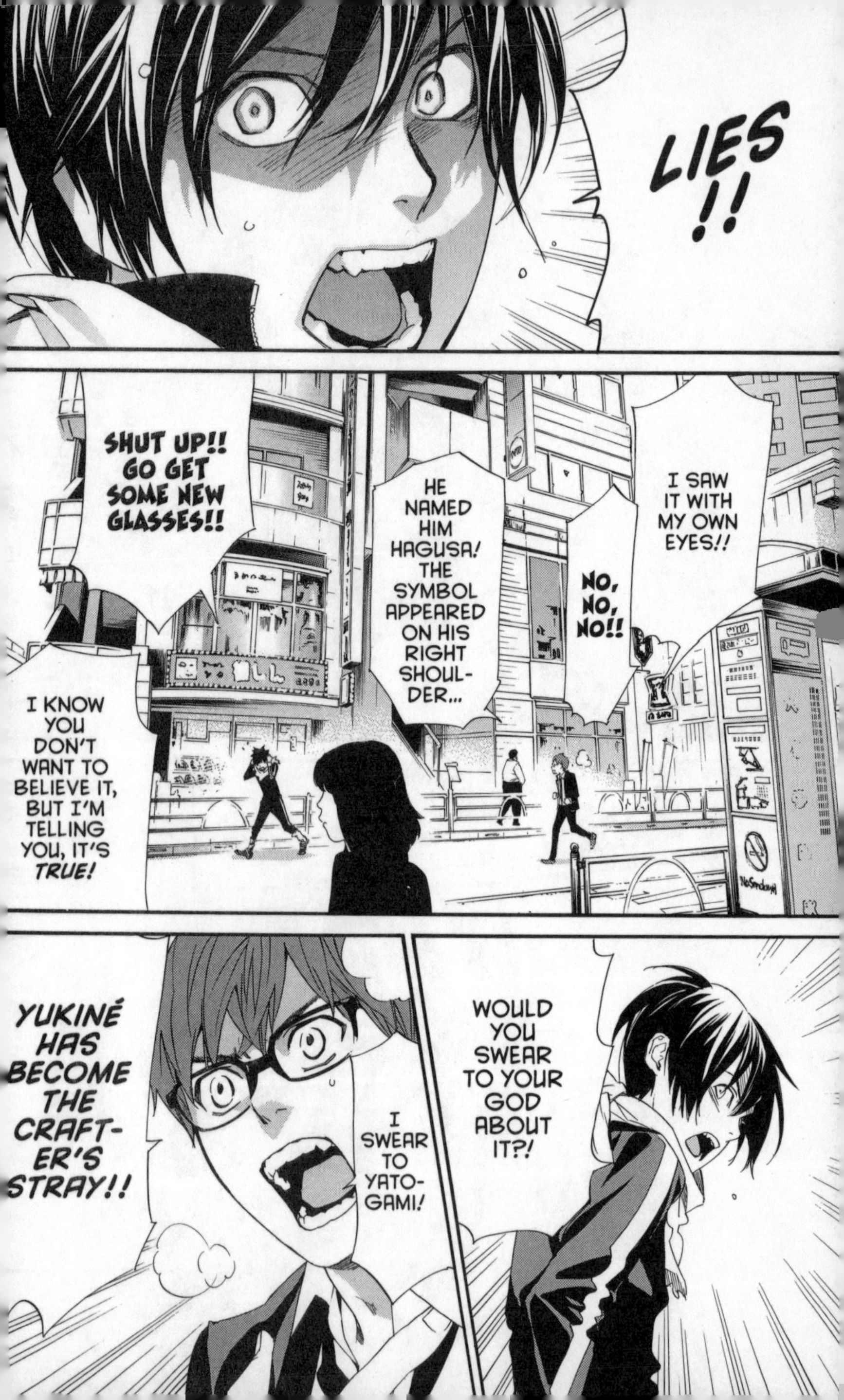
LIES!!
I SAW IT WITH MY OWN EYES!!
NO, NO, NO!!
HE NAMED HIM HAGUSA! THE SYMBOL APPEARED ON HIS RIGHT SHOULDER...
SHUT UP!! GO GET SOME NEW GLASSES!!
I KNOW YOU DON'T WANT TO BELIEVE IT, BUT I'M TELLING YOU, IT'S TRUE!
WOULD YOU SWEAR TO YOUR GOD ABOUT IT?!
I SWEAR TO YATO-GAMI!
YUKINÉ HAS BECOME THE CRAFTER'S STRAY!!

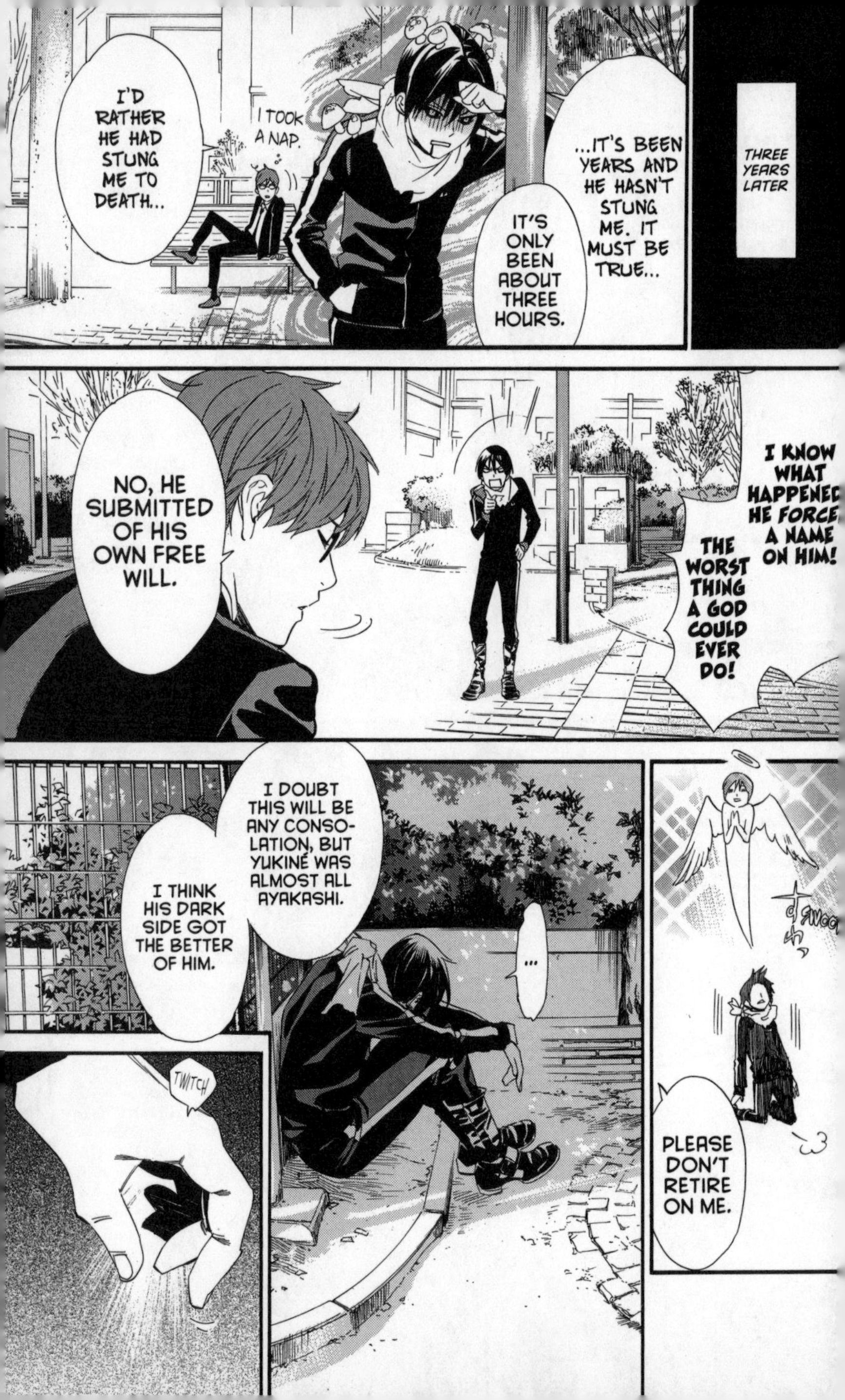
THREE YEARS LATER
...IT'S BEEN YEARS AND HE HASN'T STUNG ME. IT MUST BE TRUE...
IT'S ONLY BEEN ABOUT THREE HOURS.
I TOOK A NAP.
I'D RATHER HE HAD STUNG ME TO DEATH...
I KNOW WHAT HAPPENED HE FORCE A NAME ON HIM!
THE WORST THING A GOD COULD EVER DO!
NO, HE SUBMITTED OF HIS OWN FREE WILL.
SWOO
PLEASE DON'T RETIRE ON ME.
...
I DOUBT THIS WILL BE ANY CONSOLATION, BUT YUKINÉ WAS ALMOST ALL AYAKASHI.
I THINK HIS DARK SIDE GOT THE BETTER OF HIM.
TWITCH

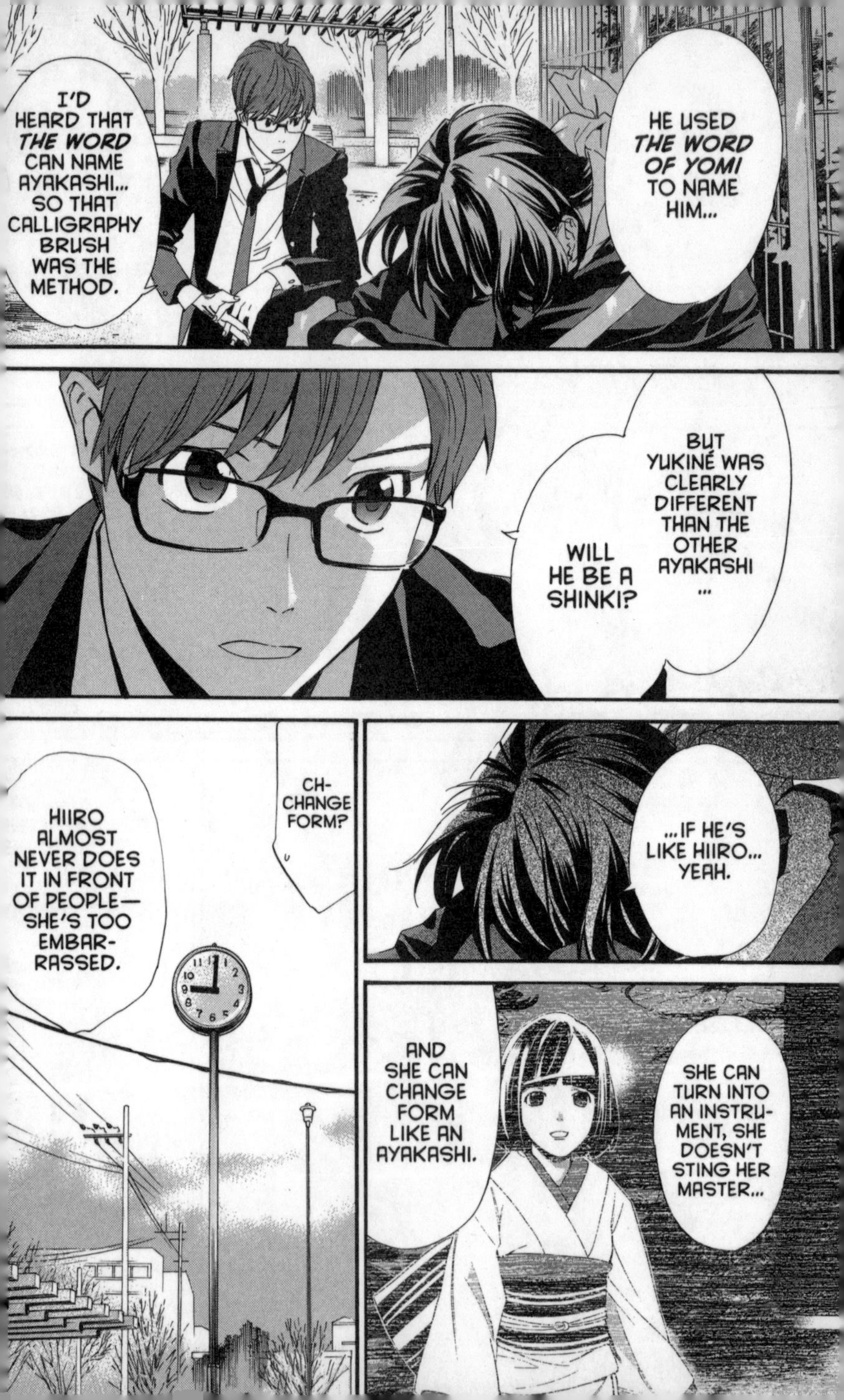
HE USED *THE WORD OF YOMI* TO NAME HIM...
I'D HEARD THAT *THE WORD* CAN NAME AYAKASHI... SO THAT CALLIGRAPHY BRUSH WAS THE METHOD.
BUT YUKINÉ WAS CLEARLY DIFFERENT THAN THE OTHER AYAKASHI...
WILL HE BE A SHINKI?
...IF HE'S LIKE HIIRO... YEAH.
SHE CAN TURN INTO AN INSTRU-MENT, SHE DOESN'T STING HER MASTER...
AND SHE CAN CHANGE FORM LIKE AN AYAKASHI.
CH- CHANGE FORM?
HIIRO ALMOST NEVER DOES IT IN FRONT OF PEOPLE—SHE'S TOO EMBAR-RASSED.

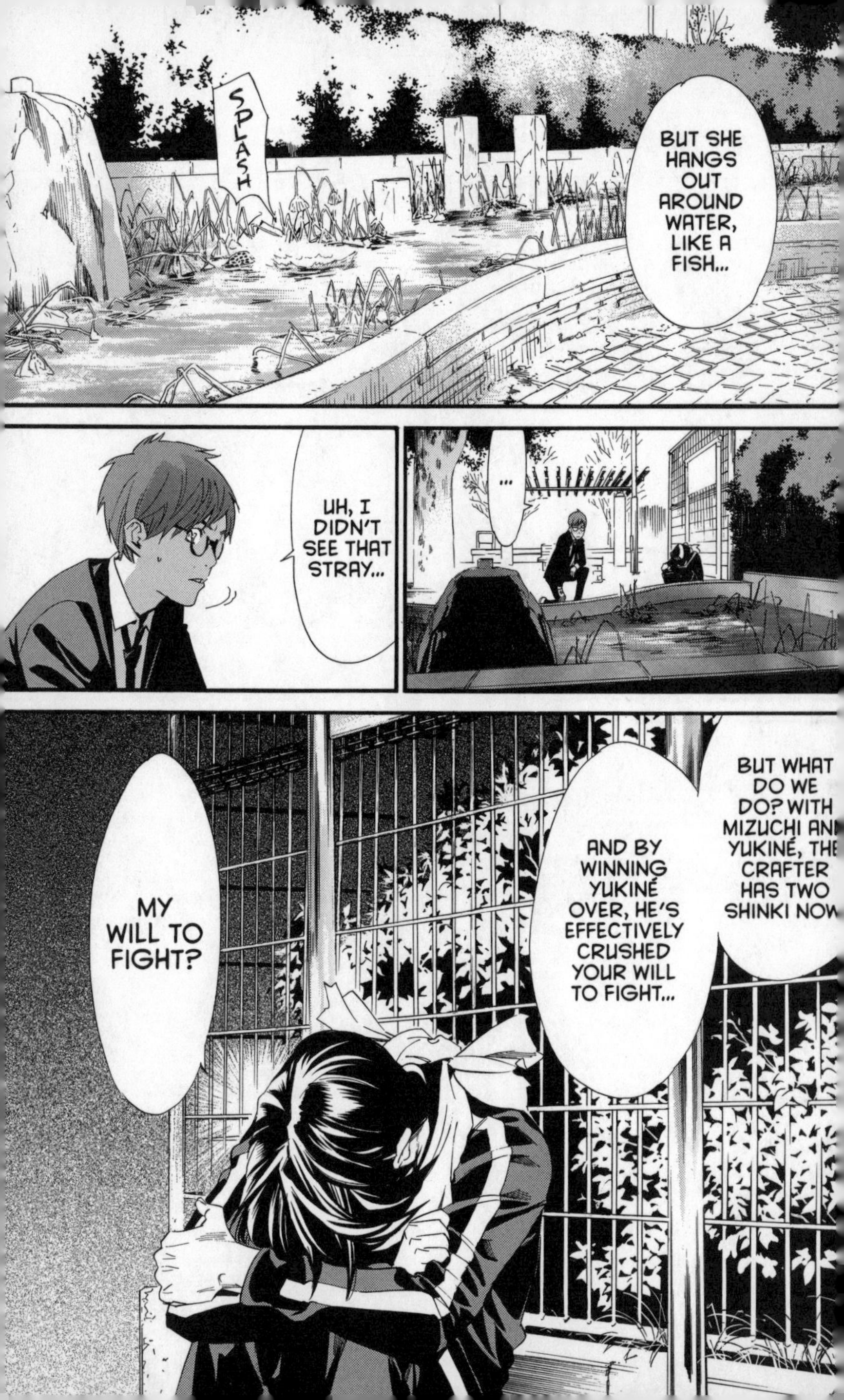
BUT SHE HANGS OUT AROUND WATER, LIKE A FISH...
SPLASH
...
UH, I DIDN'T SEE THAT STRAY...
BUT WHAT DO WE DO? WITH MIZUCHI AN YUKINÉ, TH CRAFTER HAS TWO SHINKI NOW
AND BY WINNING YUKINÉ OVER, HE'S EFFECTIVELY CRUSHED YOUR WILL TO FIGHT...
MY WILL TO FIGHT?

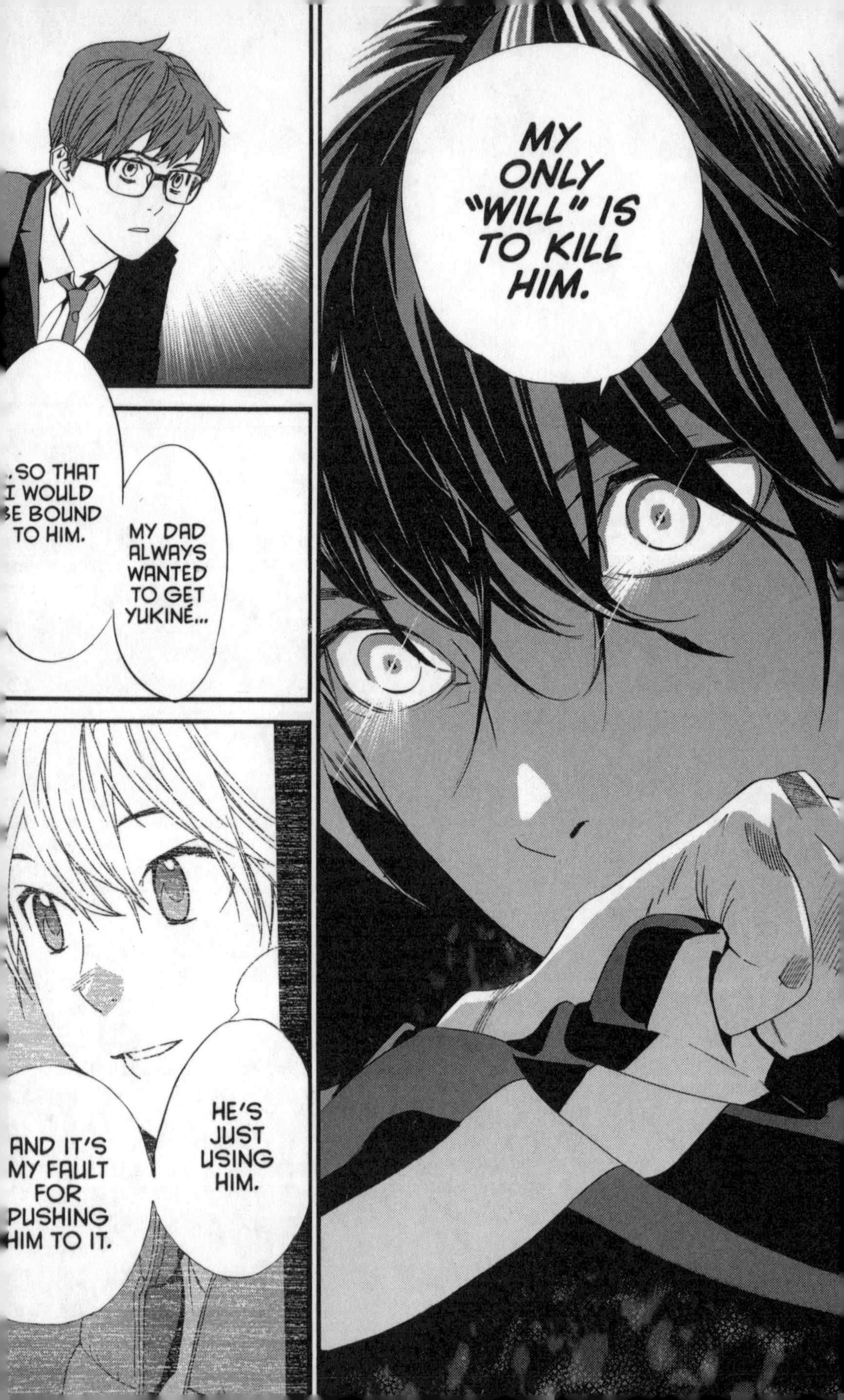
MY ONLY "WILL" IS TO KILL HIM.
MY DAD ALWAYS WANTED TO GET YUKINÉ...
.SO THAT I WOULD BE BOUND TO HIM.
HE'S JUST USING HIM.
AND IT'S MY FAULT FOR PUSHING HIM TO IT.

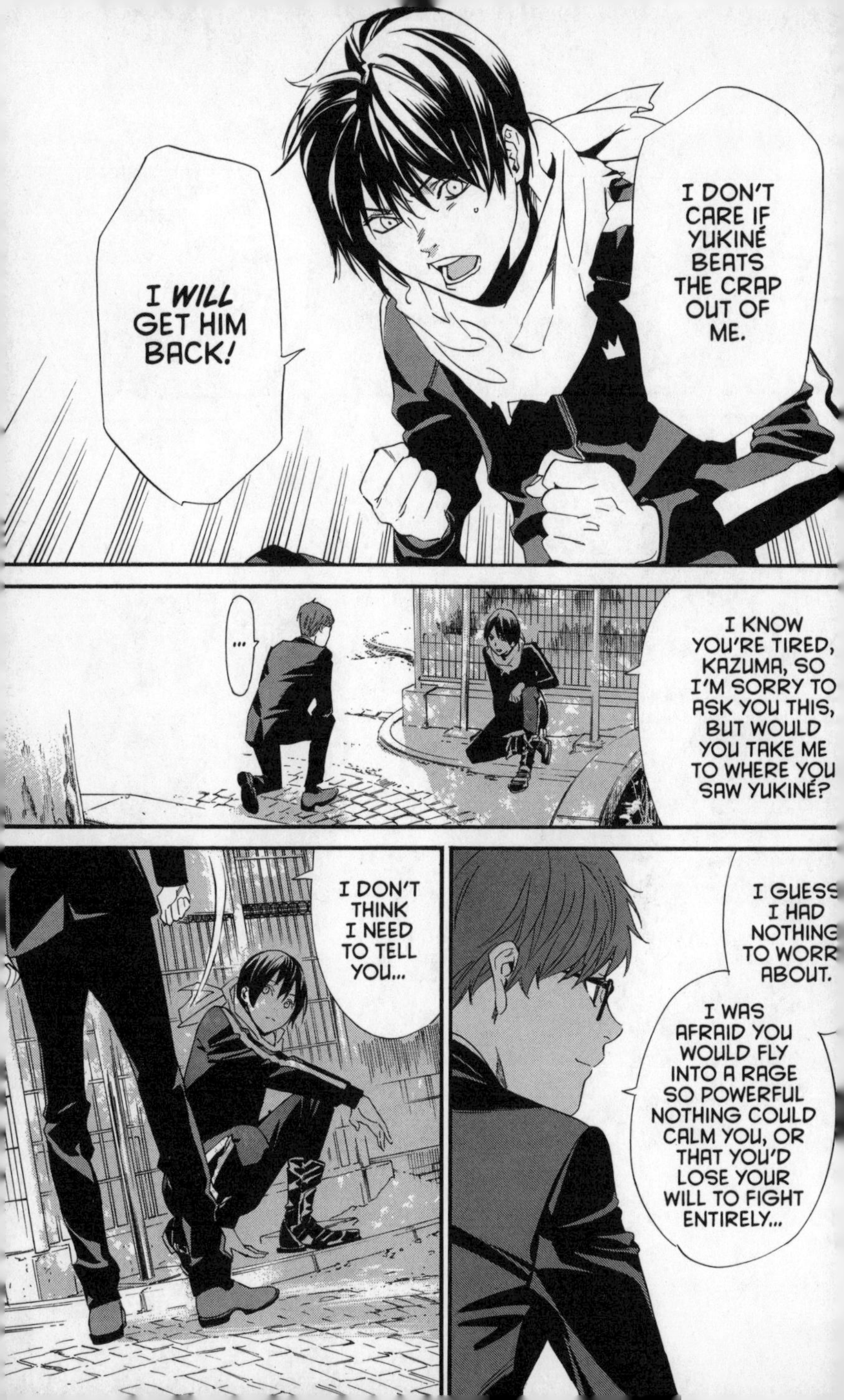
I DON'T CARE IF YUKINÉ BEATS THE CRAP OUT OF ME.
I *WILL* GET HIM BACK!
I KNOW YOU'RE TIRED, KAZUMA, SO I'M SORRY TO ASK YOU THIS, BUT WOULD YOU TAKE ME TO WHERE YOU SAW YUKINÉ?
...
I GUESS I HAD NOTHING TO WORR ABOUT.
I WAS AFRAID YOU WOULD FLY INTO A RAGE SO POWERFUL NOTHING COULD CALM YOU, OR THAT YOU'D LOSE YOUR WILL TO FIGHT ENTIRELY...
I DON'T THINK I NEED TO TELL YOU...

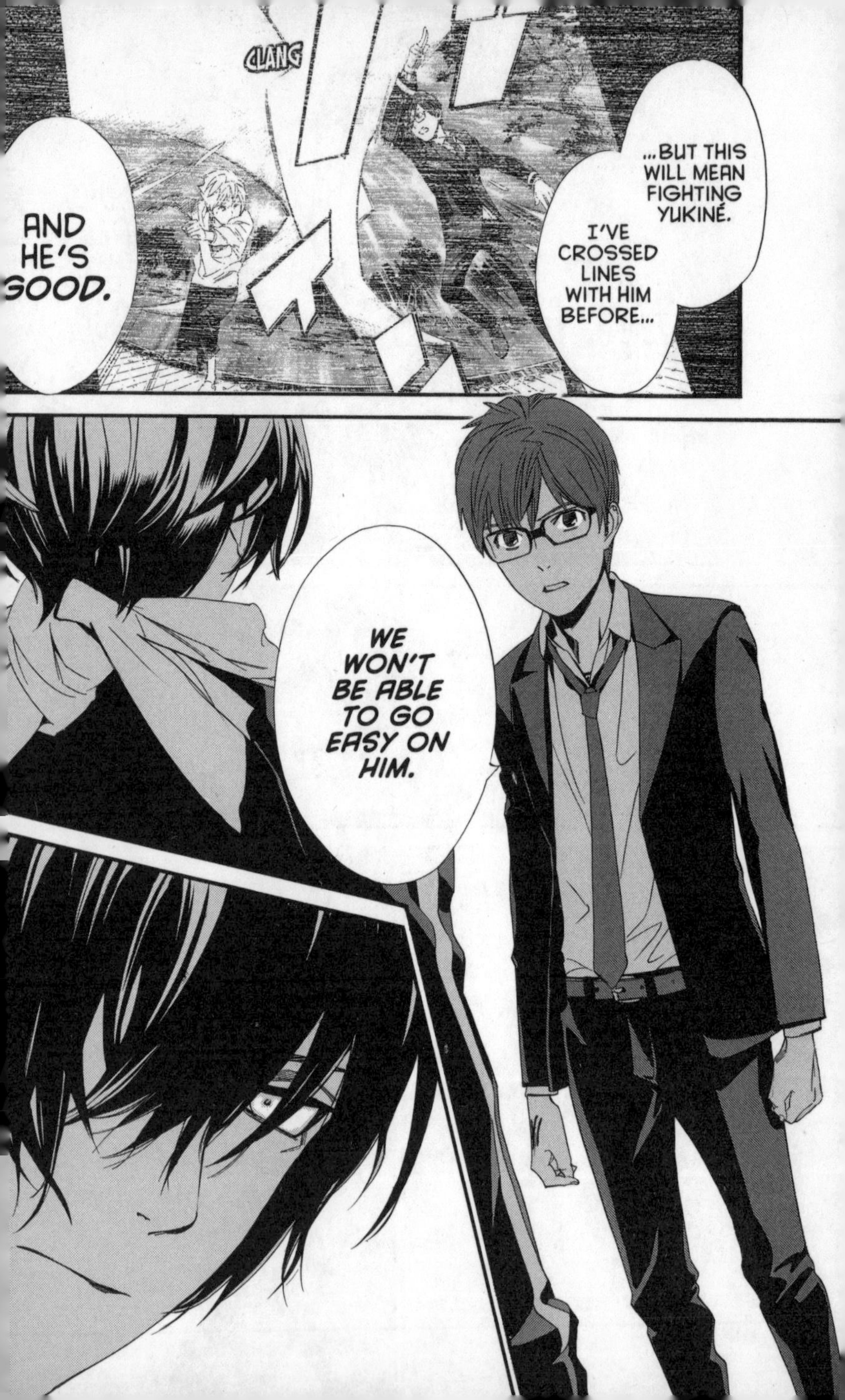
CLANG
...BUT THIS WILL MEAN FIGHTING YUKINÉ.
I'VE CROSSED LINES WITH HIM BEFORE...
AND HE'S GOOD.
WE WON'T BE ABLE TO GO EASY ON HIM.

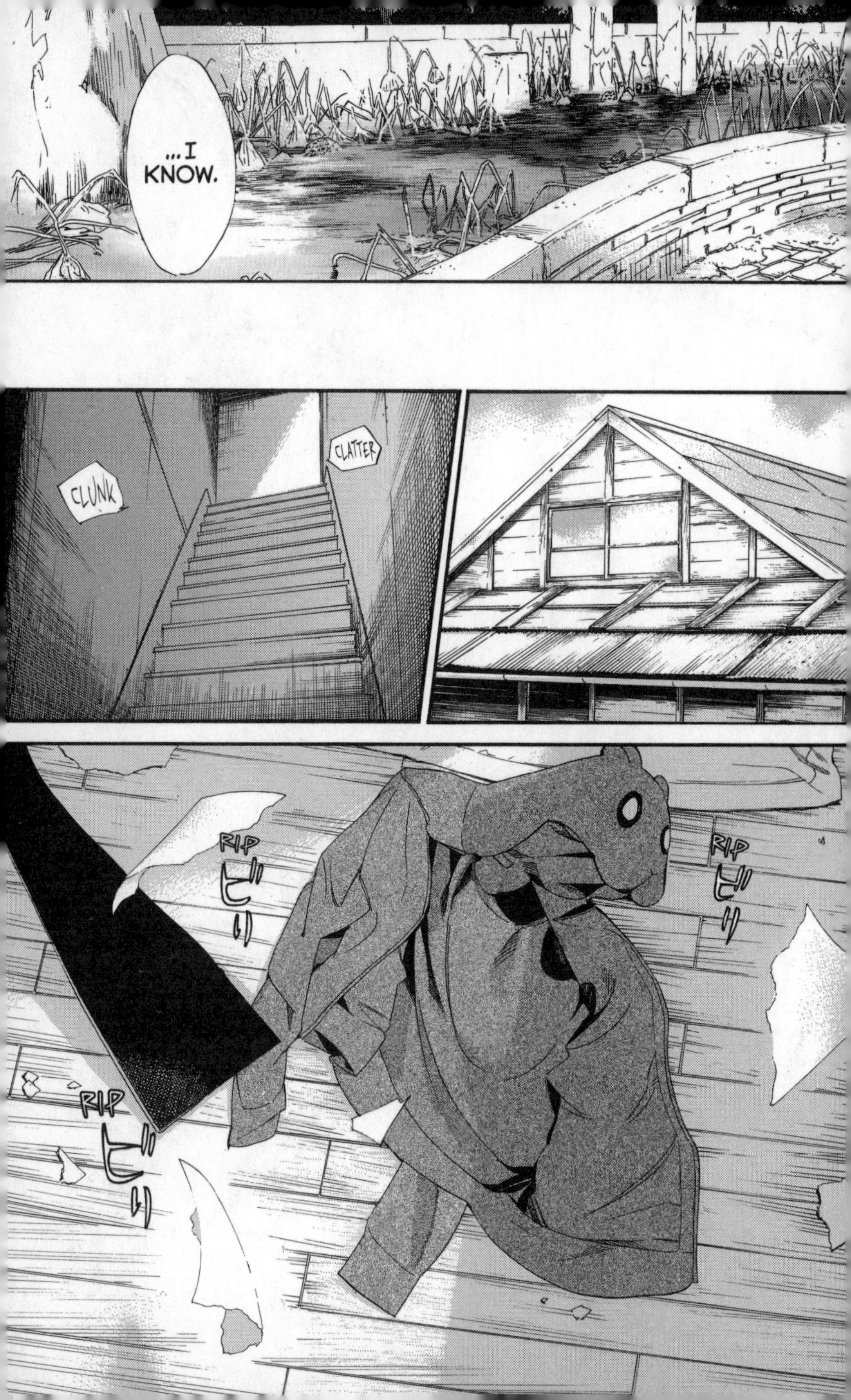
...I KNOW.
CLATTER
CLUNK
RIP
RIP
RIP

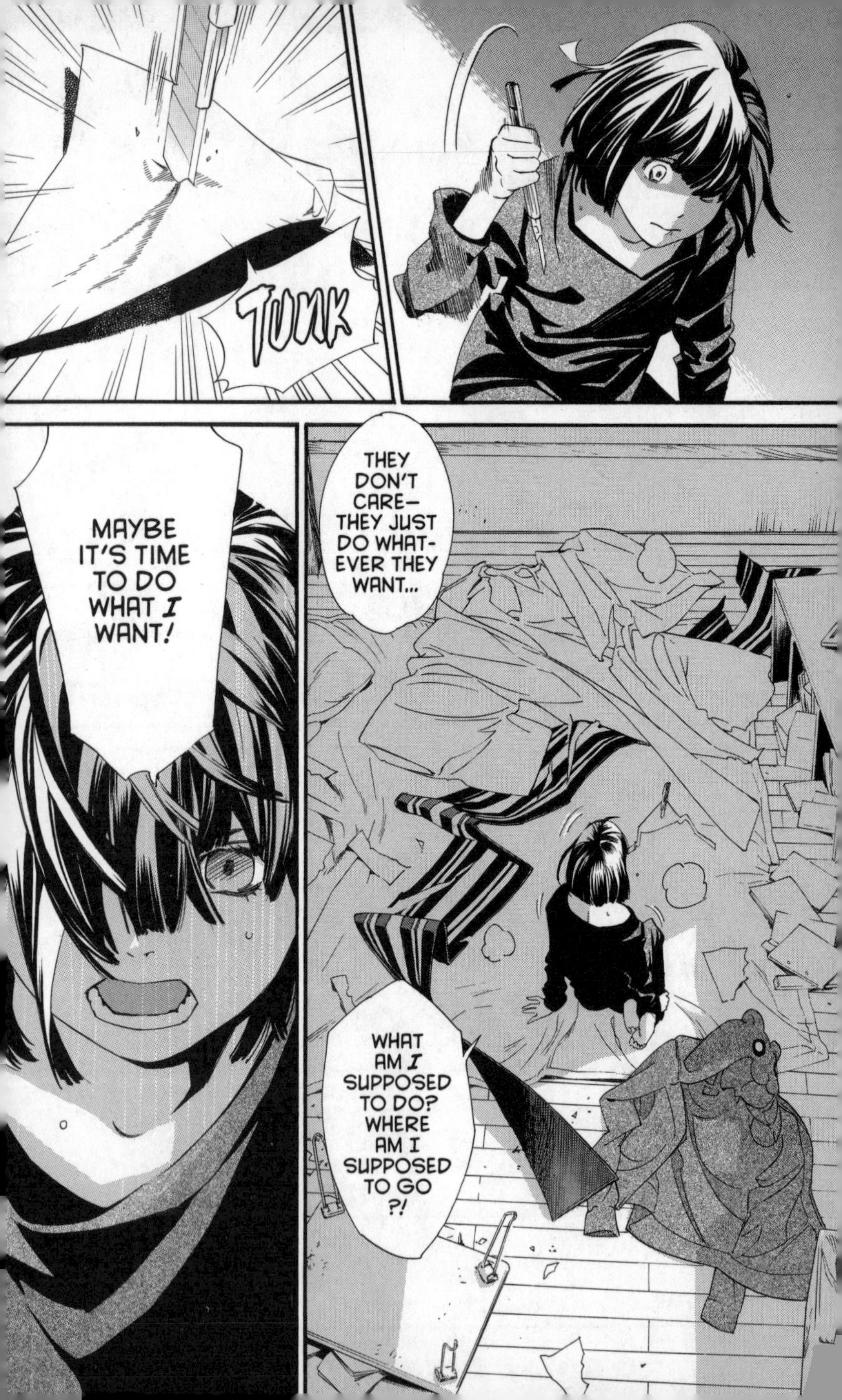
TUNK
THEY DON'T CARE—THEY JUST DO WHATEVER THEY WANT...
WHAT AM I SUPPOSED TO DO? WHERE AM I SUPPOSED TO GO?!
MAYBE IT'S TIME TO DO WHAT I WANT!

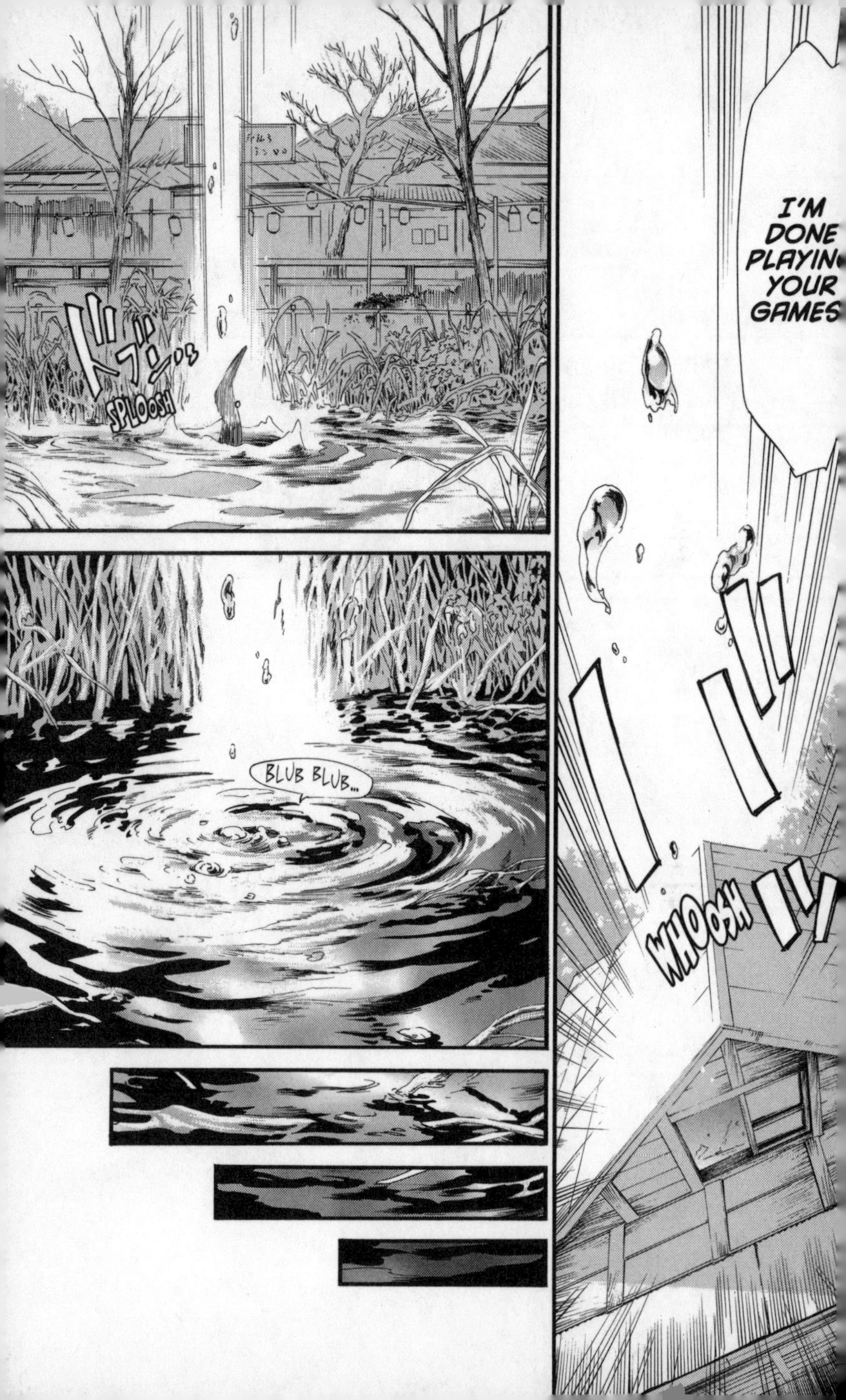
I'M DONE PLAYING YOUR GAMES
WHOOSH
SPLOOSH
BLUB BLUB...

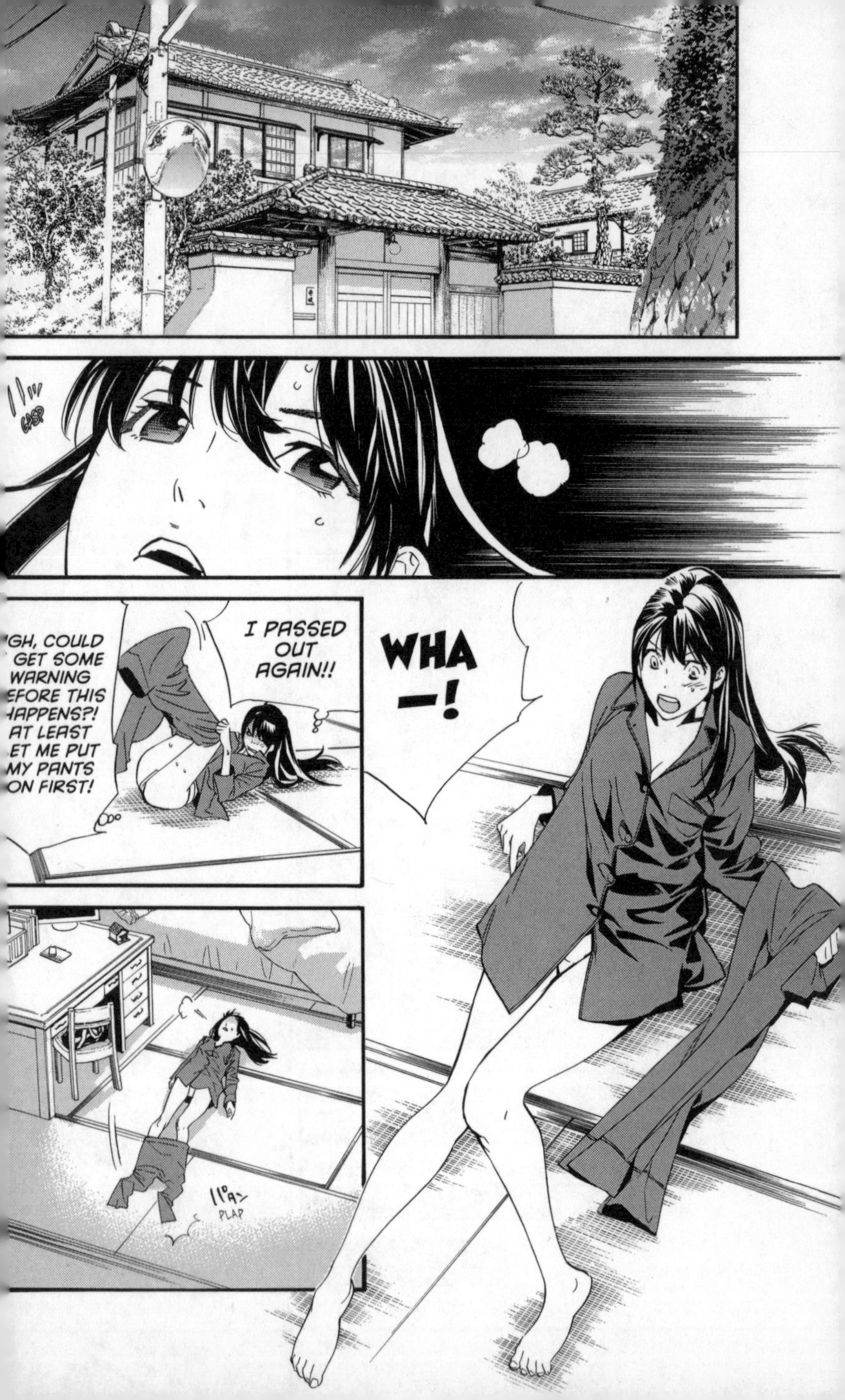
GASP
WHA—!
I PASSED OUT AGAIN!!
GH, COULD GET SOME WARNING EFORE THIS HAPPENS?! AT LEAST ET ME PUT MY PANTS ON FIRST!
PLAP

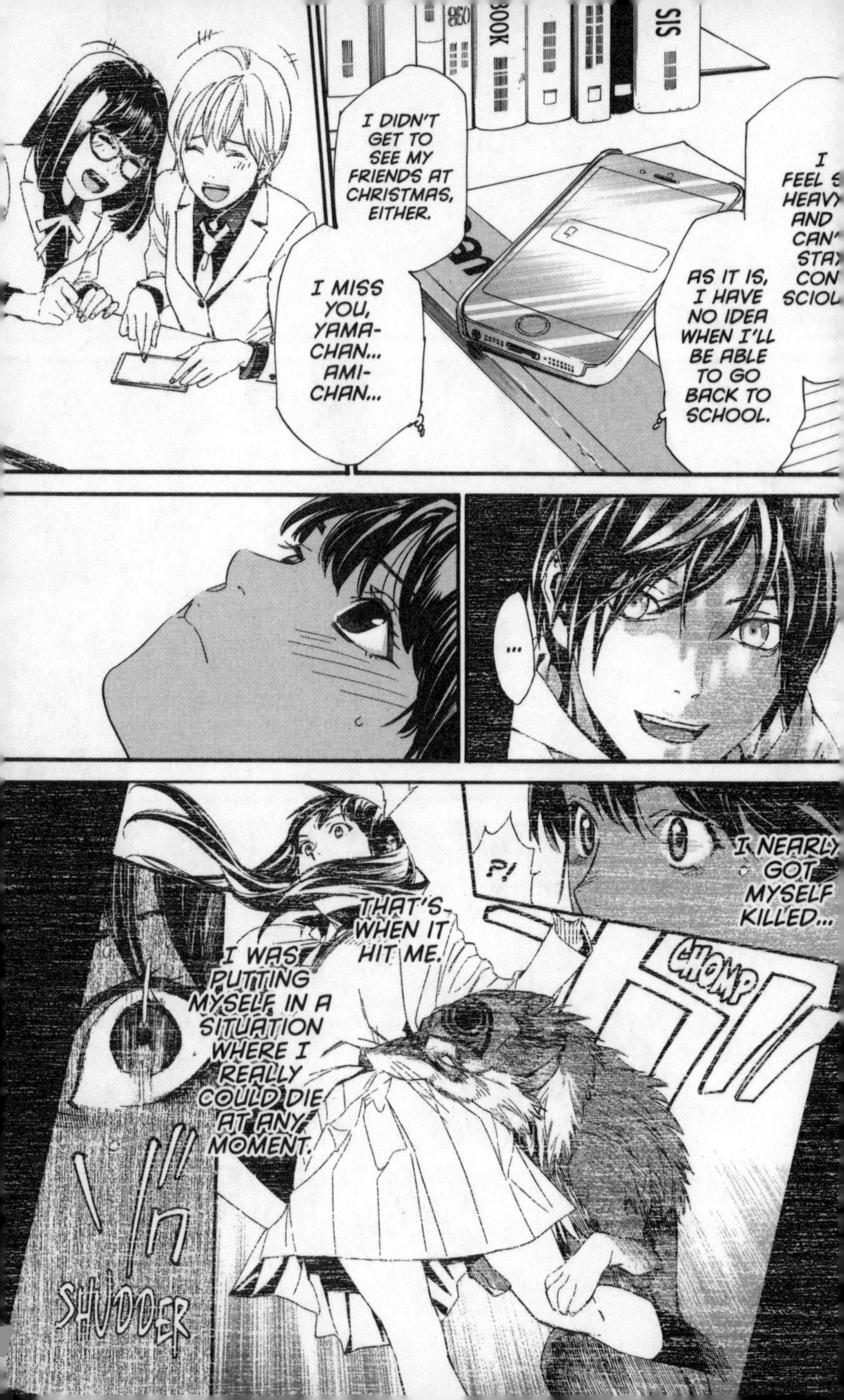
I FEEL S HEAVY AND CAN' STAY CON SCIOL
AS IT IS, I HAVE NO IDEA WHEN I'LL BE ABLE TO GO BACK TO SCHOOL.
I DIDN'T GET TO SEE MY FRIENDS AT CHRISTMAS, EITHER.
I MISS YOU, YAMA-CHAN... AMI-CHAN...
...
I NEARLY GOT MYSELF KILLED...
?!
CHOMP
THAT'S WHEN IT HIT ME.
I WAS PUTTING MYSELF IN A SITUATION WHERE I REALLY COULD DIE AT ANY MOMENT.
SHUDDER

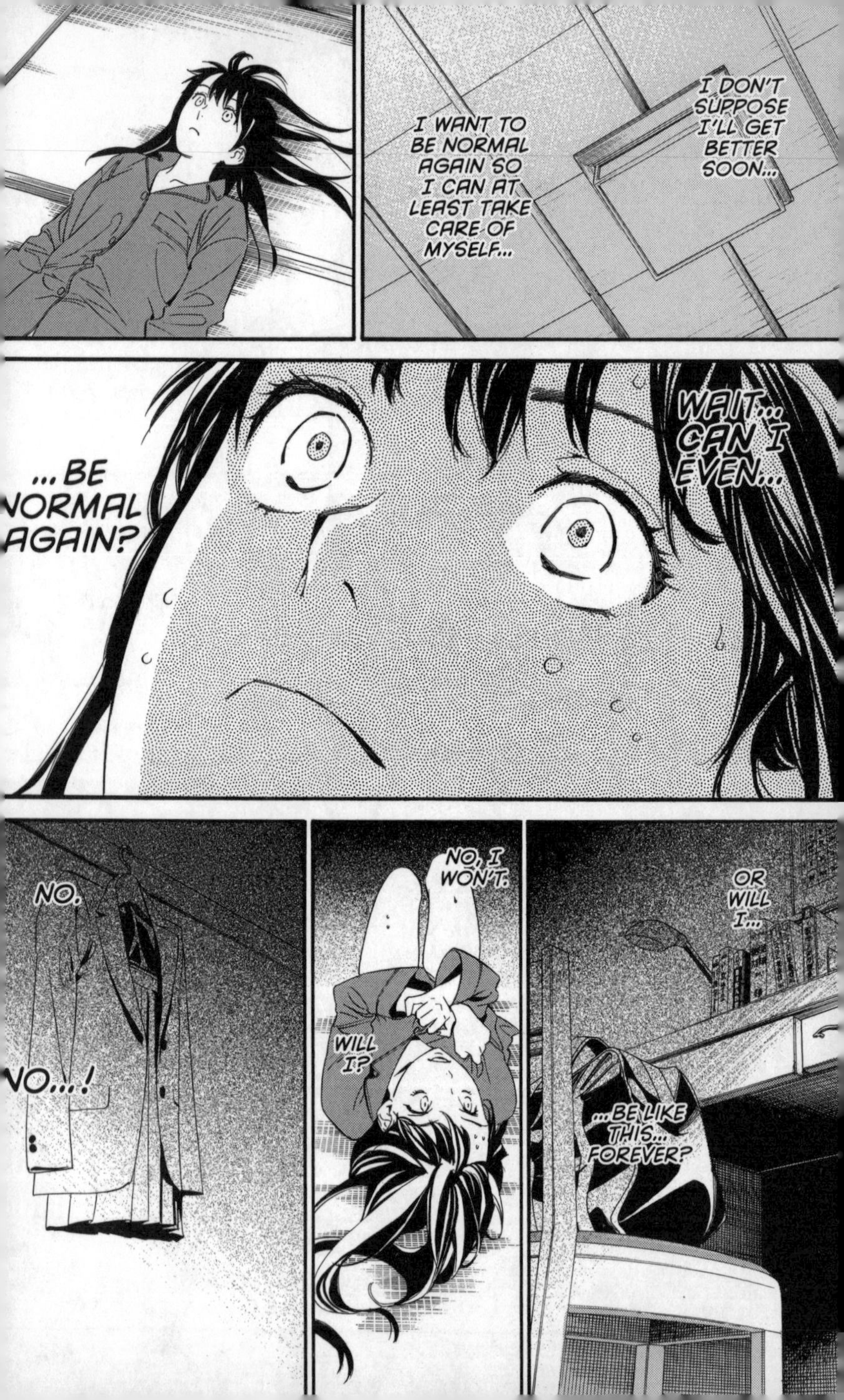
I DON'T SUPPOSE I'LL GET BETTER SOON...
I WANT TO BE NORMAL AGAIN SO I CAN AT LEAST TAKE CARE OF MYSELF...
WAIT... CAN I EVEN...
...BE NORMAL AGAIN?
OR WILL I...
...BE LIKE THIS... FOREVER?
NO, I WON'T.
WILL I?
NO.
NO...!

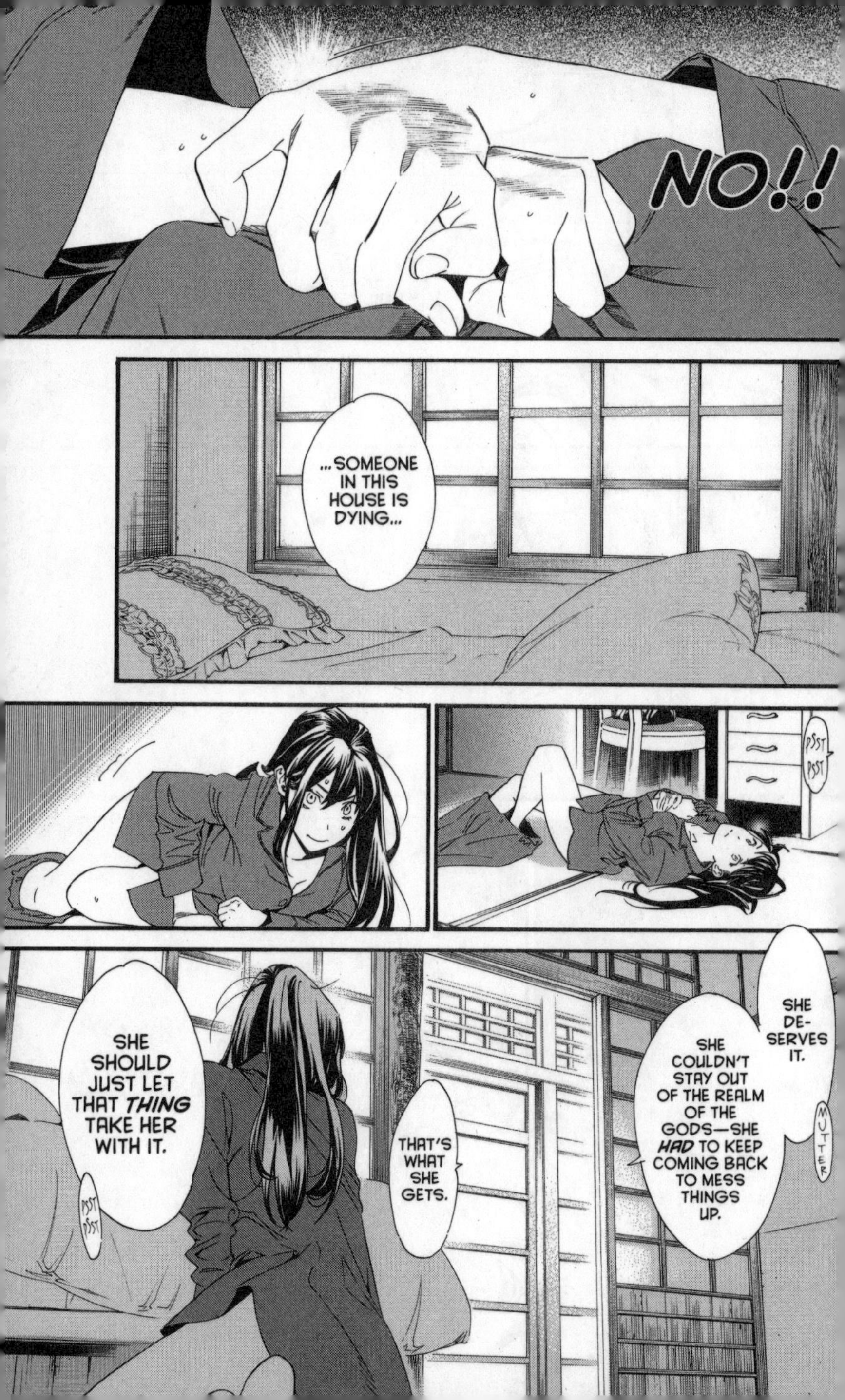
NO!!
...SOMEONE IN THIS HOUSE IS DYING...
PSST PSST
SHE DE-SERVES IT.
MUTTER
SHE COULDN'T STAY OUT OF THE REALM OF THE GODS—SHE HAD TO KEEP COMING BACK TO MESS THINGS UP.
THAT'S WHAT SHE GETS.
SHE SHOULD JUST LET THAT THING TAKE HER WITH IT.
PSST PSST

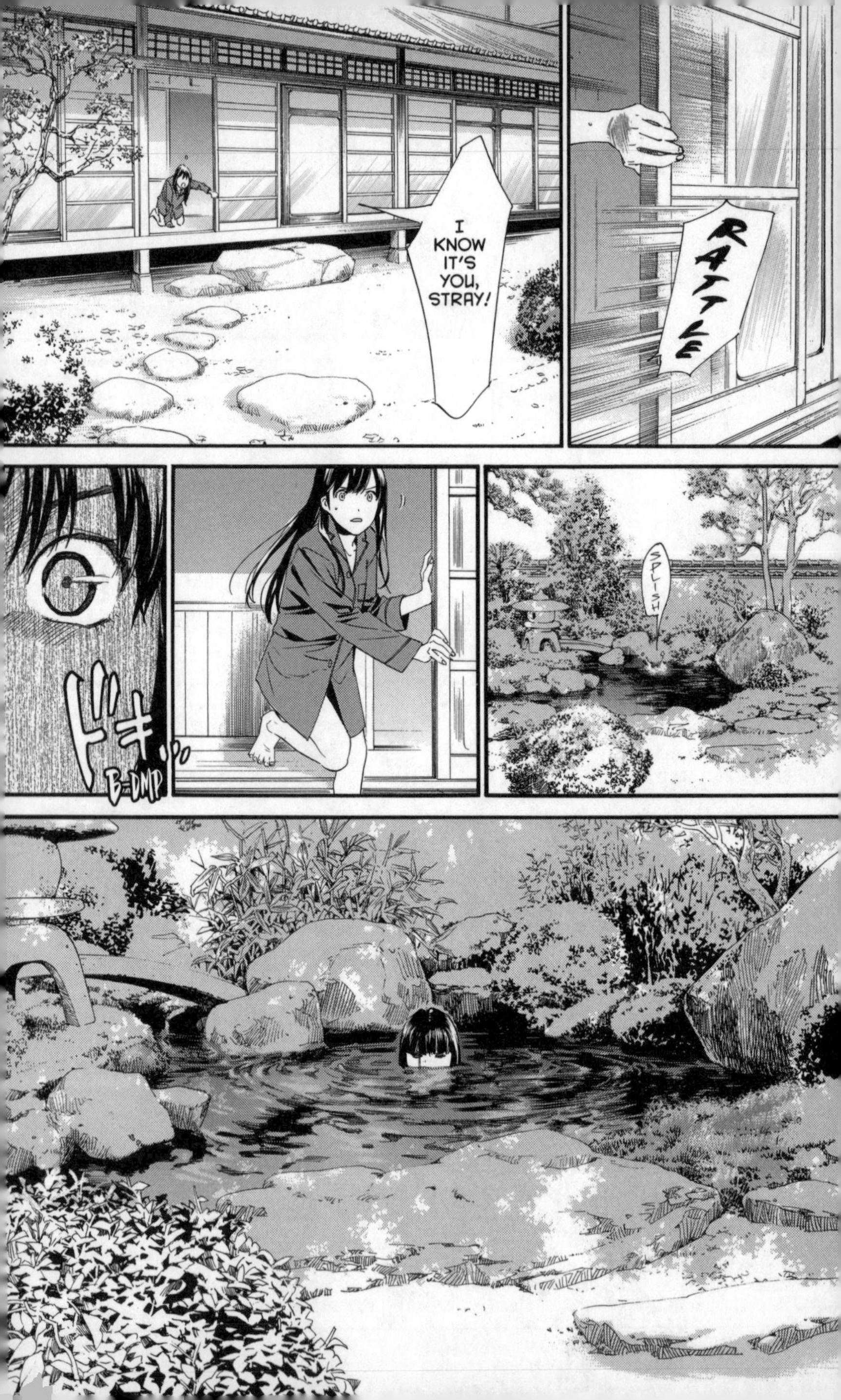
RATTLE
I KNOW IT'S YOU, STRAY!
SPLISH
ドキッ
B-DMP

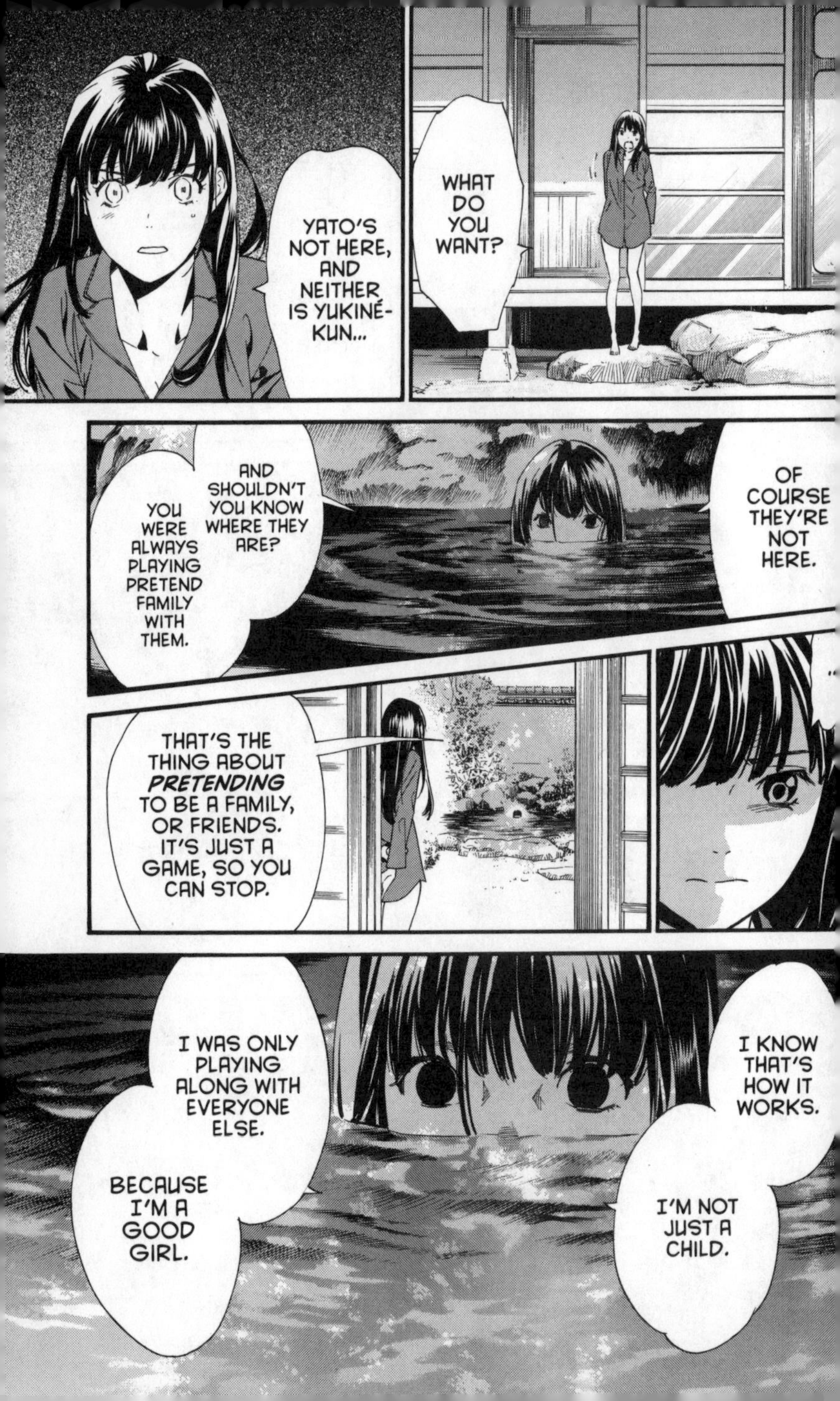
WHAT DO YOU WANT?
YATO'S NOT HERE, AND NEITHER IS YUKINÉ-KUN...
OF COURSE THEY'RE NOT HERE.
AND SHOULDN'T YOU KNOW WHERE THEY ARE?
YOU WERE ALWAYS PLAYING PRETEND FAMILY WITH THEM.
THAT'S THE THING ABOUT *PRETENDING* TO BE A FAMILY, OR FRIENDS. IT'S JUST A GAME, SO YOU CAN STOP.
I KNOW THAT'S HOW IT WORKS.
I'M NOT JUST A CHILD.
I WAS ONLY PLAYING ALONG WITH EVERYONE ELSE.
BECAUSE I'M A GOOD GIRL.

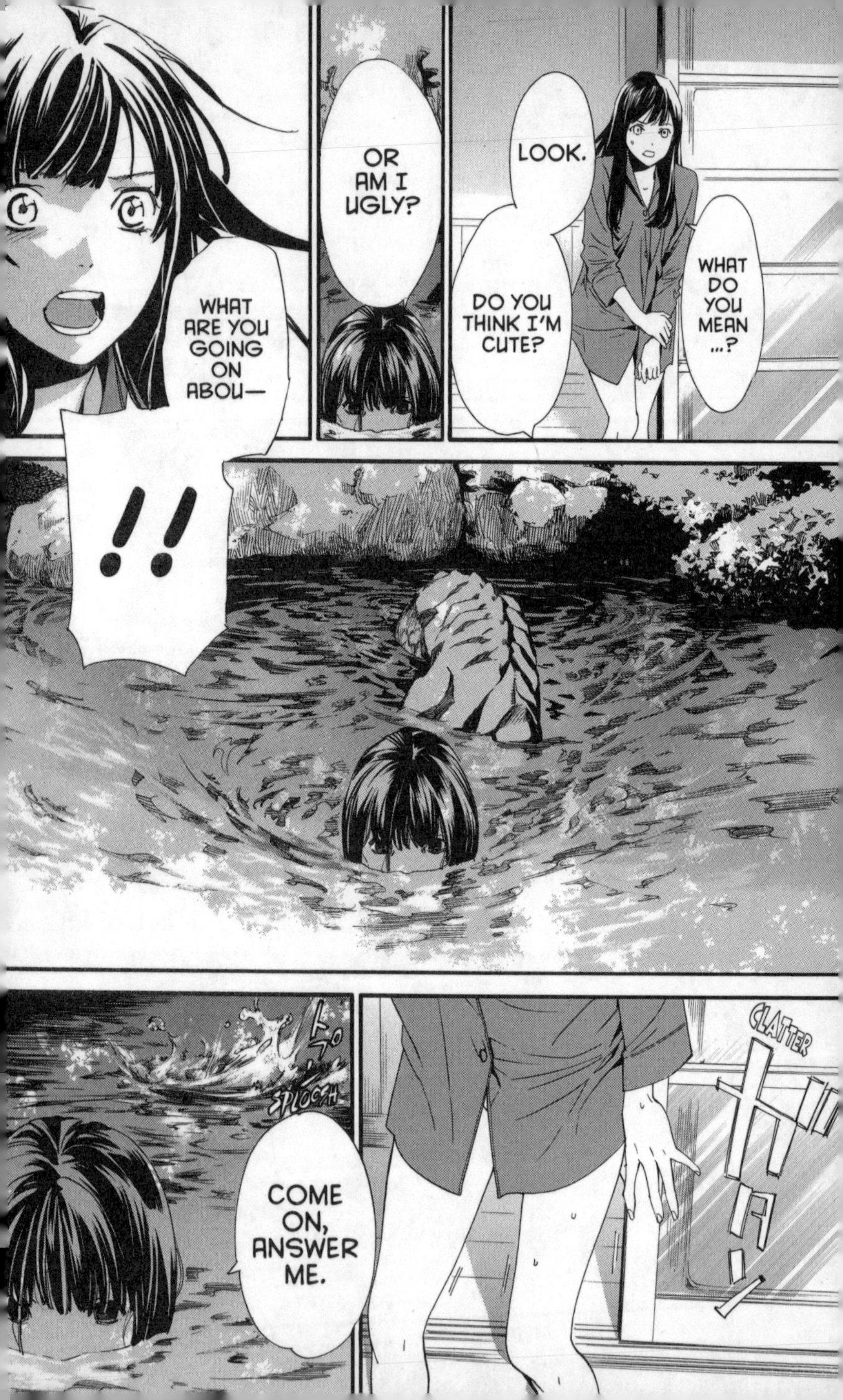
WHAT DO YOU MEAN ...?
LOOK.
DO YOU THINK I'M CUTE?
OR AM I UGLY?
WHAT ARE YOU GOING ON ABOU—
!!
CLATTER
SPLOOSH
COME ON, ANSWER ME.

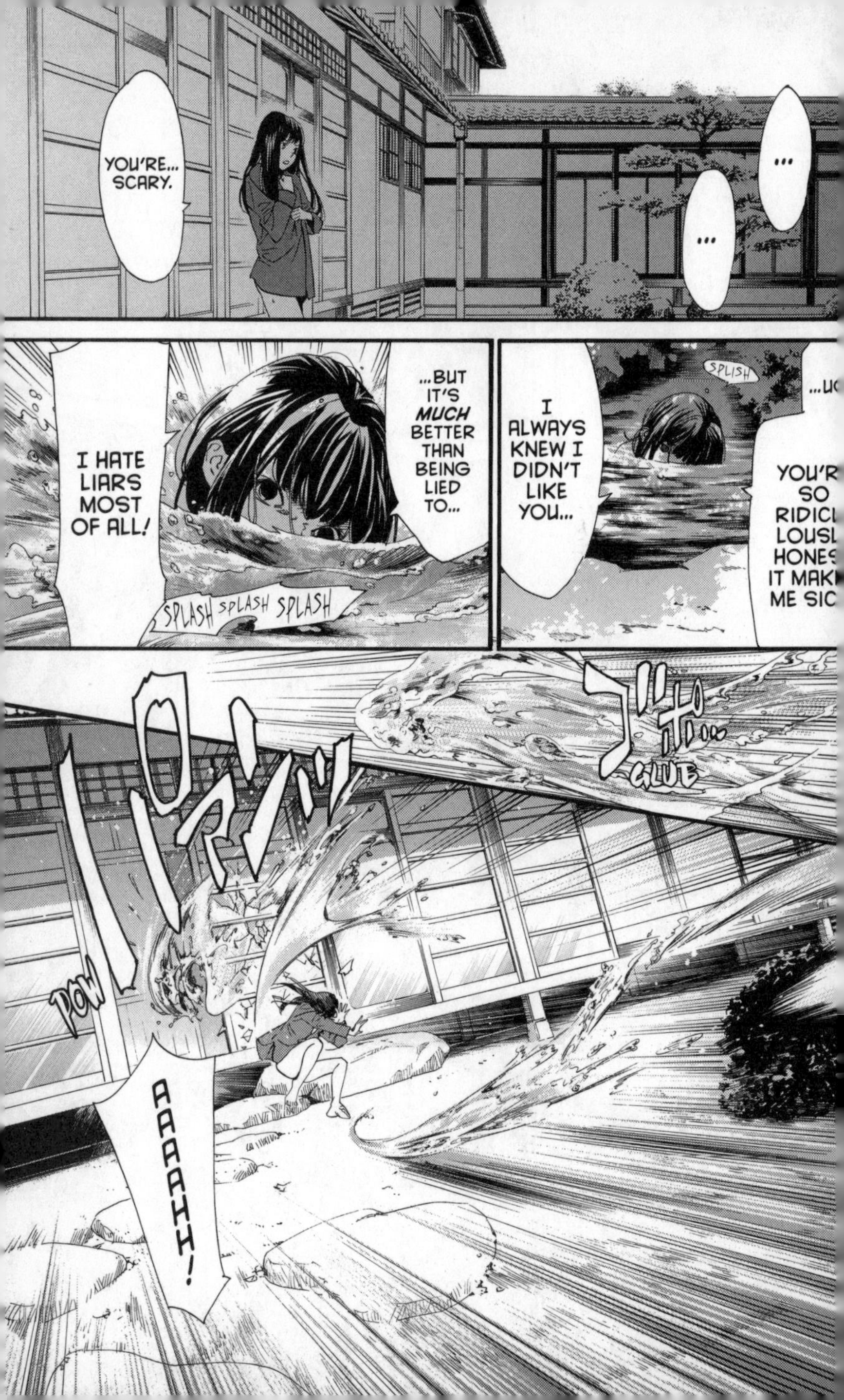
...
...
YOU'RE... SCARY.
...UG
YOU'R SO RIDICI LOUSL HONES IT MAK ME SIC
SPLASH
I ALWAYS KNEW I DIDN'T LIKE YOU...
...BUT IT'S *MUCH* BETTER THAN BEING LIED TO...
I HATE LIARS MOST OF ALL!
SPLASH SPLASH SPLASH
GLUB
POW
AAAAAHH!

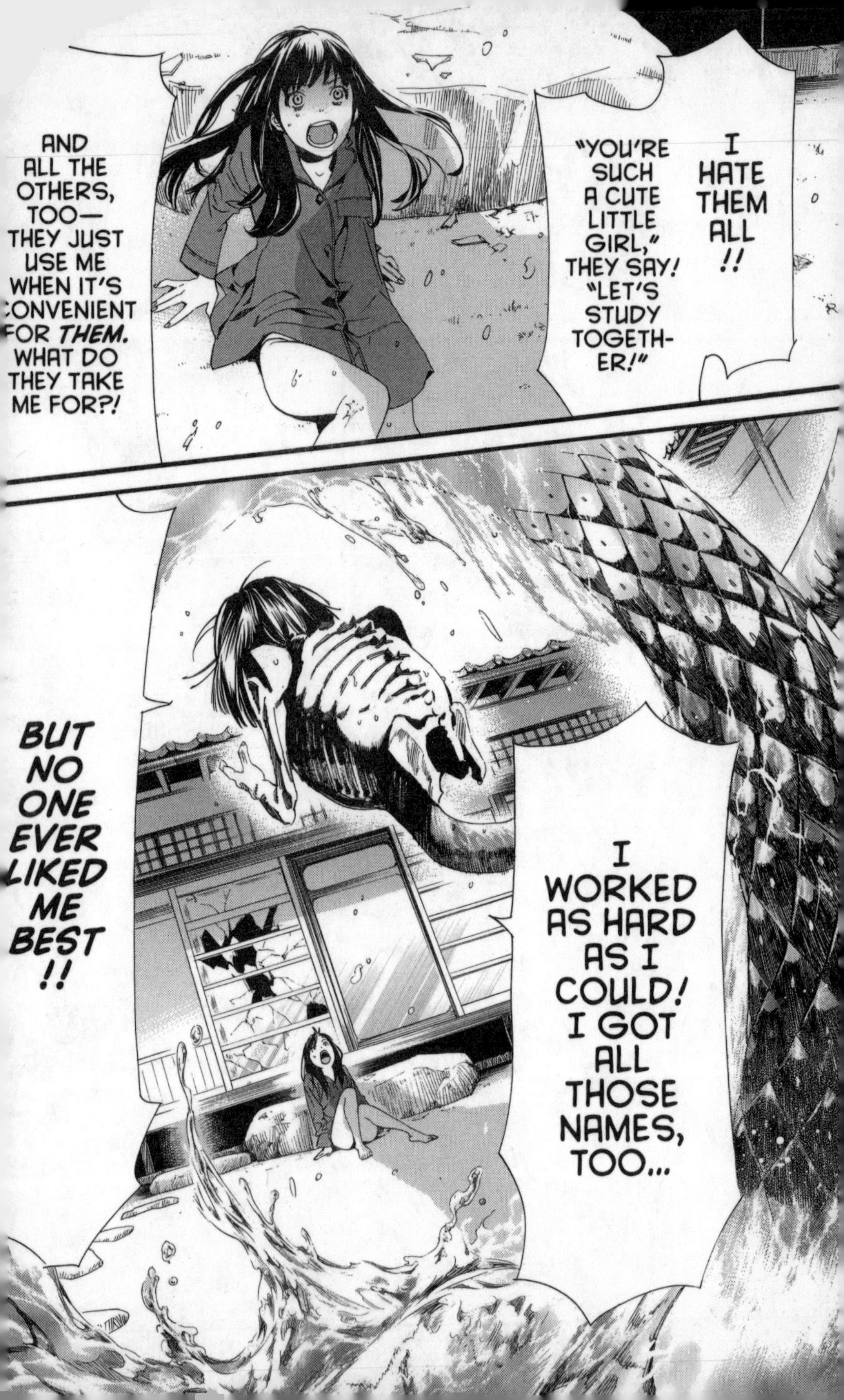

I HATE THEM ALL!!
"YOU'RE SUCH A CUTE LITTLE GIRL," THEY SAY! "LET'S STUDY TOGETH-ER!"
AND ALL THE OTHERS, TOO—THEY JUST USE ME WHEN IT'S CONVENIENT FOR *THEM.* WHAT DO THEY TAKE ME FOR?!
I WORKED AS HARD AS I COULD! I GOT ALL THOSE NAMES, TOO...
BUT NO ONE EVER LIKED ME BEST!!

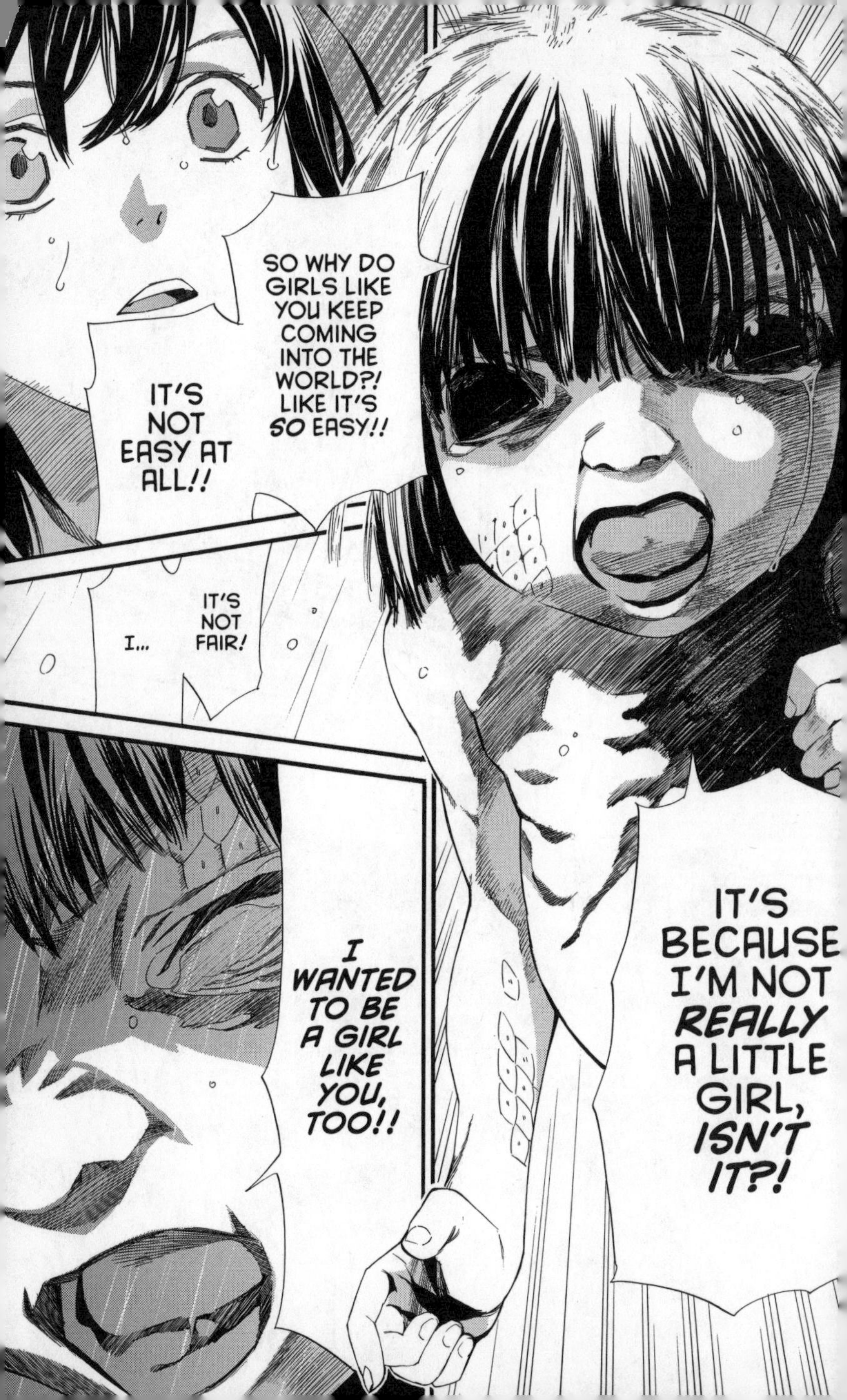
IT'S BECAUSE I'M NOT *REALLY* A LITTLE GIRL, *ISN'T IT?!*
SO WHY DO GIRLS LIKE YOU KEEP COMING INTO THE WORLD?! LIKE IT'S *SO* EASY!!
IT'S NOT EASY AT ALL!!
IT'S NOT FAIR!
I...
I WANTED TO BE A GIRL LIKE YOU, TOO!!

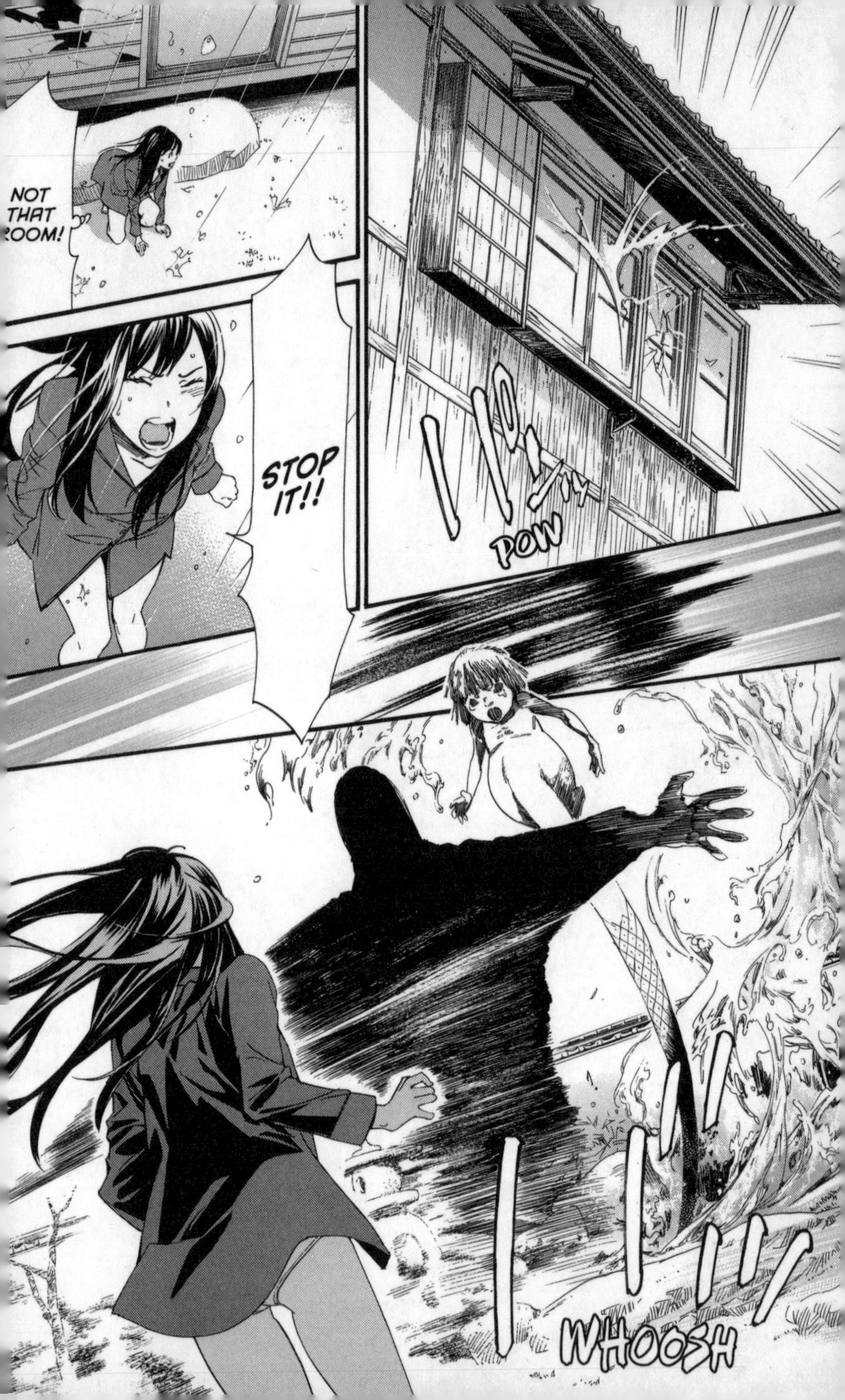
POW
NOT THAT ROOM!
STOP IT!!
WHOOSH

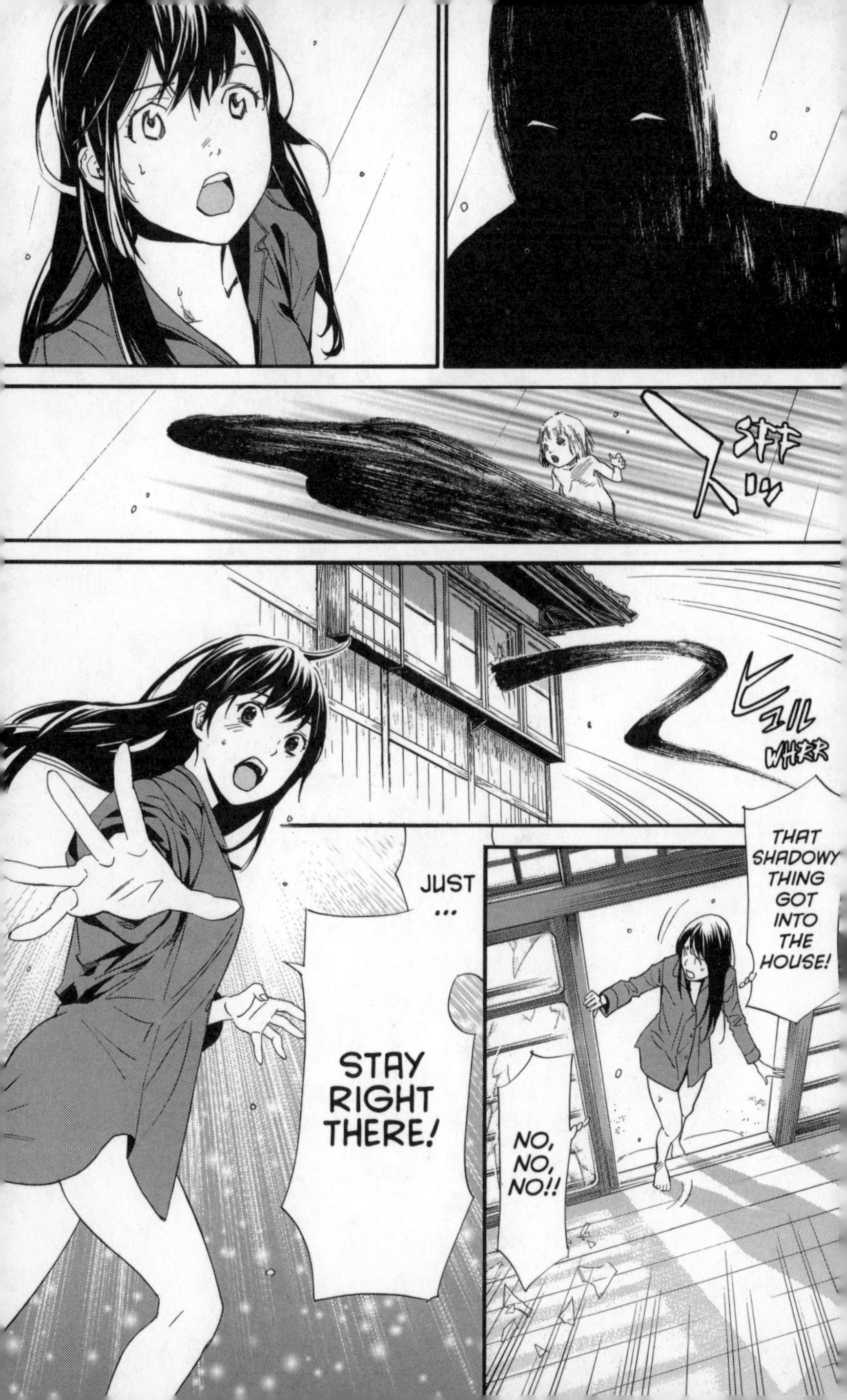
SFF
ヒュル
WHRRR
THAT SHADOWY THING GOT INTO THE HOUSE!
NO, NO, NO!!
JUST...
STAY RIGHT THERE!

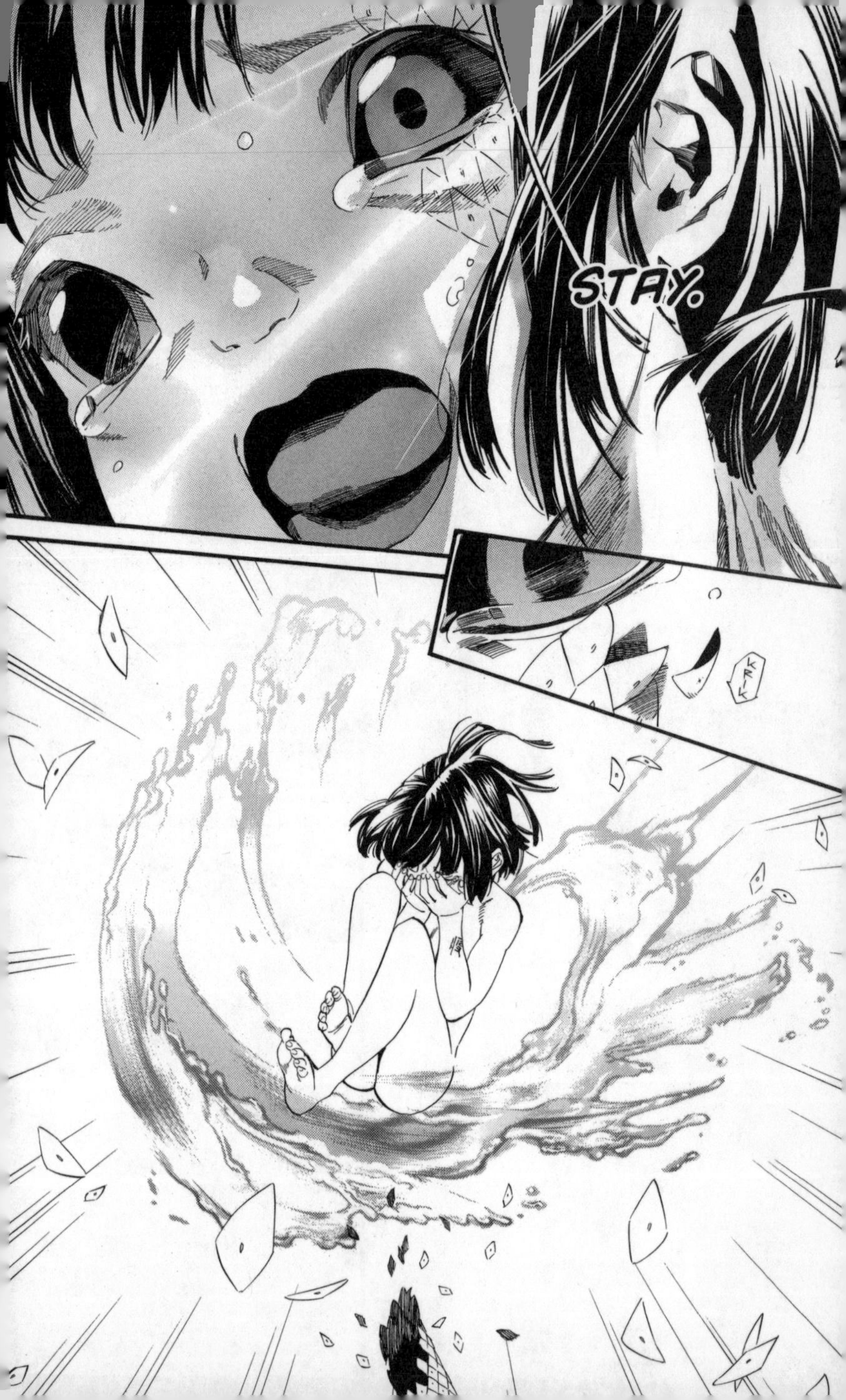
STAY.
KRIK

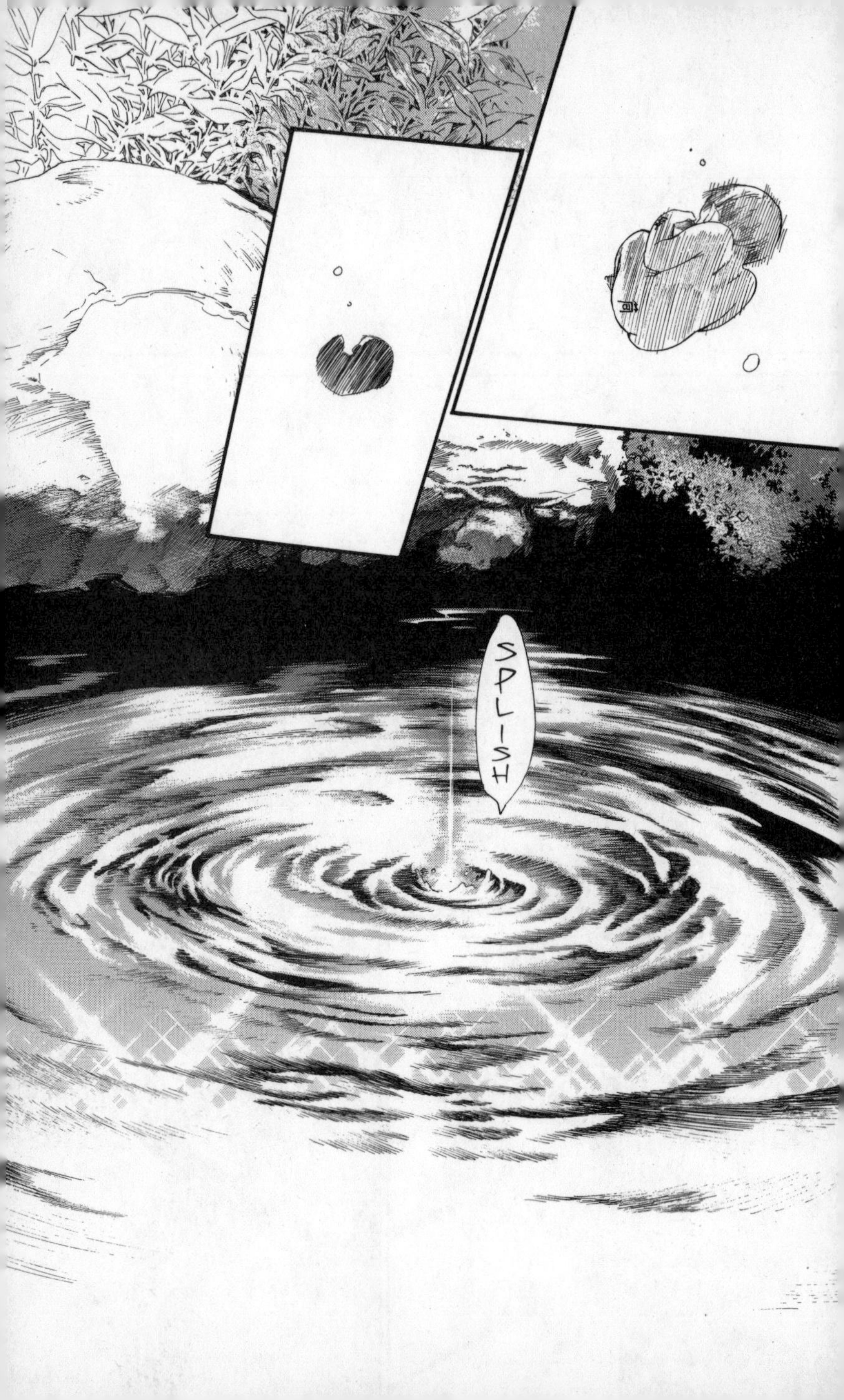
SPLISH

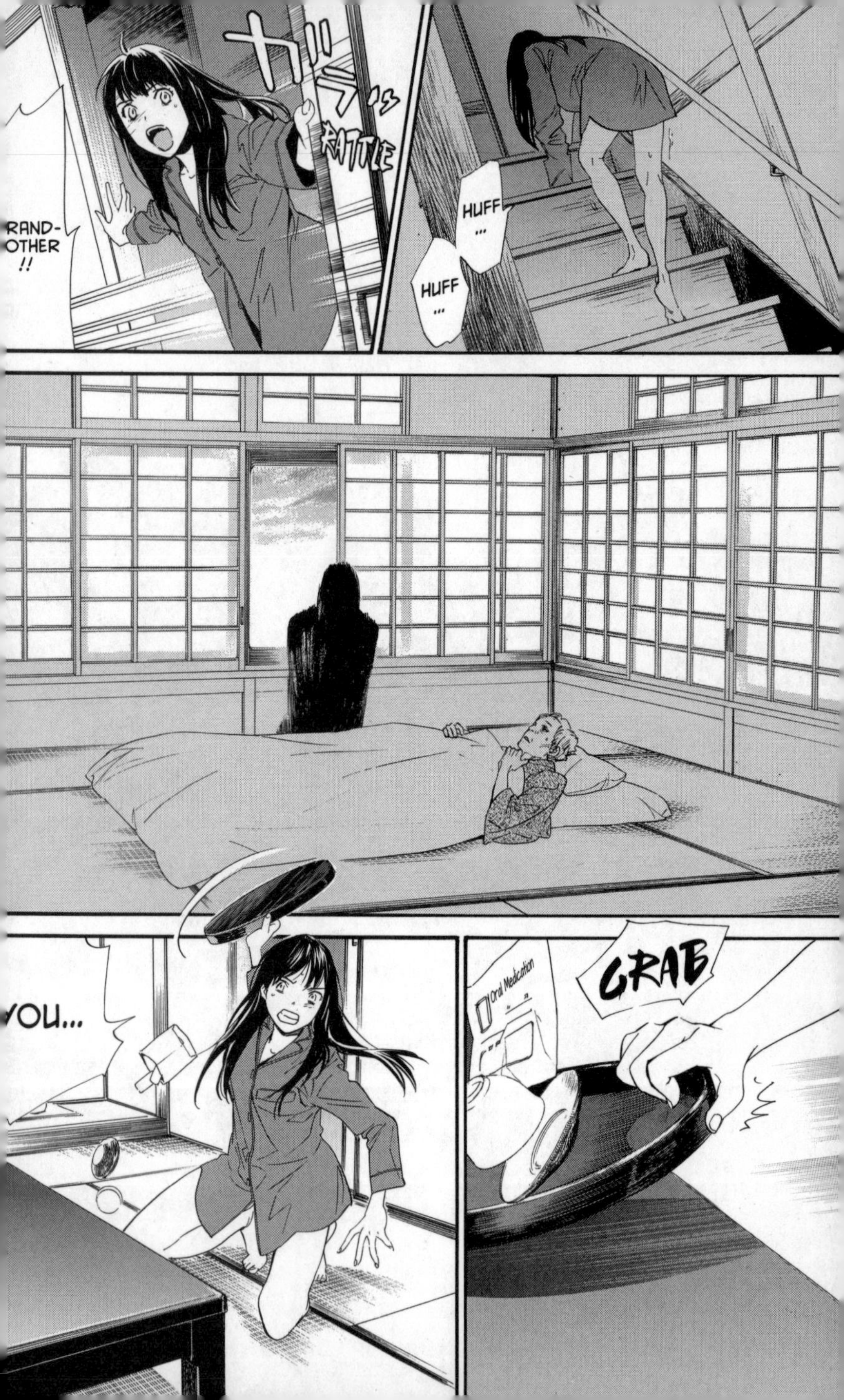
HUFF...
HUFF...
ガラッ
RATTLE
RAND-
OTHER
!!
Oral Medication
GRAB
YOU...

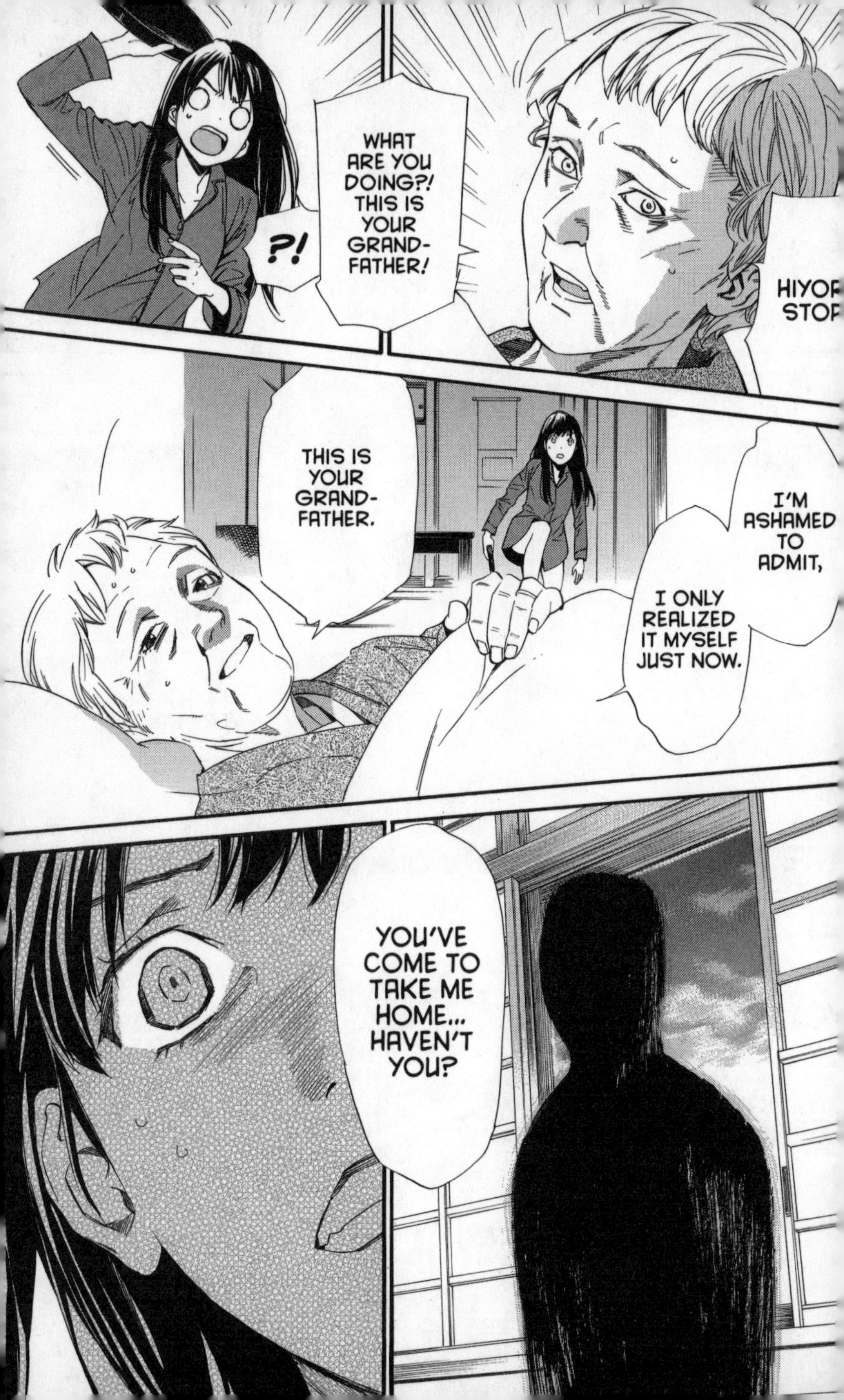
HIYOR STOP
WHAT ARE YOU DOING?! THIS IS YOUR GRAND-FATHER!
?!
I'M ASHAMED TO ADMIT,
I ONLY REALIZED IT MYSELF JUST NOW.
THIS IS YOUR GRAND-FATHER.
YOU'VE COME TO TAKE ME HOME... HAVEN'T YOU?

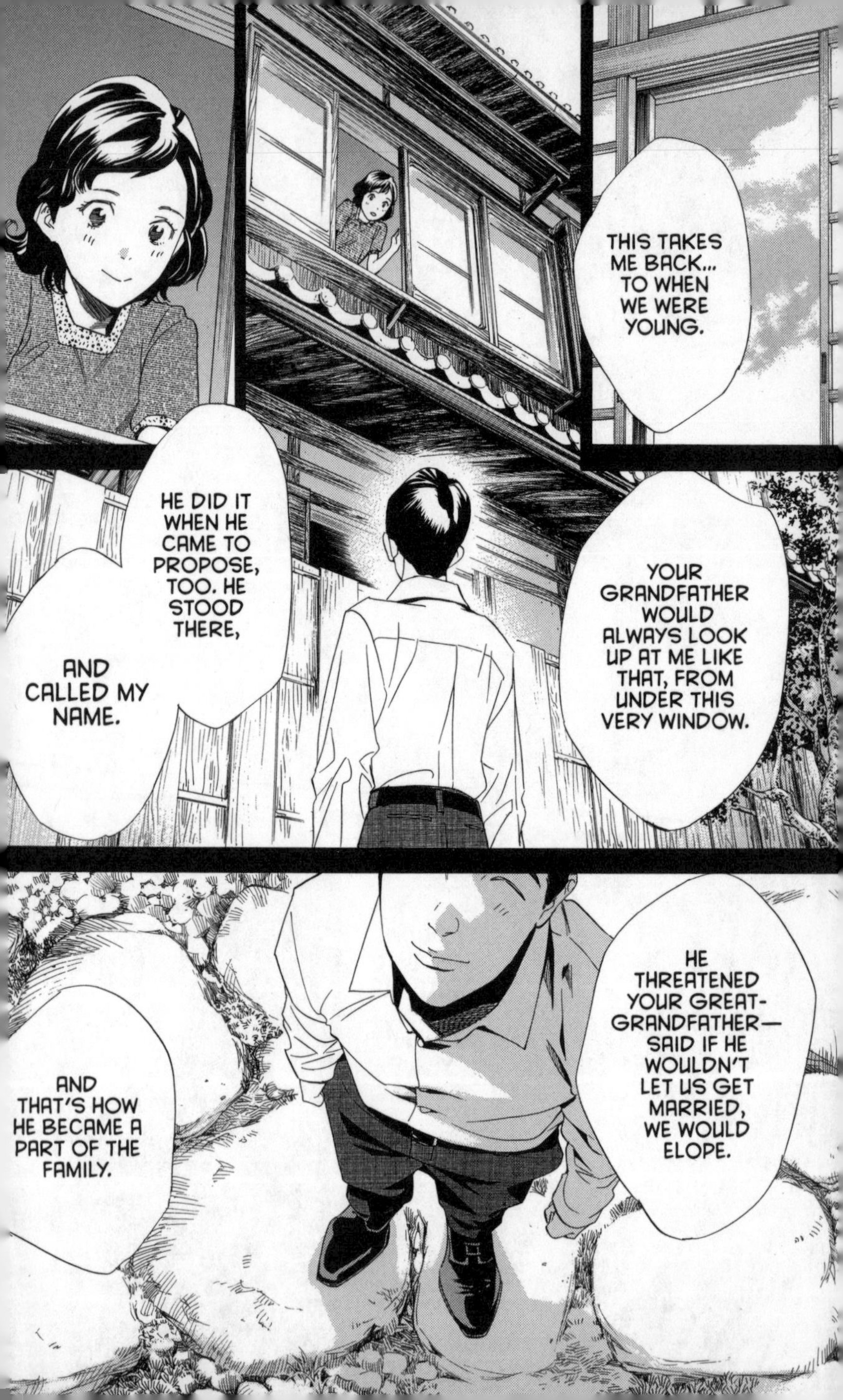
THIS TAKES ME BACK... TO WHEN WE WERE YOUNG.
YOUR GRANDFATHER WOULD ALWAYS LOOK UP AT ME LIKE THAT, FROM UNDER THIS VERY WINDOW.
HE DID IT WHEN HE CAME TO PROPOSE, TOO. HE STOOD THERE,
AND CALLED MY NAME.
HE THREATENED YOUR GREAT-GRANDFATHER—SAID IF HE WOULDN'T LET US GET MARRIED, WE WOULD ELOPE.
AND THAT'S HOW HE BECAME A PART OF THE FAMILY.

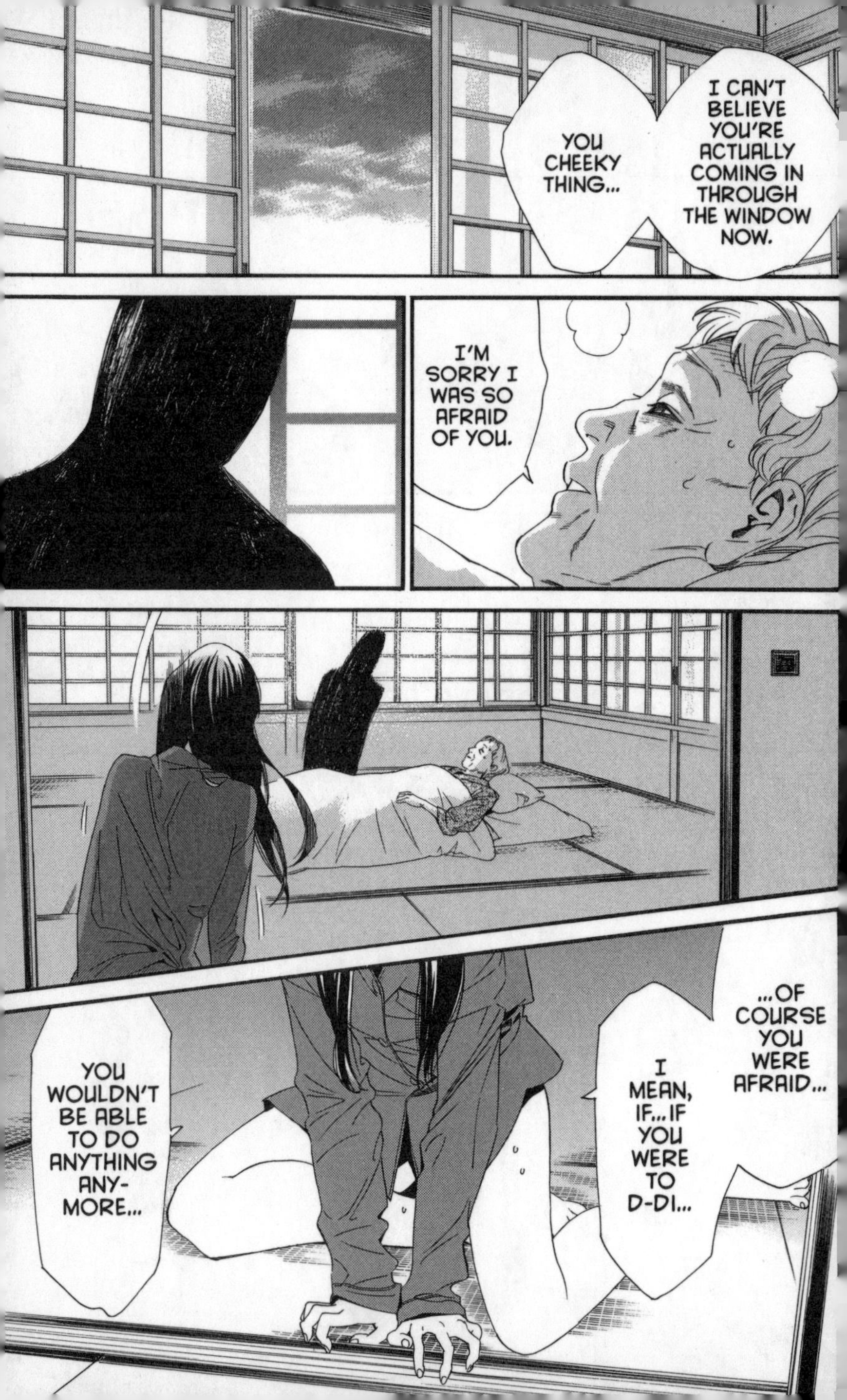

I CAN'T BELIEVE YOU'RE ACTUALLY COMING IN THROUGH THE WINDOW NOW.
YOU CHEEKY THING...
I'M SORRY I WAS SO AFRAID OF YOU.
...OF COURSE YOU WERE AFRAID...
I MEAN, IF...IF YOU WERE TO D-DI...
YOU WOULDN'T BE ABLE TO DO ANYTHING ANY-MORE...

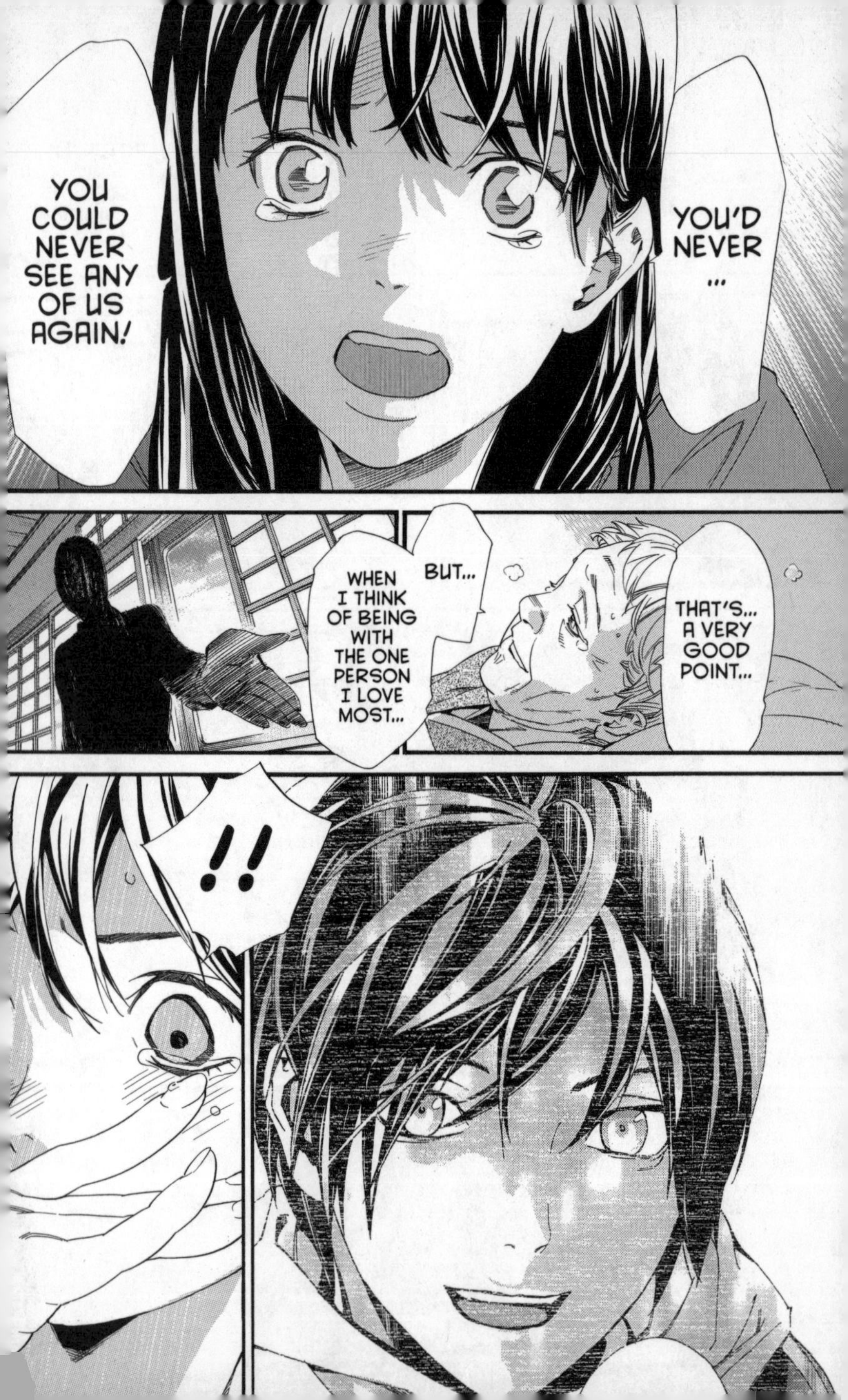

YOU'D NEVER ...
YOU COULD NEVER SEE ANY OF US AGAIN!
THAT'S... A VERY GOOD POINT...
BUT...
WHEN I THINK OF BEING WITH THE ONE PERSON I LOVE MOST...
!!

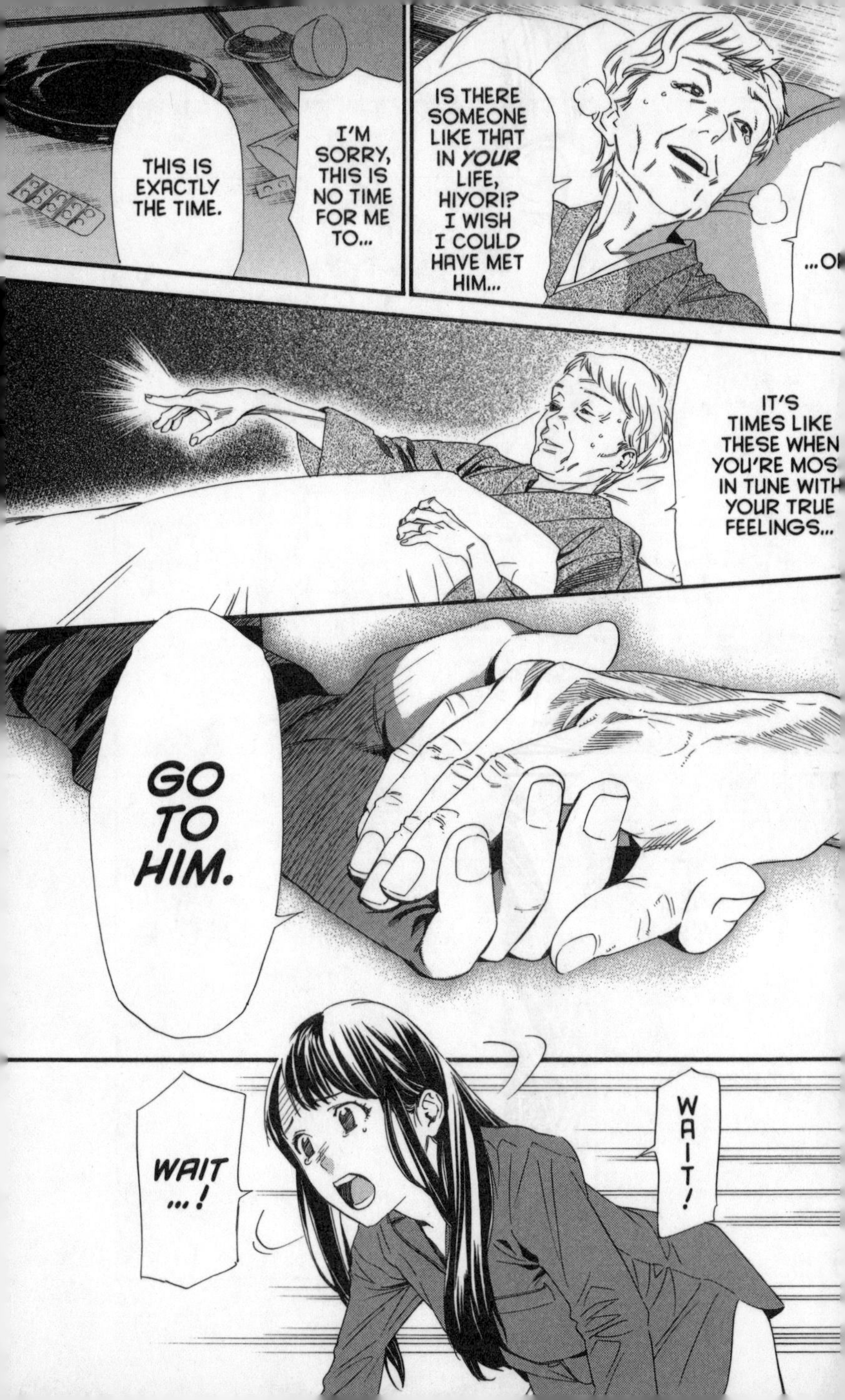
...O
IS THERE SOMEONE LIKE THAT IN *YOUR* LIFE, HIYORI? I WISH I COULD HAVE MET HIM...
I'M SORRY, THIS IS NO TIME FOR ME TO...
THIS IS EXACTLY THE TIME.
IT'S TIMES LIKE THESE WHEN YOU'RE MOS IN TUNE WITH YOUR TRUE FEELINGS...
GO TO HIM.
WAIT!
WAIT ...!

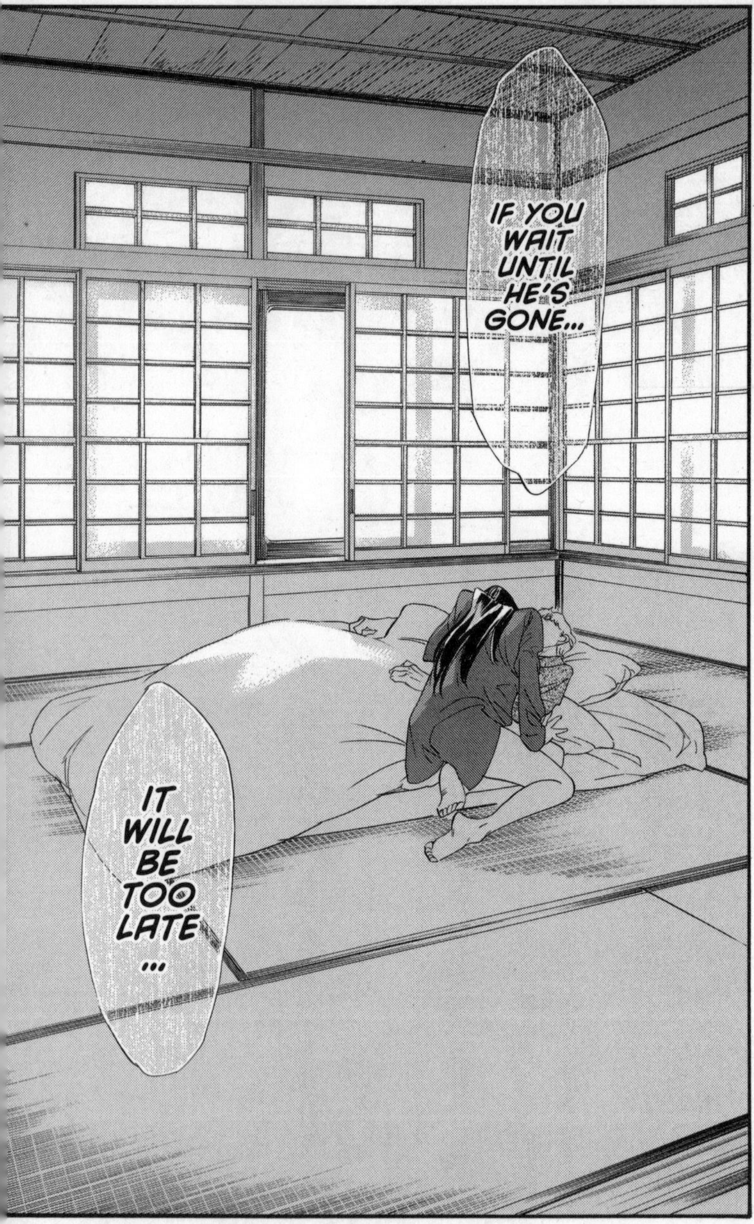
IF YOU WAIT UNTIL HE'S GONE...
IT WILL BE TOO LATE ...

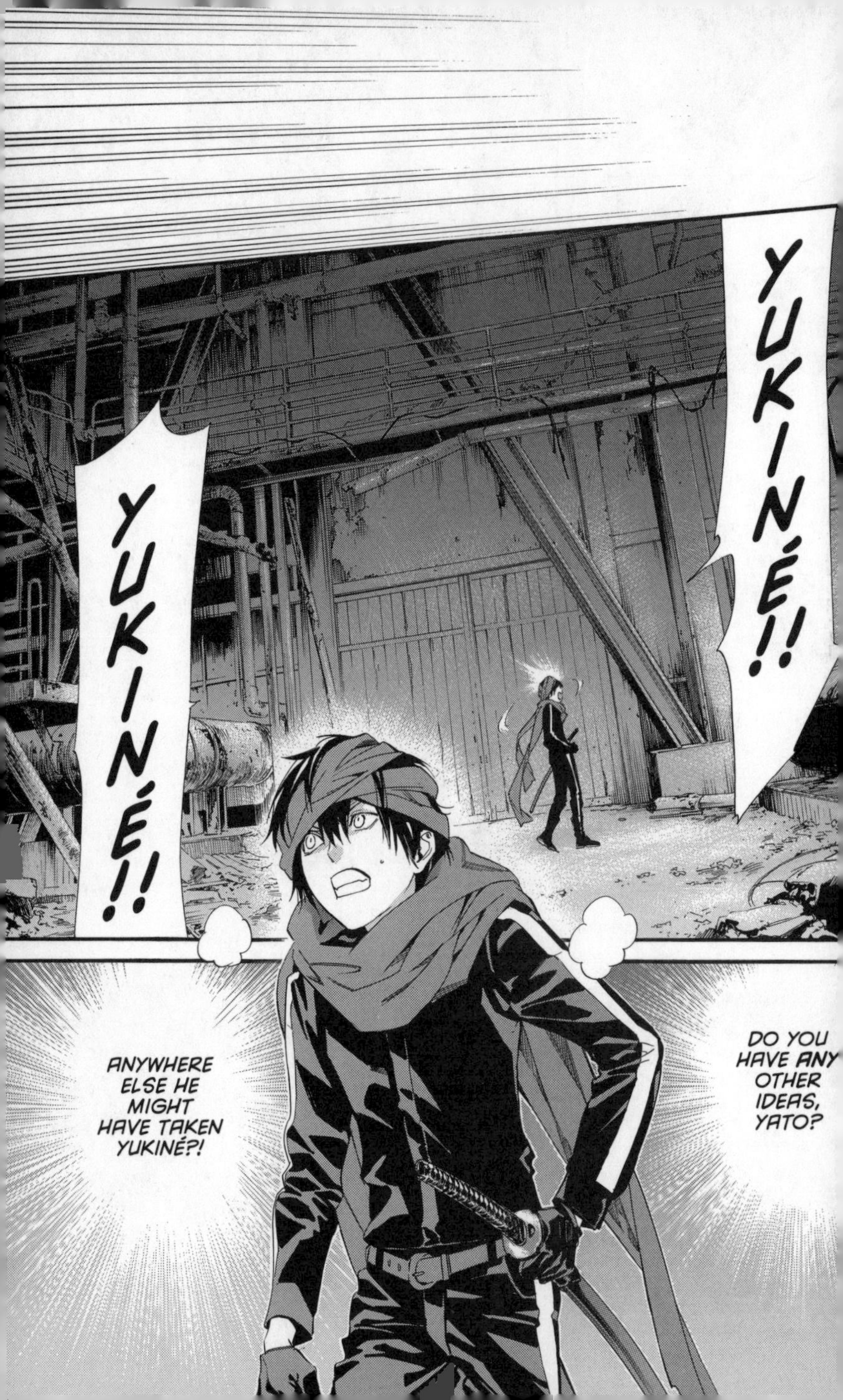
YUKINÉ!!
YUKINÉ!!
DO YOU HAVE ANY OTHER IDEAS, YATO?
ANYWHERE ELSE HE MIGHT HAVE TAKEN YUKINÉ?!

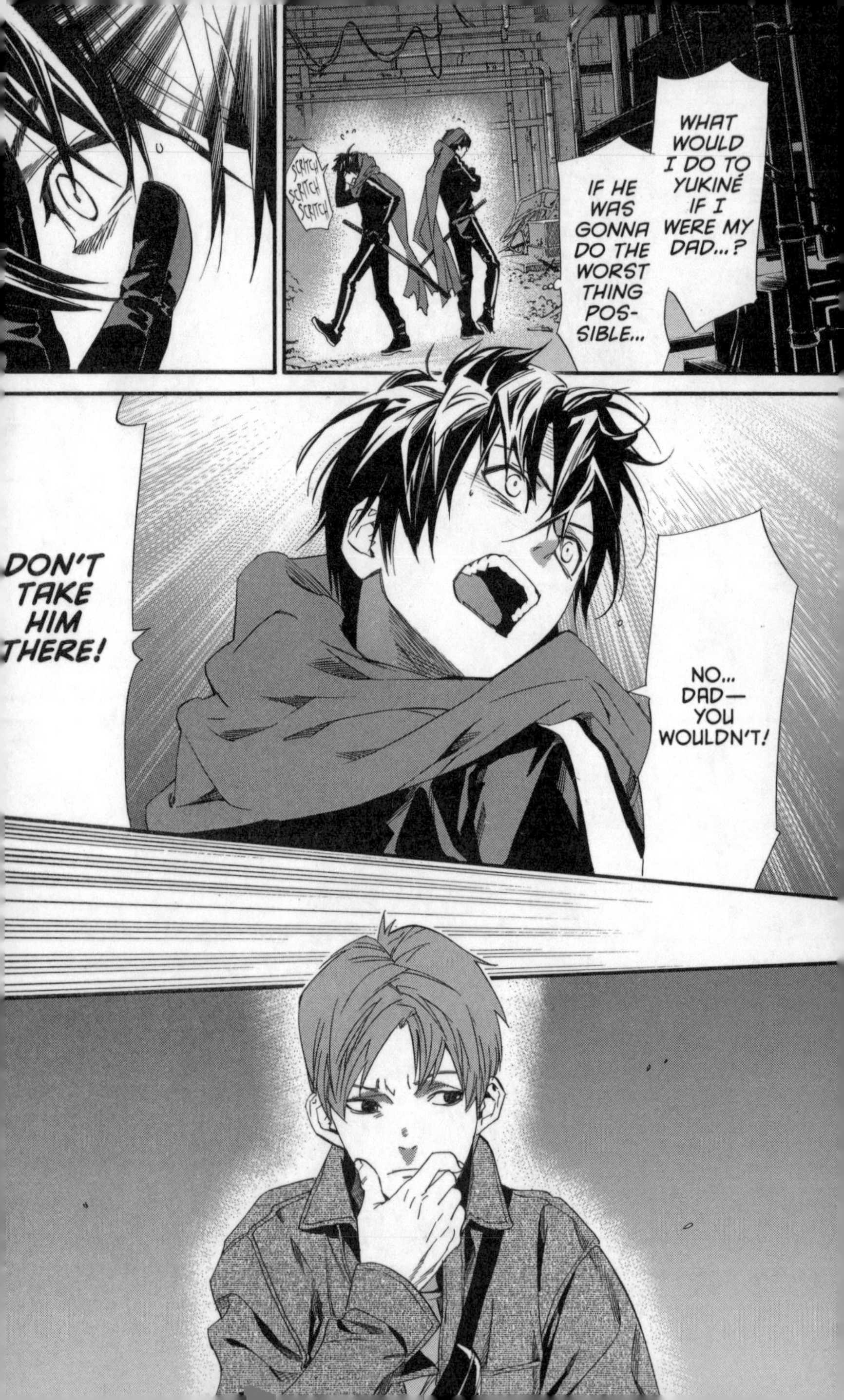
WHAT WOULD I DO TO YUKINÉ IF I WERE MY DAD...?
IF HE WAS GONNA DO THE WORST THING POS-SIBLE...
SCRATCH SCRATCH SCRATCH
NO... DAD— YOU WOULDN'T!
DON'T TAKE HIM THERE!

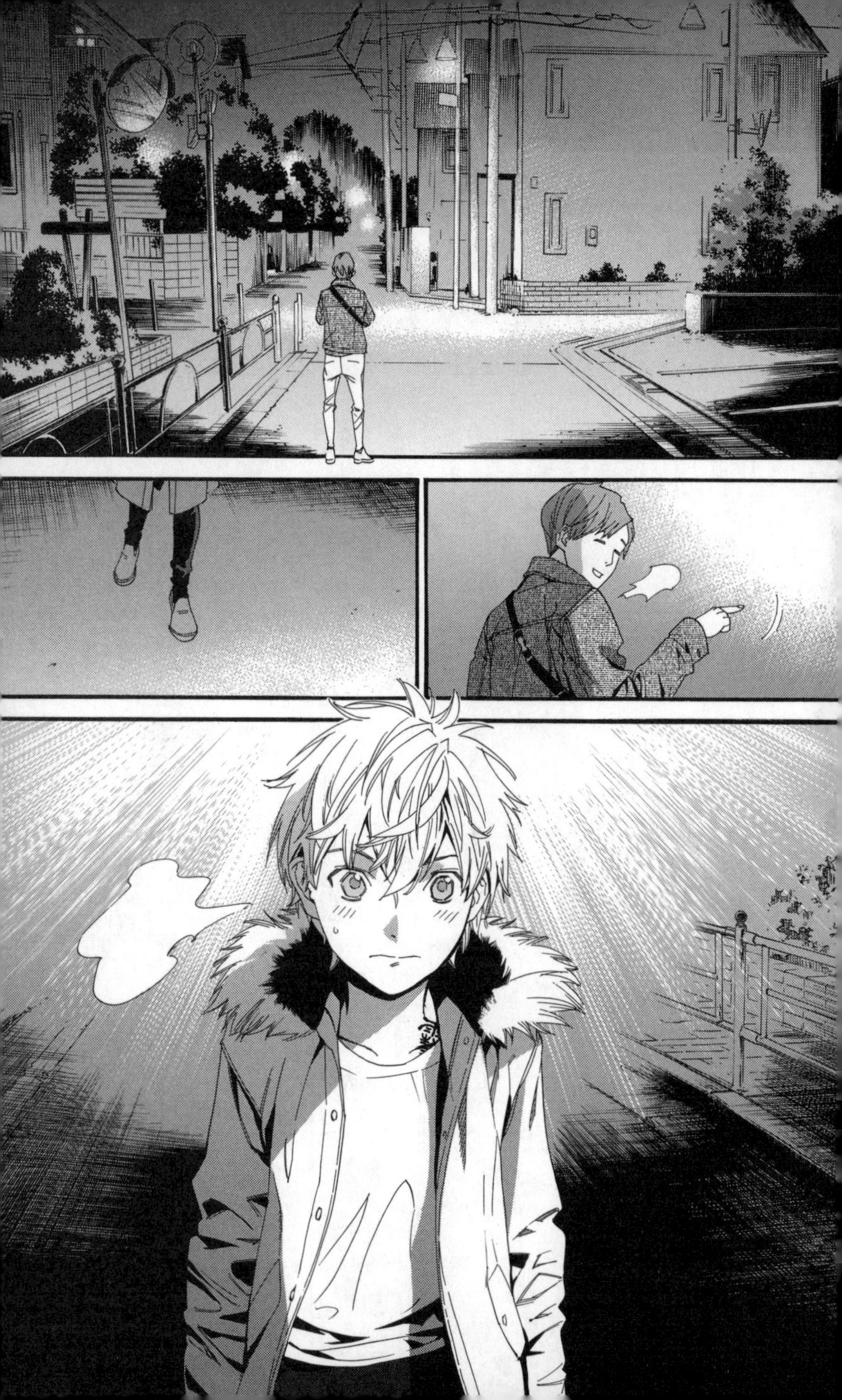

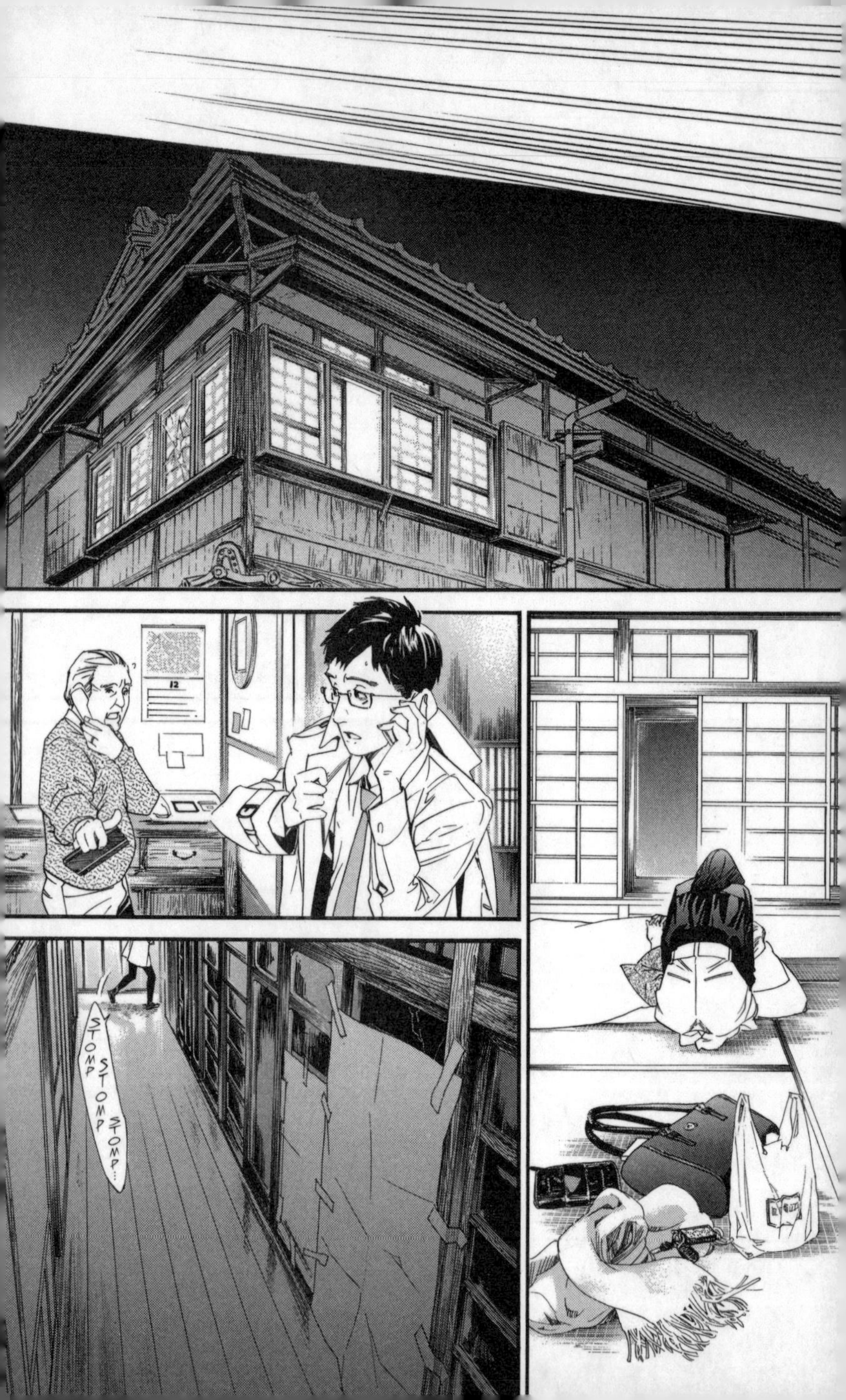
STOMP STOMP STOMP...

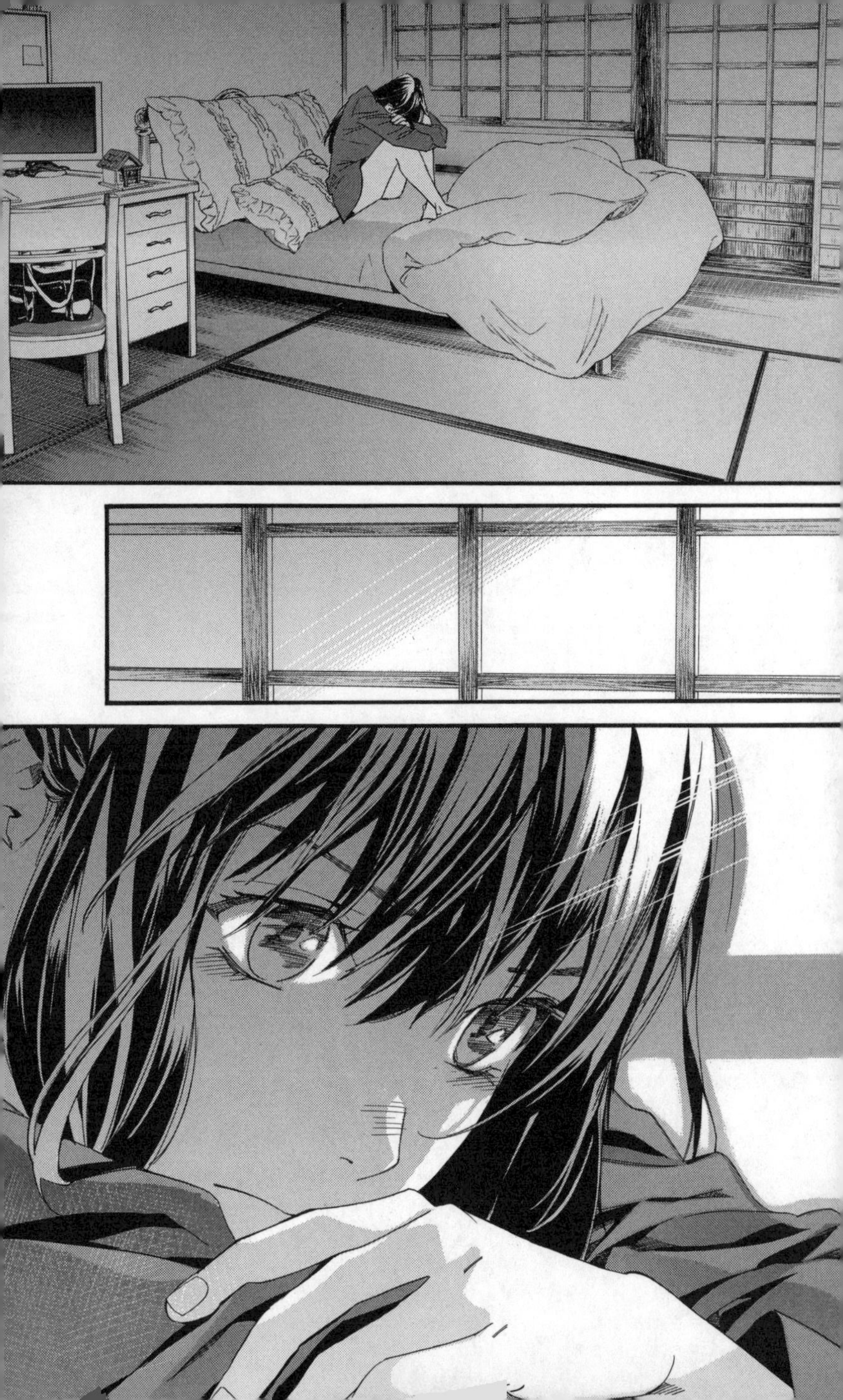

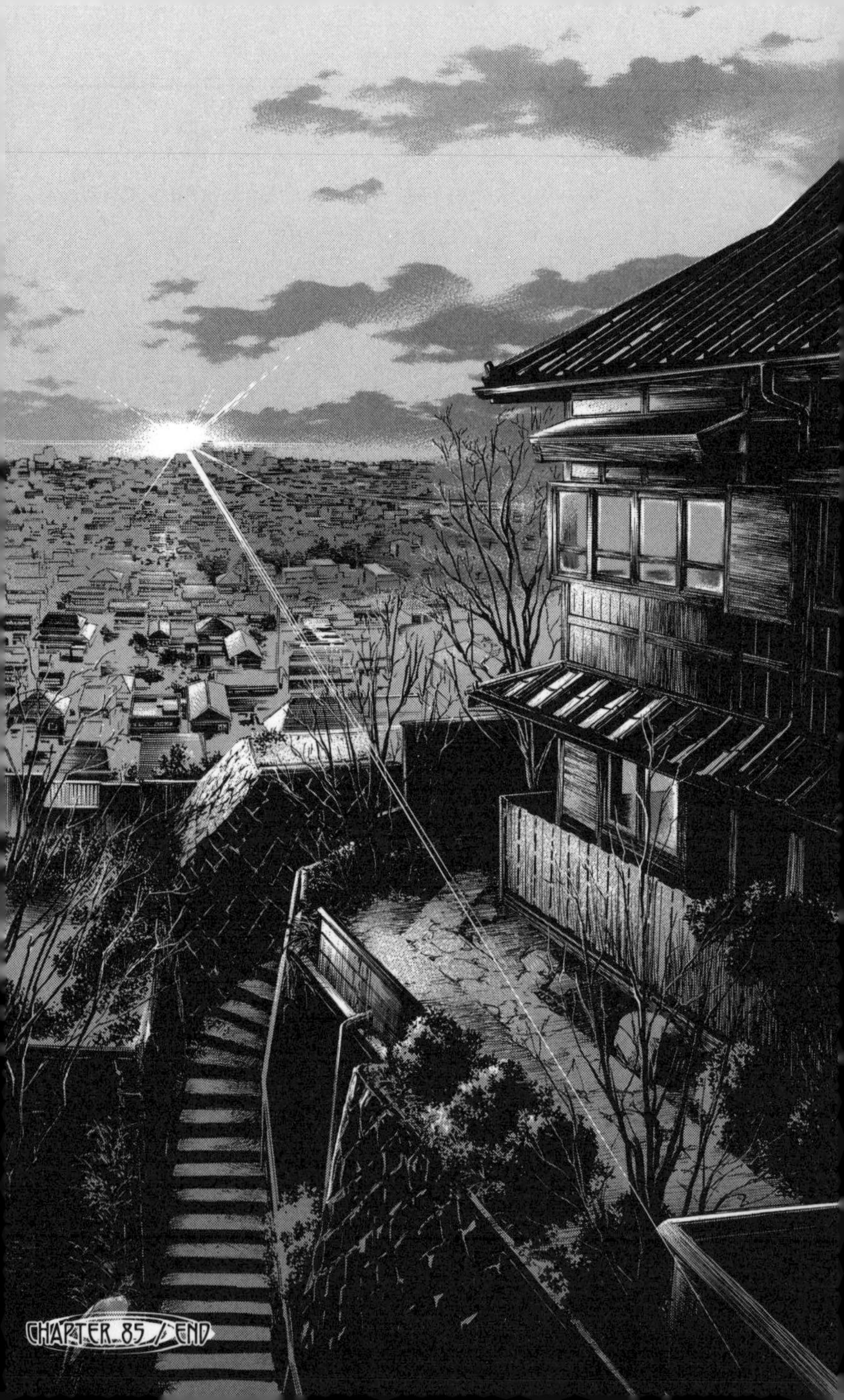
CHAPTER 85 / END

野

息

神

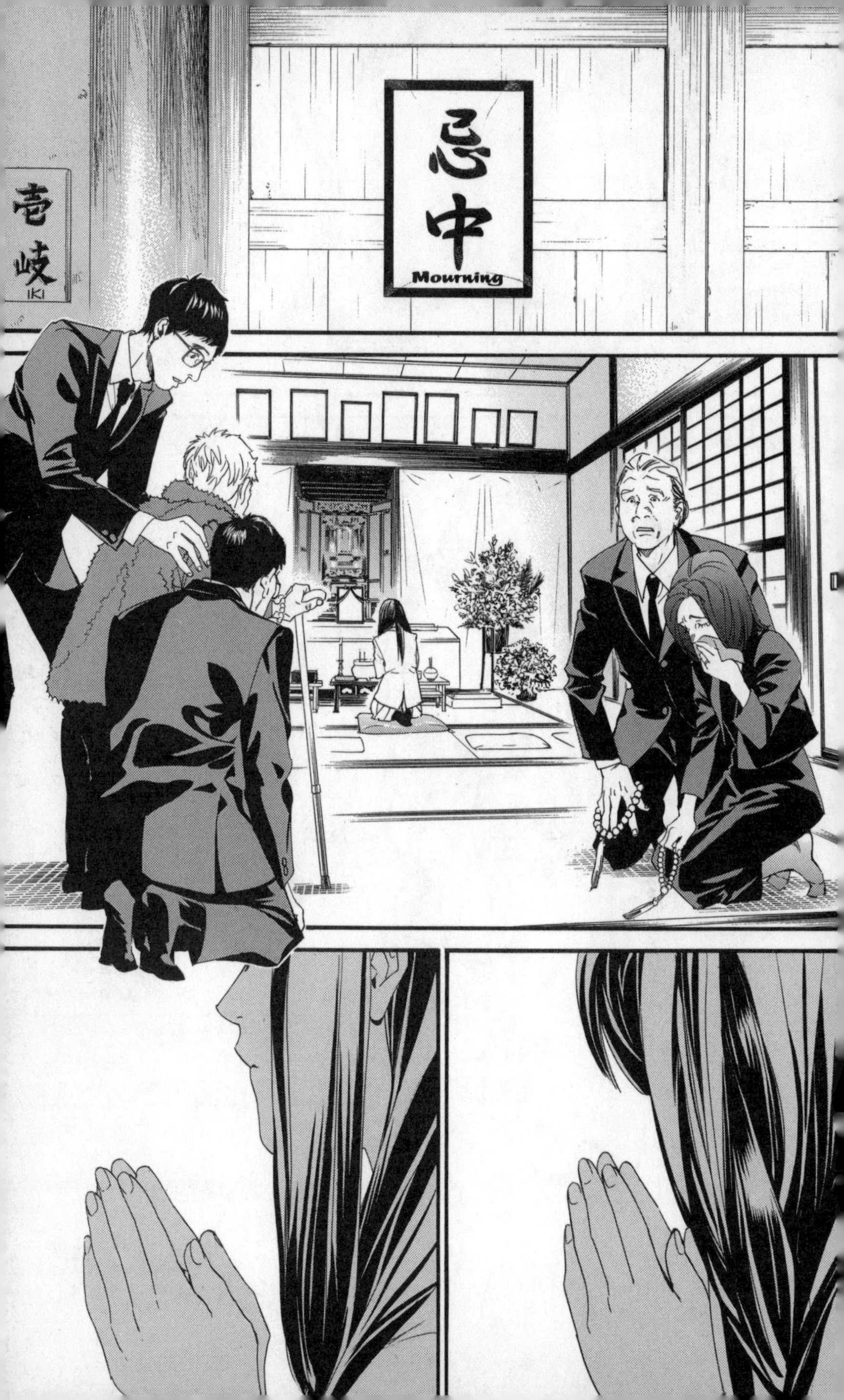
忌中
Mourning
壱岐
IKI

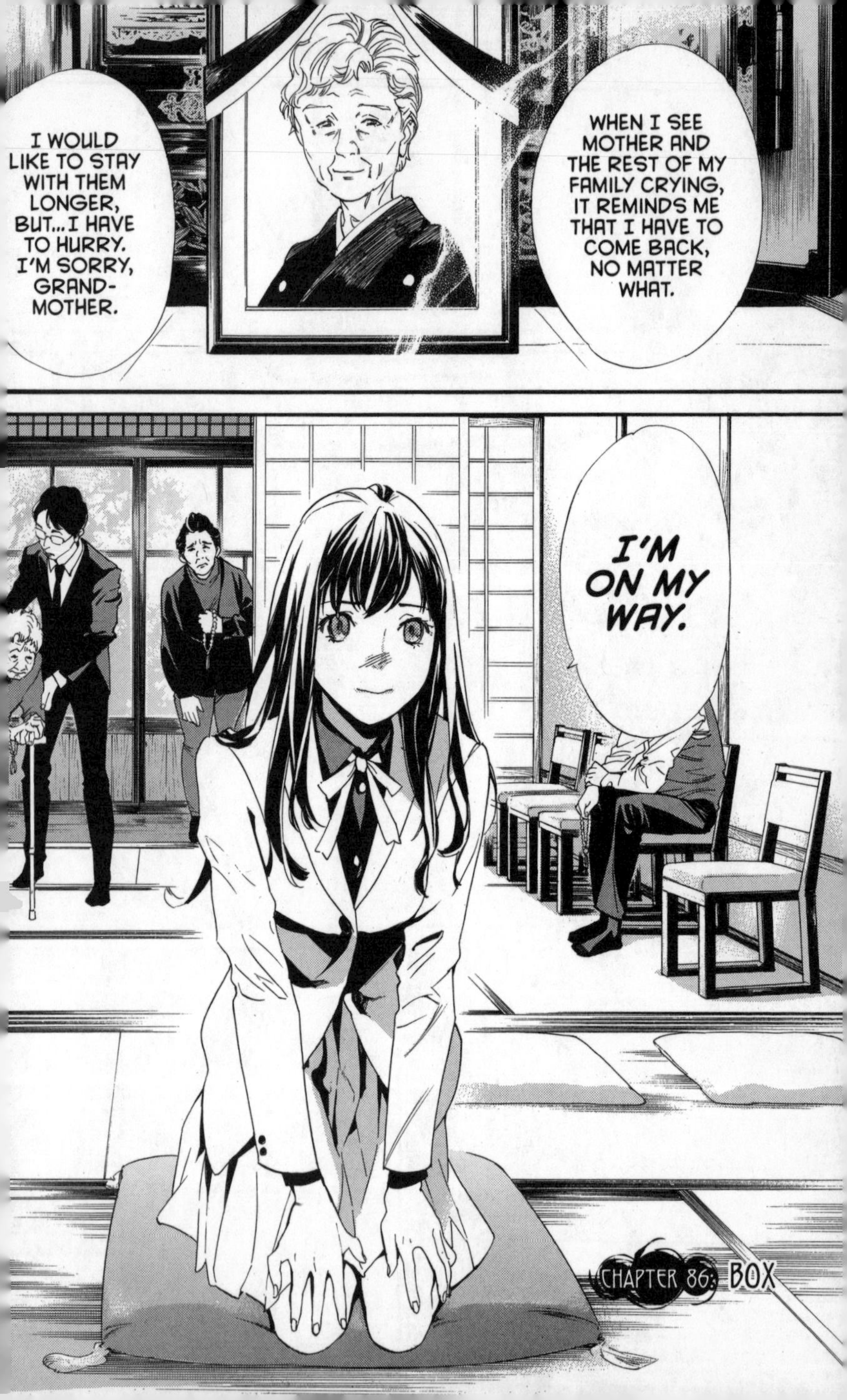
WHEN I SEE MOTHER AND THE REST OF MY FAMILY CRYING, IT REMINDS ME THAT I HAVE TO COME BACK, NO MATTER WHAT.
I WOULD LIKE TO STAY WITH THEM LONGER, BUT...I HAVE TO HURRY. I'M SORRY, GRAND-MOTHER.
I'M ON MY WAY.
CHAPTER 86: BOX

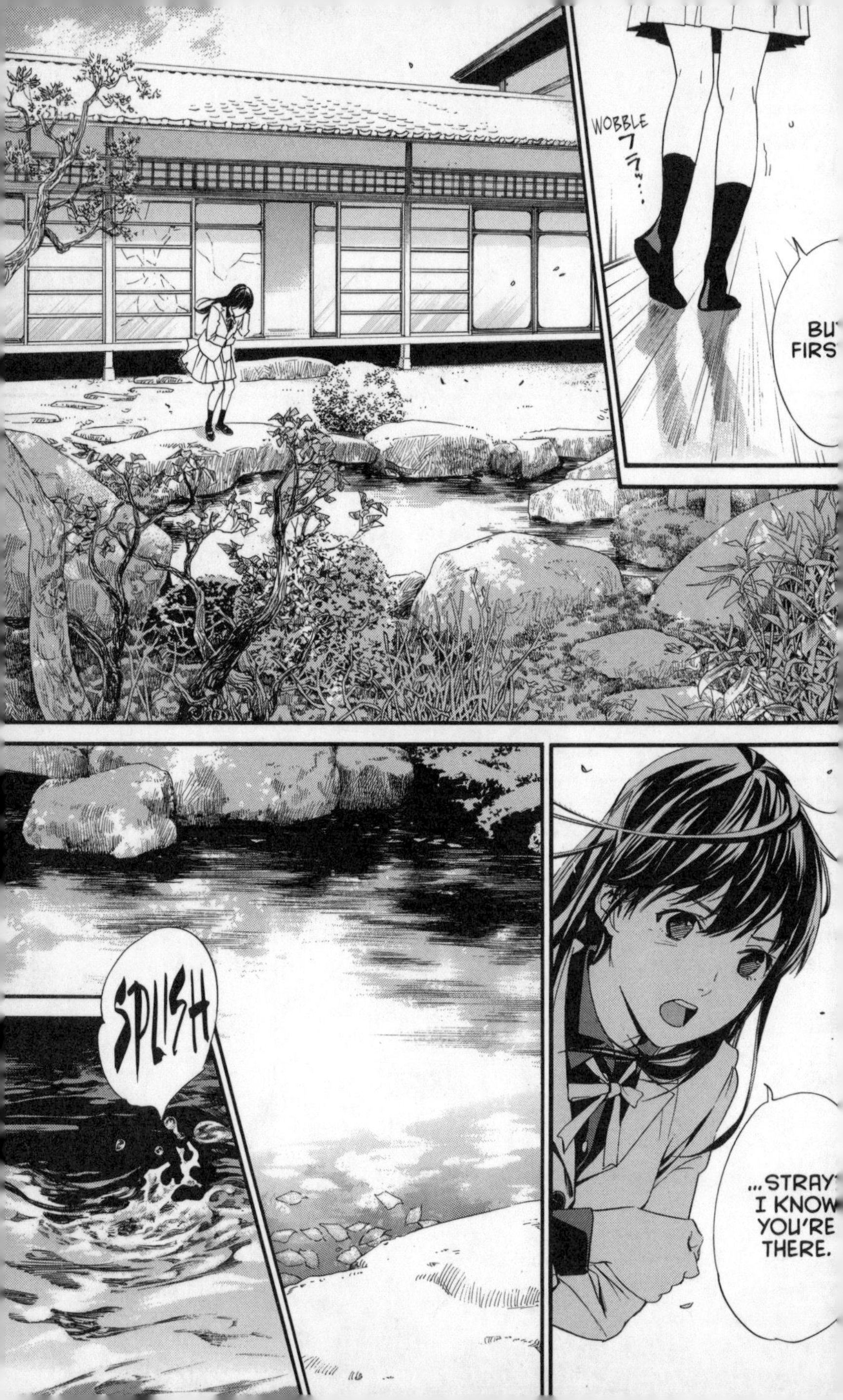
WOBBLE
BU
FIRS
...STRAY
I KNOW
YOU'RE
THERE.
SPLISH

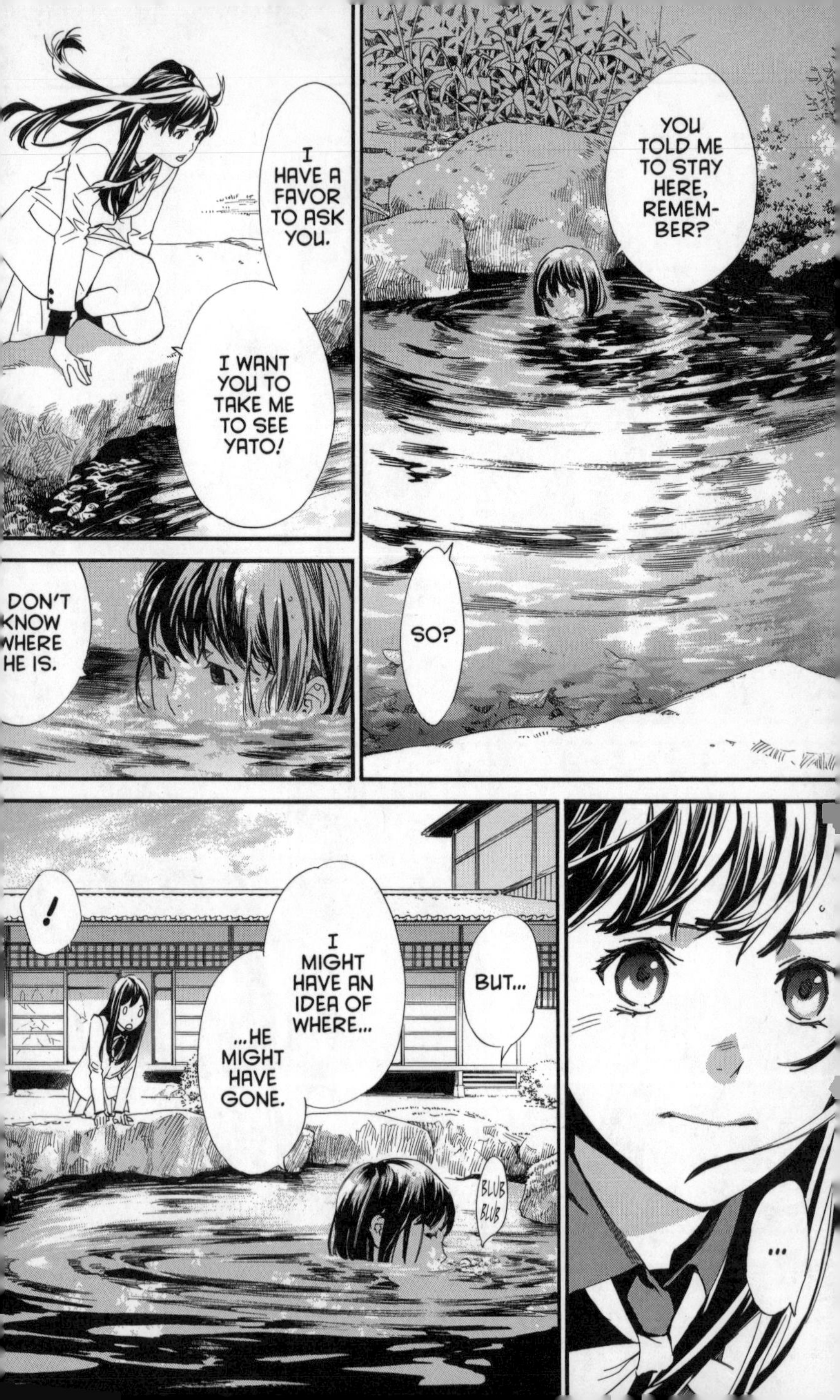
YOU TOLD ME TO STAY HERE, REMEMBER?
SO?
I HAVE A FAVOR TO ASK YOU.
I WANT YOU TO TAKE ME TO SEE YATO!
DON'T KNOW WHERE HE IS.
...
BUT...
I MIGHT HAVE AN IDEA OF WHERE...
...HE MIGHT HAVE GONE.
BLUB BLUB
!

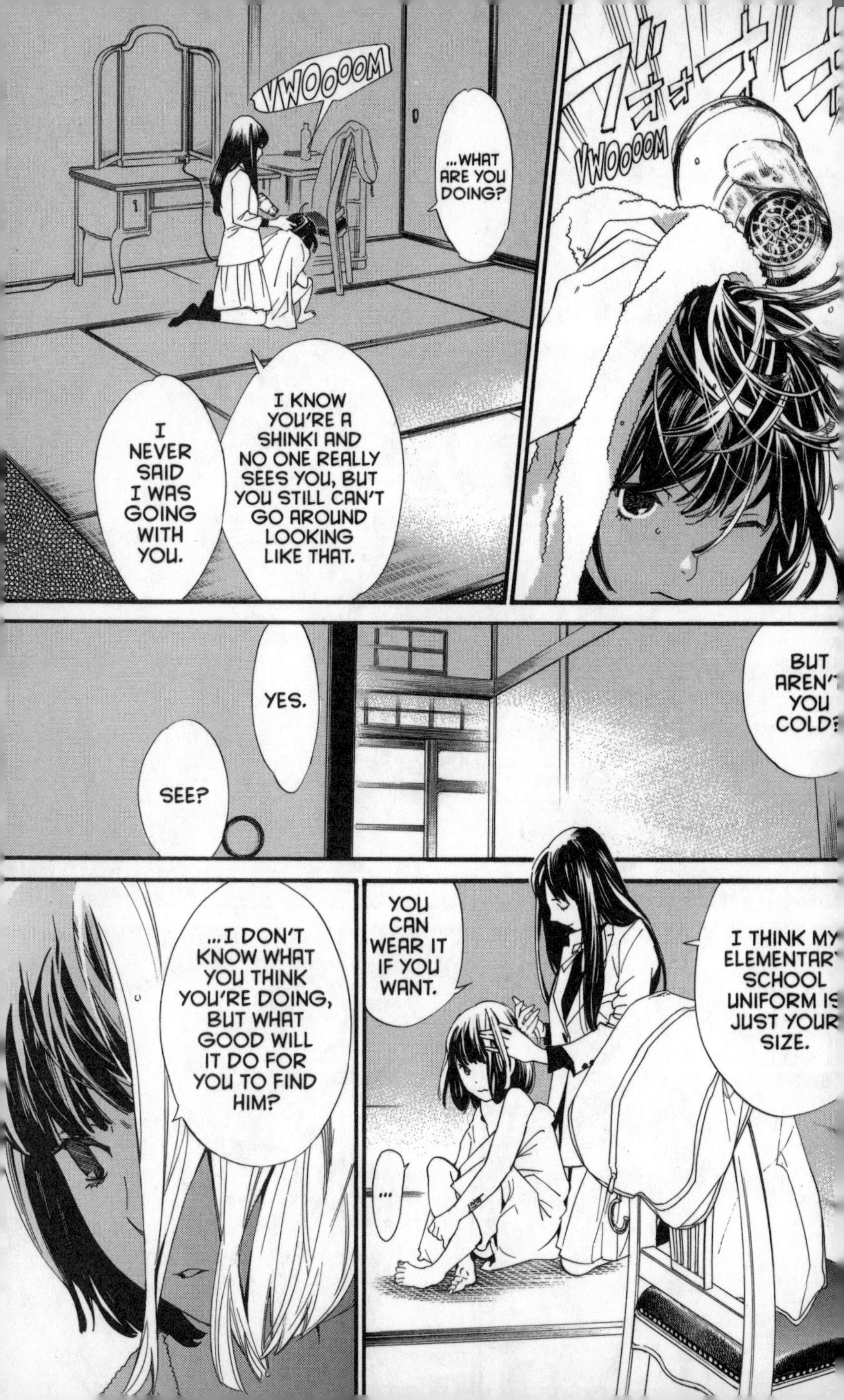
VWOOOOM
VWOOOOM
...WHAT ARE YOU DOING?
I KNOW YOU'RE A SHINKI AND NO ONE REALLY SEES YOU, BUT YOU STILL CAN'T GO AROUND LOOKING LIKE THAT.
I NEVER SAID I WAS GOING WITH YOU.
BUT AREN' YOU COLD?
YES.
SEE?
I THINK MY ELEMENTAR' SCHOOL UNIFORM IS JUST YOUR SIZE.
YOU CAN WEAR IT IF YOU WANT.
...
...I DON'T KNOW WHAT YOU THINK YOU'RE DOING, BUT WHAT GOOD WILL IT DO FOR YOU TO FIND HIM?

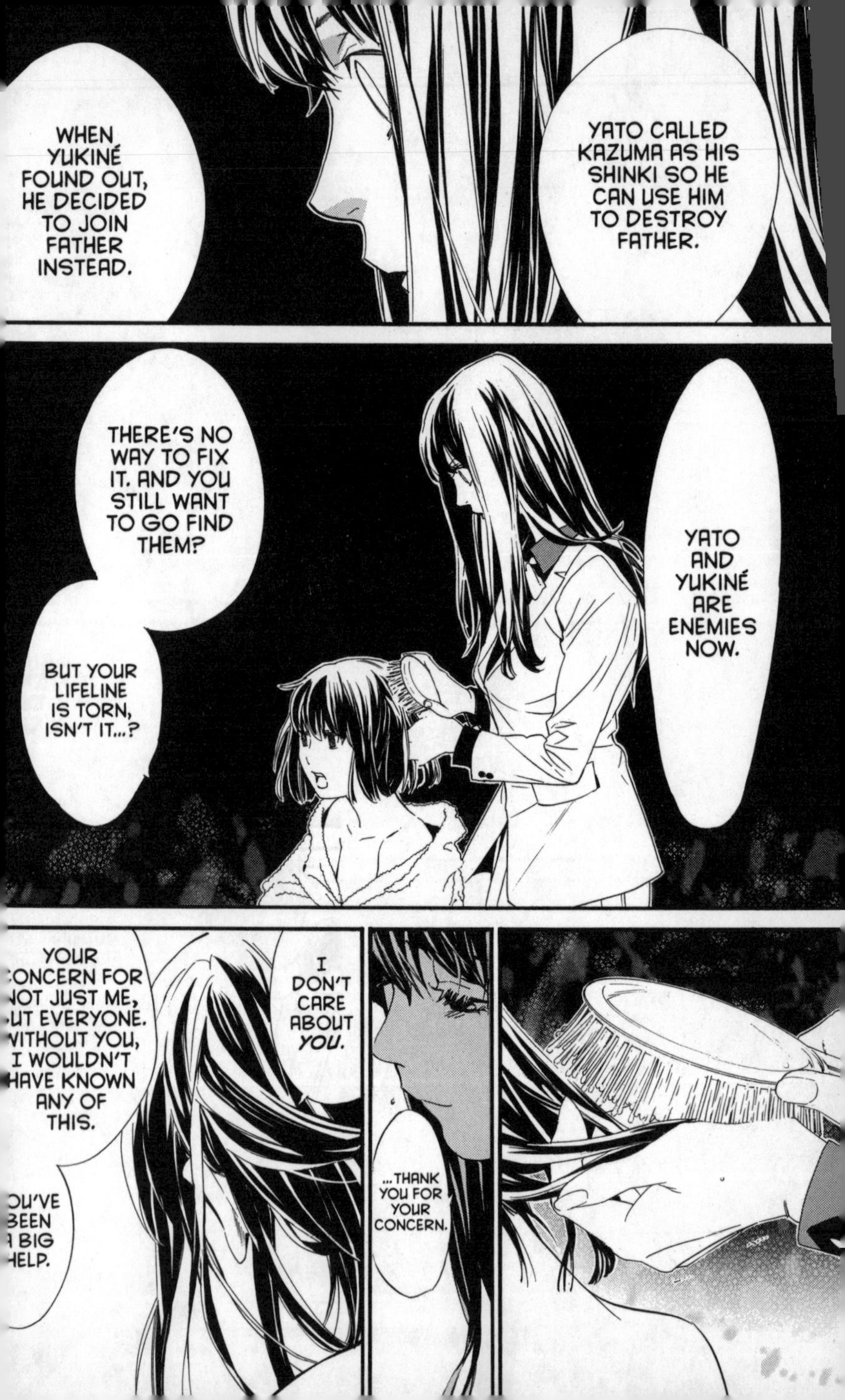
YATO CALLED KAZUMA AS HIS SHINKI SO HE CAN USE HIM TO DESTROY FATHER.
WHEN YUKINÉ FOUND OUT, HE DECIDED TO JOIN FATHER INSTEAD.
YATO AND YUKINÉ ARE ENEMIES NOW.
THERE'S NO WAY TO FIX IT. AND YOU STILL WANT TO GO FIND THEM?
BUT YOUR LIFELINE IS TORN, ISN'T IT...?
...THANK YOU FOR YOUR CONCERN.
I DON'T CARE ABOUT *YOU*.
YOUR CONCERN FOR NOT JUST ME, BUT EVERYONE. WITHOUT YOU, I WOULDN'T HAVE KNOWN ANY OF THIS.
YOU'VE BEEN A BIG HELP.

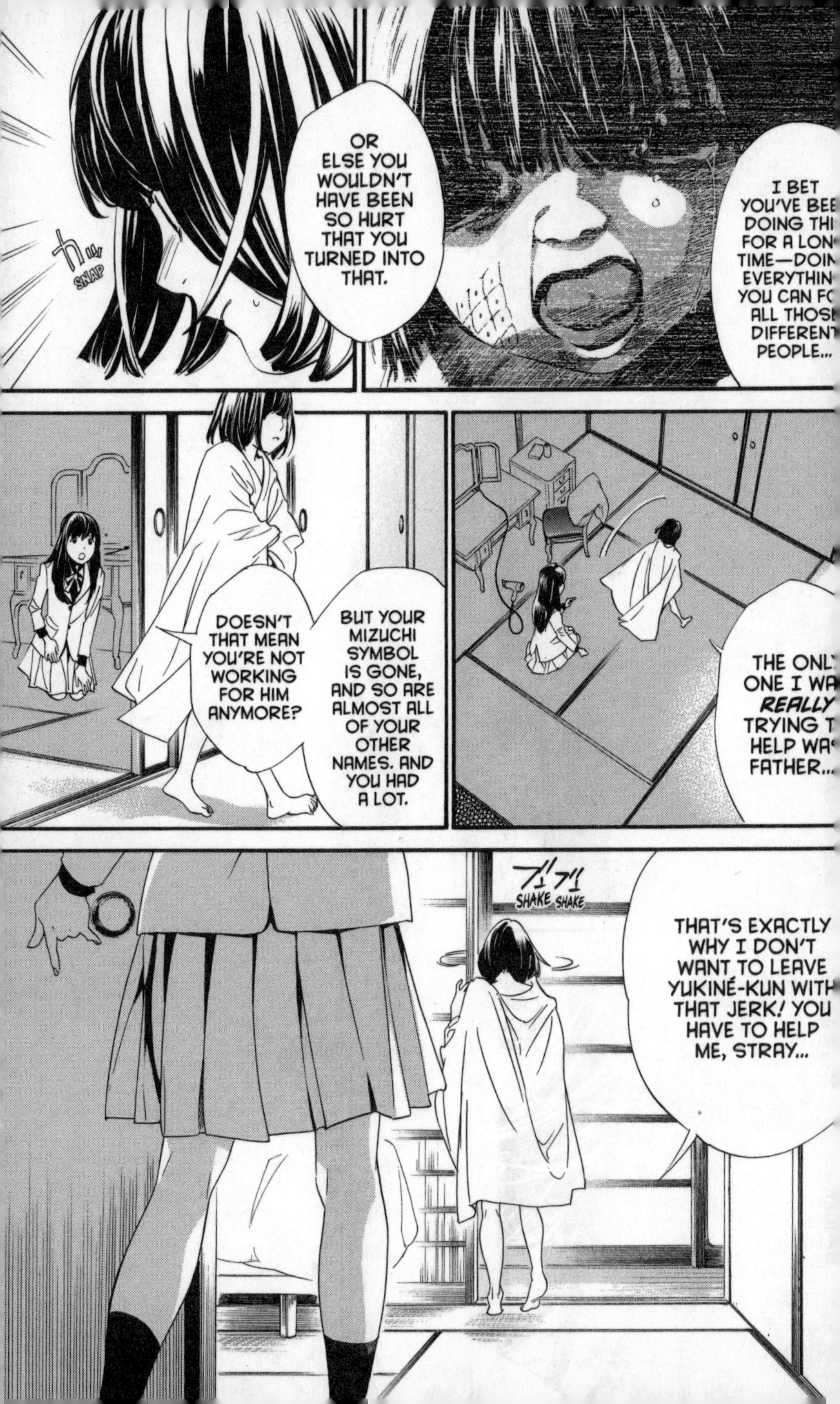
I BET YOU'VE BEE DOING THI FOR A LON TIME—DOIN EVERYTHIN YOU CAN FO ALL THOSE DIFFERENT PEOPLE...
OR ELSE YOU WOULDN'T HAVE BEEN SO HURT THAT YOU TURNED INTO THAT.
SNAP
THE ONL ONE I WA *REALLY* TRYING T HELP WA FATHER...
BUT YOUR MIZUCHI SYMBOL IS GONE, AND SO ARE ALMOST ALL OF YOUR OTHER NAMES. AND YOU HAD A LOT.
DOESN'T THAT MEAN YOU'RE NOT WORKING FOR HIM ANYMORE?
SHAKE SHAKE
THAT'S EXACTLY WHY I DON'T WANT TO LEAVE YUKINÉ-KUN WITH THAT JERK! YOU HAVE TO HELP ME, STRAY...

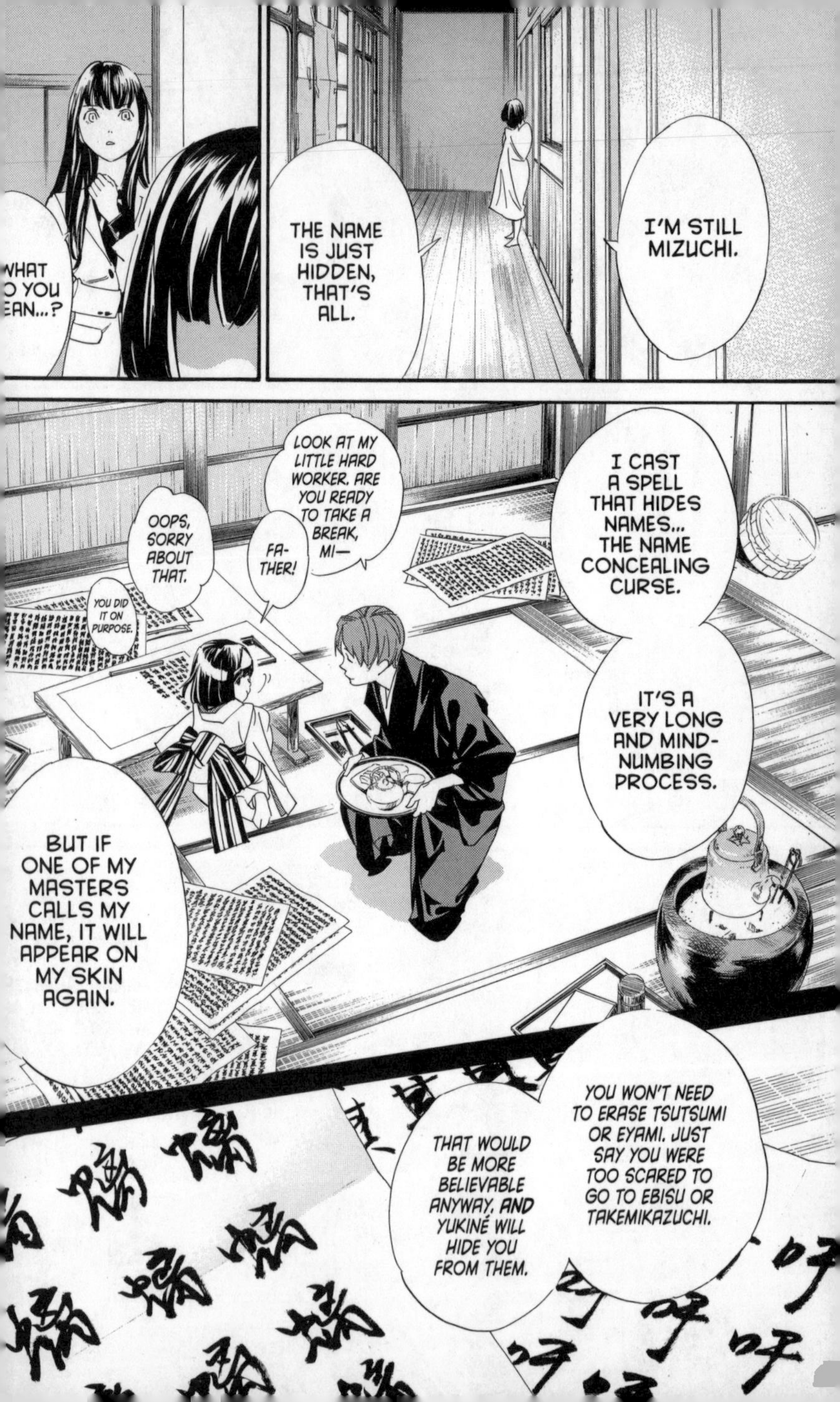
I'M STILL MIZUCHI.
THE NAME IS JUST HIDDEN, THAT'S ALL.
WHAT O YOU EAN...?
I CAST A SPELL THAT HIDES NAMES... THE NAME CONCEALING CURSE.
IT'S A VERY LONG AND MIND-NUMBING PROCESS.
LOOK AT MY LITTLE HARD WORKER. ARE YOU READY TO TAKE A BREAK, MI—
FA-THER!
OOPS, SORRY ABOUT THAT.
YOU DID IT ON PURPOSE.
BUT IF ONE OF MY MASTERS CALLS MY NAME, IT WILL APPEAR ON MY SKIN AGAIN.
YOU WON'T NEED TO ERASE TSUTSUMI OR EYAMI. JUST SAY YOU WERE TOO SCARED TO GO TO EBISU OR TAKEMIKAZUCHI.
THAT WOULD BE MORE BELIEVABLE ANYWAY, AND YUKINÉ WILL HIDE YOU FROM THEM.

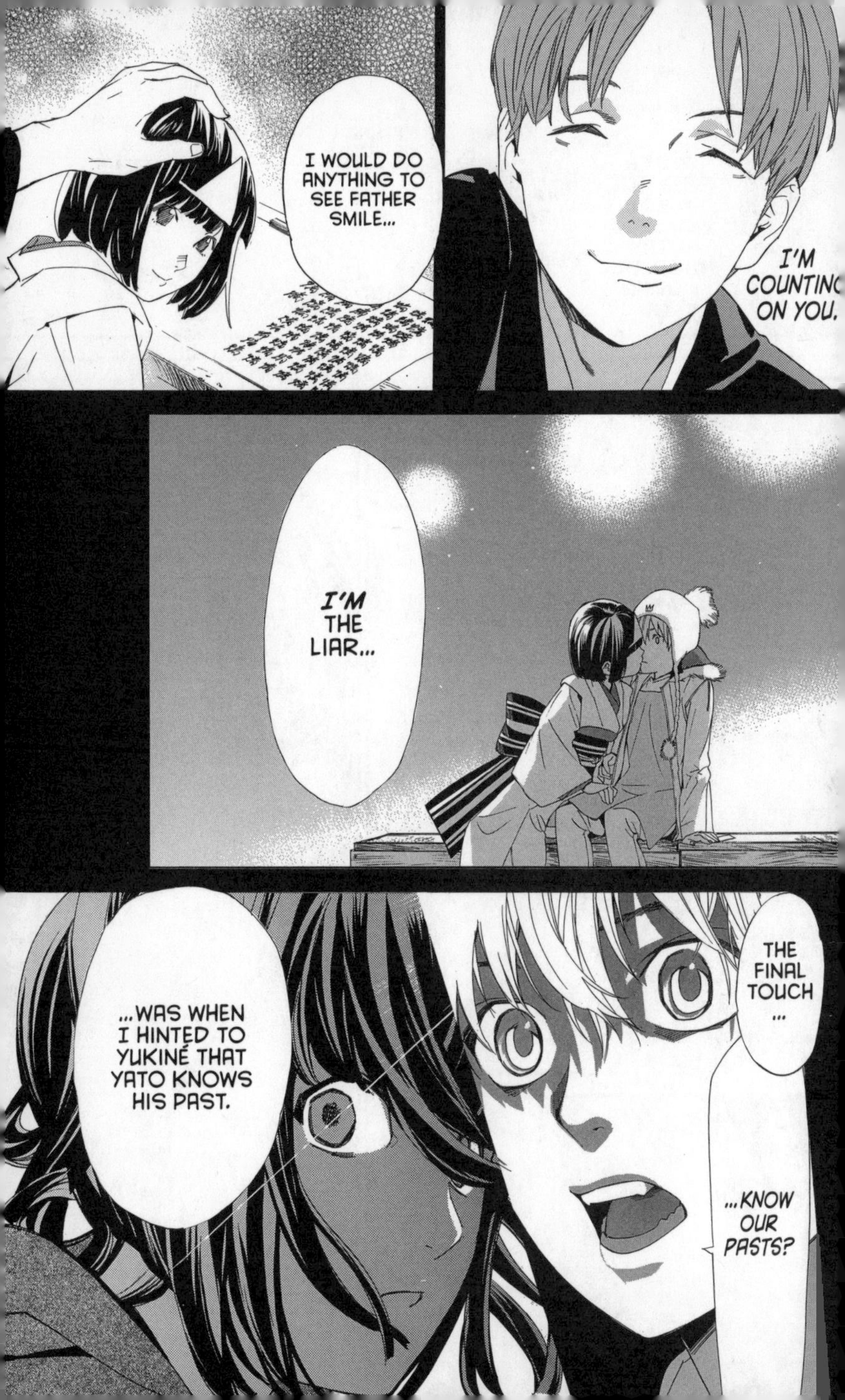
I'M COUNTING ON YOU.
I WOULD DO ANYTHING TO SEE FATHER SMILE...
I'M THE LIAR...
THE FINAL TOUCH...
...WAS WHEN I HINTED TO YUKINÉ THAT YATO KNOWS HIS PAST.
...KNOW OUR PASTS?

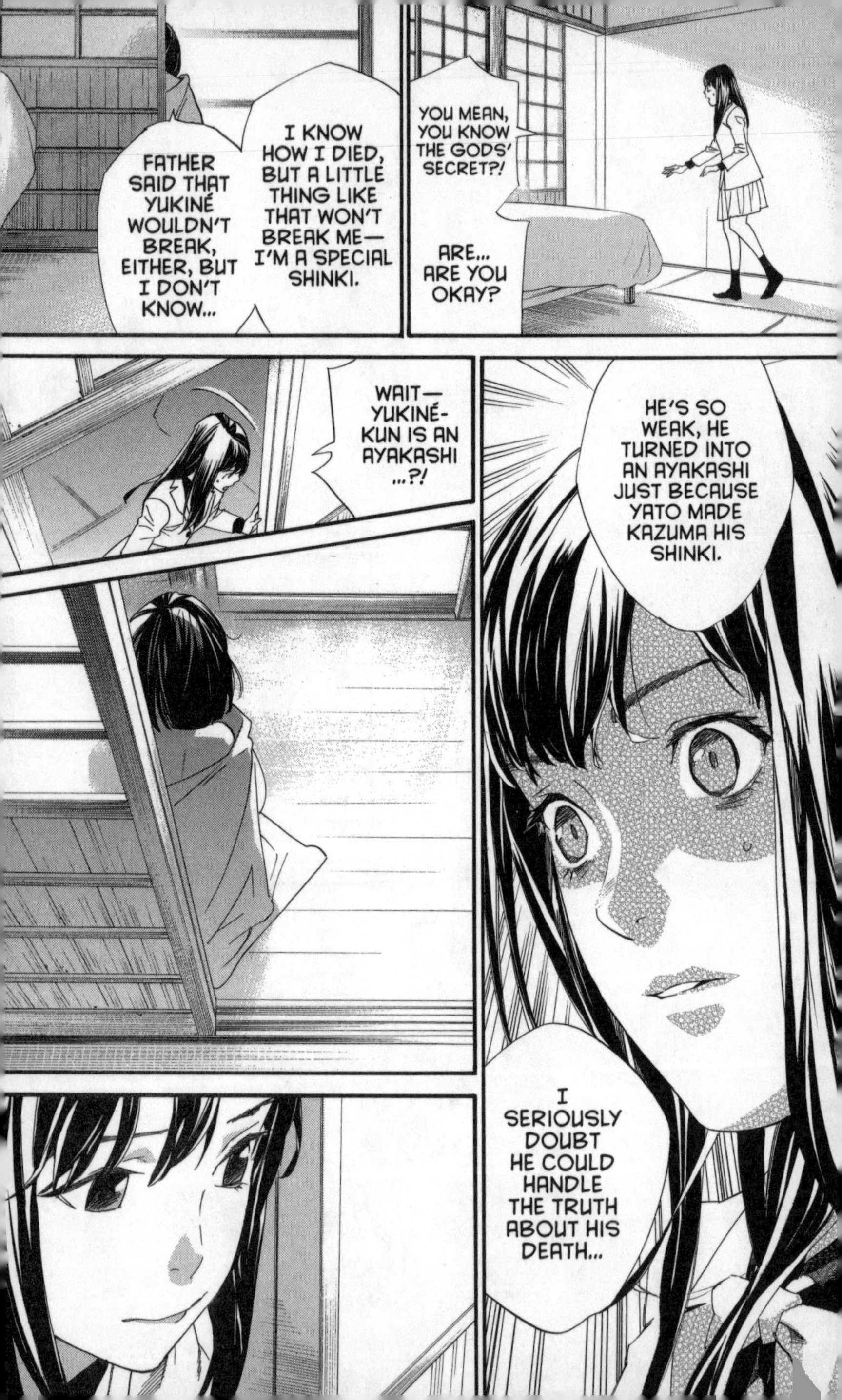
YOU MEAN, YOU KNOW THE GODS' SECRET?!
ARE... ARE YOU OKAY?
I KNOW HOW I DIED, BUT A LITTLE THING LIKE THAT WON'T BREAK ME— I'M A SPECIAL SHINKI.
FATHER SAID THAT YUKINÉ WOULDN'T BREAK, EITHER, BUT I DON'T KNOW...
HE'S SO WEAK, HE TURNED INTO AN AYAKASHI JUST BECAUSE YATO MADE KAZUMA HIS SHINKI.
I SERIOUSLY DOUBT HE COULD HANDLE THE TRUTH ABOUT HIS DEATH...
WAIT— YUKINÉ-KUN IS AN AYAKASHI ...?!

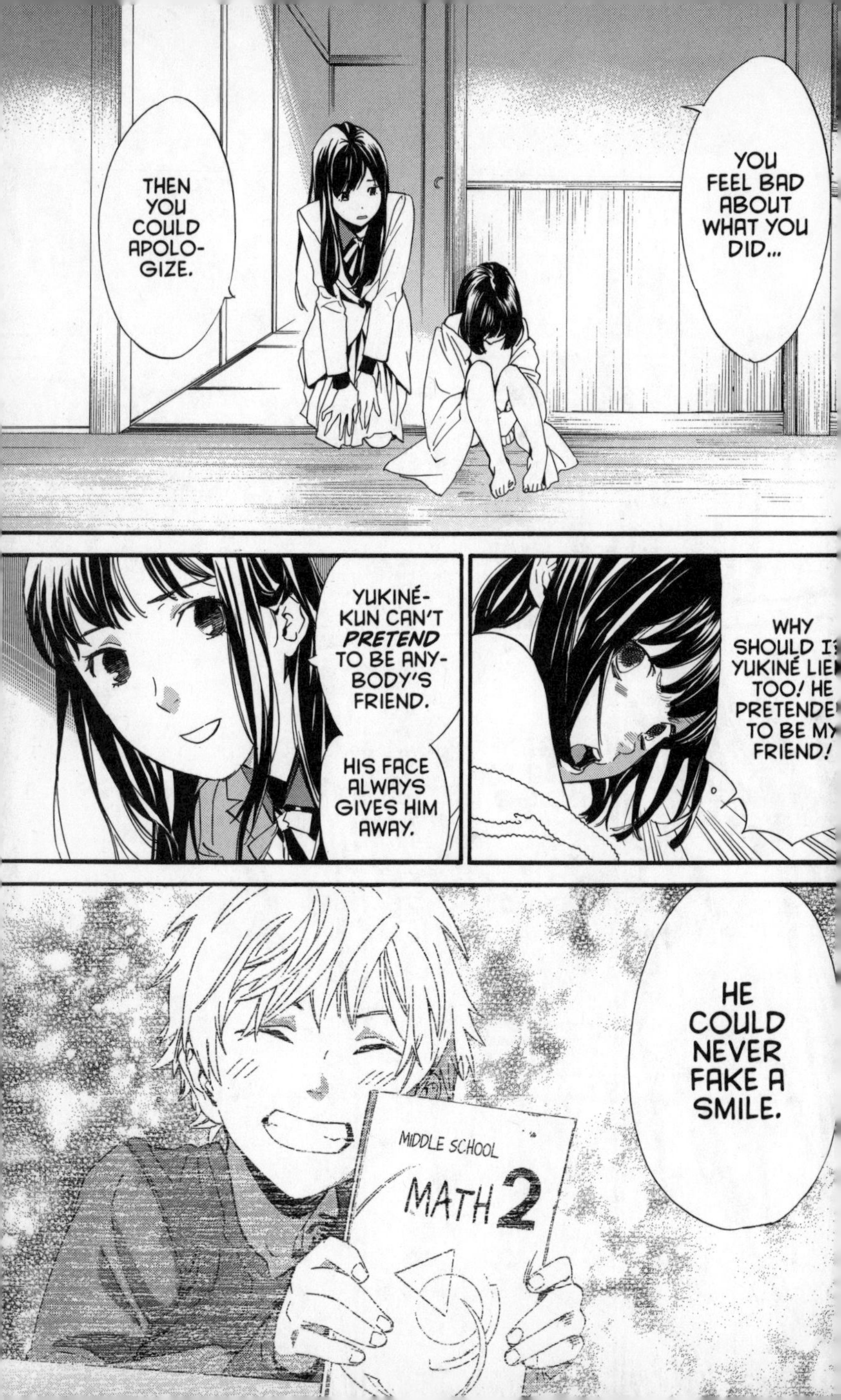
YOU FEEL BAD ABOUT WHAT YOU DID...
THEN YOU COULD APOLO-GIZE.
WHY SHOULD I? YUKINÉ LIED TOO! HE PRETENDED TO BE MY FRIEND!
YUKINÉ-KUN CAN'T *PRETEND* TO BE ANY-BODY'S FRIEND.
HIS FACE ALWAYS GIVES HIM AWAY.
HE COULD NEVER FAKE A SMILE.
MIDDLE SCHOOL
MATH 2

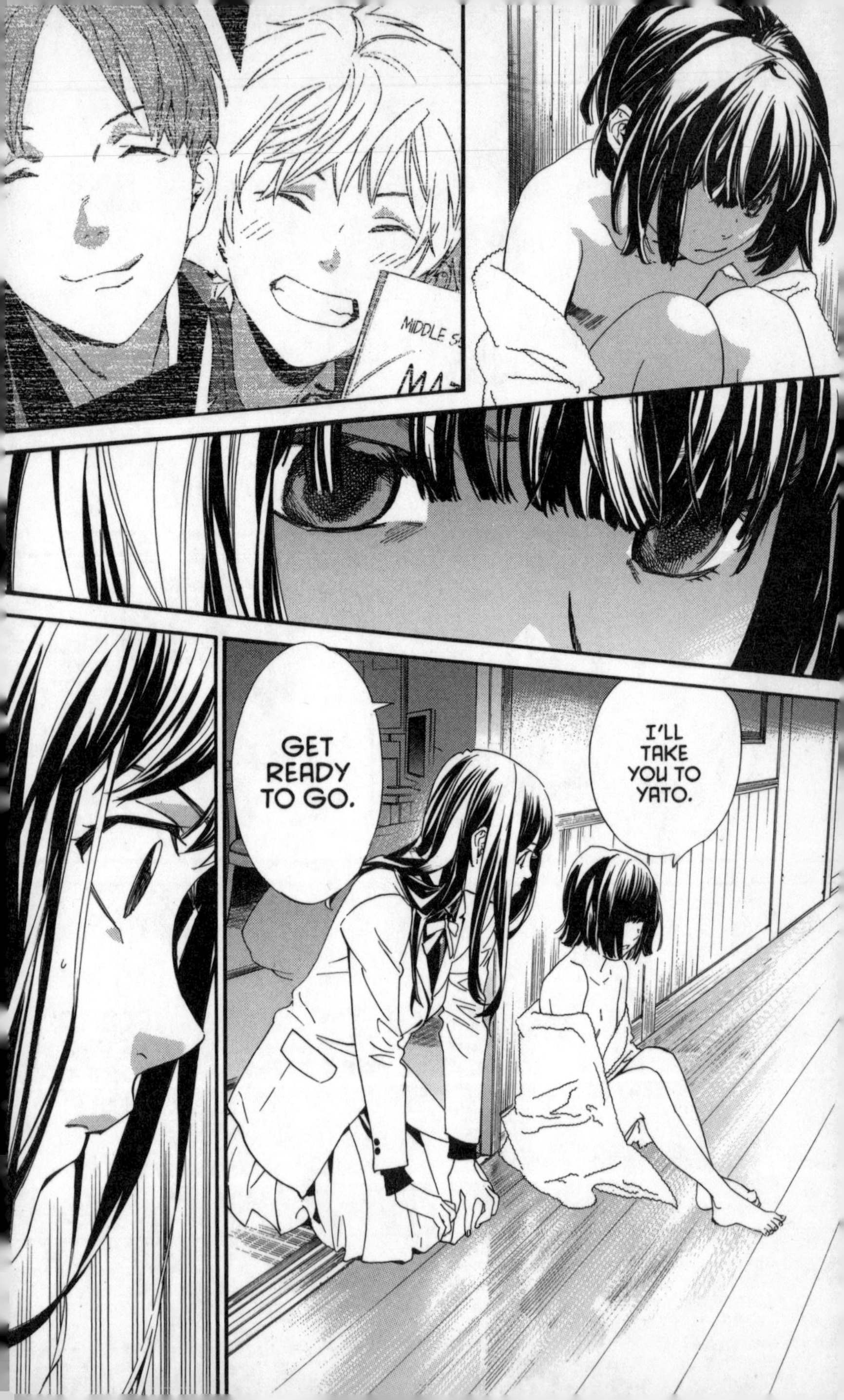
I'LL TAKE YOU TO YATO.
GET READY TO GO.

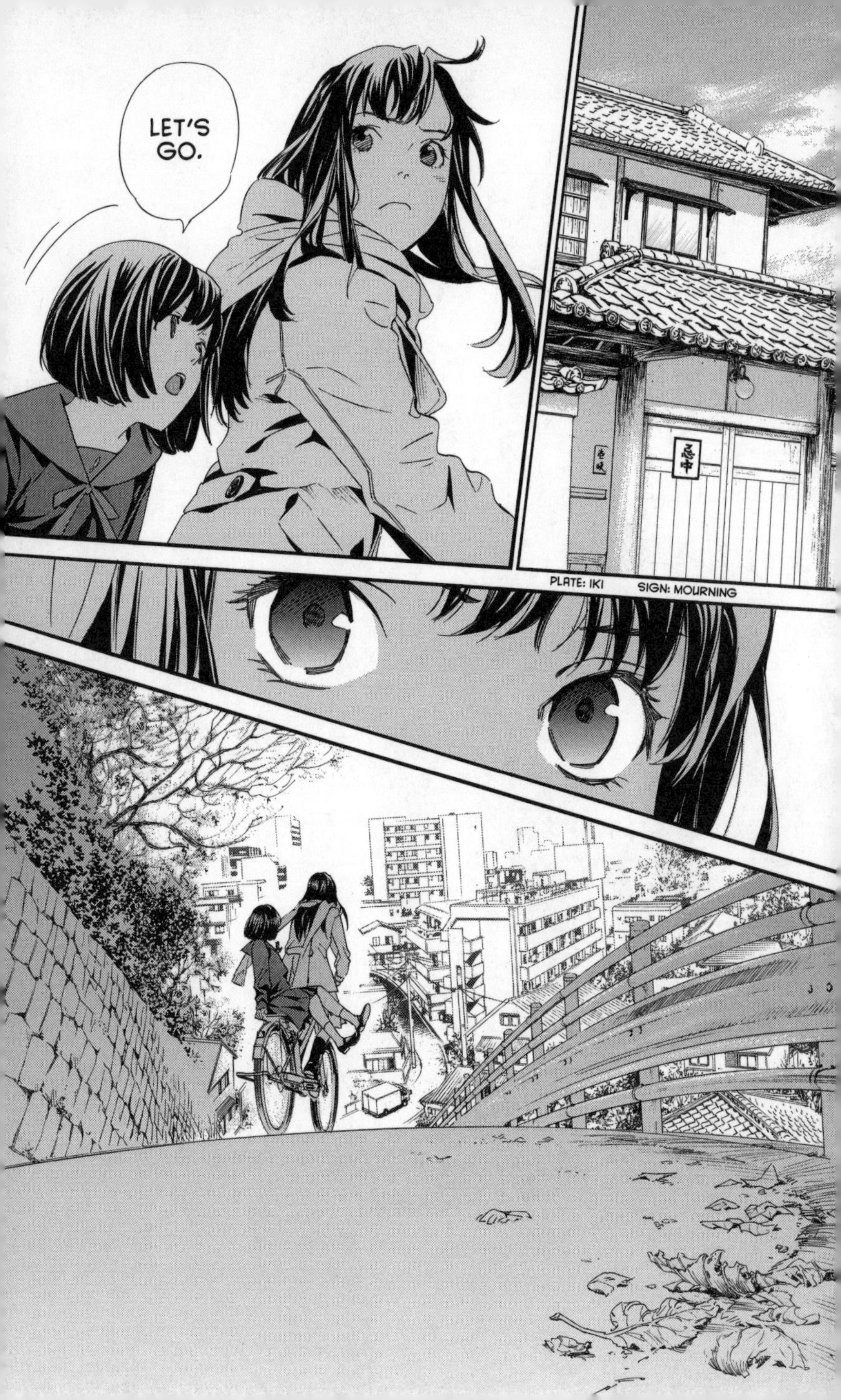

LET'S GO.
SIGN: MOURNING
PLATE: IKI

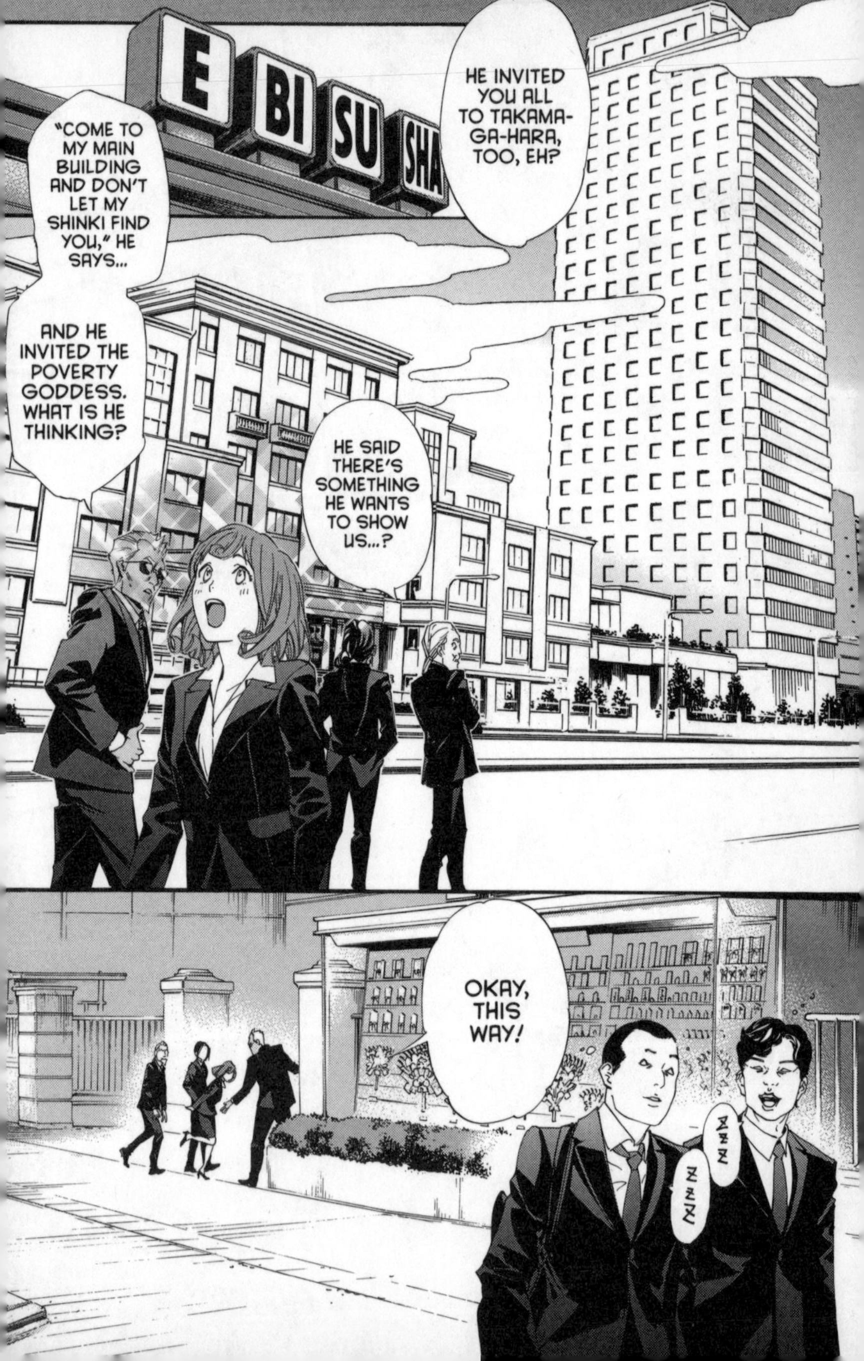
E BI SU SHA
HE INVITED YOU ALL TO TAKAMA-GA-HARA, TOO, EH?
"COME TO MY MAIN BUILDING AND DON'T LET MY SHINKI FIND YOU," HE SAYS...
AND HE INVITED THE POVERTY GODDESS. WHAT IS HE THINKING?
HE SAID THERE'S SOMETHING HE WANTS TO SHOW US...?
OKAY, THIS WAY!
ZZZ
ZZZ

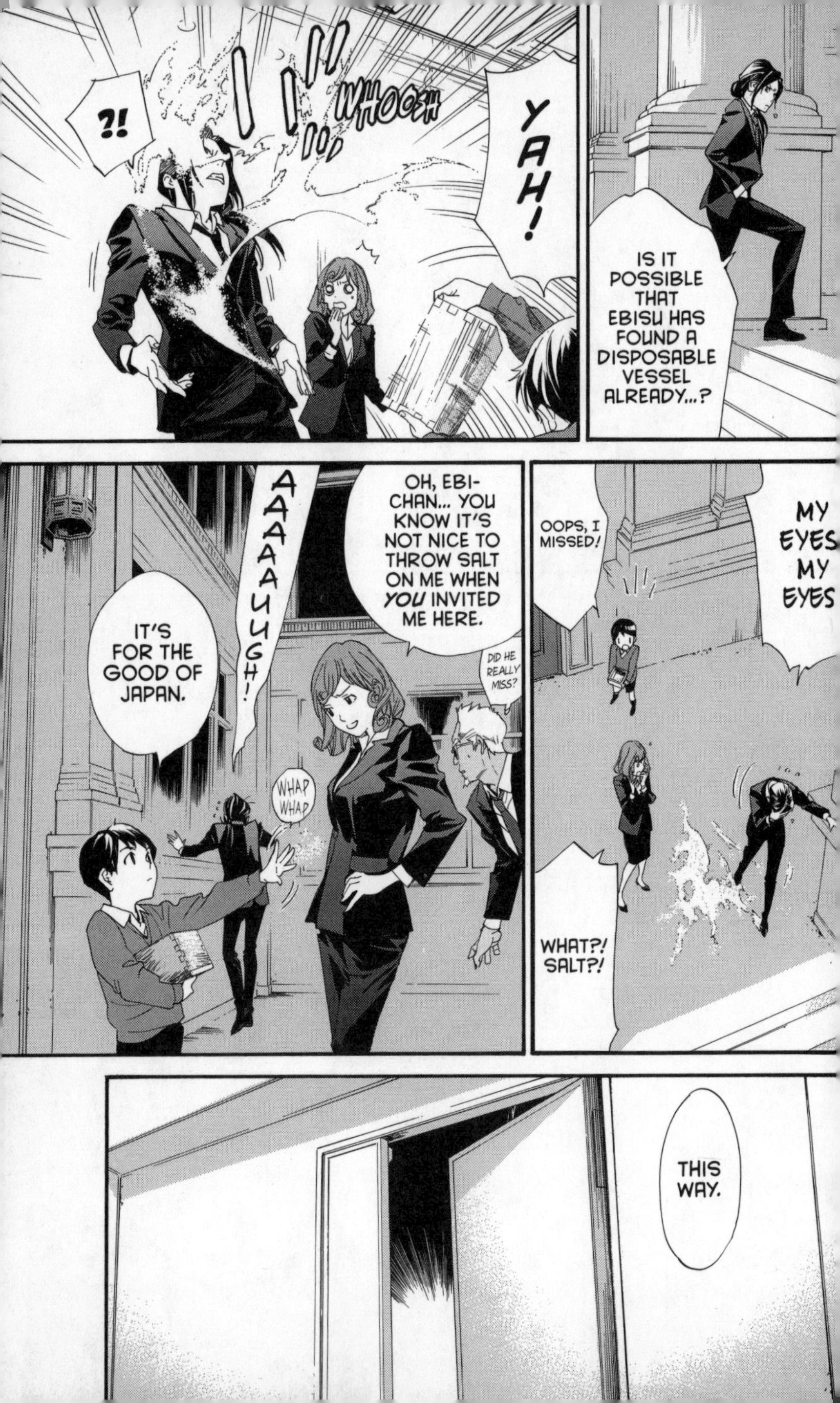
IS IT POSSIBLE THAT EBISU HAS FOUND A DISPOSABLE VESSEL ALREADY...?
YAH!
WHOOSH
?!
MY EYES MY EYES
OOPS, I MISSED!
WHAT?! SALT?!
OH, EBI-CHAN... YOU KNOW IT'S NOT NICE TO THROW SALT ON ME WHEN *YOU* INVITED ME HERE.
AAAAAAUUGH!
IT'S FOR THE GOOD OF JAPAN.
DID HE REALLY MISS?
WHAP WHAP
THIS WAY.

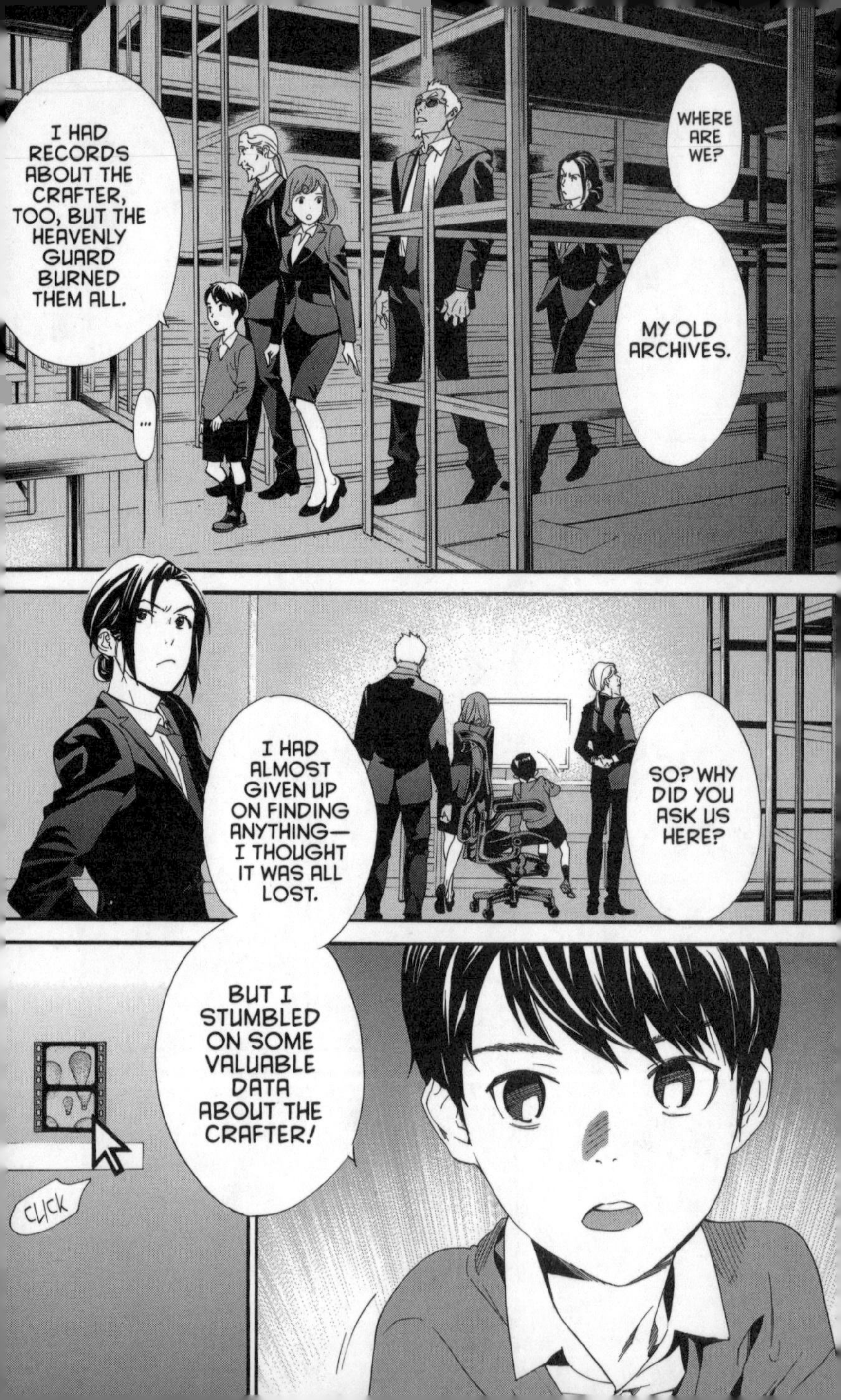
WHERE ARE WE?
MY OLD ARCHIVES.
I HAD RECORDS ABOUT THE CRAFTER, TOO, BUT THE HEAVENLY GUARD BURNED THEM ALL.
...
SO? WHY DID YOU ASK US HERE?
I HAD ALMOST GIVEN UP ON FINDING ANYTHING— I THOUGHT IT WAS ALL LOST.
BUT I STUMBLED ON SOME VALUABLE DATA ABOUT THE CRAFTER!
CLICK

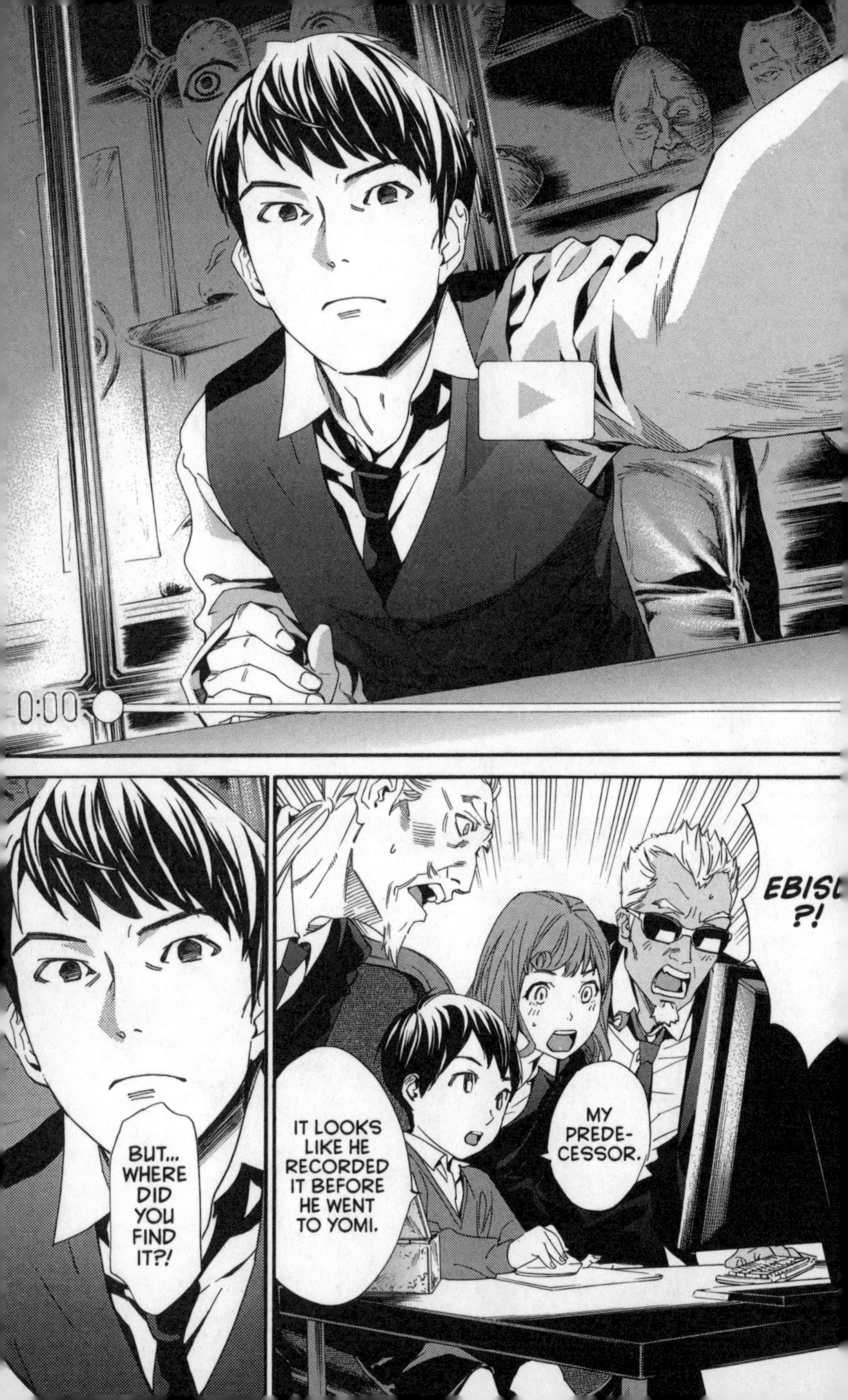
0:00
EBISU ?!
MY PREDECESSOR.
IT LOOKS LIKE HE RECORDED IT BEFORE HE WENT TO YOMI.
BUT... WHERE DID YOU FIND IT?!

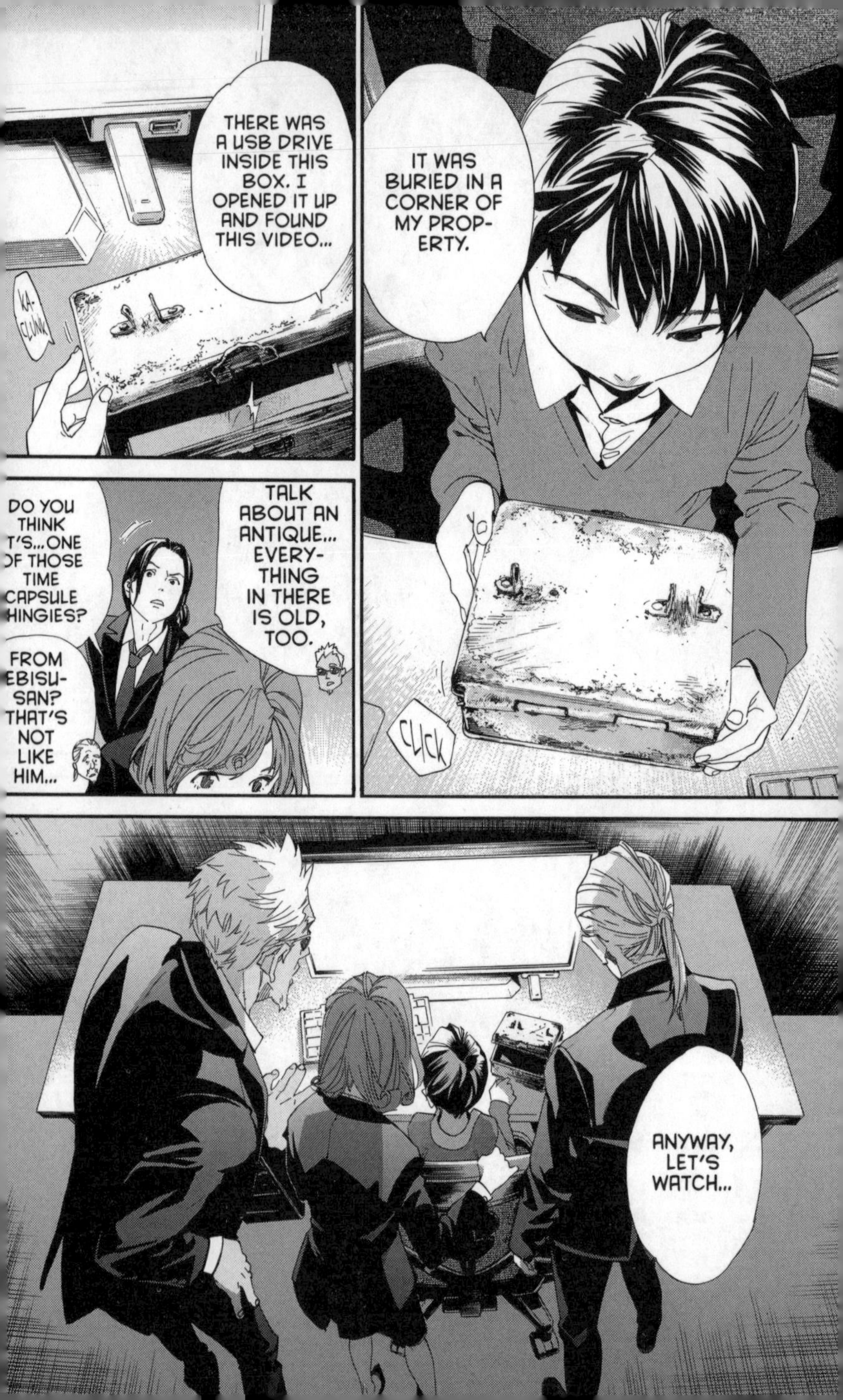

IT WAS BURIED IN A CORNER OF MY PROP-ERTY.
CLICK
THERE WAS A USB DRIVE INSIDE THIS BOX. I OPENED IT UP AND FOUND THIS VIDEO...
KA-CLUNK
TALK ABOUT AN ANTIQUE... EVERY-THING IN THERE IS OLD, TOO.
DO YOU THINK T'S...ONE OF THOSE TIME CAPSULE HINGIES?
FROM EBISU-SAN? THAT'S NOT LIKE HIM...
ANYWAY, LET'S WATCH...

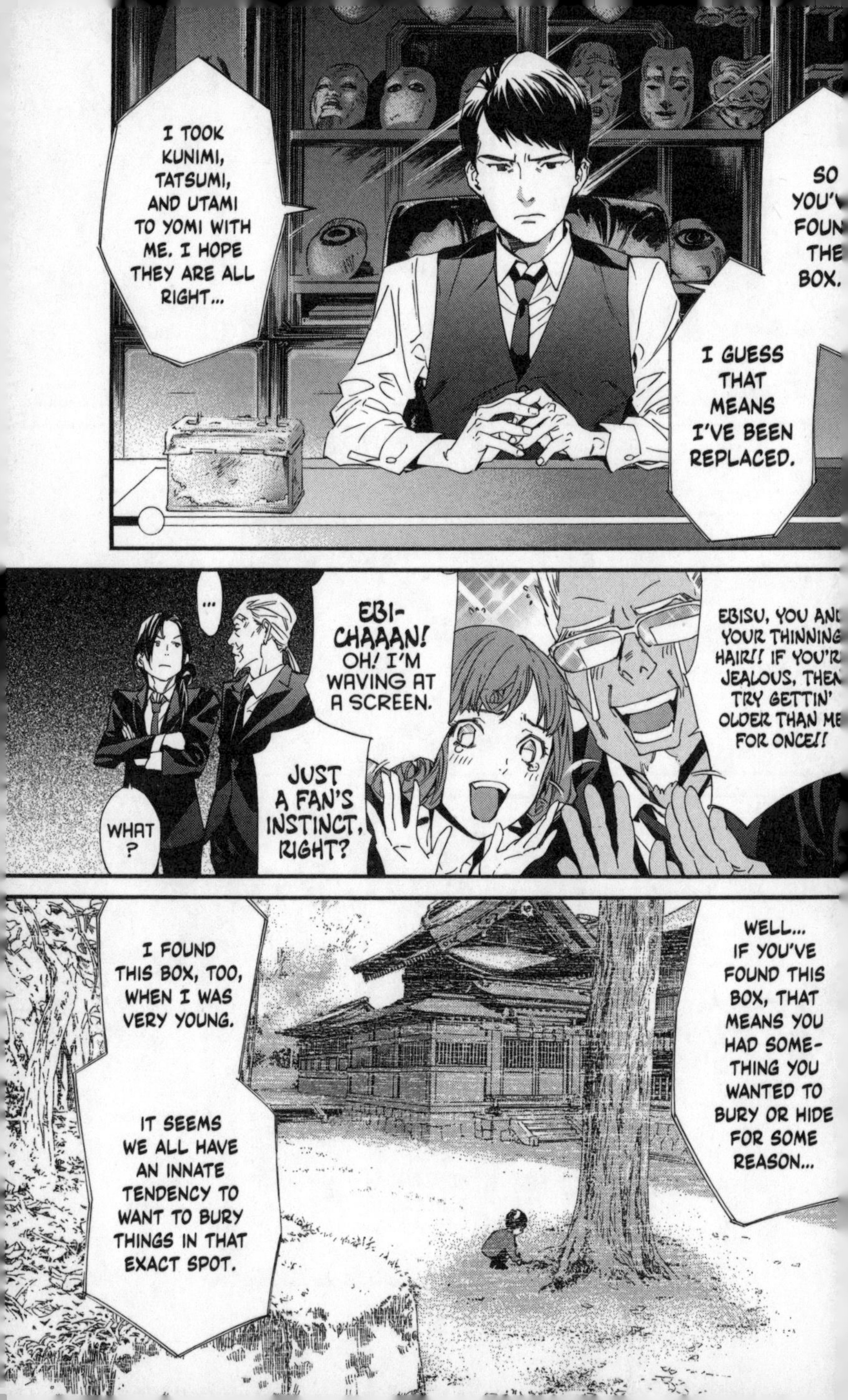
SO YOU'V FOUN THE BOX.
I GUESS THAT MEANS I'VE BEEN REPLACED.
I TOOK KUNIMI, TATSUMI, AND UTAMI TO YOMI WITH ME. I HOPE THEY ARE ALL RIGHT...
EBISU, YOU AN YOUR THINNING HAIR!! IF YOU'R JEALOUS, THEN TRY GETTIN' OLDER THAN ME FOR ONCE!!
EBI-CHAAAN! OH! I'M WAVING AT A SCREEN.
JUST A FAN'S INSTINCT, RIGHT?
...
WHAT?
WELL... IF YOU'VE FOUND THIS BOX, THAT MEANS YOU HAD SOME-THING YOU WANTED TO BURY OR HIDE FOR SOME REASON...
I FOUND THIS BOX, TOO, WHEN I WAS VERY YOUNG.
IT SEEMS WE ALL HAVE AN INNATE TENDENCY TO WANT TO BURY THINGS IN THAT EXACT SPOT.

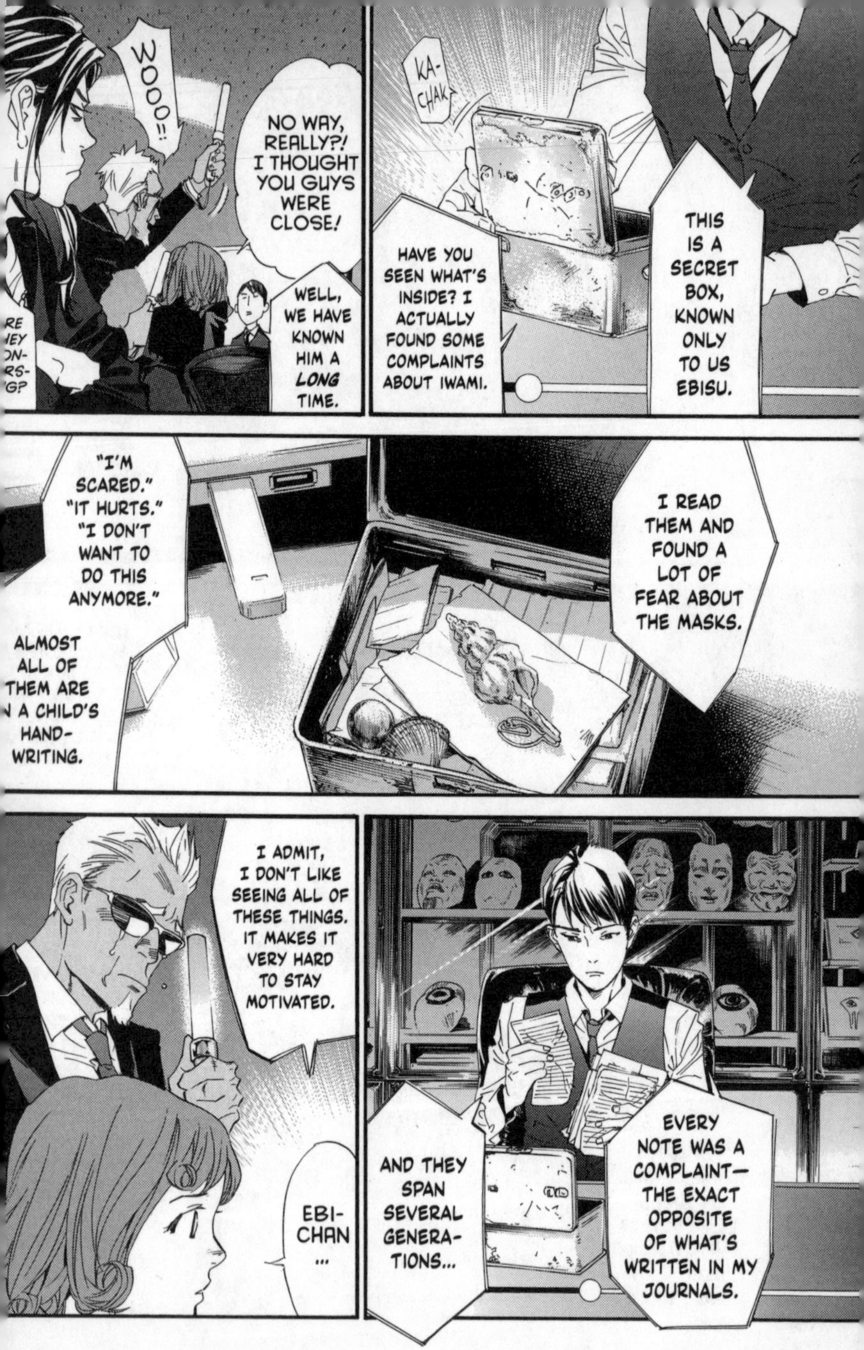
KA-CHAK
THIS IS A SECRET BOX, KNOWN ONLY TO US EBISU.
HAVE YOU SEEN WHAT'S INSIDE? I ACTUALLY FOUND SOME COMPLAINTS ABOUT IWAMI.
NO WAY, REALLY?! I THOUGHT YOU GUYS WERE CLOSE!
WOOOO!!
WELL, WE HAVE KNOWN HIM A *LONG* TIME.
I READ THEM AND FOUND A LOT OF FEAR ABOUT THE MASKS.
"I'M SCARED." "IT HURTS." "I DON'T WANT TO DO THIS ANYMORE."
ALMOST ALL OF THEM ARE N A CHILD'S HANDWRITING.
EVERY NOTE WAS A COMPLAINT—THE EXACT OPPOSITE OF WHAT'S WRITTEN IN MY JOURNALS.
AND THEY SPAN SEVERAL GENERATIONS...
I ADMIT, I DON'T LIKE SEEING ALL OF THESE THINGS. IT MAKES IT VERY HARD TO STAY MOTIVATED.
EBI-CHAN ...

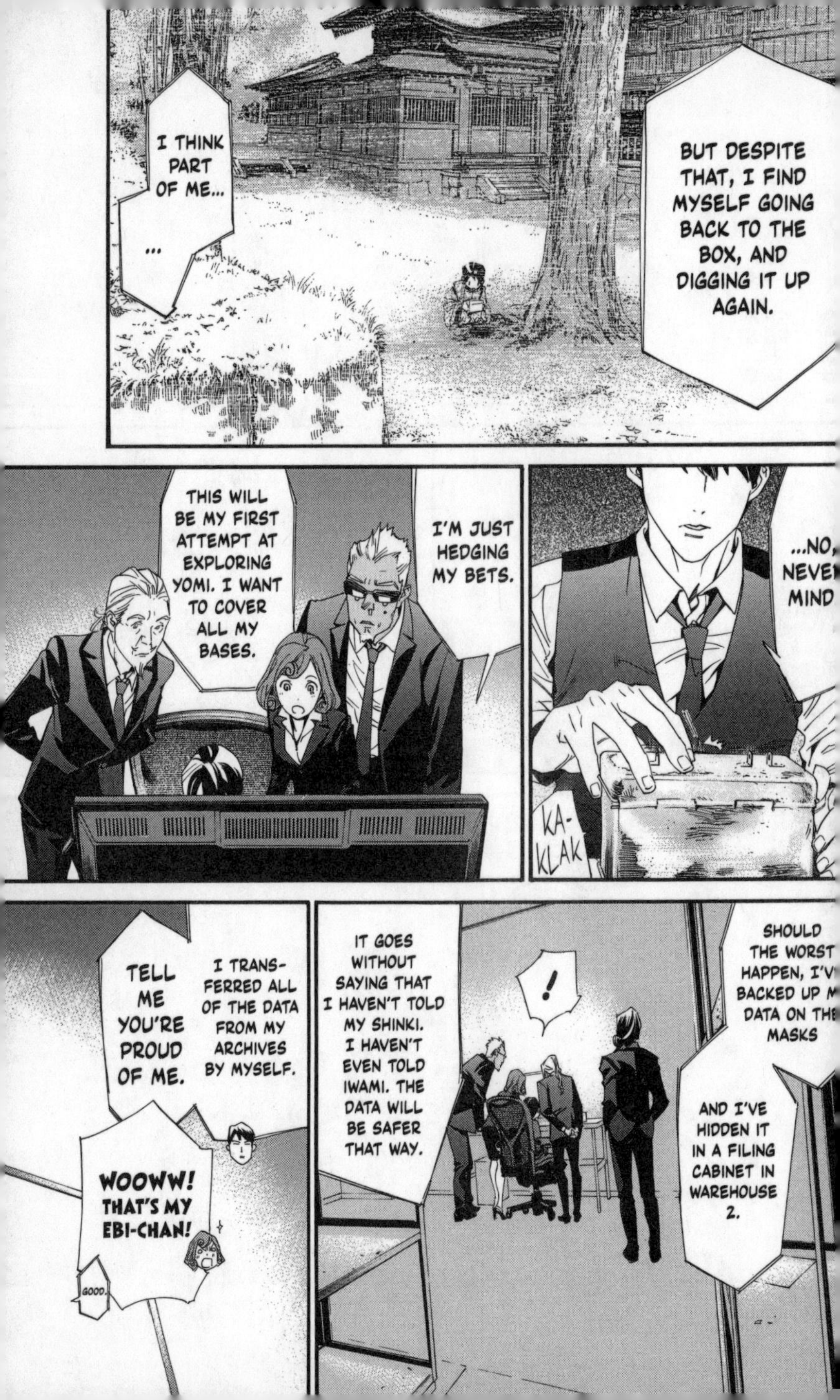

BUT DESPITE THAT, I FIND MYSELF GOING BACK TO THE BOX, AND DIGGING IT UP AGAIN.
I THINK PART OF ME...
...
...NO, NEVE MIND
KA-KLAK
I'M JUST HEDGING MY BETS.
THIS WILL BE MY FIRST ATTEMPT AT EXPLORING YOMI. I WANT TO COVER ALL MY BASES.
SHOULD THE WORST HAPPEN, I'V BACKED UP M DATA ON THE MASKS
AND I'VE HIDDEN IT IN A FILING CABINET IN WAREHOUSE 2.
!
IT GOES WITHOUT SAYING THAT I HAVEN'T TOLD MY SHINKI. I HAVEN'T EVEN TOLD IWAMI. THE DATA WILL BE SAFER THAT WAY.
I TRANS-FERRED ALL OF THE DATA FROM MY ARCHIVES BY MYSELF.
TELL ME YOU'RE PROUD OF ME.
WOOWW! THAT'S MY EBI-CHAN!
GOOD.

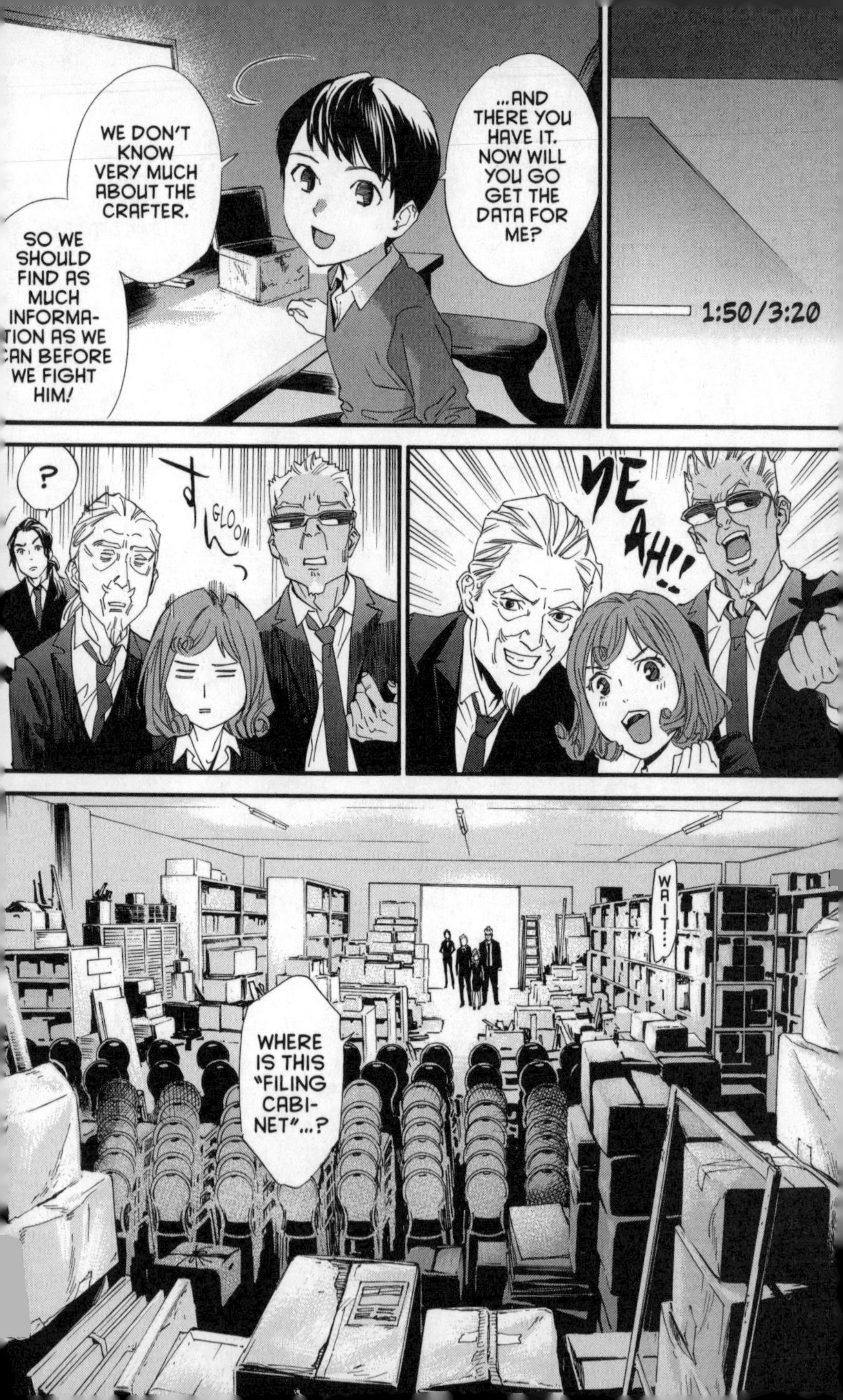
1:50/3:20
...AND THERE YOU HAVE IT. NOW WILL YOU GO GET THE DATA FOR ME?
WE DON'T KNOW VERY MUCH ABOUT THE CRAFTER.
SO WE SHOULD FIND AS MUCH INFORMATION AS WE CAN BEFORE WE FIGHT HIM!
YEAH!!
GLOOM
?
WAIT...
WHERE IS THIS "FILING CABINET"...?

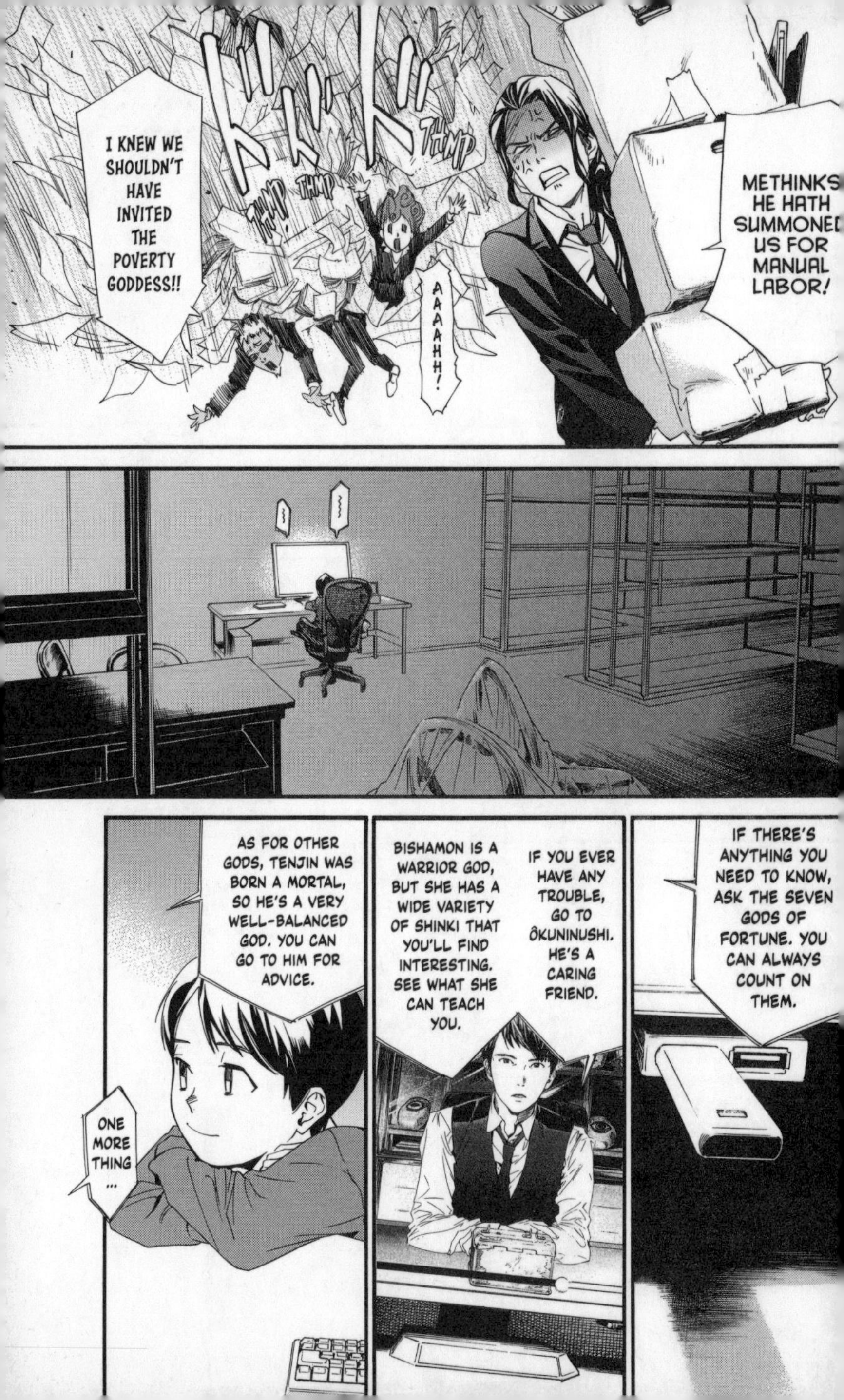
METHINKS HE HATH SUMMONED US FOR MANUAL LABOR!
THMP
THMP THMP
AAAAHH!
I KNEW WE SHOULDN'T HAVE INVITED THE POVERTY GODDESS!!
IF THERE'S ANYTHING YOU NEED TO KNOW, ASK THE SEVEN GODS OF FORTUNE. YOU CAN ALWAYS COUNT ON THEM.
IF YOU EVER HAVE ANY TROUBLE, GO TO ÔKUNINUSHI. HE'S A CARING FRIEND.
BISHAMON IS A WARRIOR GOD, BUT SHE HAS A WIDE VARIETY OF SHINKI THAT YOU'LL FIND INTERESTING. SEE WHAT SHE CAN TEACH YOU.
AS FOR OTHER GODS, TENJIN WAS BORN A MORTAL, SO HE'S A VERY WELL-BALANCED GOD. YOU CAN GO TO HIM FOR ADVICE.
ONE MORE THING...

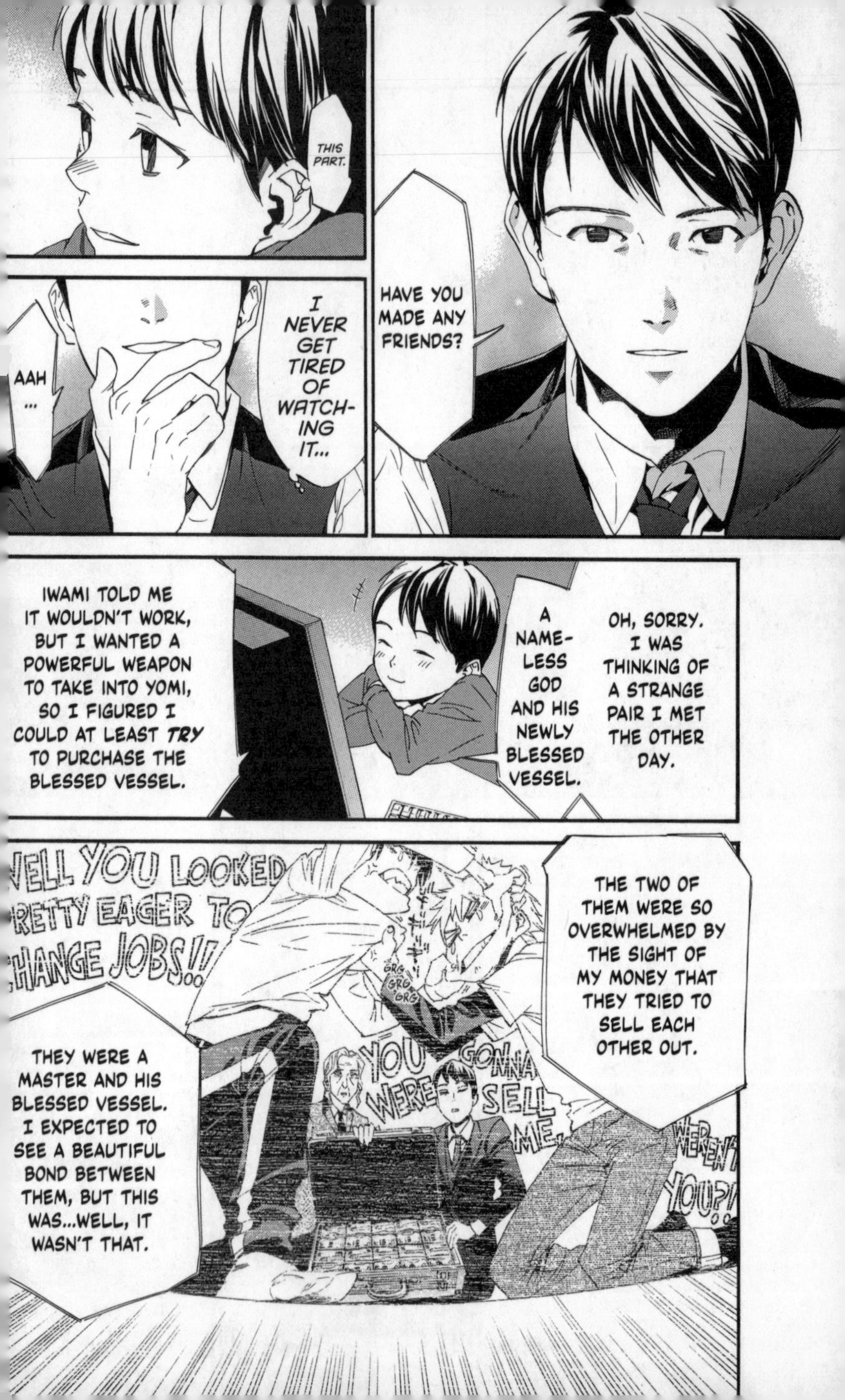
HAVE YOU MADE ANY FRIENDS?
THIS PART.
I NEVER GET TIRED OF WATCHING IT...
AAH...
OH, SORRY. I WAS THINKING OF A STRANGE PAIR I MET THE OTHER DAY.
A NAMELESS GOD AND HIS NEWLY BLESSED VESSEL.
IWAMI TOLD ME IT WOULDN'T WORK, BUT I WANTED A POWERFUL WEAPON TO TAKE INTO YOMI, SO I FIGURED I COULD AT LEAST *TRY* TO PURCHASE THE BLESSED VESSEL.
THE TWO OF THEM WERE SO OVERWHELMED BY THE SIGHT OF MY MONEY THAT THEY TRIED TO SELL EACH OTHER OUT.
WEREN'T YOU?!
YOU WERE GONNA SELL ME,
WELL YOU LOOKED PRETTY EAGER TO CHANGE JOBS!!
GRG GRG GRG
THEY WERE A MASTER AND HIS BLESSED VESSEL. I EXPECTED TO SEE A BEAUTIFUL BOND BETWEEN THEM, BUT THIS WAS...WELL, IT WASN'T THAT.

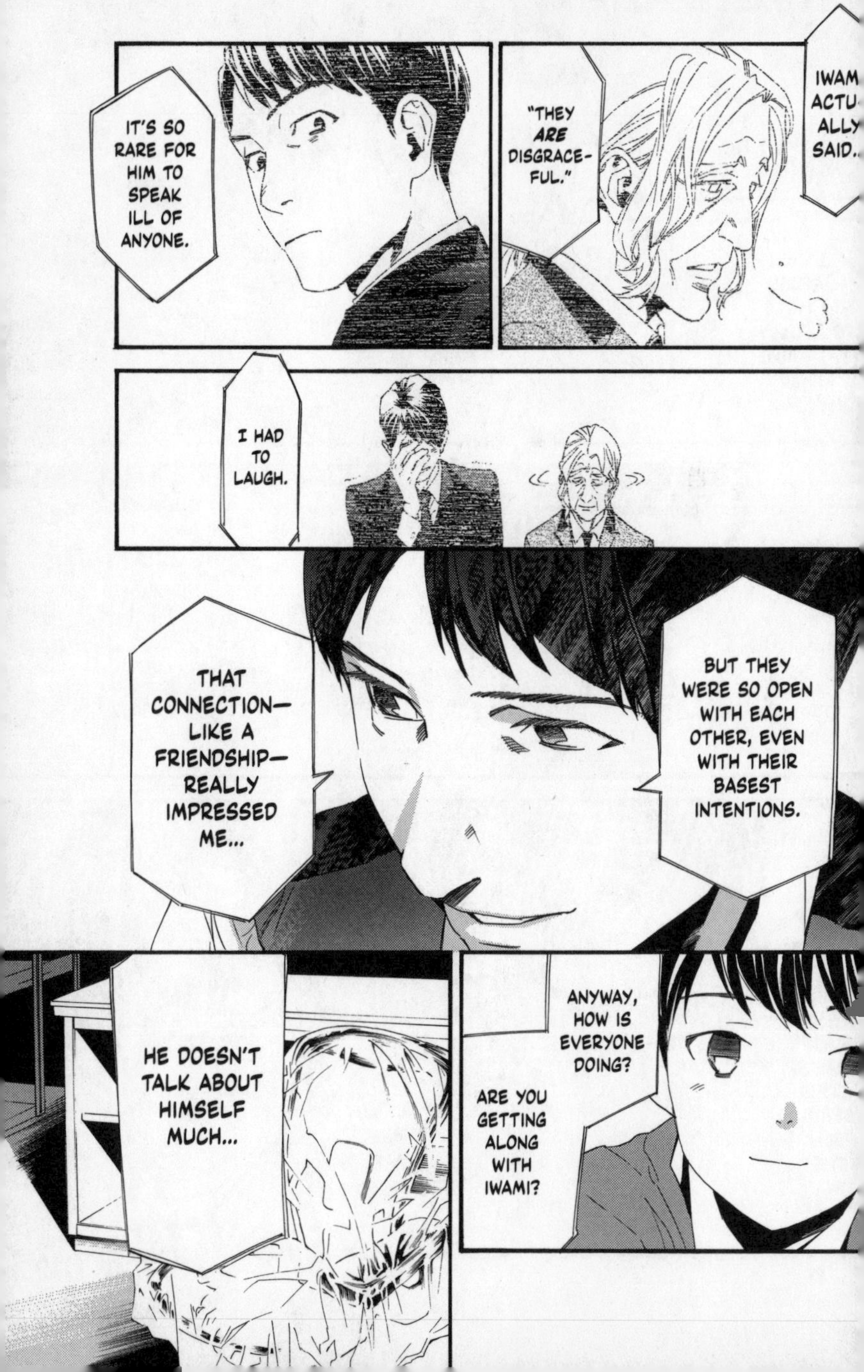
IWAM ACTU-ALLY SAID..
"THEY *ARE* DISGRACE-FUL."
IT'S SO RARE FOR HIM TO SPEAK ILL OF ANYONE.
I HAD TO LAUGH.
BUT THEY WERE SO OPEN WITH EACH OTHER, EVEN WITH THEIR BASEST INTENTIONS.
THAT CONNECTION—LIKE A FRIENDSHIP—REALLY IMPRESSED ME...
ANYWAY, HOW IS EVERYONE DOING?
ARE YOU GETTING ALONG WITH IWAMI?
HE DOESN'T TALK ABOUT HIMSELF MUCH...

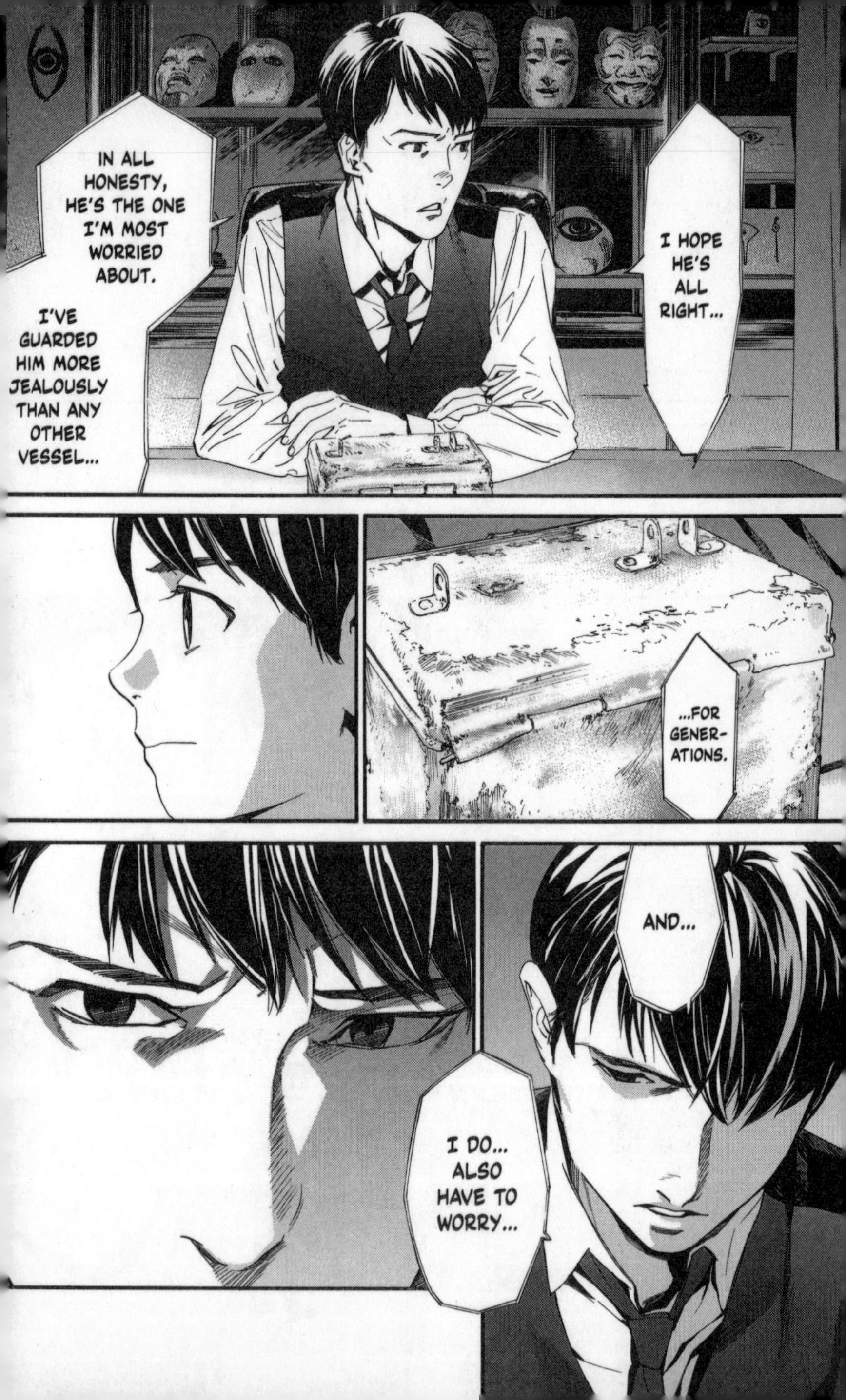
I HOPE HE'S ALL RIGHT...
IN ALL HONESTY, HE'S THE ONE I'M MOST WORRIED ABOUT.
I'VE GUARDED HIM MORE JEALOUSLY THAN ANY OTHER VESSEL...
...FOR GENER-ATIONS.
AND...
I DO... ALSO HAVE TO WORRY...

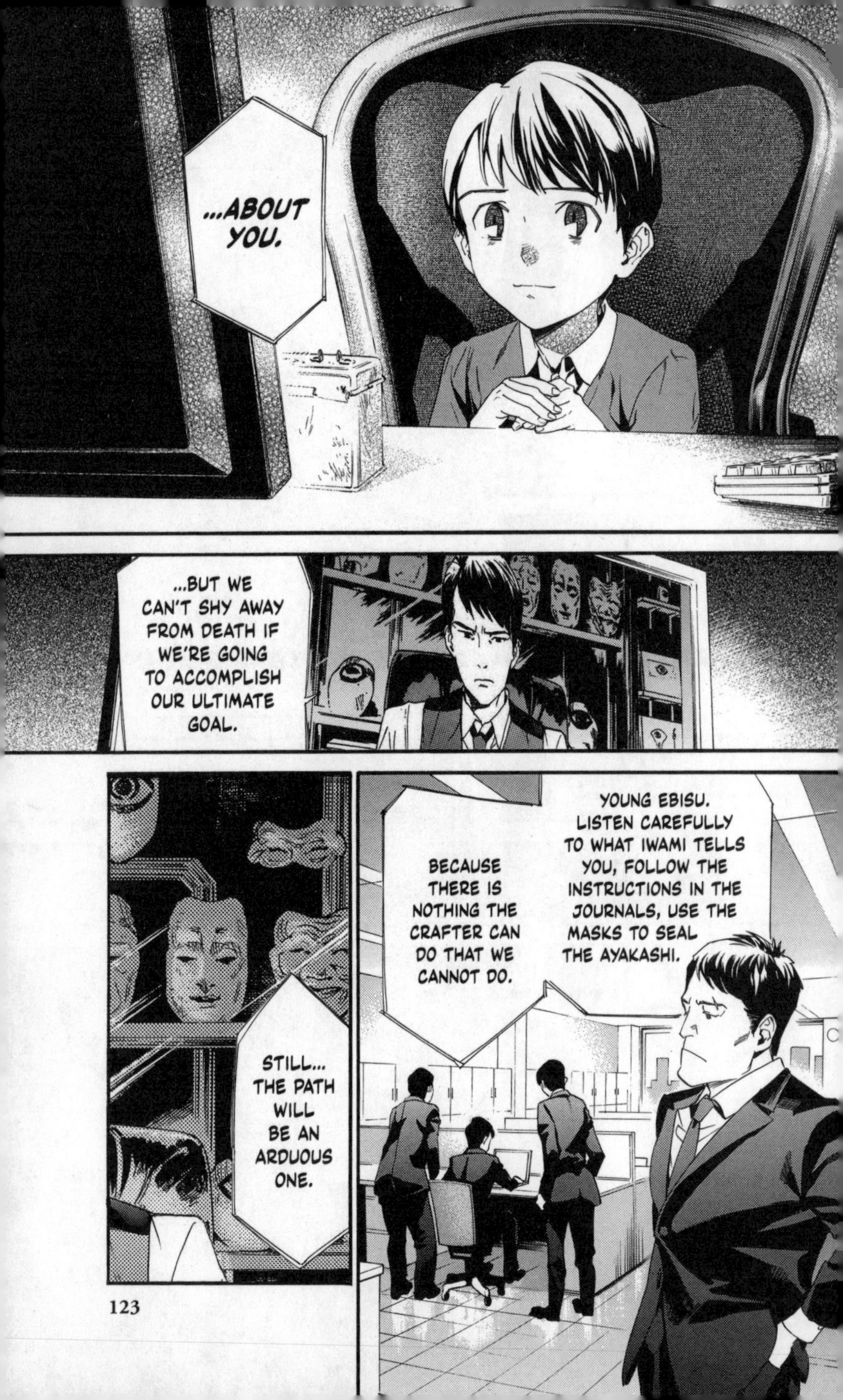

...ABOUT YOU.
...BUT WE CAN'T SHY AWAY FROM DEATH IF WE'RE GOING TO ACCOMPLISH OUR ULTIMATE GOAL.
YOUNG EBISU. LISTEN CAREFULLY TO WHAT IWAMI TELLS YOU, FOLLOW THE INSTRUCTIONS IN THE JOURNALS, USE THE MASKS TO SEAL THE AYAKASHI.
BECAUSE THERE IS NOTHING THE CRAFTER CAN DO THAT WE CANNOT DO.
STILL... THE PATH WILL BE AN ARDUOUS ONE.

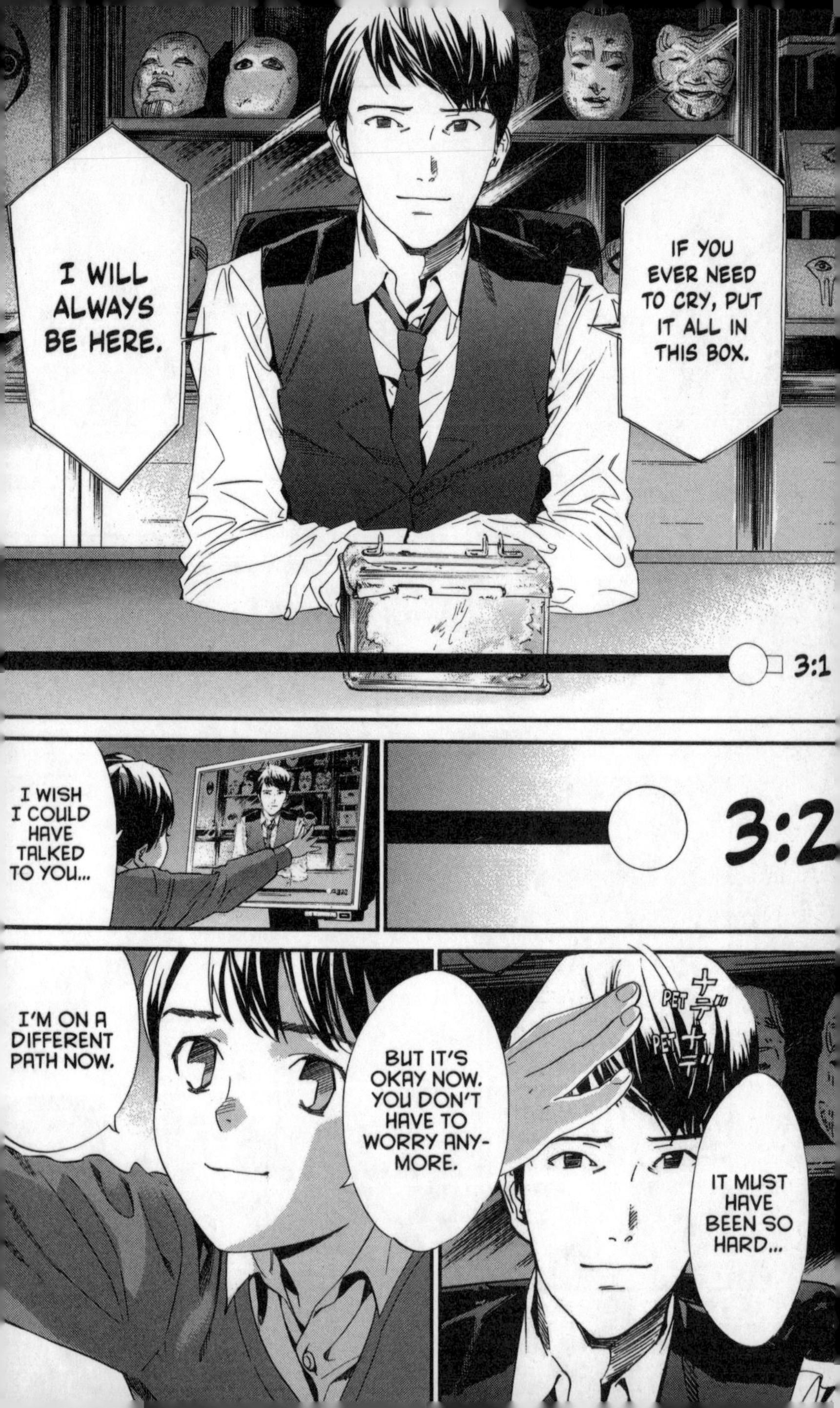
IF YOU EVER NEED TO CRY, PUT IT ALL IN THIS BOX.
I WILL ALWAYS BE HERE.
3:1
3:2
I WISH I COULD HAVE TALKED TO YOU...
PET ナデ
PET ナデ
IT MUST HAVE BEEN SO HARD...
BUT IT'S OKAY NOW. YOU DON'T HAVE TO WORRY ANY-MORE.
I'M ON A DIFFERENT PATH NOW.

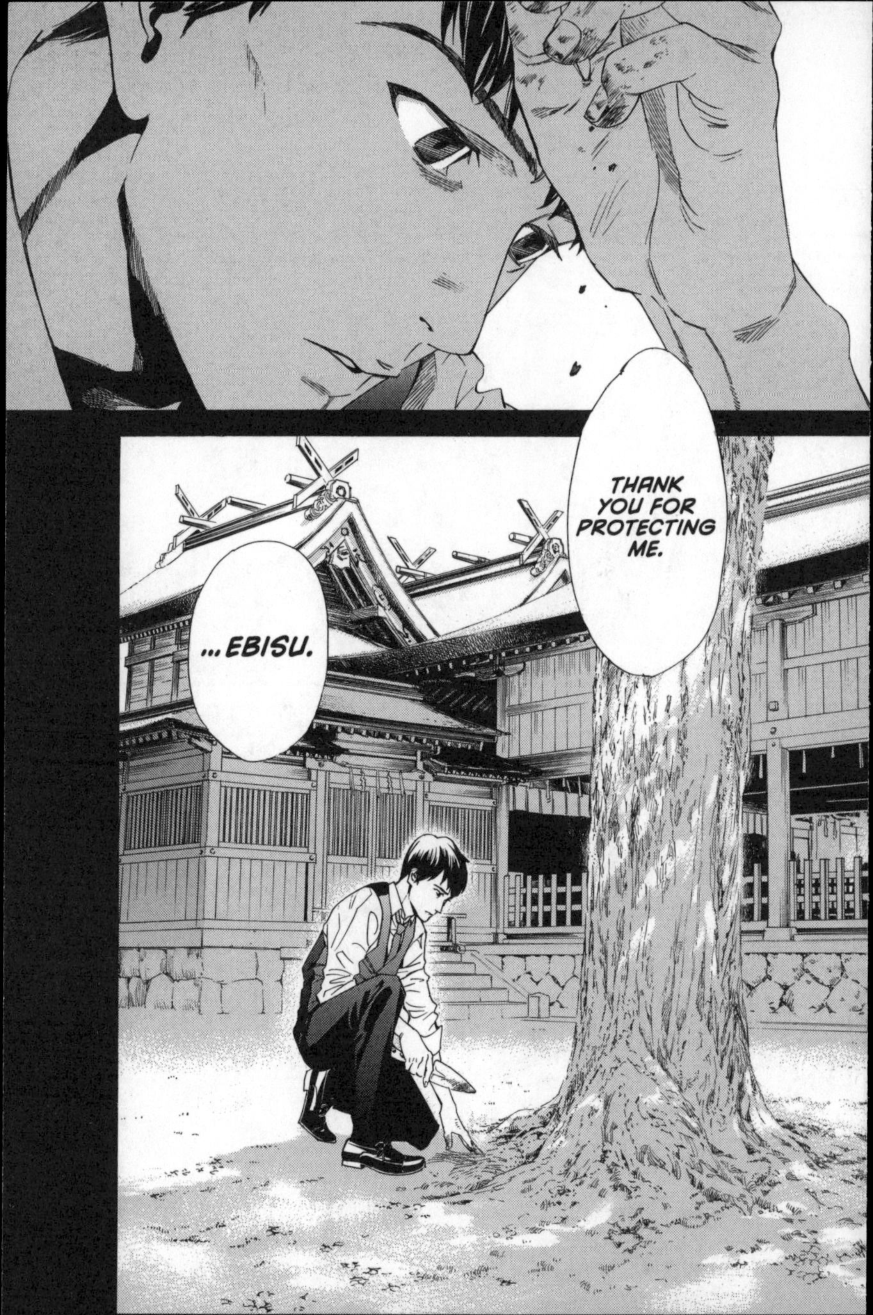
THANK YOU FOR PROTECTING ME.
...EBISU.

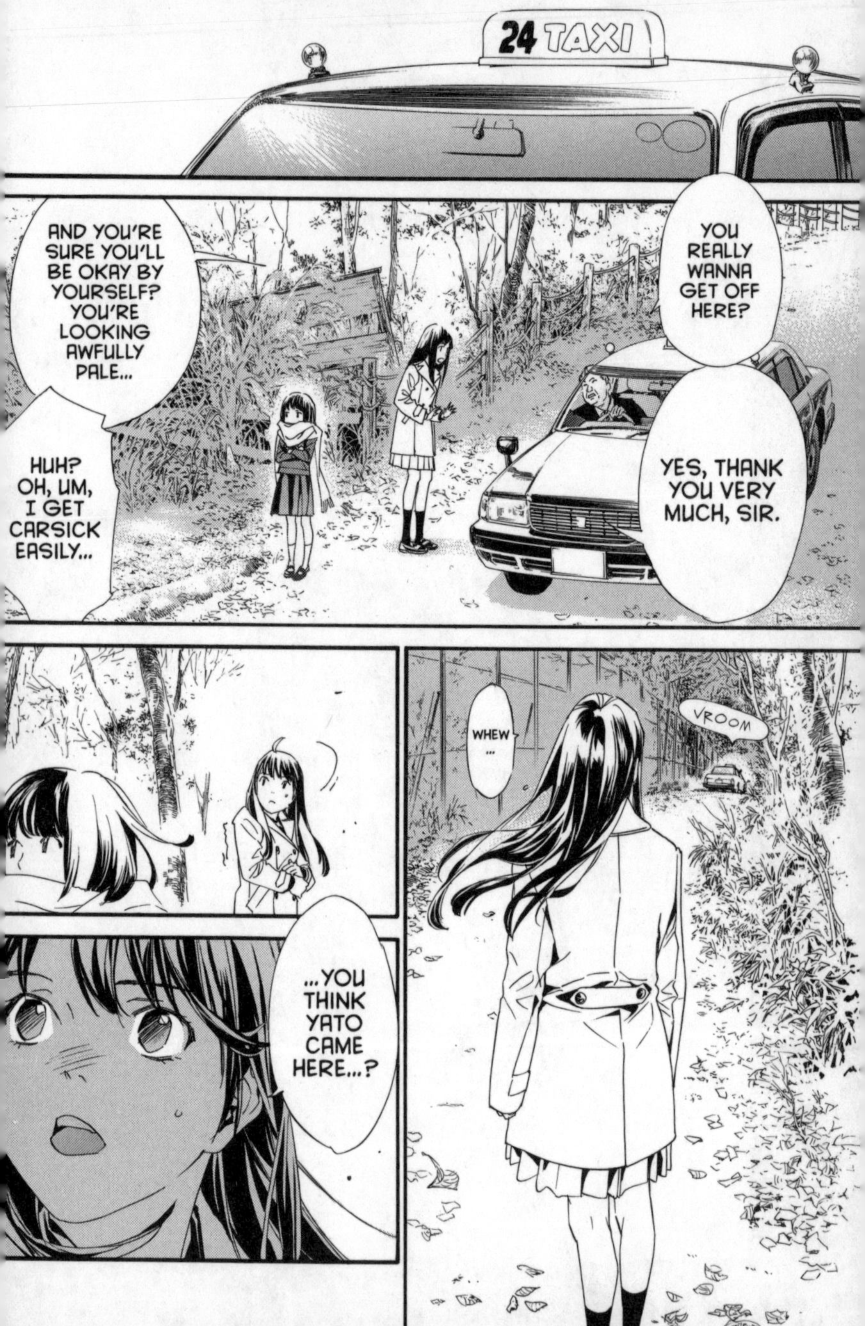
24 TAXI
YOU REALLY WANNA GET OFF HERE?
YES, THANK YOU VERY MUCH, SIR.
AND YOU'RE SURE YOU'LL BE OKAY BY YOURSELF? YOU'RE LOOKING AWFULLY PALE...
HUH? OH, UM, I GET CARSICK EASILY...
VROOM
WHEW ...
...YOU THINK YATO CAME HERE...?

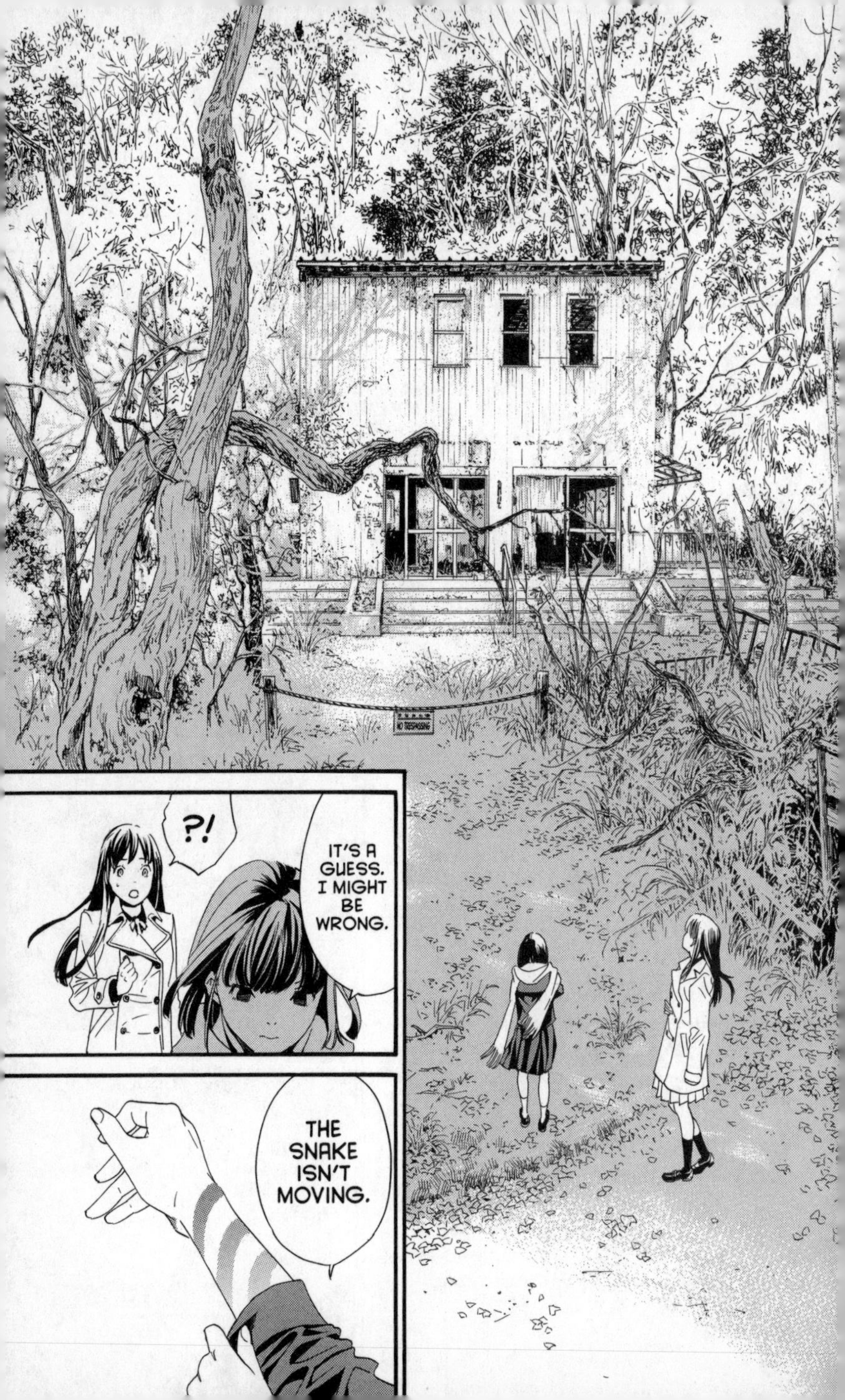
NO TRESPASSING
IT'S A GUESS. I MIGHT BE WRONG.
?!
THE SNAKE ISN'T MOVING.

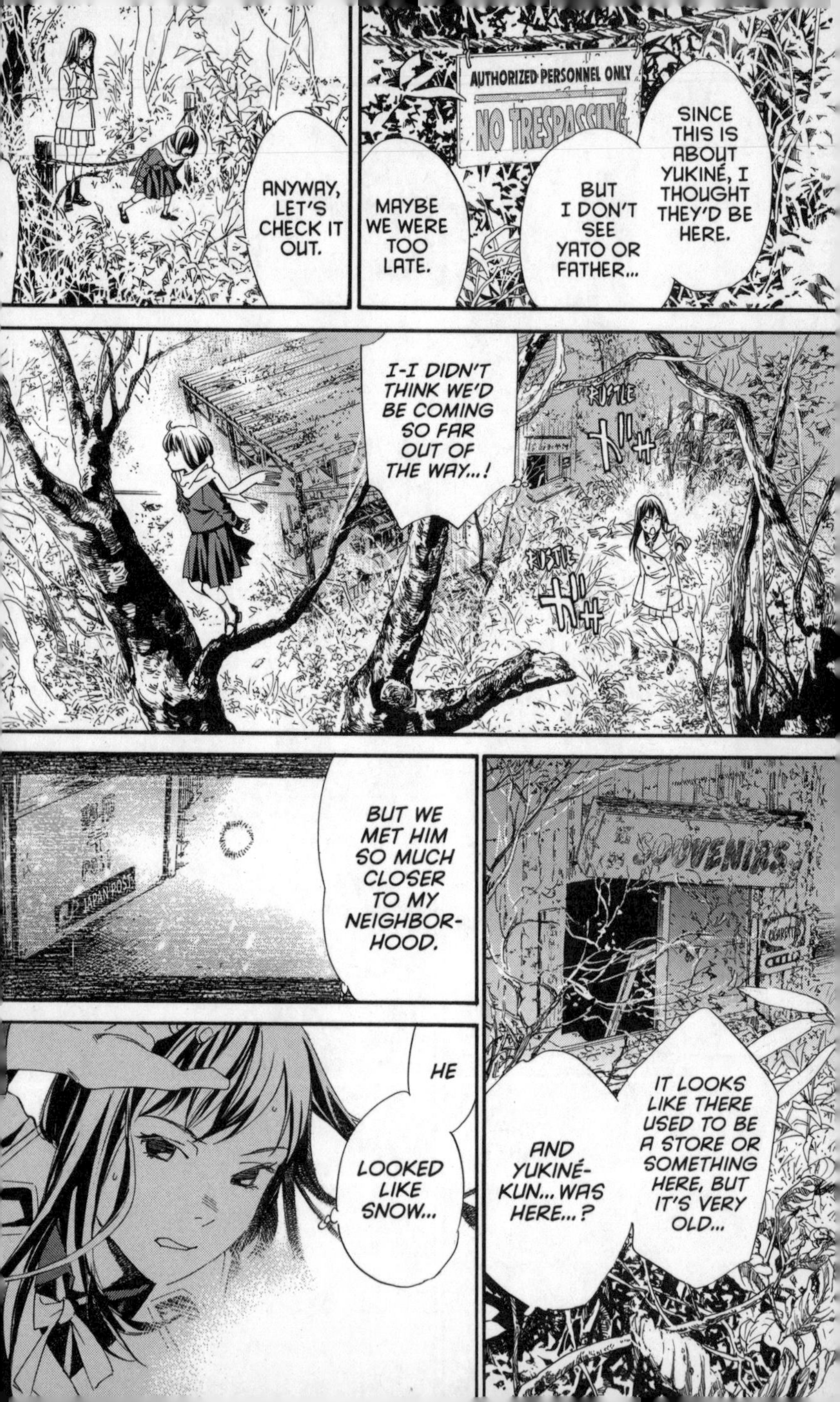
AUTHORIZED PERSONNEL ONLY
NO TRESPASSING
SINCE THIS IS ABOUT YUKINÉ, I THOUGHT THEY'D BE HERE.
BUT I DON'T SEE YATO OR FATHER...
MAYBE WE WERE TOO LATE.
ANYWAY, LET'S CHECK IT OUT.
RUSTLE
I-I DIDN'T THINK WE'D BE COMING SO FAR OUT OF THE WAY...!
RUSTLE
SOUVENIRS
IT LOOKS LIKE THERE USED TO BE A STORE OR SOMETHING HERE, BUT IT'S VERY OLD...
AND YUKINÉ-KUN...WAS HERE...?
JAPAN POST
BUT WE MET HIM SO MUCH CLOSER TO MY NEIGHBORHOOD.
HE
LOOKED LIKE SNOW...

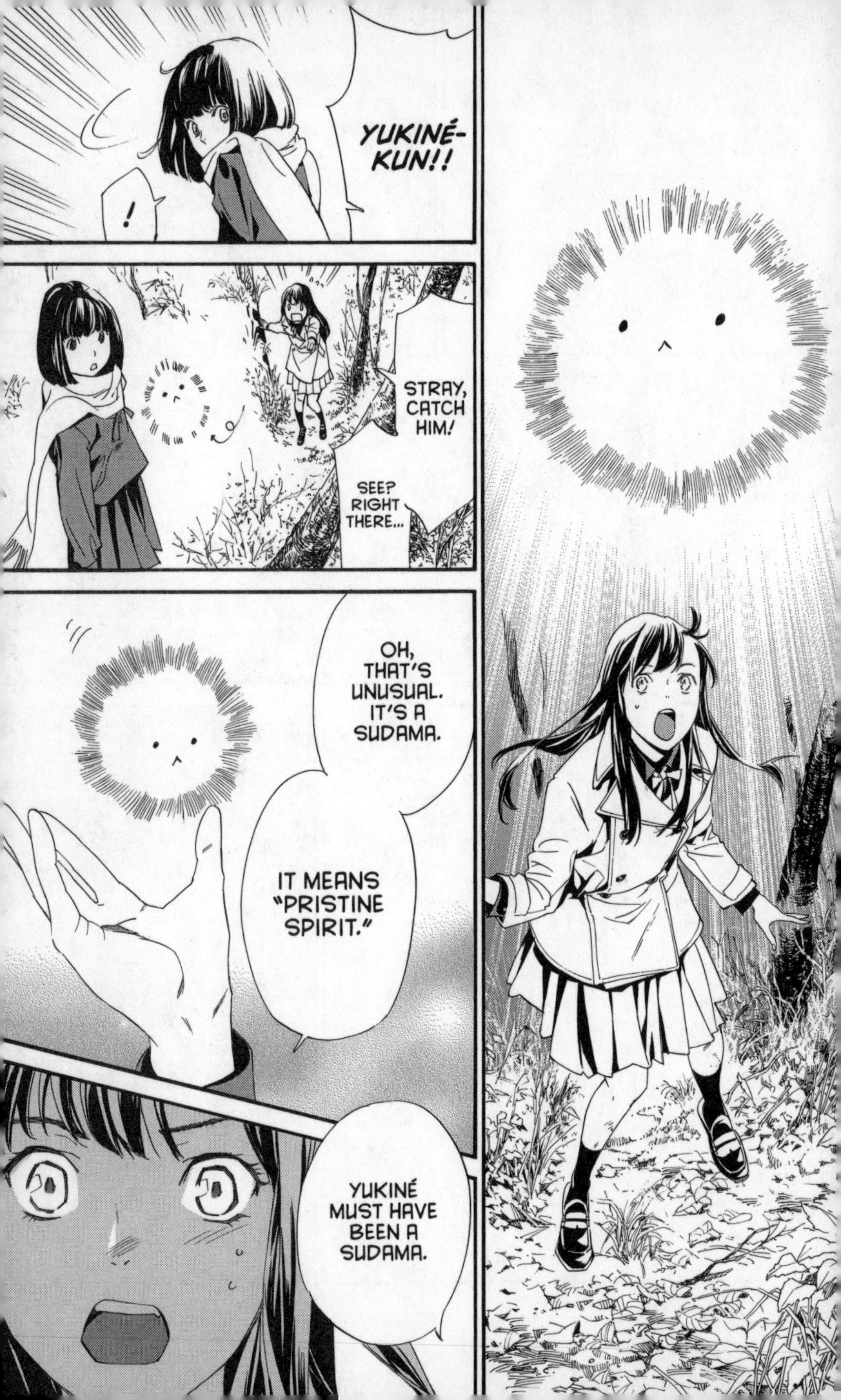
YUKINÉ-KUN!!
!
STRAY, CATCH HIM!
SEE? RIGHT THERE...
OH, THAT'S UNUSUAL. IT'S A SUDAMA.
IT MEANS "PRISTINE SPIRIT."
YUKINÉ MUST HAVE BEEN A SUDAMA.

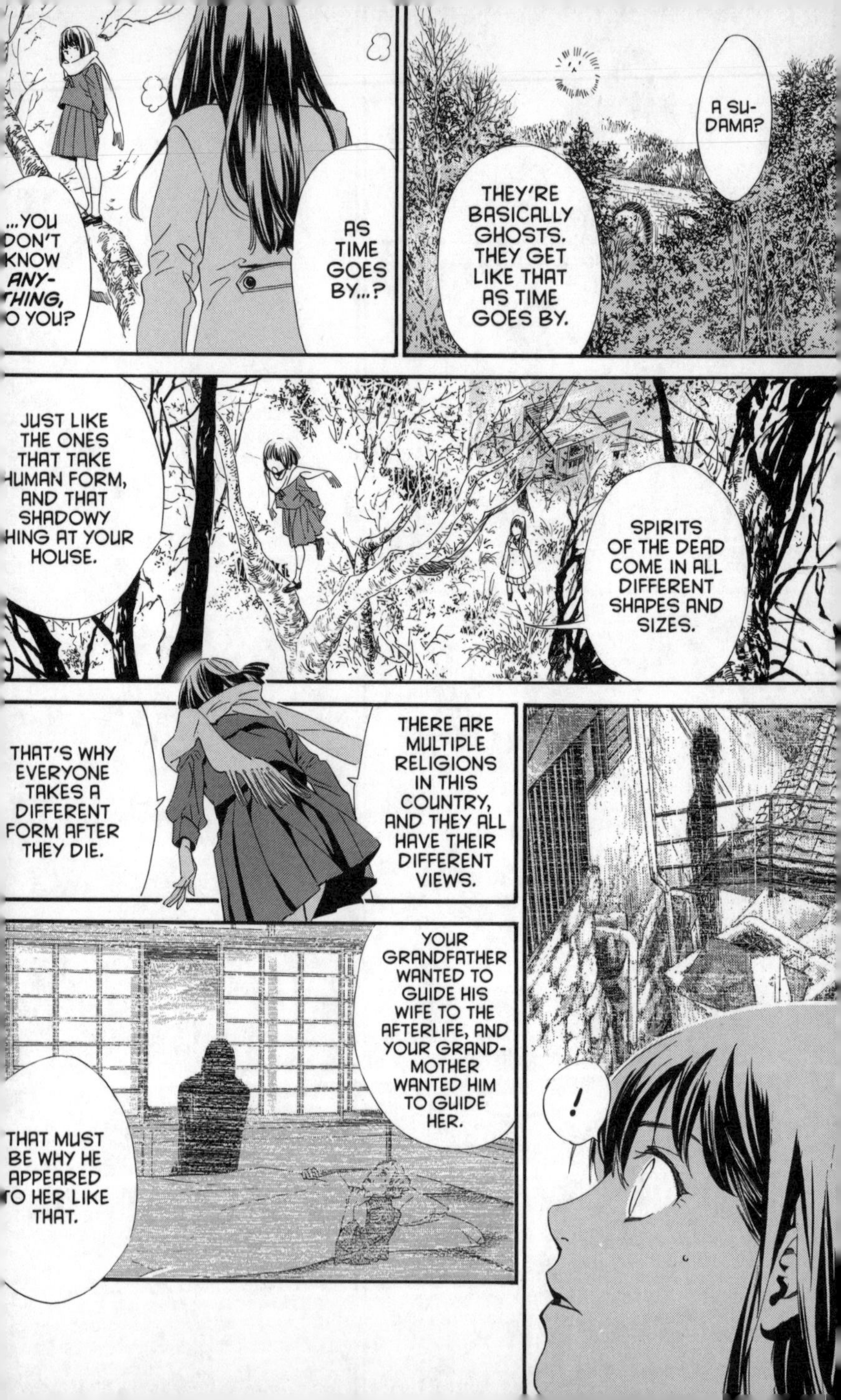

A SU-DAMA?
THEY'RE BASICALLY GHOSTS. THEY GET LIKE THAT AS TIME GOES BY.
AS TIME GOES BY...?
...YOU DON'T KNOW *ANY-THING,* O YOU?
SPIRITS OF THE DEAD COME IN ALL DIFFERENT SHAPES AND SIZES.
JUST LIKE THE ONES THAT TAKE HUMAN FORM, AND THAT SHADOWY HING AT YOUR HOUSE.
!
THERE ARE MULTIPLE RELIGIONS IN THIS COUNTRY, AND THEY ALL HAVE THEIR DIFFERENT VIEWS.
THAT'S WHY EVERYONE TAKES A DIFFERENT FORM AFTER THEY DIE.
YOUR GRANDFATHER WANTED TO GUIDE HIS WIFE TO THE AFTERLIFE, AND YOUR GRAND-MOTHER WANTED HIM TO GUIDE HER.
THAT MUST BE WHY HE APPEARED TO HER LIKE THAT.

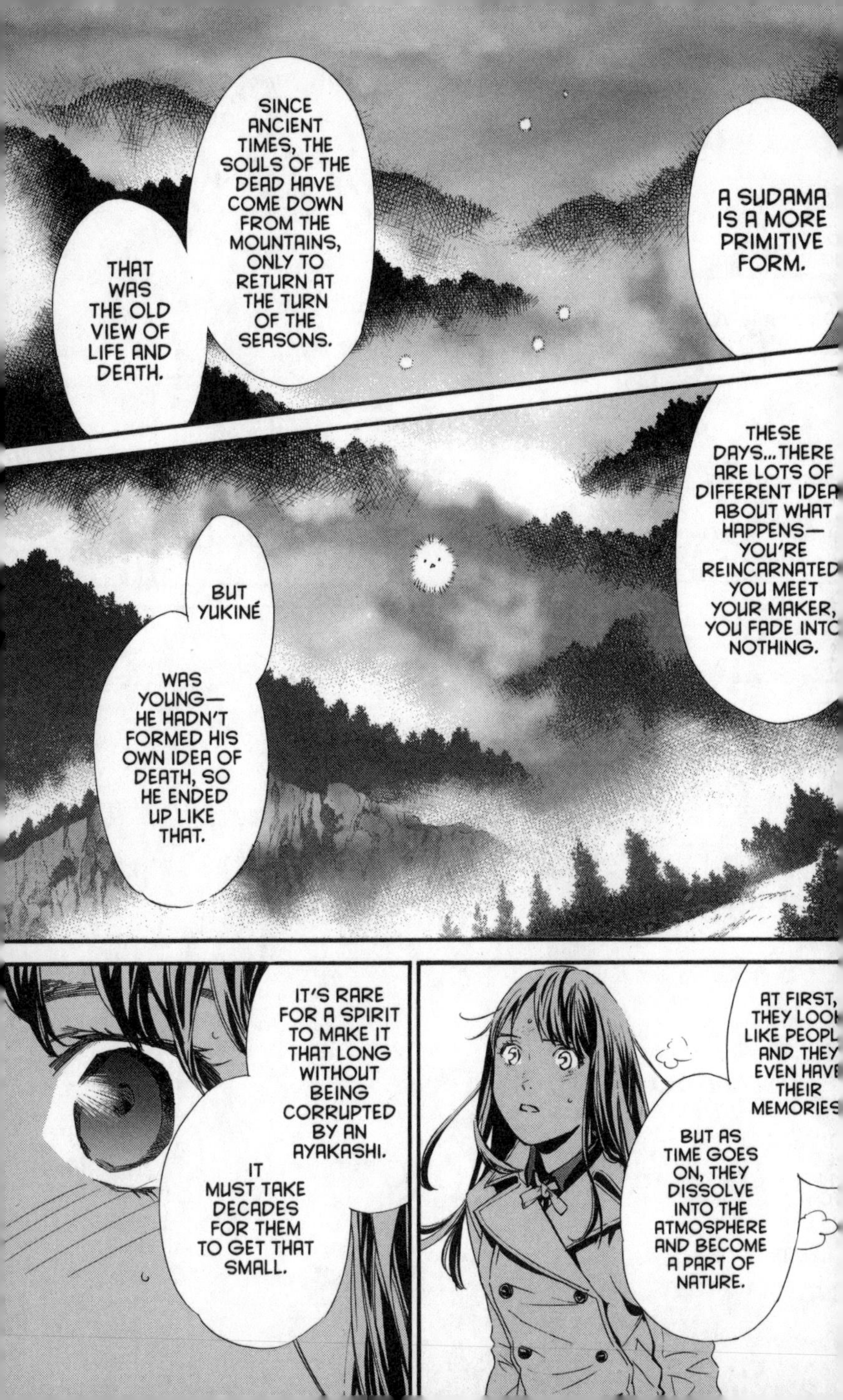
A SUDAMA IS A MORE PRIMITIVE FORM.
SINCE ANCIENT TIMES, THE SOULS OF THE DEAD HAVE COME DOWN FROM THE MOUNTAINS, ONLY TO RETURN AT THE TURN OF THE SEASONS.
THAT WAS THE OLD VIEW OF LIFE AND DEATH.
THESE DAYS...THERE ARE LOTS OF DIFFERENT IDEA ABOUT WHAT HAPPENS—YOU'RE REINCARNATED YOU MEET YOUR MAKER, YOU FADE INTO NOTHING.
BUT YUKINÉ
WAS YOUNG—HE HADN'T FORMED HIS OWN IDEA OF DEATH, SO HE ENDED UP LIKE THAT.
AT FIRST, THEY LOOK LIKE PEOPL AND THEY EVEN HAVE THEIR MEMORIES
BUT AS TIME GOES ON, THEY DISSOLVE INTO THE ATMOSPHERE AND BECOME A PART OF NATURE.
IT'S RARE FOR A SPIRIT TO MAKE IT THAT LONG WITHOUT BEING CORRUPTED BY AN AYAKASHI.
IT MUST TAKE DECADES FOR THEM TO GET THAT SMALL.

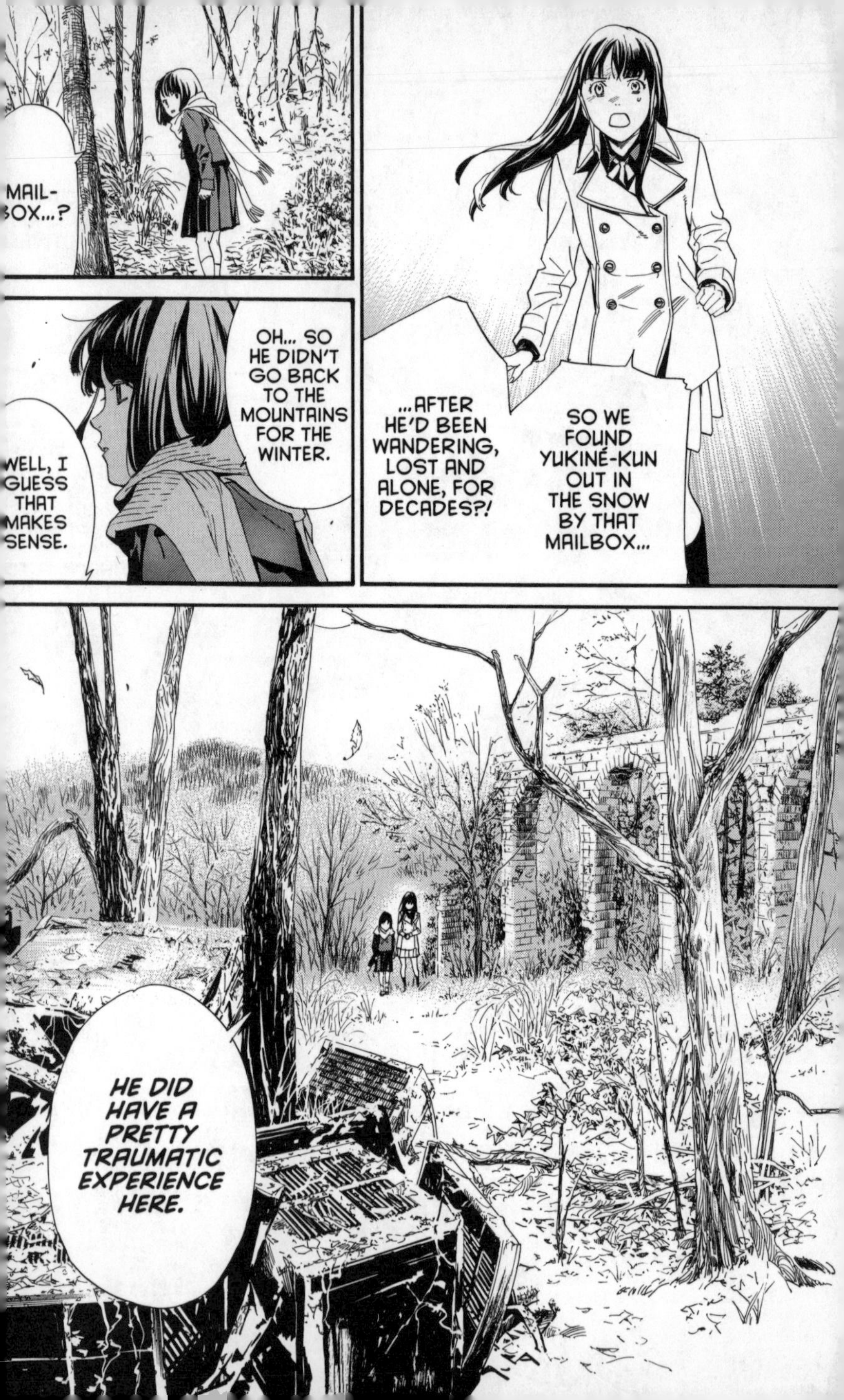
SO WE FOUND YUKINÉ-KUN OUT IN THE SNOW BY THAT MAILBOX...
...AFTER HE'D BEEN WANDERING, LOST AND ALONE, FOR DECADES?!
MAIL-BOX...?
OH... SO HE DIDN'T GO BACK TO THE MOUNTAINS FOR THE WINTER.
WELL, I GUESS THAT MAKES SENSE.
HE DID HAVE A PRETTY TRAUMATIC EXPERIENCE HERE.

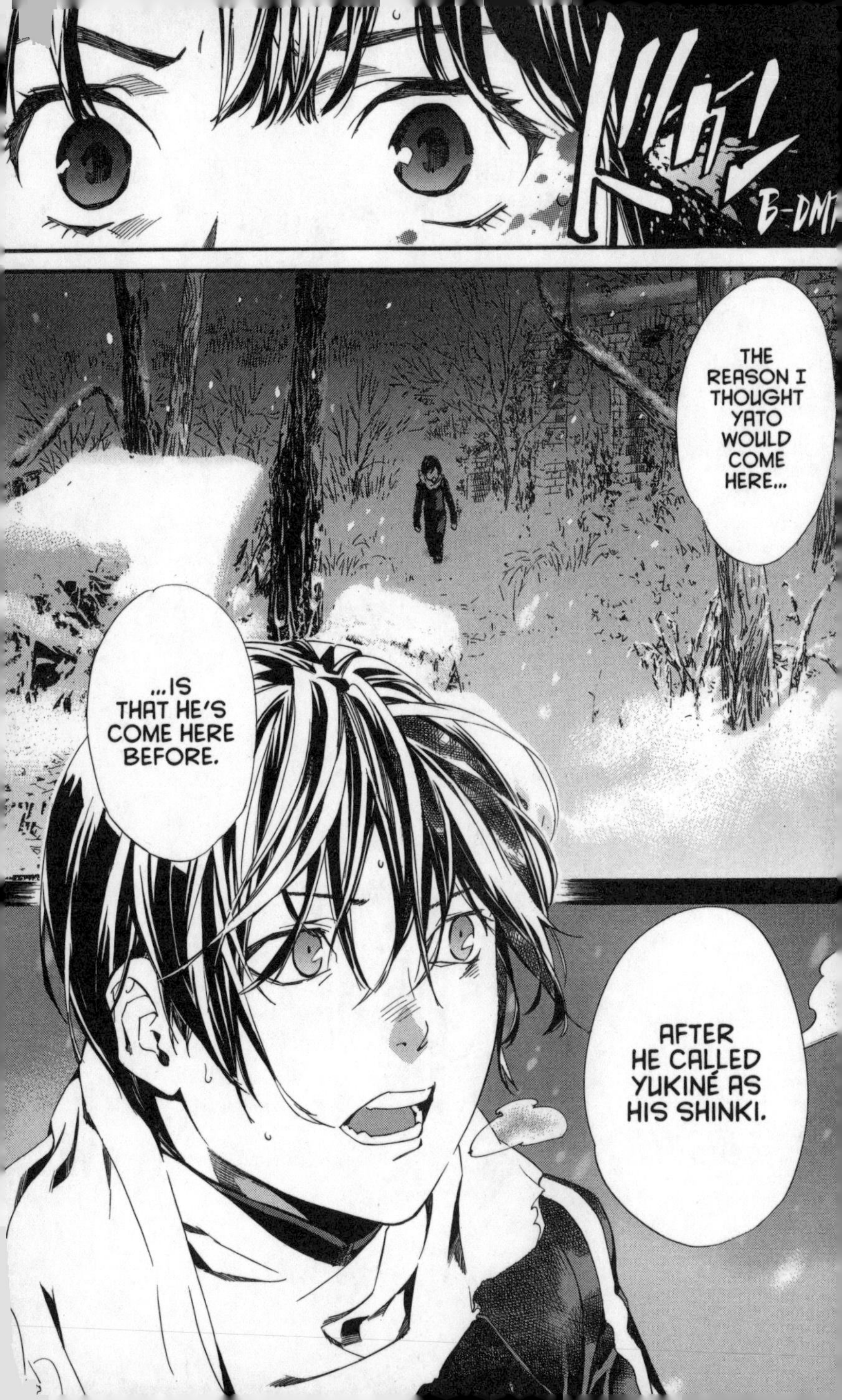
B-DM
THE REASON I THOUGHT YATO WOULD COME HERE...
...IS THAT HE'S COME HERE BEFORE.
AFTER HE CALLED YUKINÉ AS HIS SHINKI.

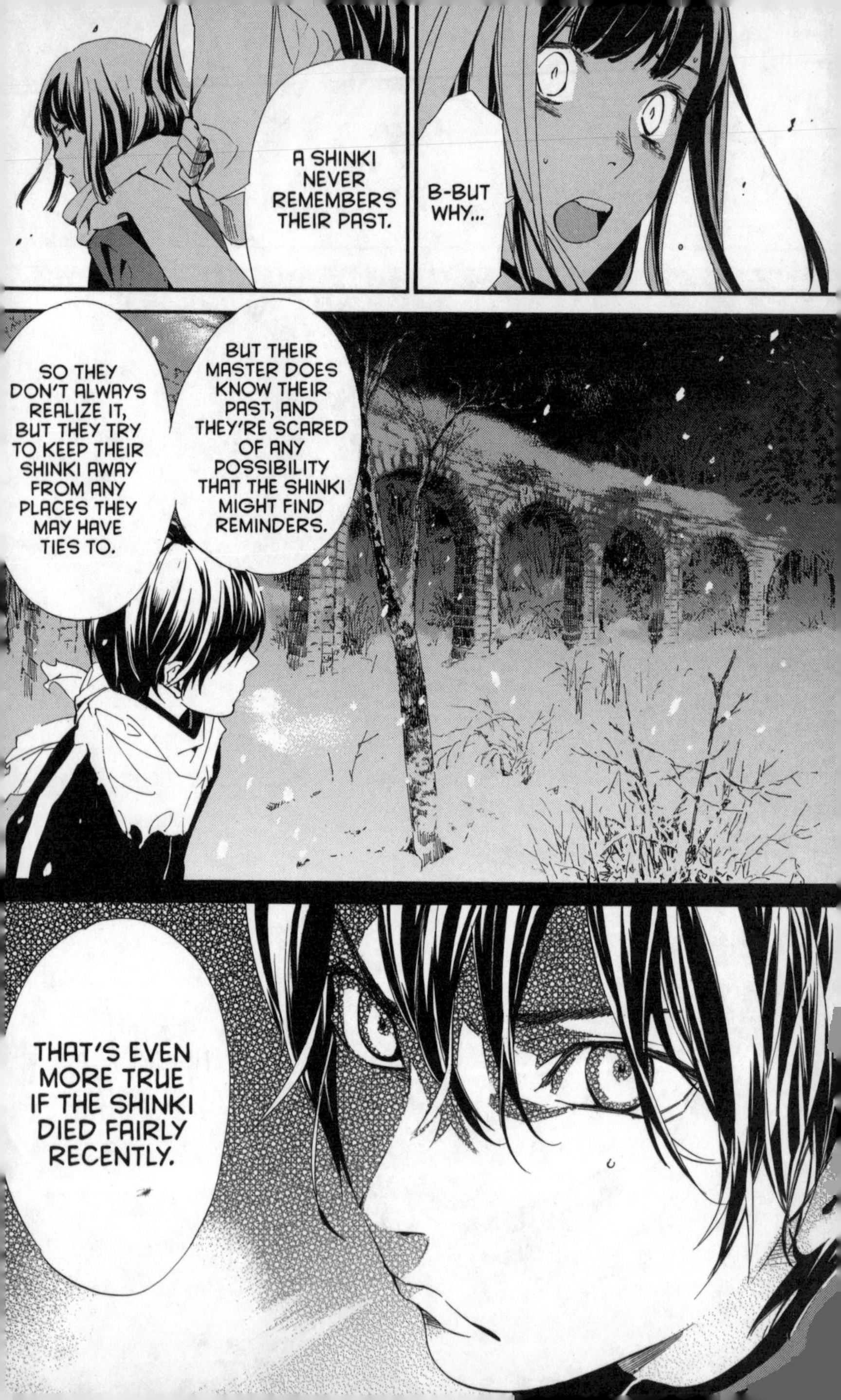
B-BUT WHY...
A SHINKI NEVER REMEMBERS THEIR PAST.
BUT THEIR MASTER DOES KNOW THEIR PAST, AND THEY'RE SCARED OF ANY POSSIBILITY THAT THE SHINKI MIGHT FIND REMINDERS.
SO THEY DON'T ALWAYS REALIZE IT, BUT THEY TRY TO KEEP THEIR SHINKI AWAY FROM ANY PLACES THEY MAY HAVE TIES TO.
THAT'S EVEN MORE TRUE IF THE SHINKI DIED FAIRLY RECENTLY.

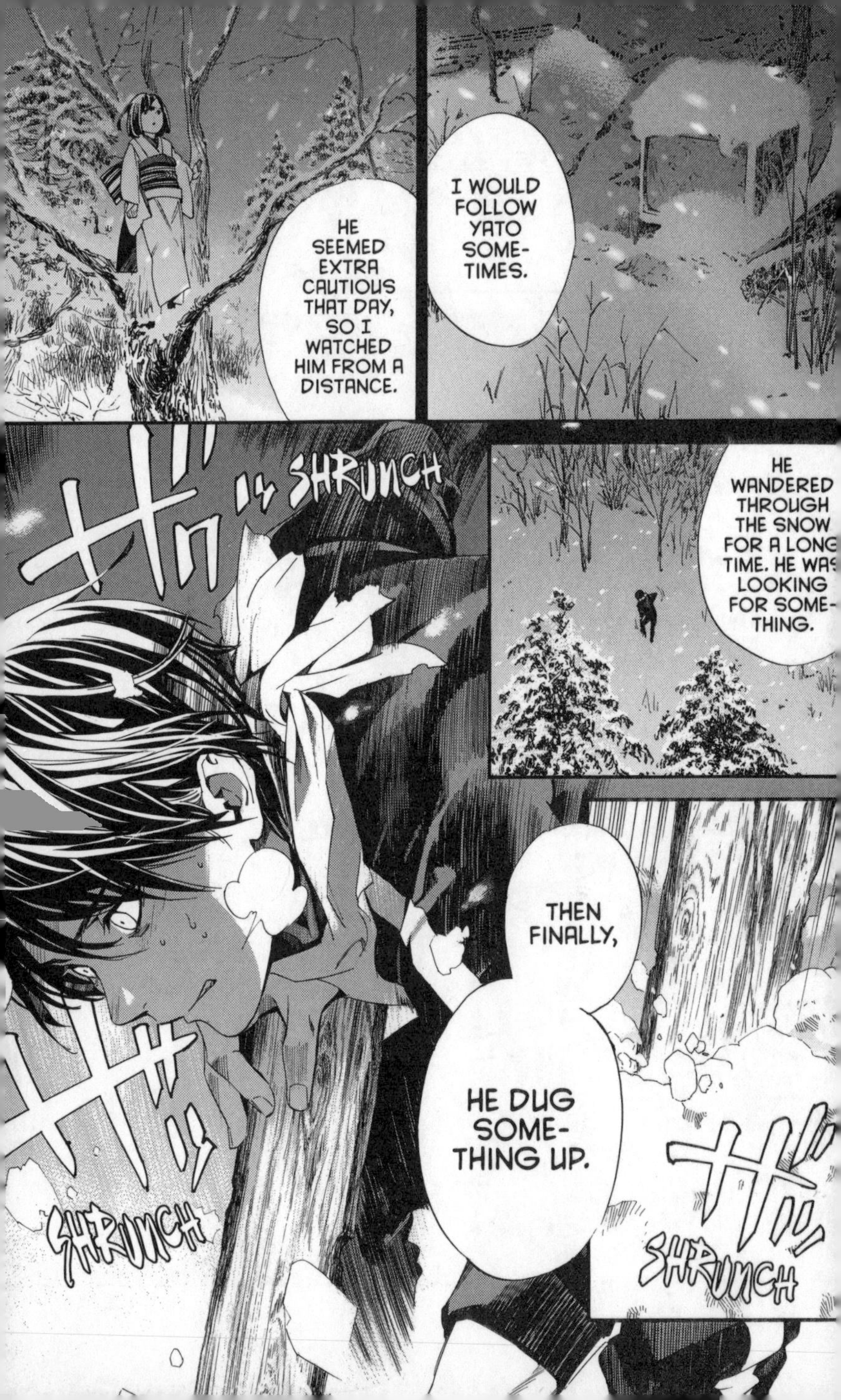
I WOULD FOLLOW YATO SOMETIMES.
HE SEEMED EXTRA CAUTIOUS THAT DAY, SO I WATCHED HIM FROM A DISTANCE.
HE WANDERED THROUGH THE SNOW FOR A LONG TIME. HE WAS LOOKING FOR SOMETHING.
THEN FINALLY,
HE DUG SOMETHING UP.
SHRUNCH
SHRUNCH
SHRUNCH

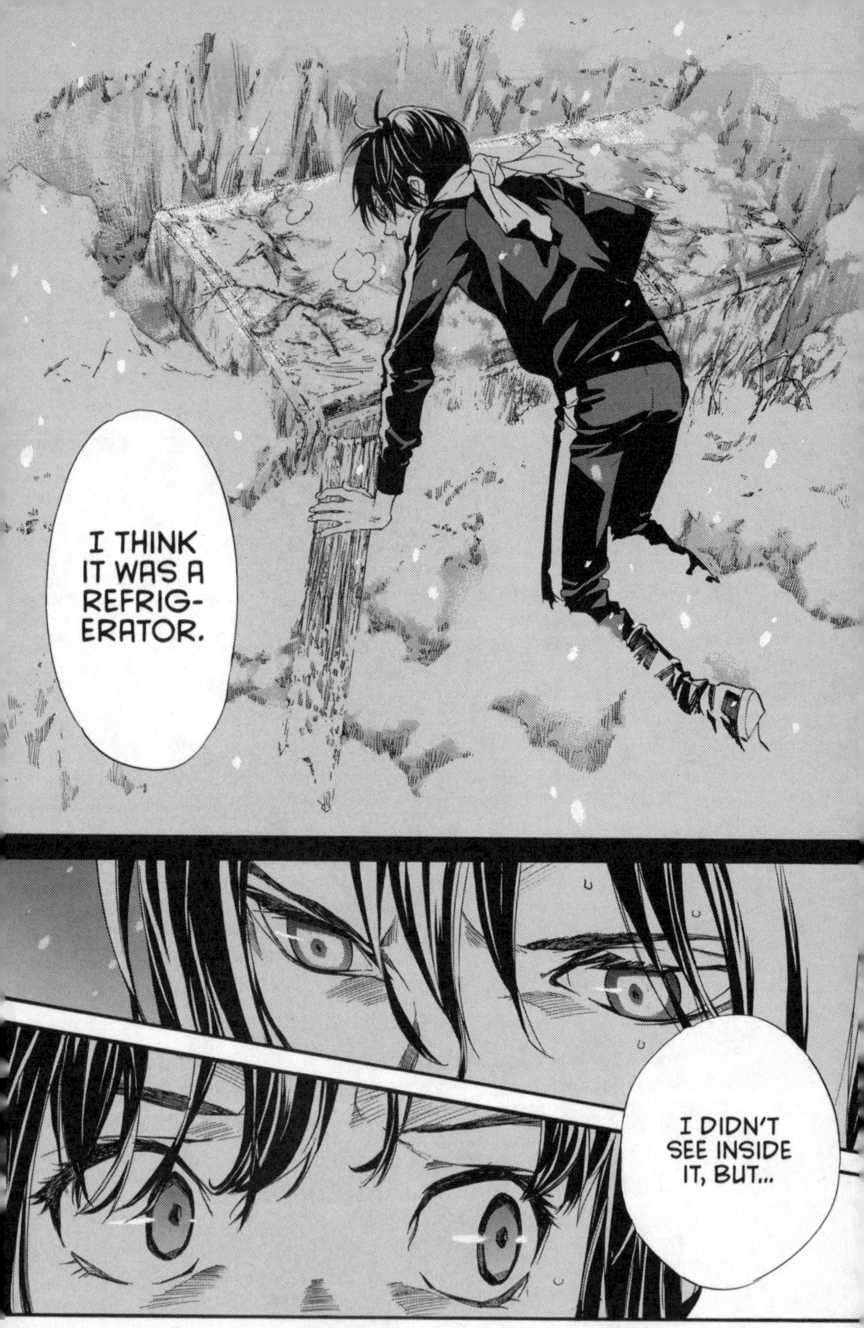
I THINK IT WAS A REFRIG-ERATOR.
I DIDN'T SEE INSIDE IT, BUT...

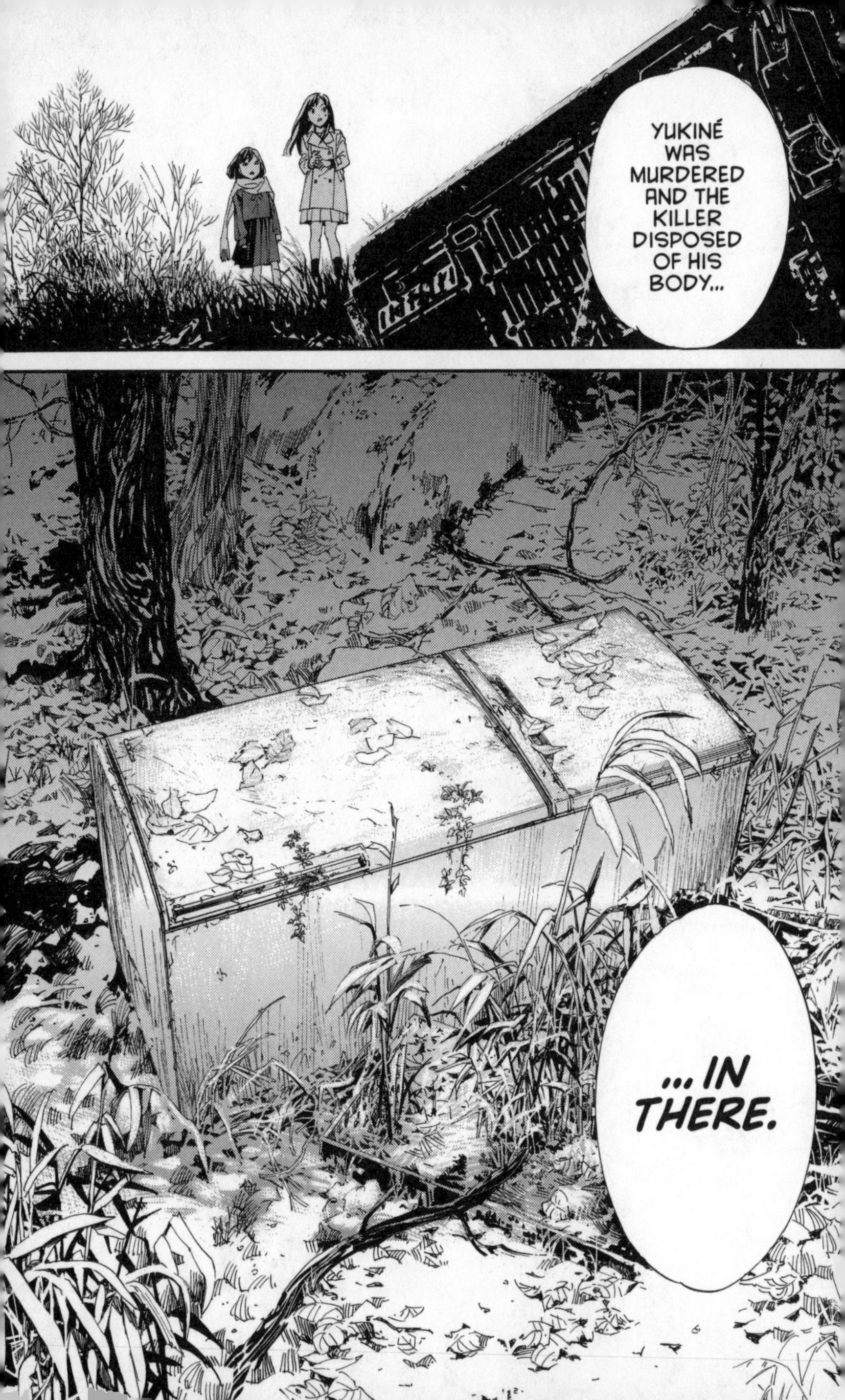
YUKINÉ WAS MURDERED AND THE KILLER DISPOSED OF HIS BODY...
...IN THERE.

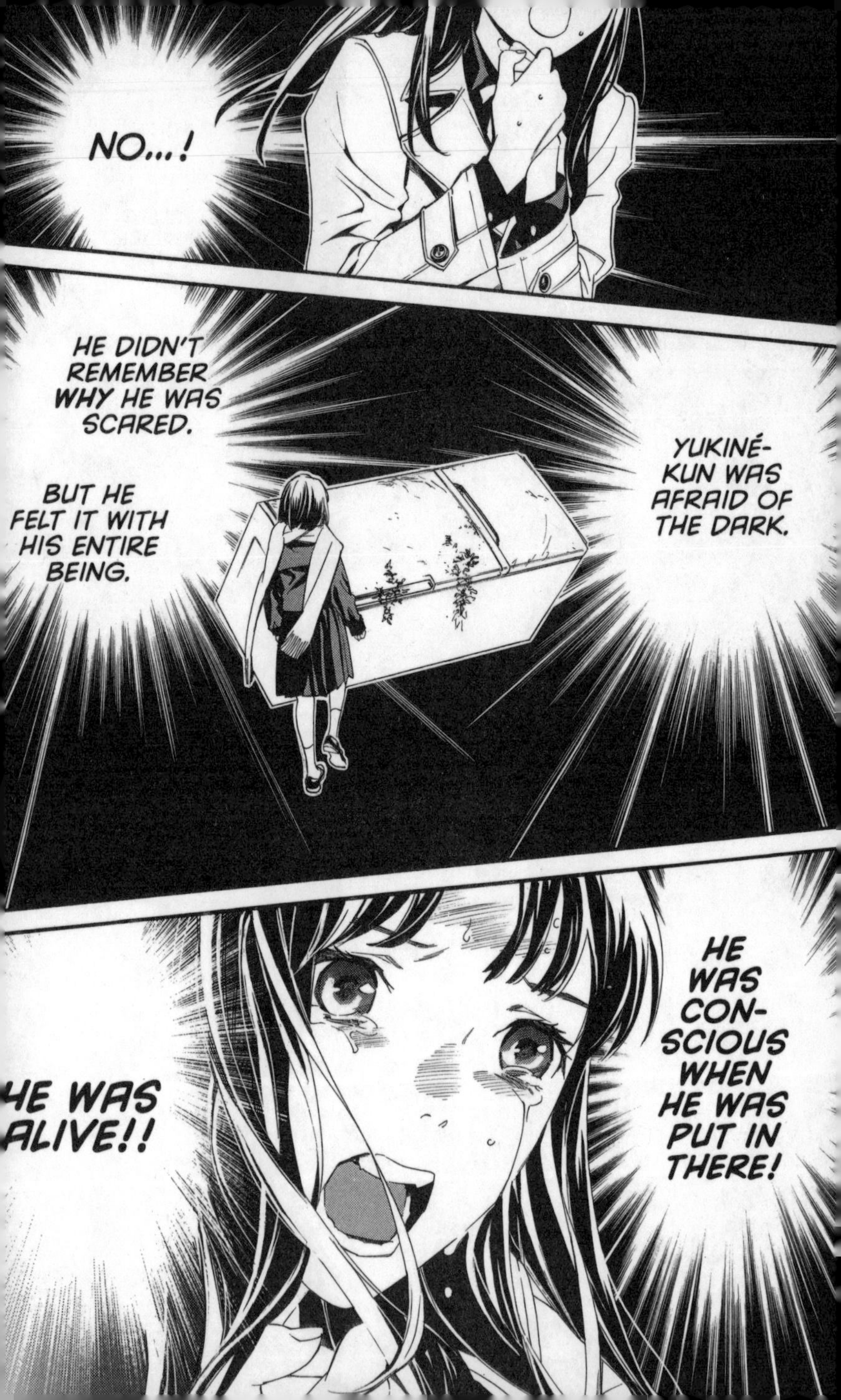
NO...!
YUKINÉ-KUN WAS AFRAID OF THE DARK.
HE DIDN'T REMEMBER WHY HE WAS SCARED.
BUT HE FELT IT WITH HIS ENTIRE BEING.
HE WAS CONSCIOUS WHEN HE WAS PUT IN THERE!
HE WAS ALIVE!!

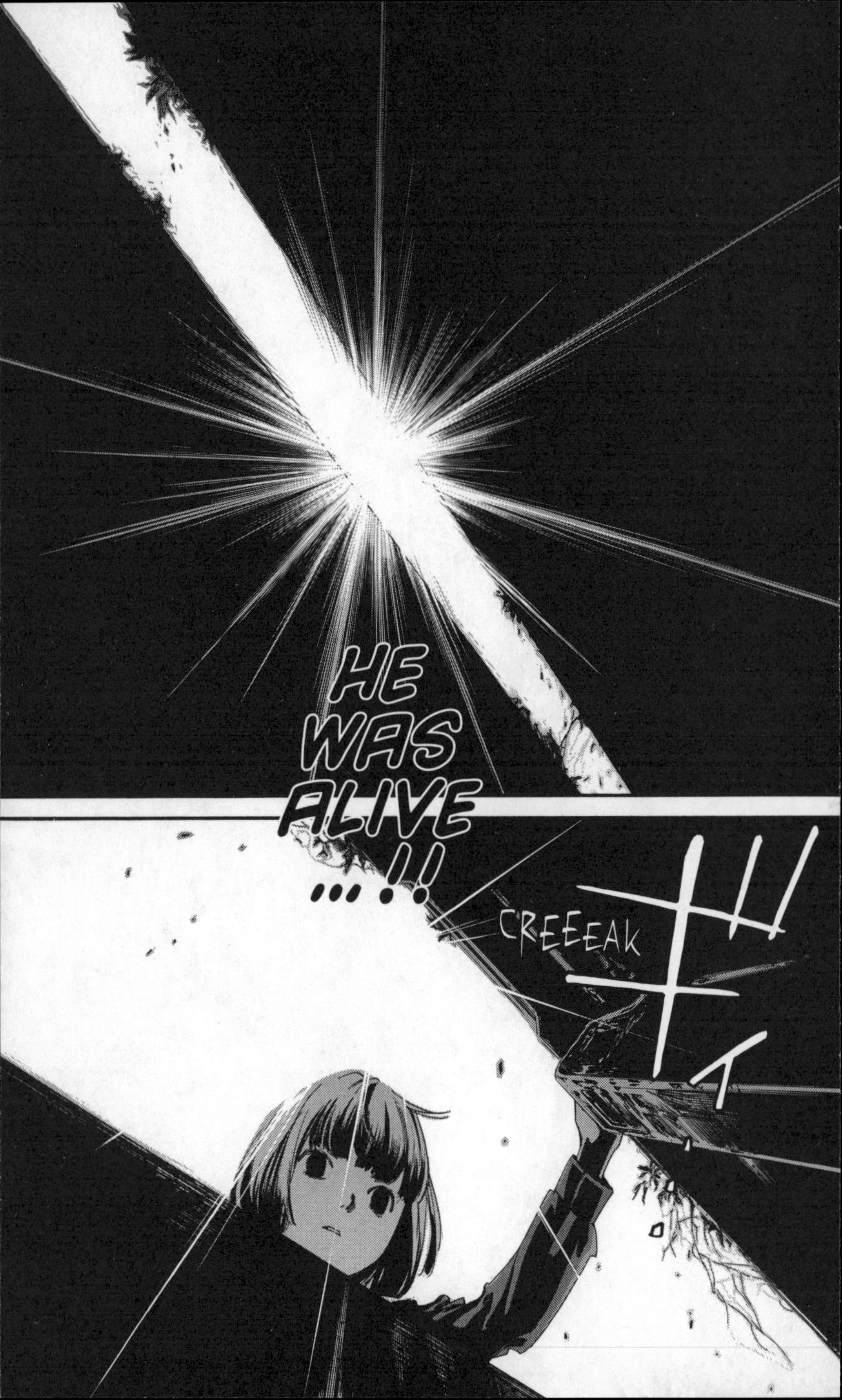
HE WAS ALIVE ...!!
CREEEAK

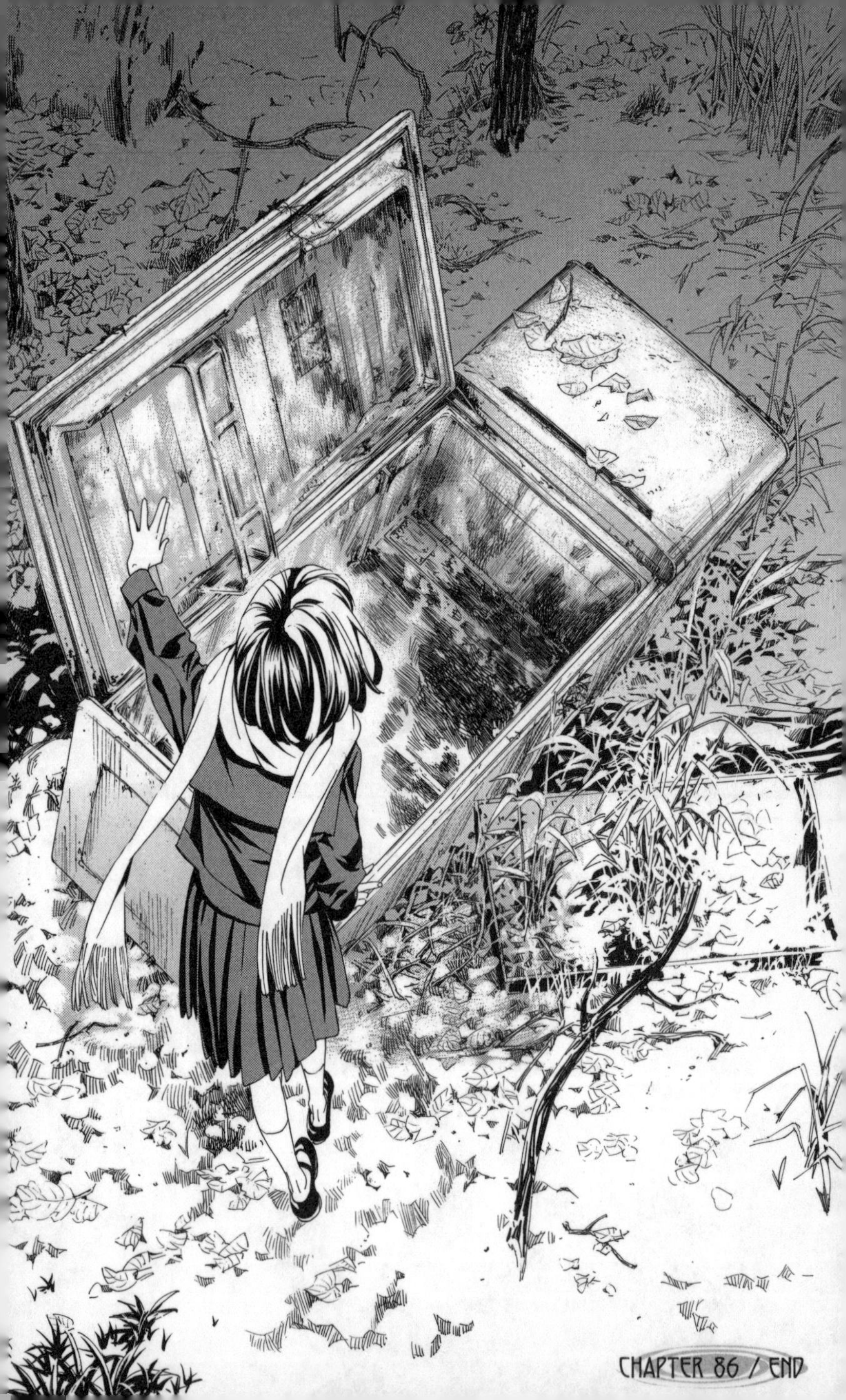
CHAPTER 86 / END

野

覺

神

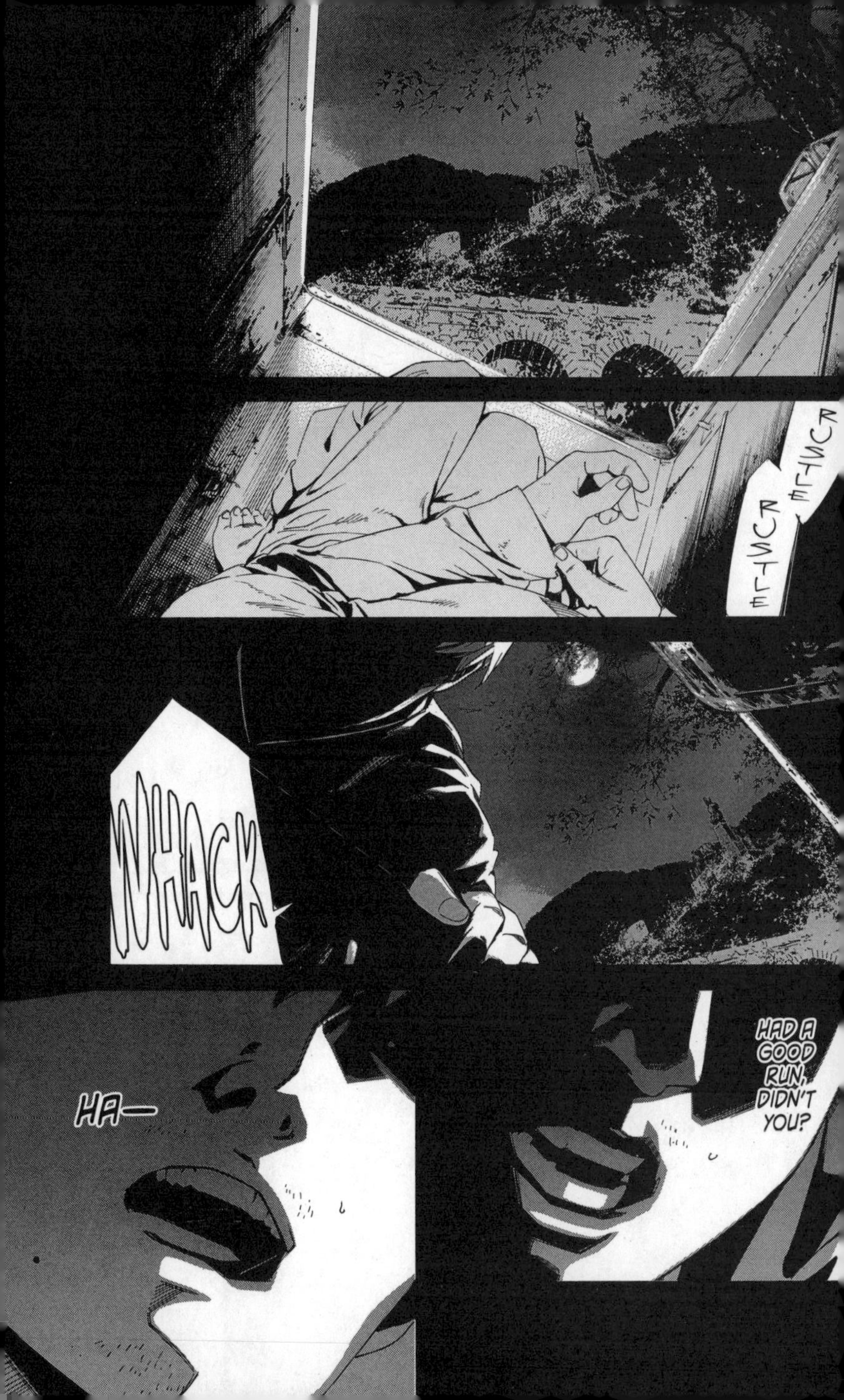
RUSTLE
RUSTLE
WHACK
HAD A GOOD RUN, DIDN'T YOU?
HA—

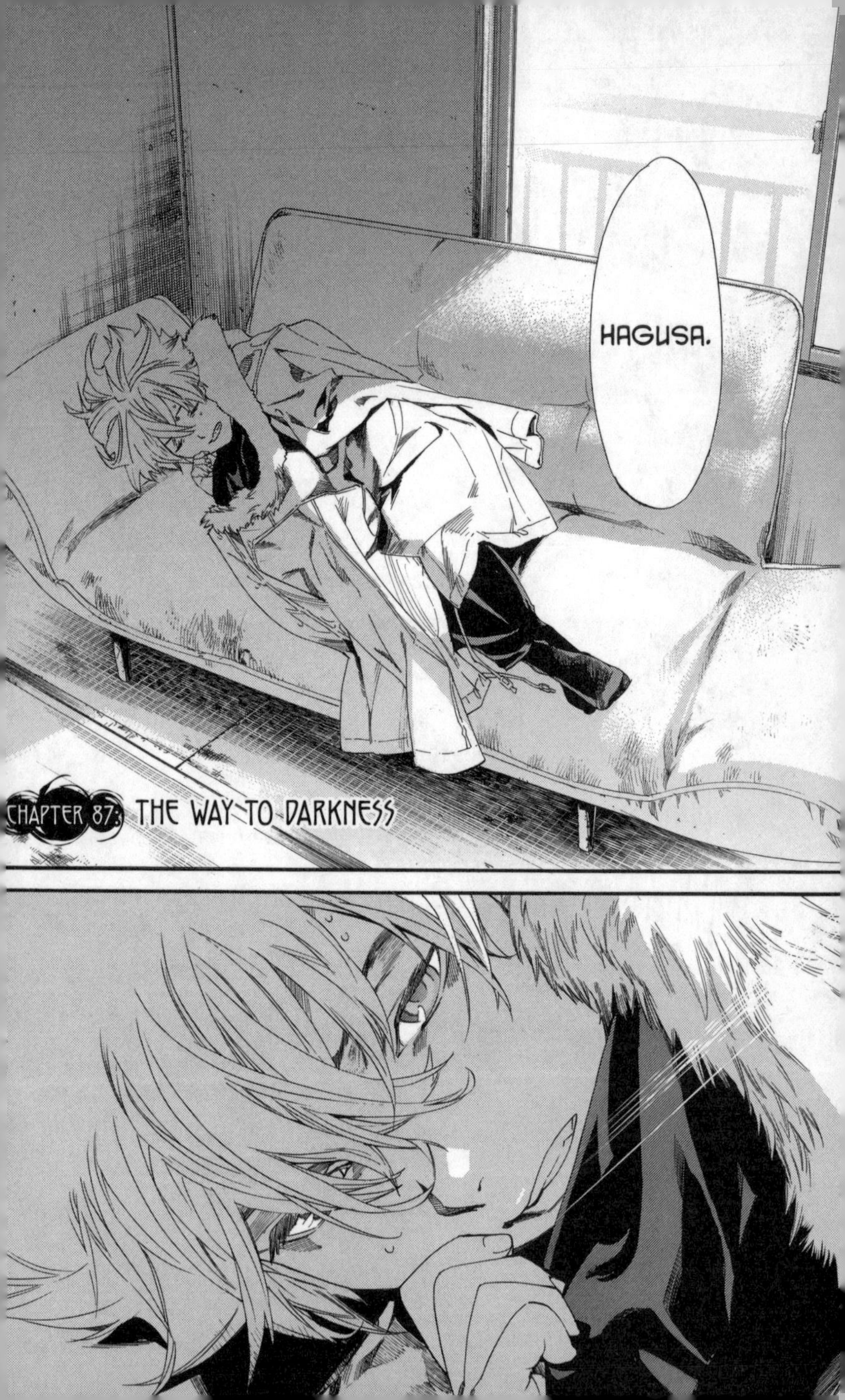
HAGUSA.
CHAPTER 87: THE WAY TO DARKNESS

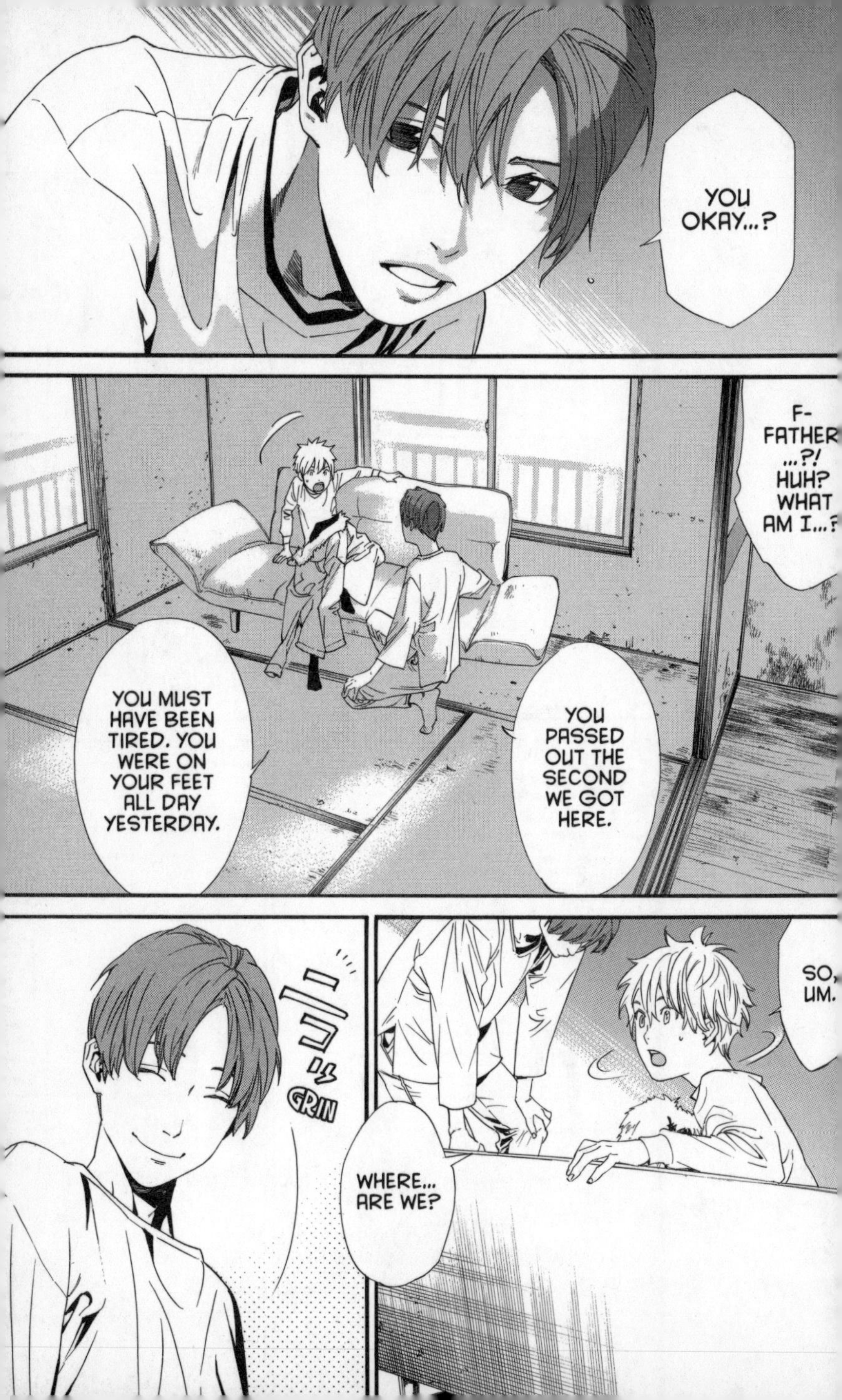
YOU OKAY...?
F-FATHER ...?! HUH? WHAT AM I...?
YOU PASSED OUT THE SECOND WE GOT HERE.
YOU MUST HAVE BEEN TIRED. YOU WERE ON YOUR FEET ALL DAY YESTERDAY.
SO, UM.
WHERE... ARE WE?
GRIN

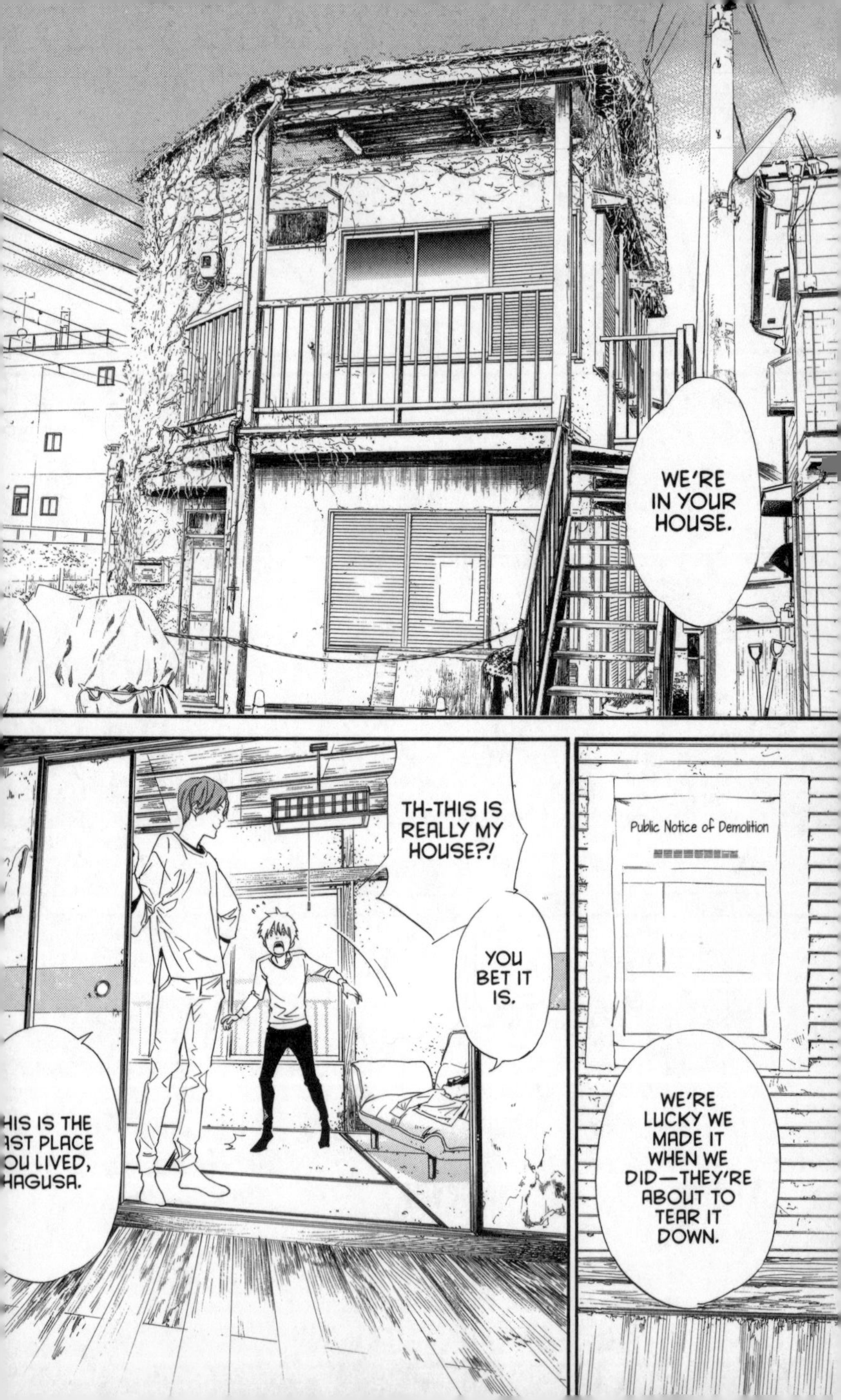
WE'RE IN YOUR HOUSE.
Public Notice of Demolition
WE'RE LUCKY WE MADE IT WHEN WE DID—THEY'RE ABOUT TO TEAR IT DOWN.
TH-THIS IS REALLY MY HOUSE?!
YOU BET IT IS.
HIS IS THE AST PLACE OU LIVED, HAGUSA.

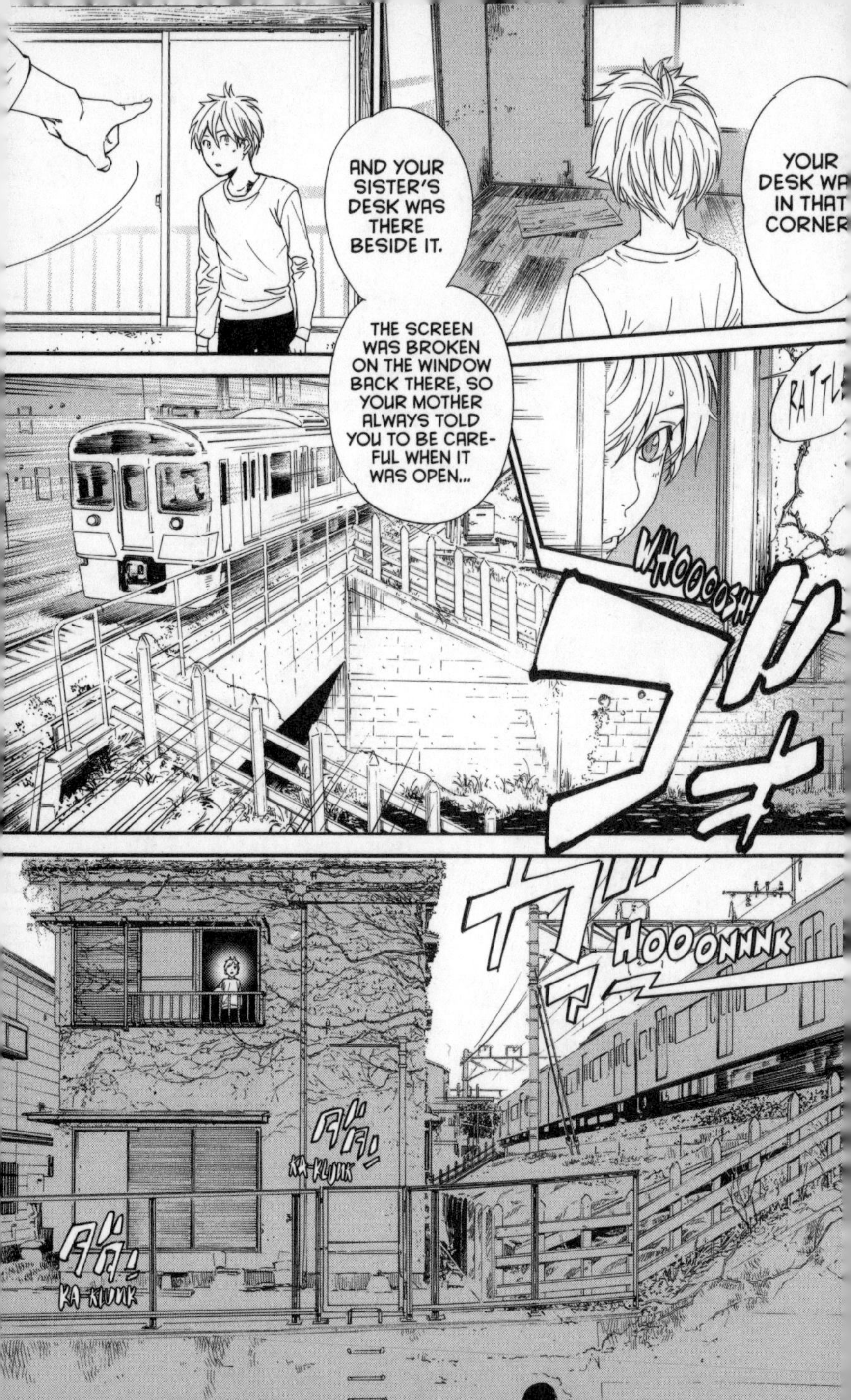
YOUR DESK WA IN THAT CORNER
AND YOUR SISTER'S DESK WAS THERE BESIDE IT.
THE SCREEN WAS BROKEN ON THE WINDOW BACK THERE, SO YOUR MOTHER ALWAYS TOLD YOU TO BE CARE-FUL WHEN IT WAS OPEN...
RATTL
WHOOOOOSH
HOOONNNK
KA-KLUNK
KA-KLUNK

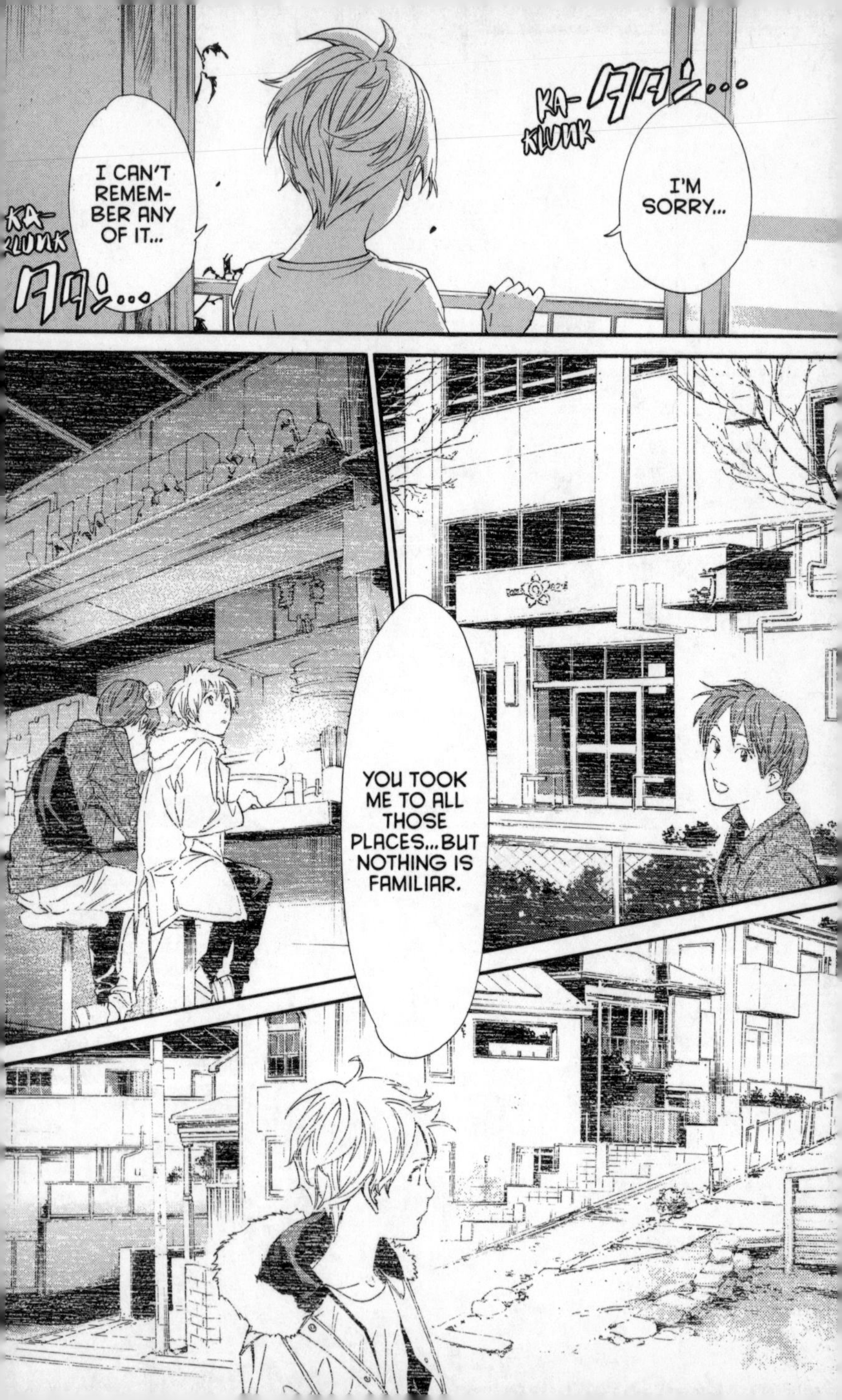
KA-KLUNK
I'M SORRY...
I CAN'T REMEMBER ANY OF IT...
KA-KLUNK
YOU TOOK ME TO ALL THOSE PLACES...BUT NOTHING IS FAMILIAR.

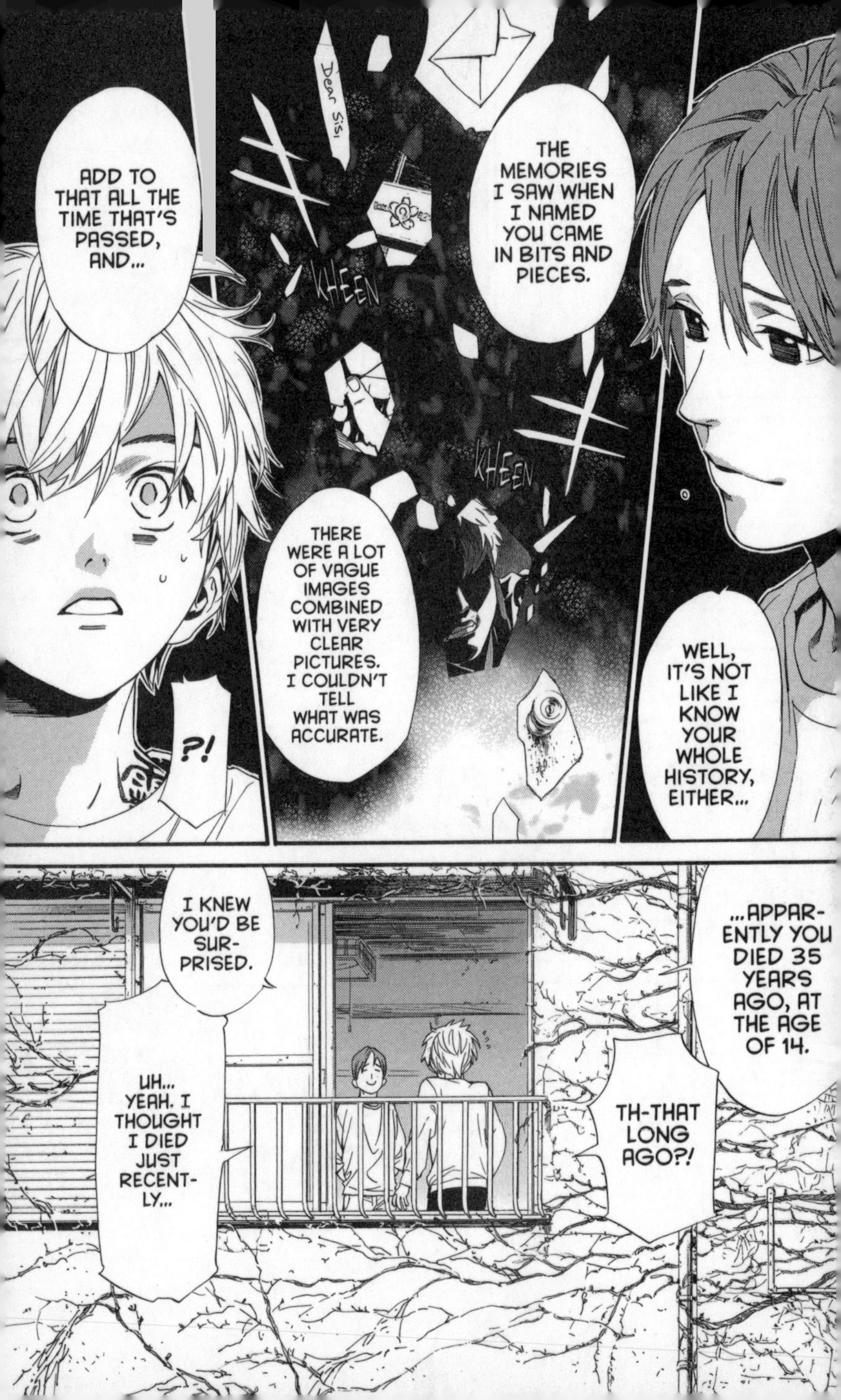
WELL, IT'S NOT LIKE I KNOW YOUR WHOLE HISTORY, EITHER...
THE MEMORIES I SAW WHEN I NAMED YOU CAME IN BITS AND PIECES.
Dear Sisi
KHEEN
KHEEN
THERE WERE A LOT OF VAGUE IMAGES COMBINED WITH VERY CLEAR PICTURES. I COULDN'T TELL WHAT WAS ACCURATE.
ADD TO THAT ALL THE TIME THAT'S PASSED, AND...
?!
...APPARENTLY YOU DIED 35 YEARS AGO, AT THE AGE OF 14.
TH-THAT LONG AGO?!
I KNEW YOU'D BE SUR-PRISED.
UH... YEAH. I THOUGHT I DIED JUST RECENT-LY...

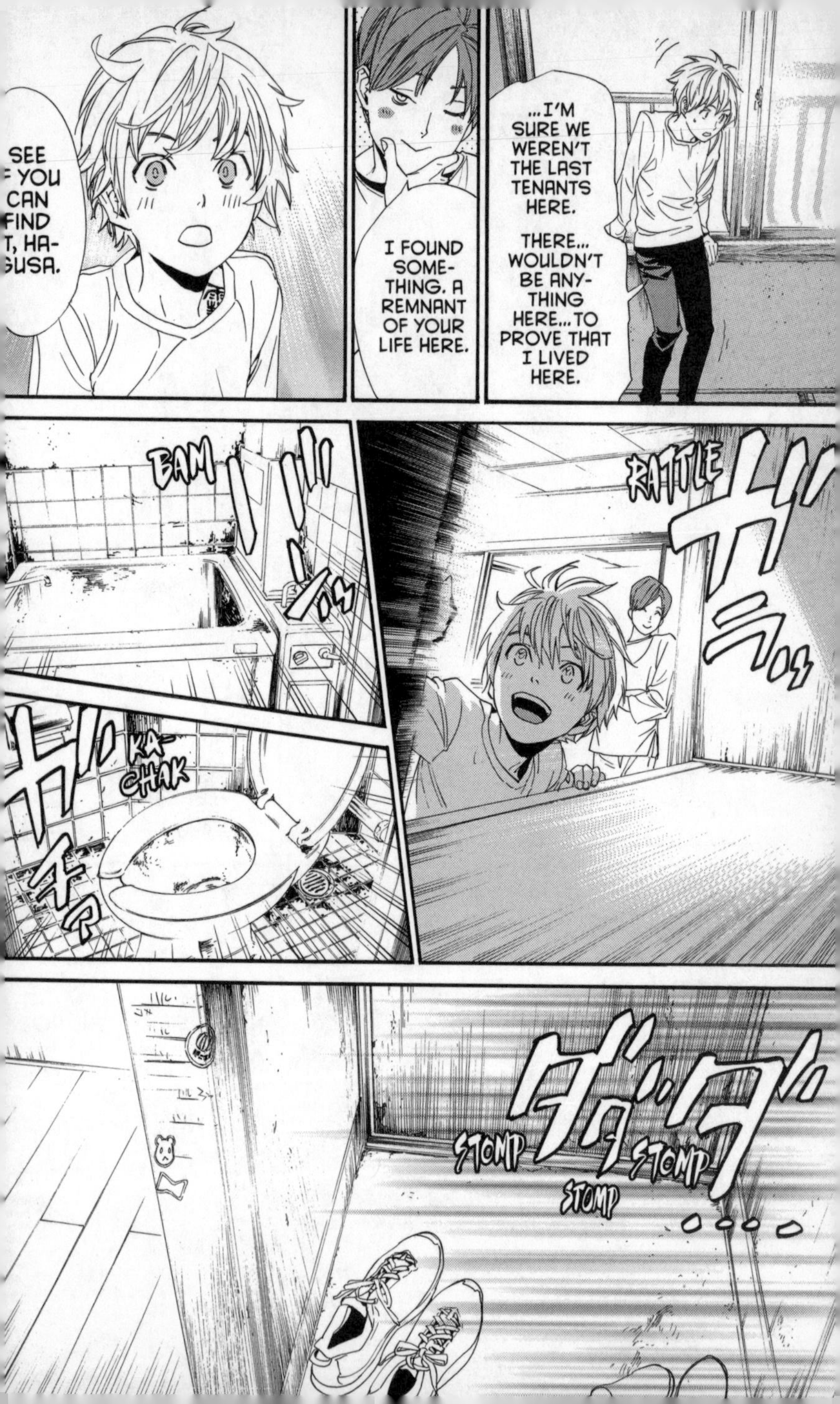
...I'M SURE WE WEREN'T THE LAST TENANTS HERE.
THERE... WOULDN'T BE ANYTHING HERE... TO PROVE THAT I LIVED HERE.
I FOUND SOMETHING. A REMNANT OF YOUR LIFE HERE.
SEE F YOU CAN FIND T, HA-GUSA.
RATTLE
BAM
KA-CHAK
STOMP
STOMP
STOMP

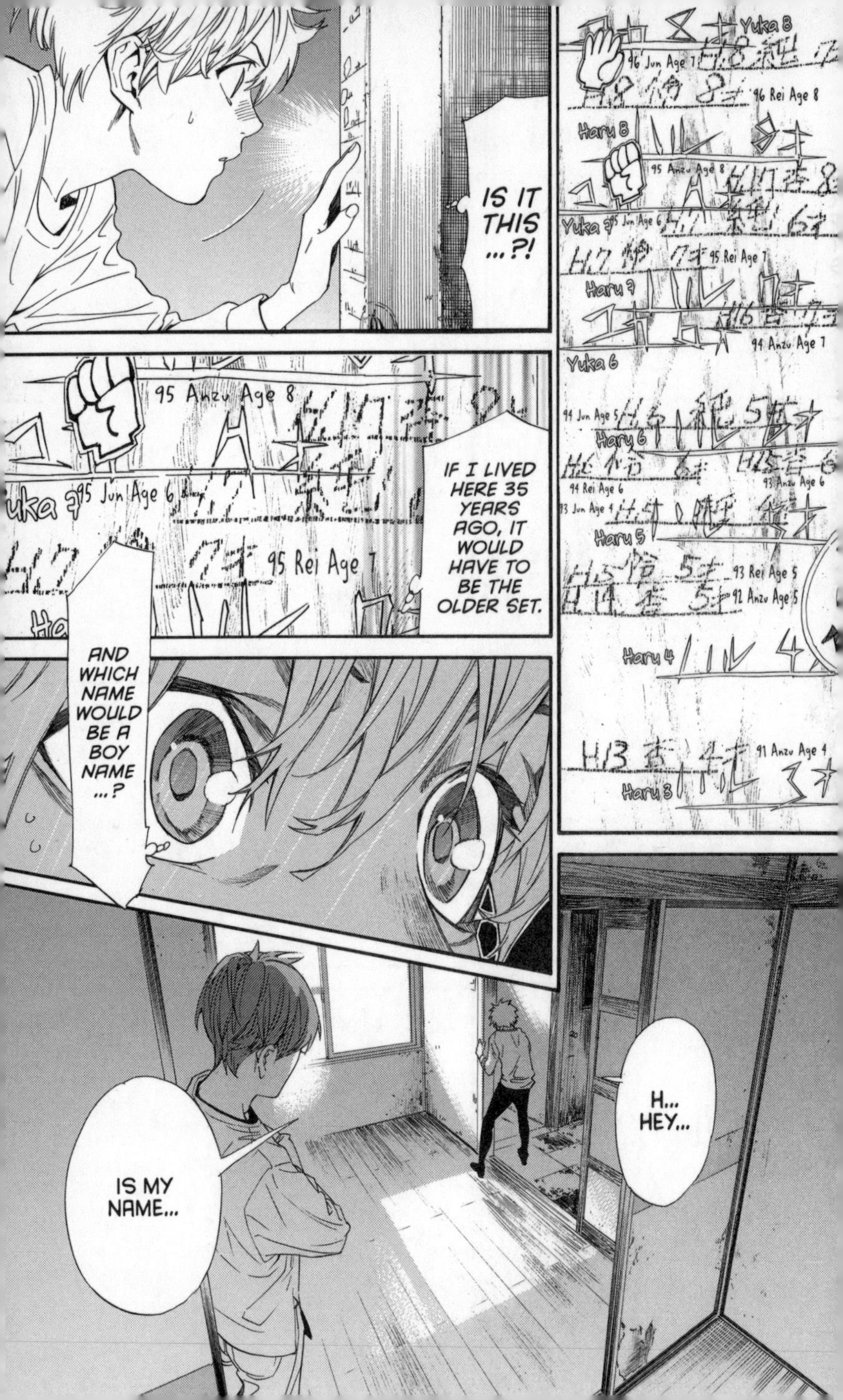
Yuka 8
96 Jun Age 7
96 Rei Age 8
Haru 8
95 Anzu Age 8
Yuka 7
95 Jun Age 6
95 Rei Age 7
Haru 7
94 Anzu Age 7
Yuka 6
94 Jun Age 5
Haru 6
94 Rei Age 6
93 Anzu Age 6
93 Jun Age 4
Haru 5
93 Rei Age 5
92 Anzu Age 5
Haru 4
91 Anzu Age 4
Haru 3
IS IT THIS ...?!
95 Anzu Age 8
Yuka 7
95 Jun Age 6
95 Rei Age 7
IF I LIVED HERE 35 YEARS AGO, IT WOULD HAVE TO BE THE OLDER SET.
AND WHICH NAME WOULD BE A BOY NAME ...?
IS MY NAME...
H... HEY...

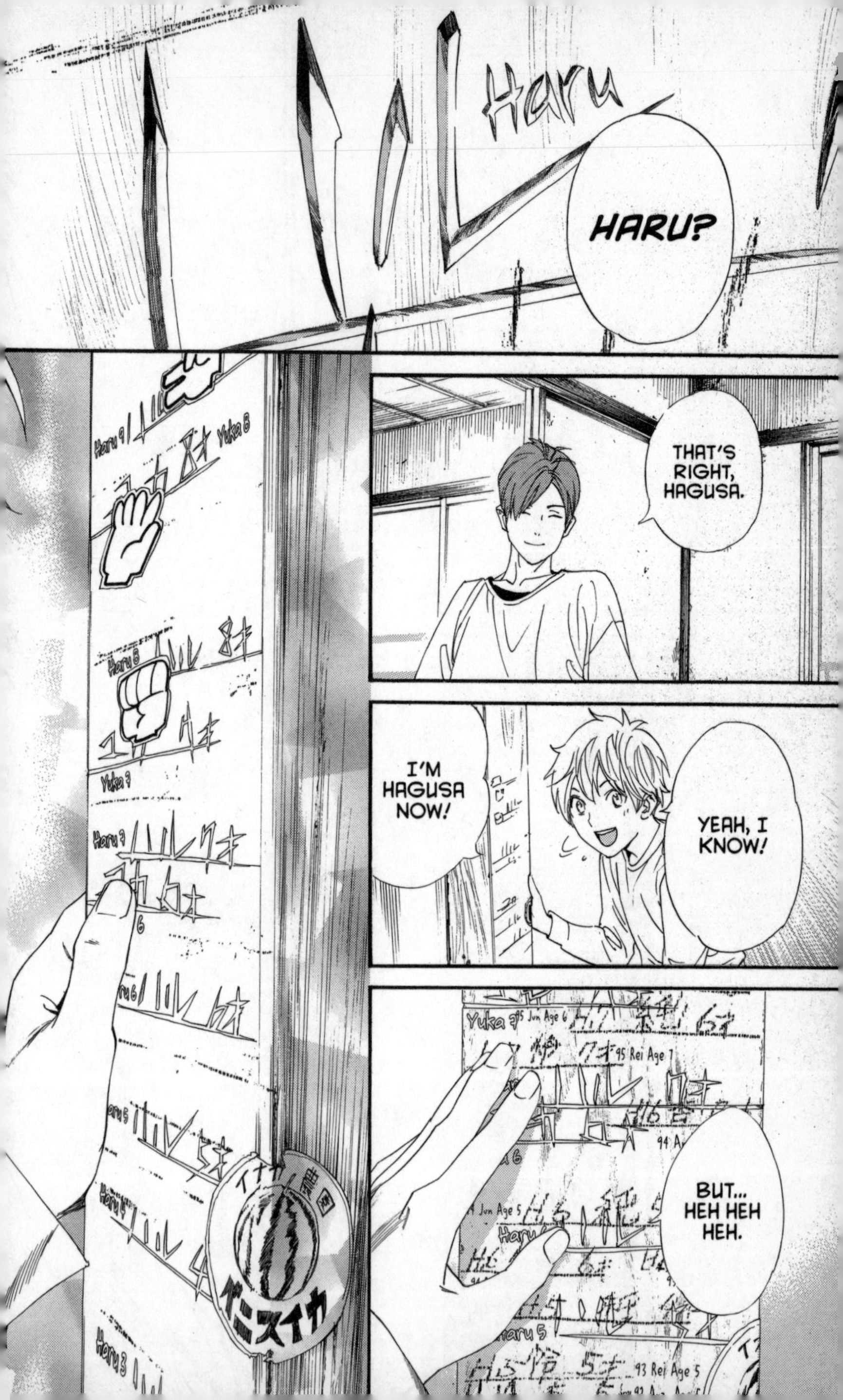
Haru
HARU?
THAT'S RIGHT, HAGUSA.
YEAH, I KNOW!
I'M HAGUSA NOW!
BUT... HEH HEH HEH.

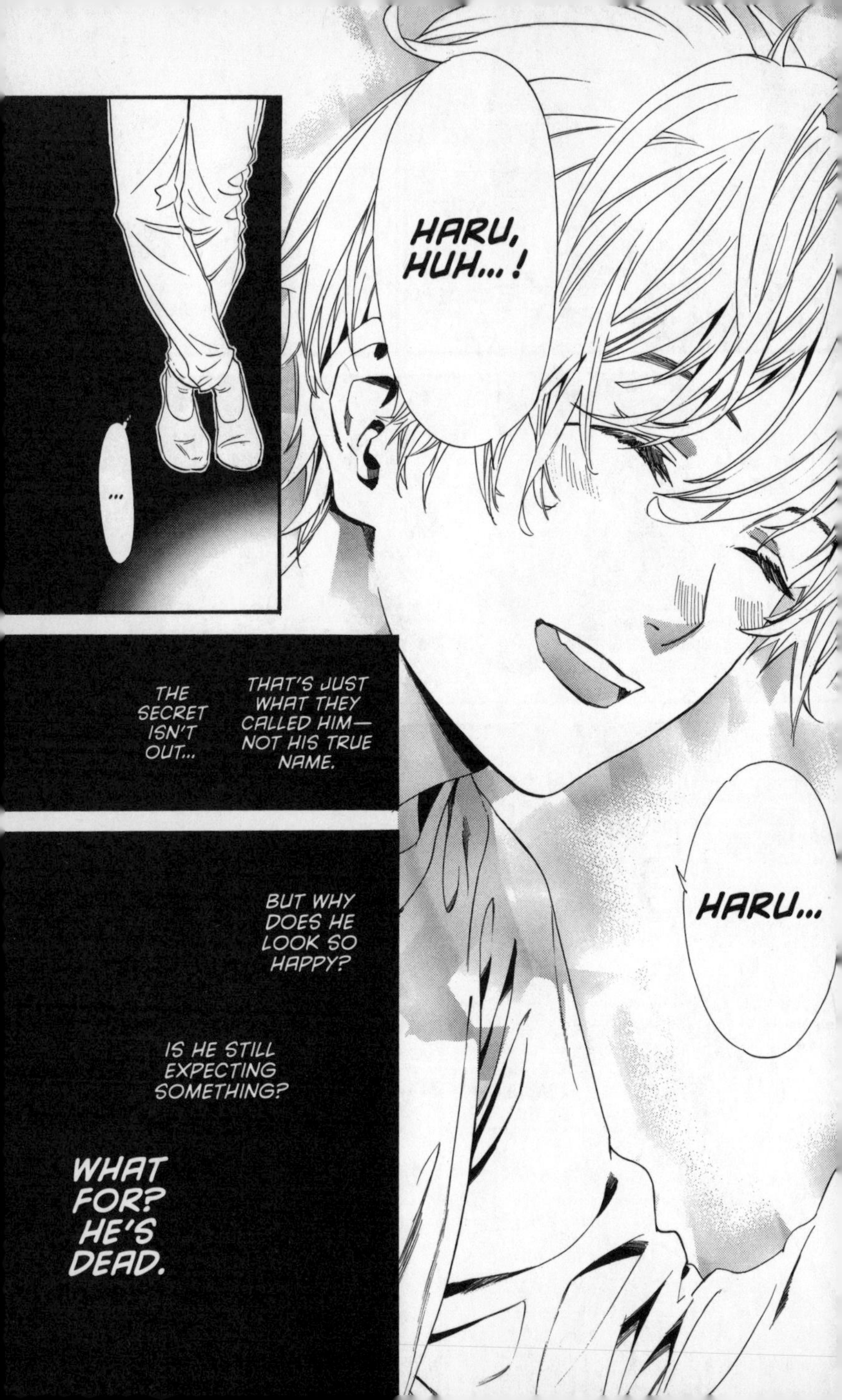
HARU, HUH...!
HARU...
...
THAT'S JUST WHAT THEY CALLED HIM—NOT HIS TRUE NAME.
THE SECRET ISN'T OUT...
BUT WHY DOES HE LOOK SO HAPPY?
IS HE STILL EXPECTING SOMETHING?
WHAT FOR? HE'S DEAD.

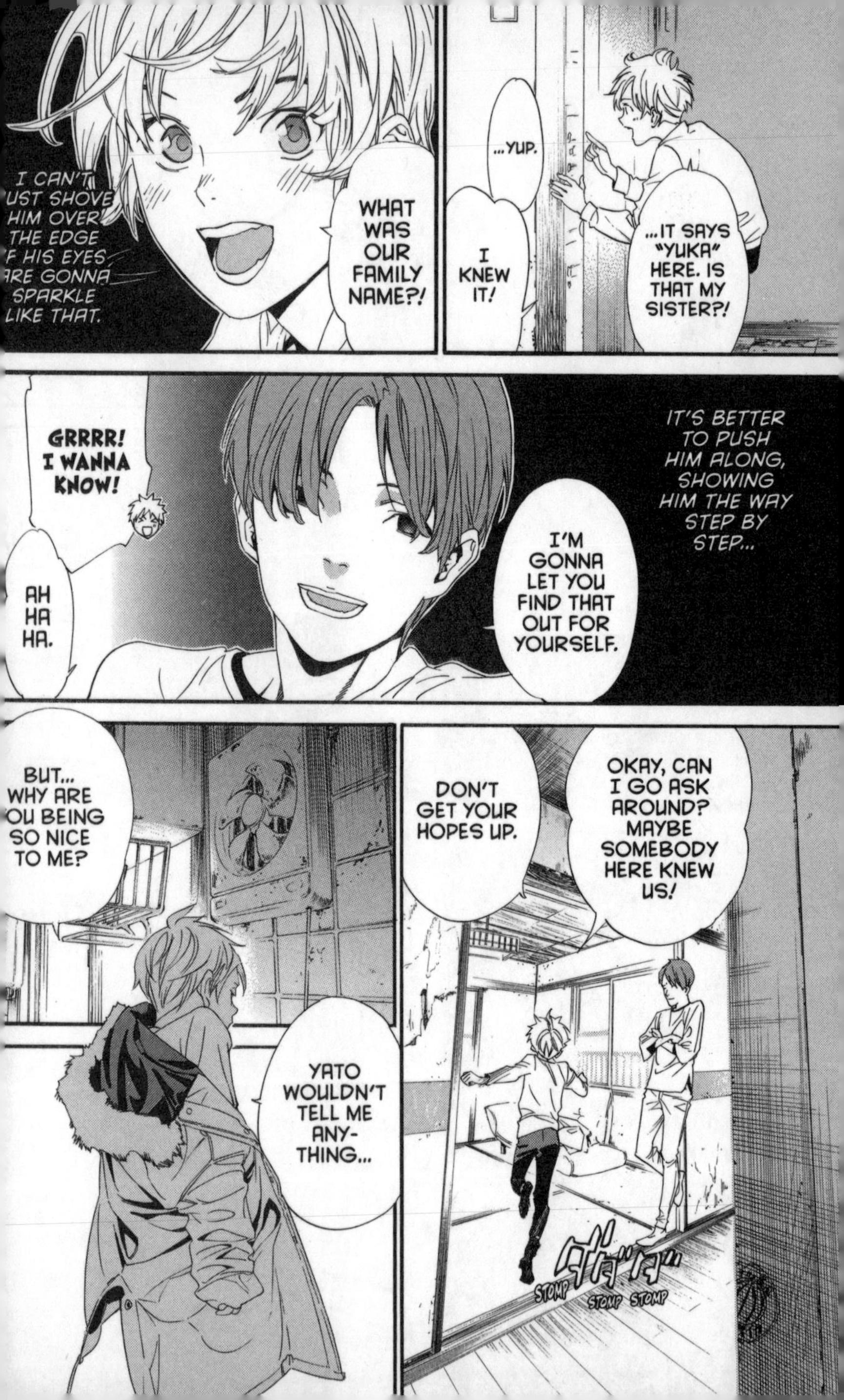
...IT SAYS "YUKA" HERE. IS THAT MY SISTER?!
...YUP.
I KNEW IT!
WHAT WAS OUR FAMILY NAME?!
I CAN'T UST SHOVE HIM OVER THE EDGE F HIS EYES ARE GONNA SPARKLE LIKE THAT.
IT'S BETTER TO PUSH HIM ALONG, SHOWING HIM THE WAY STEP BY STEP...
I'M GONNA LET YOU FIND THAT OUT FOR YOURSELF.
GRRRR! I WANNA KNOW!
AH HA HA.
OKAY, CAN I GO ASK AROUND? MAYBE SOMEBODY HERE KNEW US!
DON'T GET YOUR HOPES UP.
STOMP STOMP STOMP
BUT... WHY ARE OU BEING SO NICE TO ME?
YATO WOULDN'T TELL ME ANY-THING...

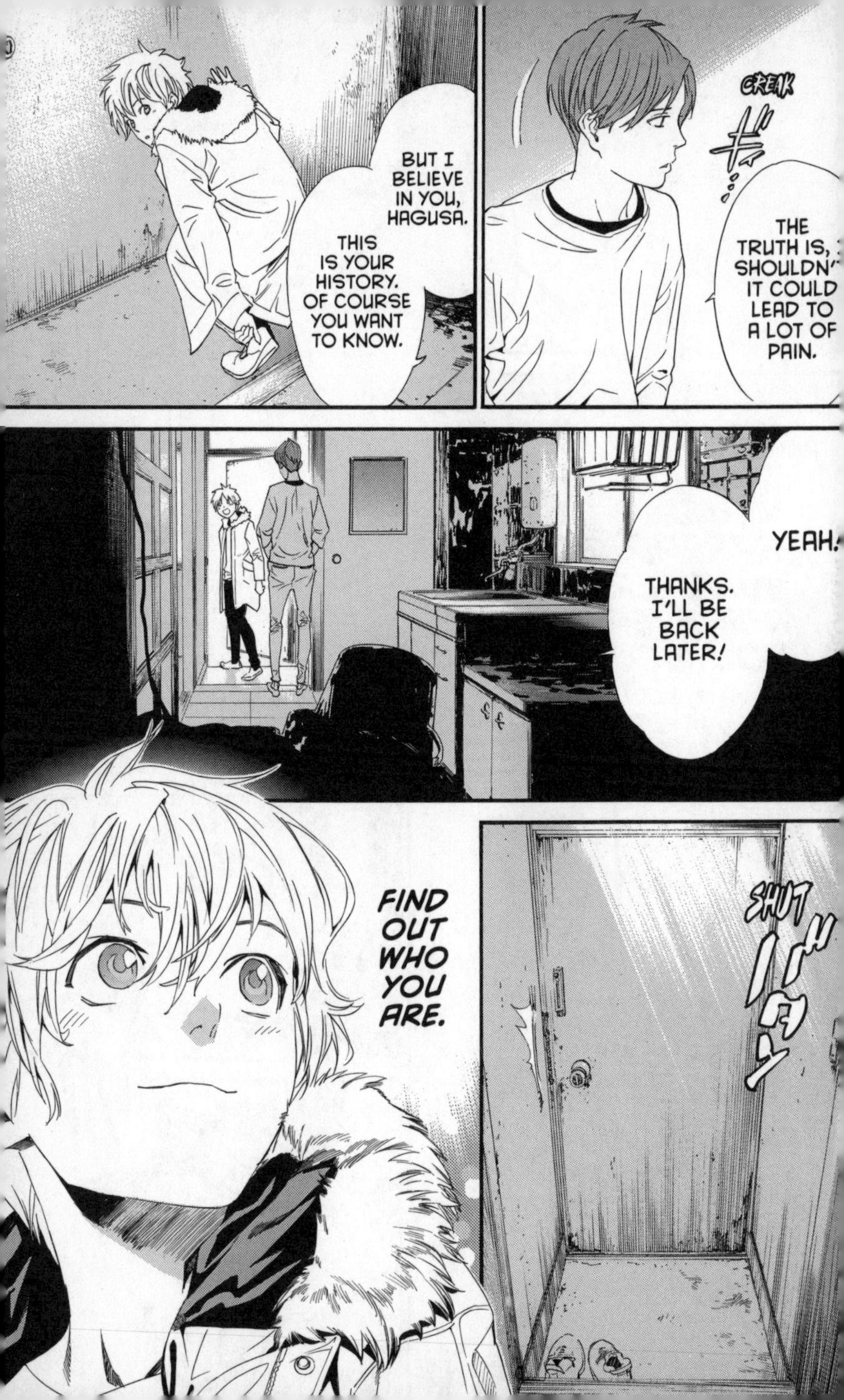
CREAK
THE TRUTH IS, SHOULDN' IT COULD LEAD TO A LOT OF PAIN.
BUT I BELIEVE IN YOU, HAGUSA.
THIS IS YOUR HISTORY. OF COURSE YOU WANT TO KNOW.
YEAH.
THANKS. I'LL BE BACK LATER!
SHUT
FIND OUT WHO YOU ARE.

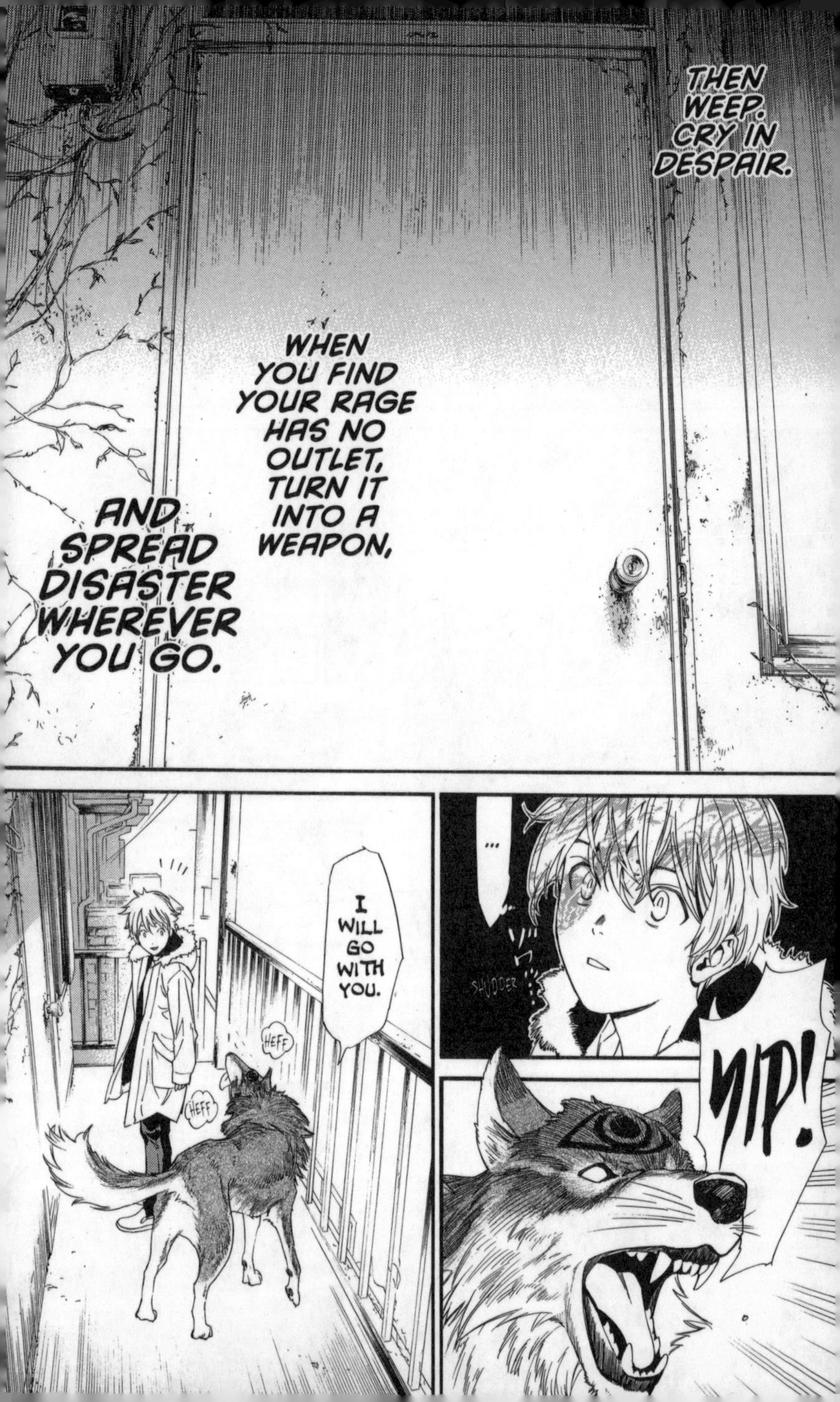
THEN WEEP. CRY IN DESPAIR.
WHEN YOU FIND YOUR RAGE HAS NO OUTLET, TURN IT INTO A WEAPON,
AND SPREAD DISASTER WHEREVER YOU GO.
...
SHUDDER
YIP!
I WILL GO WITH YOU.
HEFF
HEFF

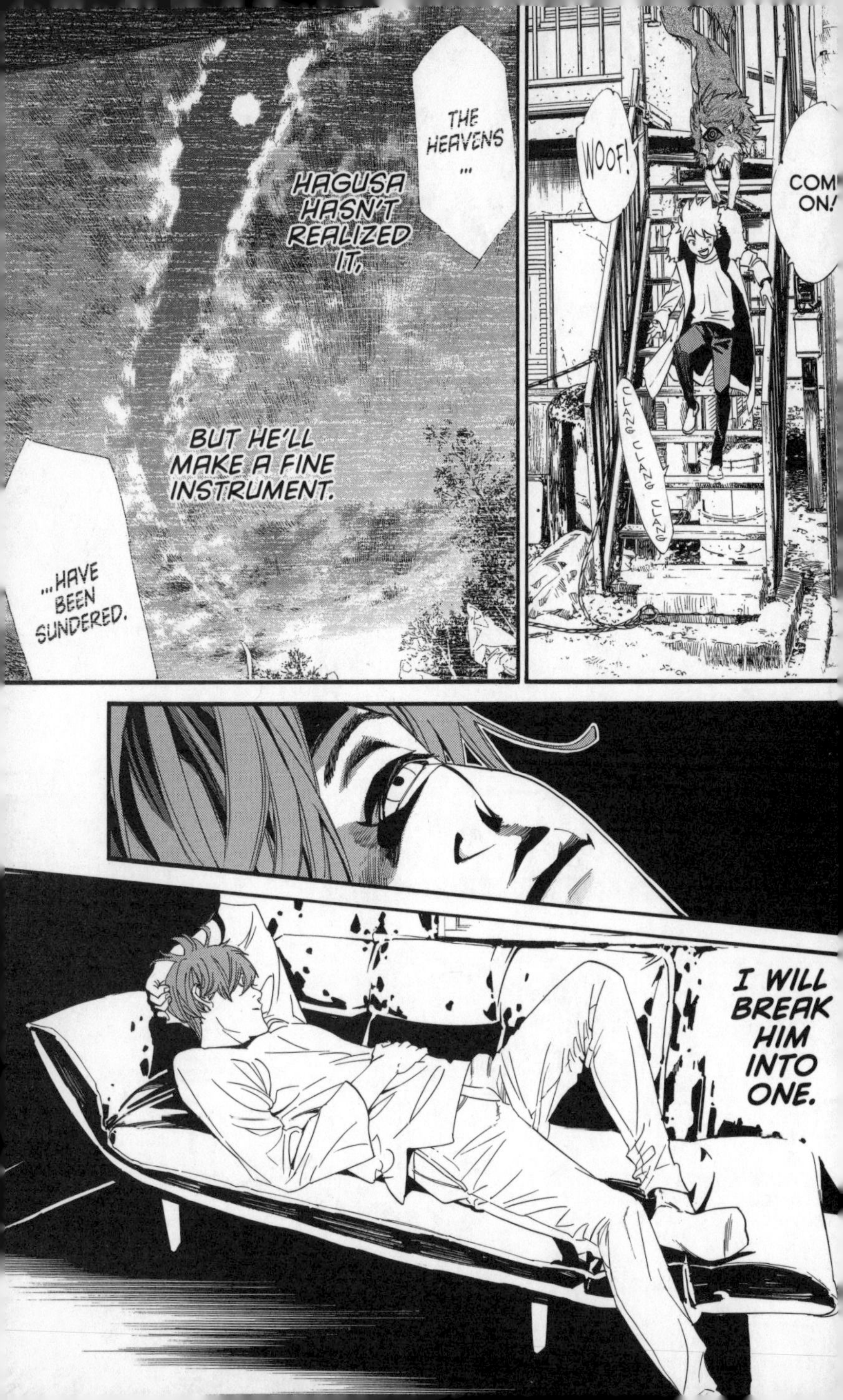
COM ON!
WOOF!
CLANG CLANG CLANG CLANG
THE HEAVENS ...
HAGUSA HASN'T REALIZED IT,
BUT HE'LL MAKE A FINE INSTRUMENT.
...HAVE BEEN SUNDERED.
I WILL BREAK HIM INTO ONE.

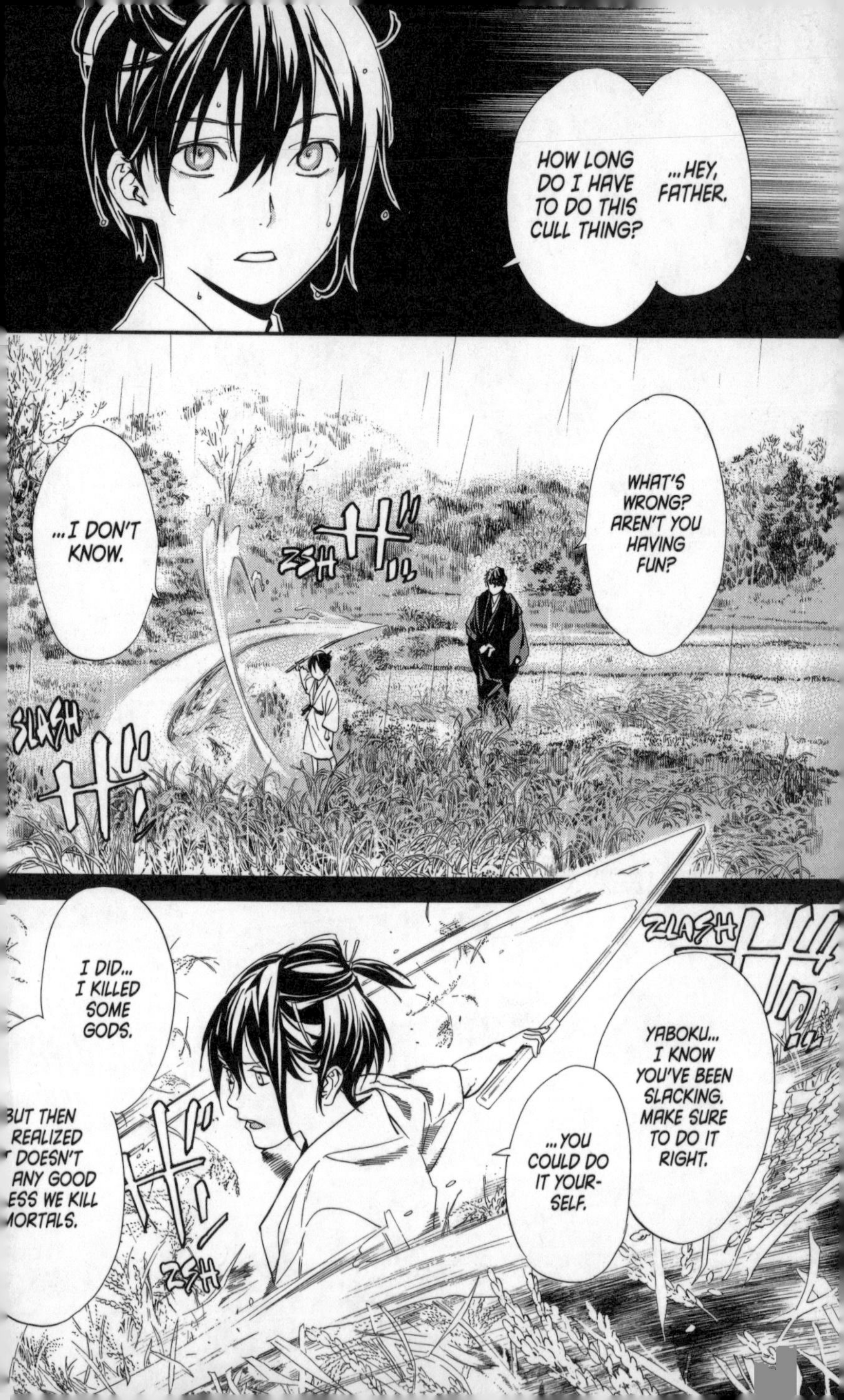
...HEY, FATHER.
HOW LONG DO I HAVE TO DO THIS CULL THING?
WHAT'S WRONG? AREN'T YOU HAVING FUN?
ZSH
...I DON'T KNOW.
SLASH
ZLASH
YABOKU... I KNOW YOU'VE BEEN SLACKING. MAKE SURE TO DO IT RIGHT.
...YOU COULD DO IT YOURSELF.
I DID... I KILLED SOME GODS.
BUT THEN REALIZED DOESN'T ANY GOOD ESS WE KILL MORTALS.
ZSH

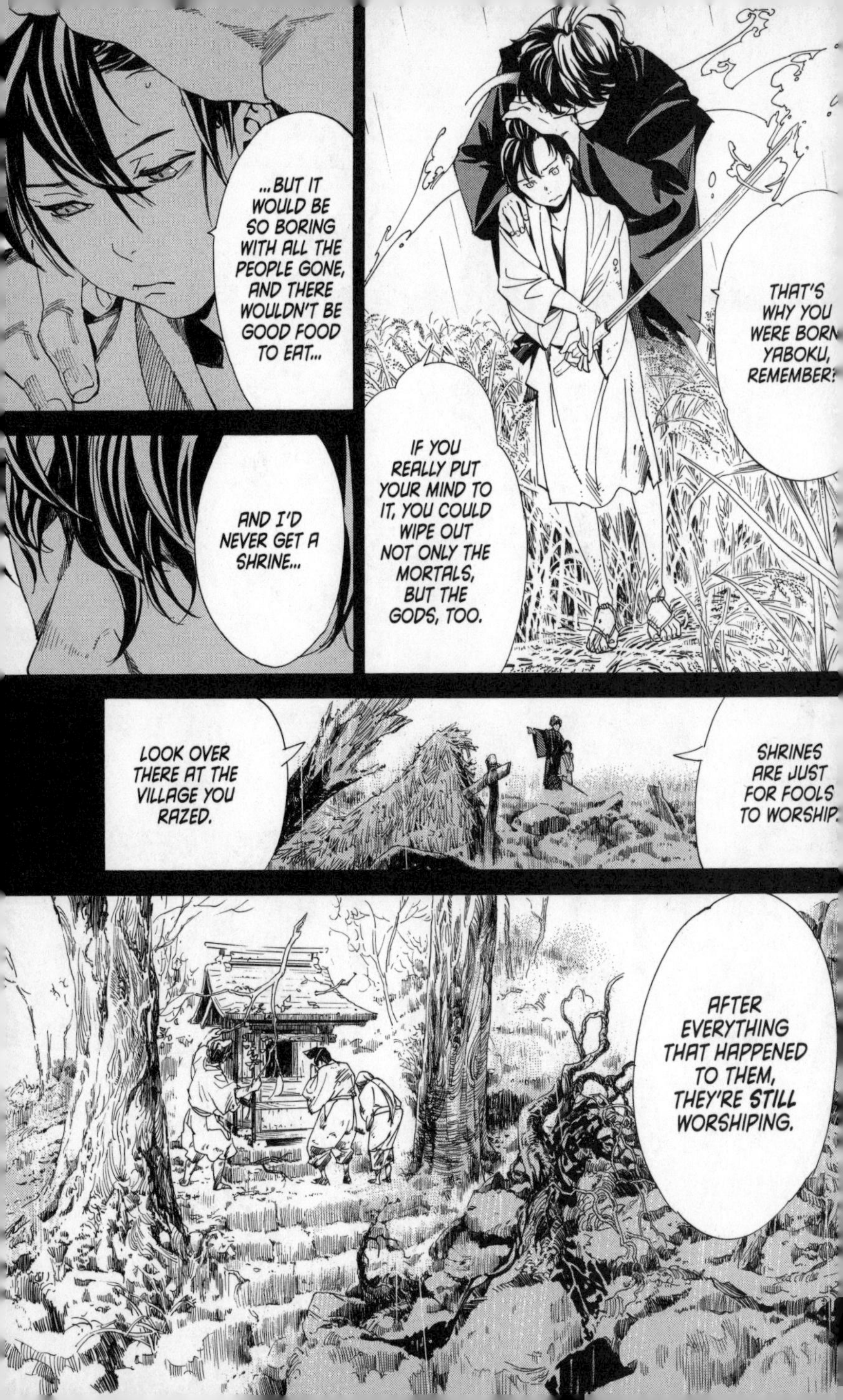
THAT'S WHY YOU WERE BORN YABOKU, REMEMBER?
IF YOU REALLY PUT YOUR MIND TO IT, YOU COULD WIPE OUT NOT ONLY THE MORTALS, BUT THE GODS, TOO.
...BUT IT WOULD BE SO BORING WITH ALL THE PEOPLE GONE, AND THERE WOULDN'T BE GOOD FOOD TO EAT...
AND I'D NEVER GET A SHRINE...
SHRINES ARE JUST FOR FOOLS TO WORSHIP.
LOOK OVER THERE AT THE VILLAGE YOU RAZED.
AFTER EVERYTHING THAT HAPPENED TO THEM, THEY'RE **STILL** WORSHIPING.

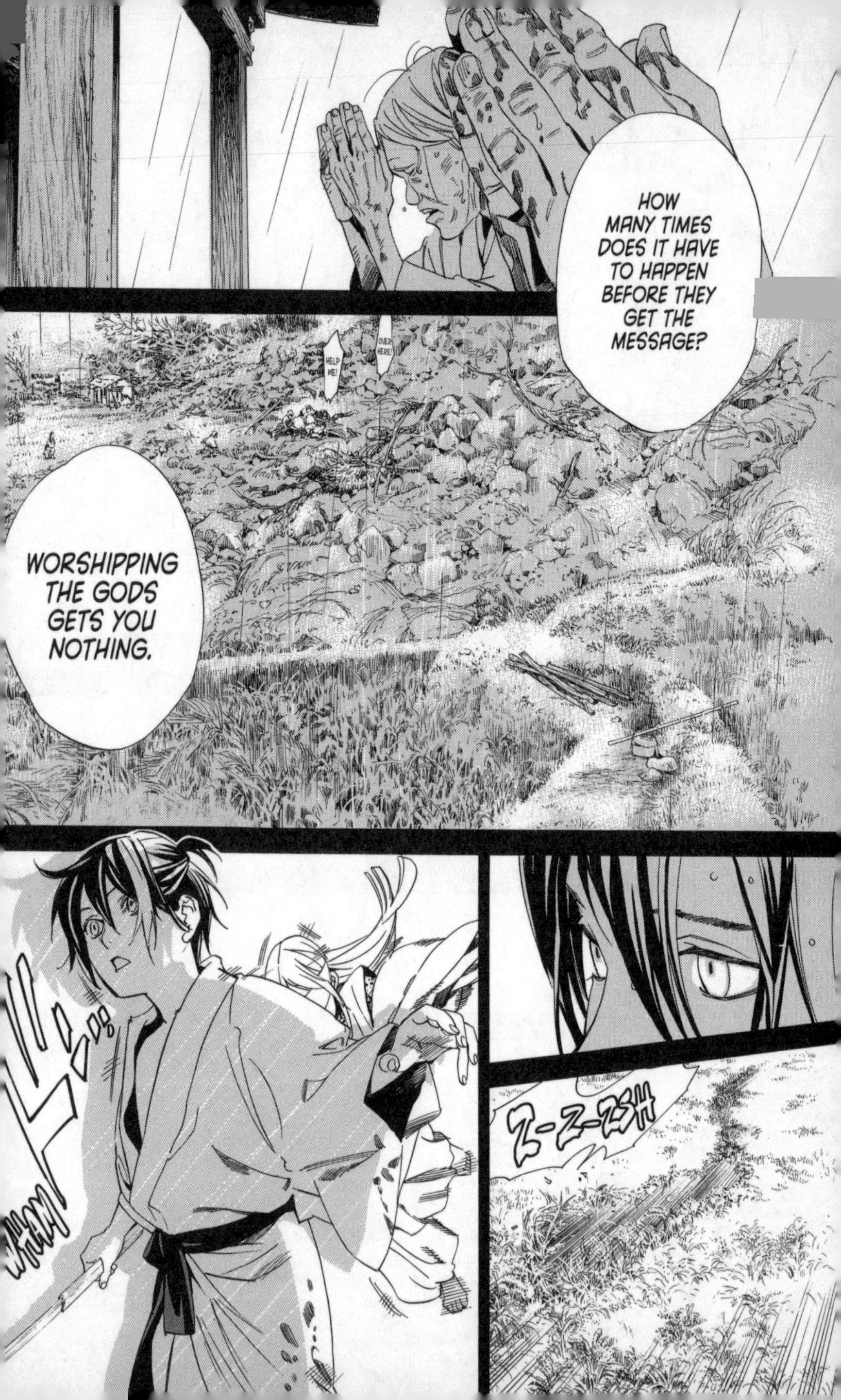
HOW MANY TIMES DOES IT HAVE TO HAPPEN BEFORE THEY GET THE MESSAGE?
OVER HERE!
HELP ME!
WORSHIPPING THE GODS GETS YOU NOTHING.
Z-Z-ZSH

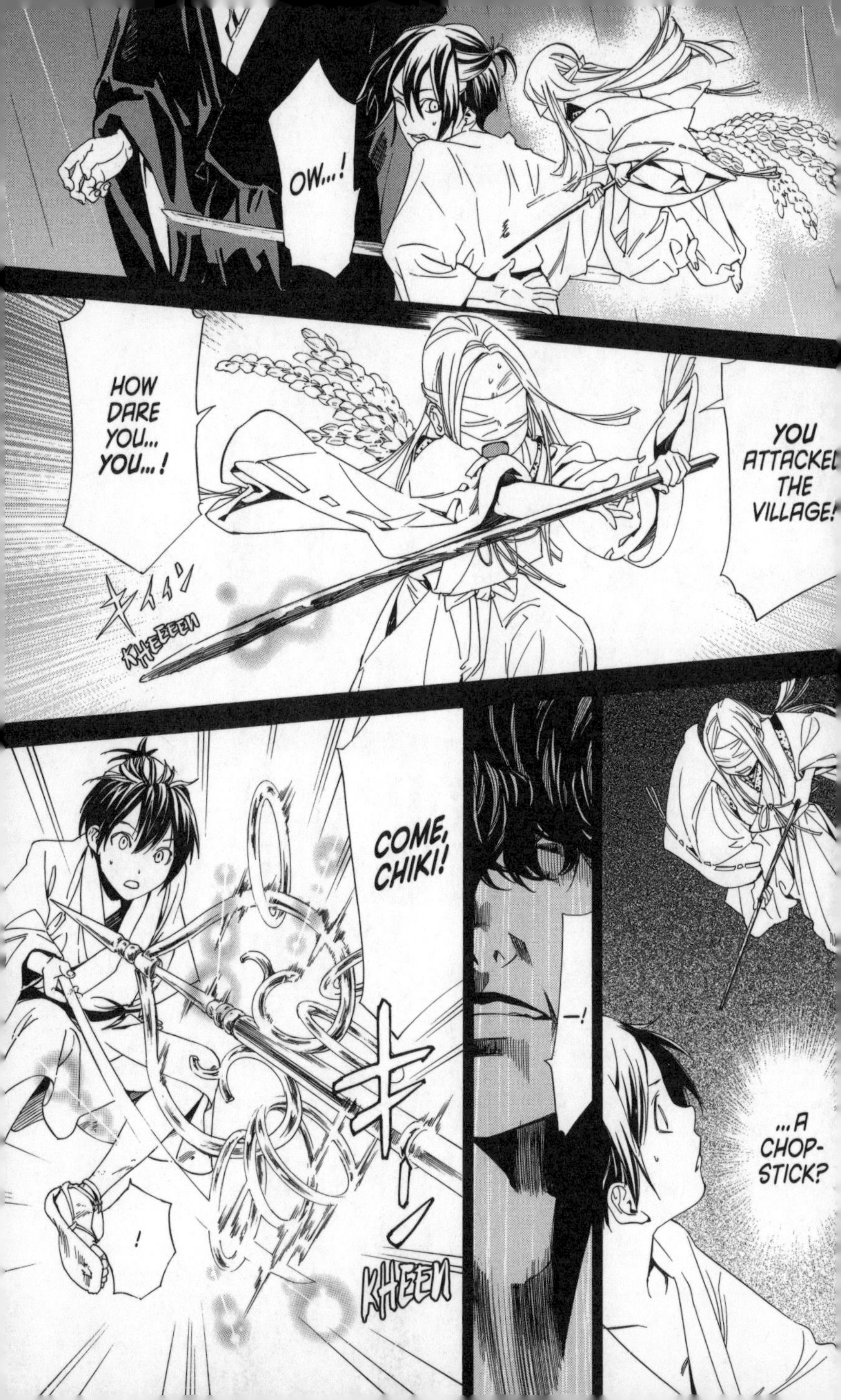
OW...!
YOU ATTACKED THE VILLAGE!
HOW DARE YOU... YOU...!
KHEEEEN
...A CHOP-STICK?
—!
COME, CHIKI!
KHEEN
!

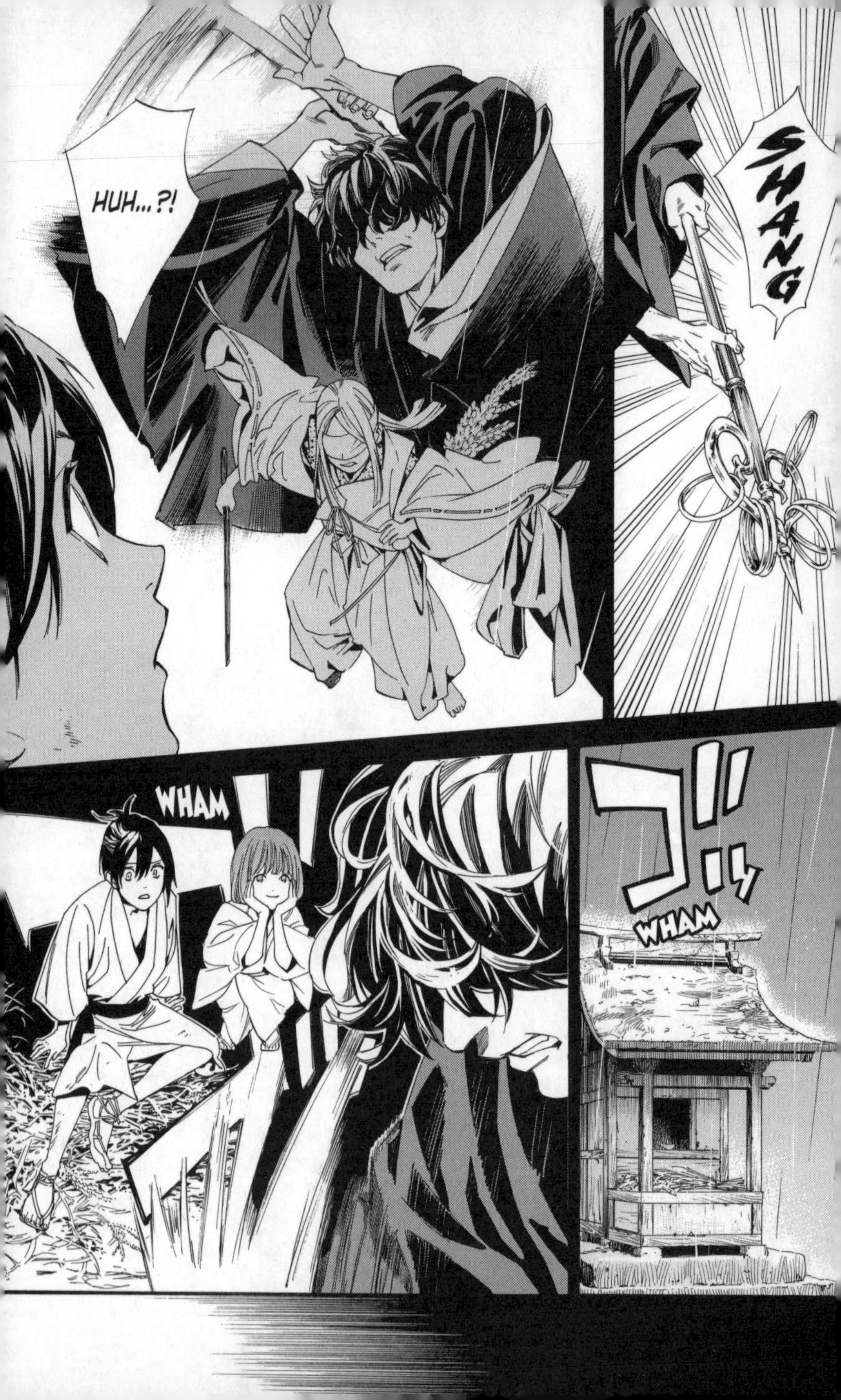
SHANG
HUH...?!
ゴッ
WHAM
WHAM

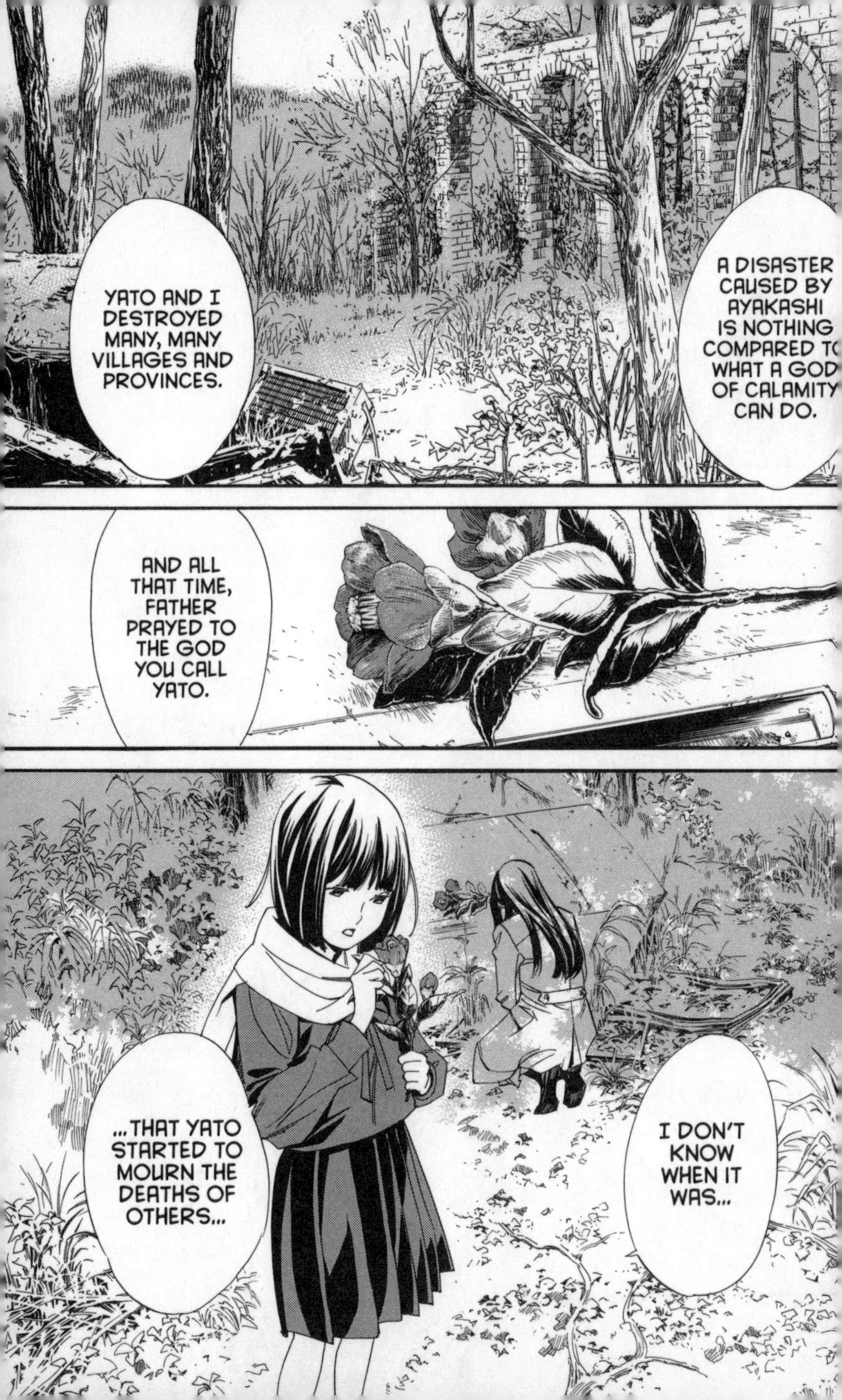
A DISASTER CAUSED BY AYAKASHI IS NOTHING COMPARED TO WHAT A GOD OF CALAMITY CAN DO.
YATO AND I DESTROYED MANY, MANY VILLAGES AND PROVINCES.
AND ALL THAT TIME, FATHER PRAYED TO THE GOD YOU CALL YATO.
I DON'T KNOW WHEN IT WAS...
...THAT YATO STARTED TO MOURN THE DEATHS OF OTHERS...

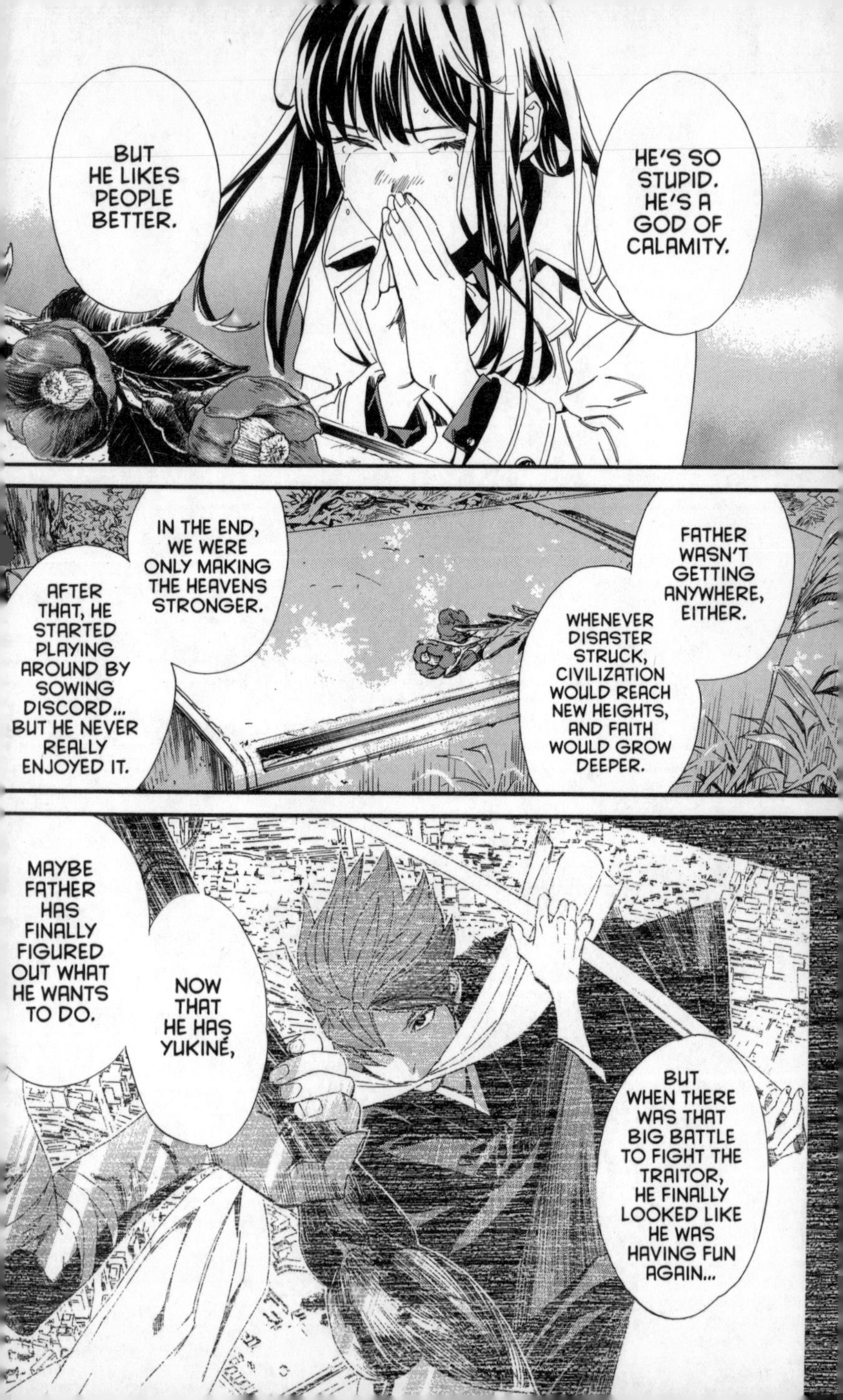
HE'S SO STUPID. HE'S A GOD OF CALAMITY.
BUT HE LIKES PEOPLE BETTER.
FATHER WASN'T GETTING ANYWHERE, EITHER.
WHENEVER DISASTER STRUCK, CIVILIZATION WOULD REACH NEW HEIGHTS, AND FAITH WOULD GROW DEEPER.
IN THE END, WE WERE ONLY MAKING THE HEAVENS STRONGER.
AFTER THAT, HE STARTED PLAYING AROUND BY SOWING DISCORD... BUT HE NEVER REALLY ENJOYED IT.
BUT WHEN THERE WAS THAT BIG BATTLE TO FIGHT THE TRAITOR, HE FINALLY LOOKED LIKE HE WAS HAVING FUN AGAIN...
NOW THAT HE HAS YUKINÉ,
MAYBE FATHER HAS FINALLY FIGURED OUT WHAT HE WANTS TO DO.

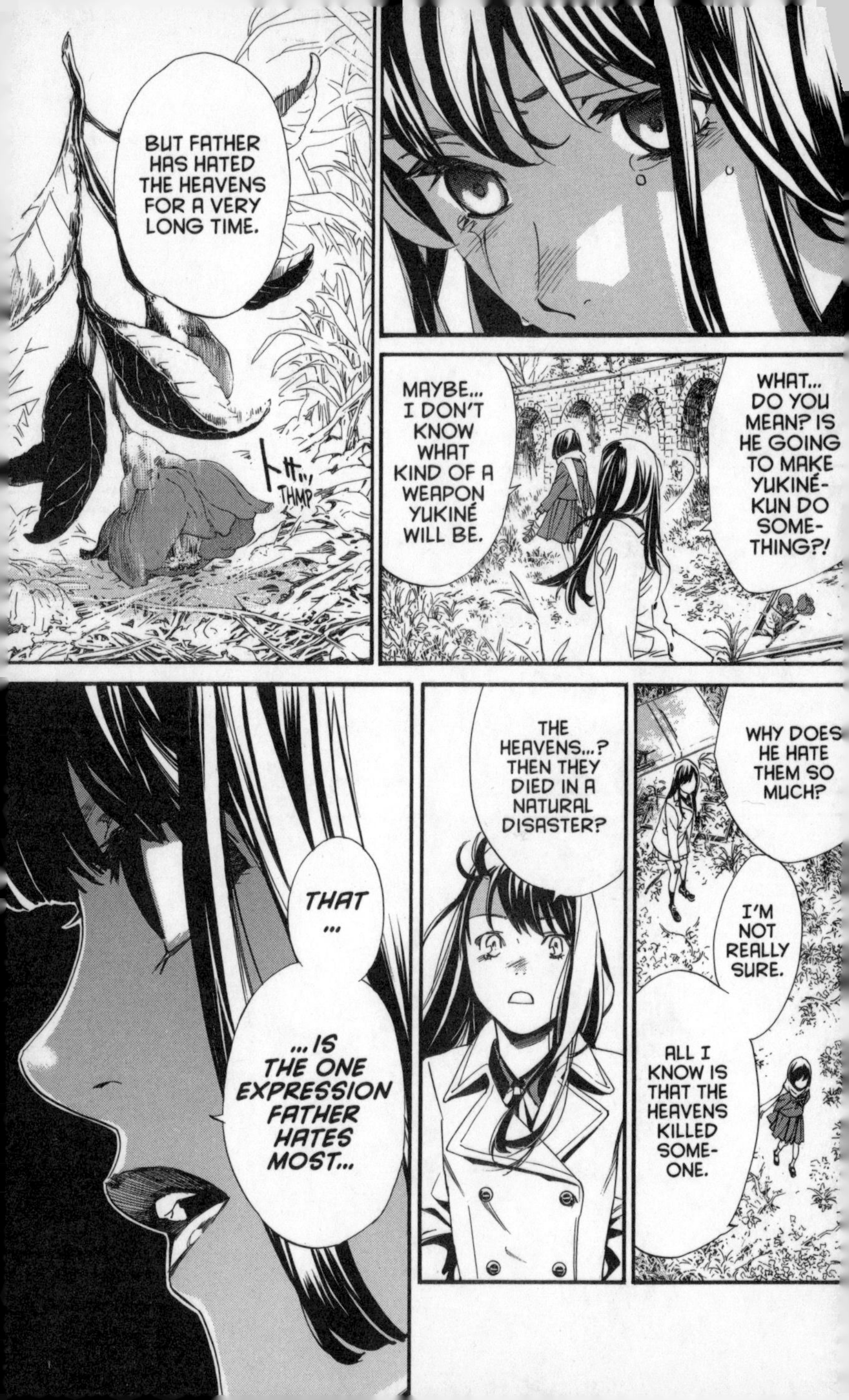
WHAT... DO YOU MEAN? IS HE GOING TO MAKE YUKINÉ-KUN DO SOME-THING?!
MAYBE... I DON'T KNOW WHAT KIND OF A WEAPON YUKINÉ WILL BE.
BUT FATHER HAS HATED THE HEAVENS FOR A VERY LONG TIME.
THMP
WHY DOES HE HATE THEM SO MUCH?
I'M NOT REALLY SURE.
ALL I KNOW IS THAT THE HEAVENS KILLED SOME-ONE.
THE HEAVENS...? THEN THEY DIED IN A NATURAL DISASTER?
THAT...
...IS THE ONE EXPRESSION FATHER HATES MOST...

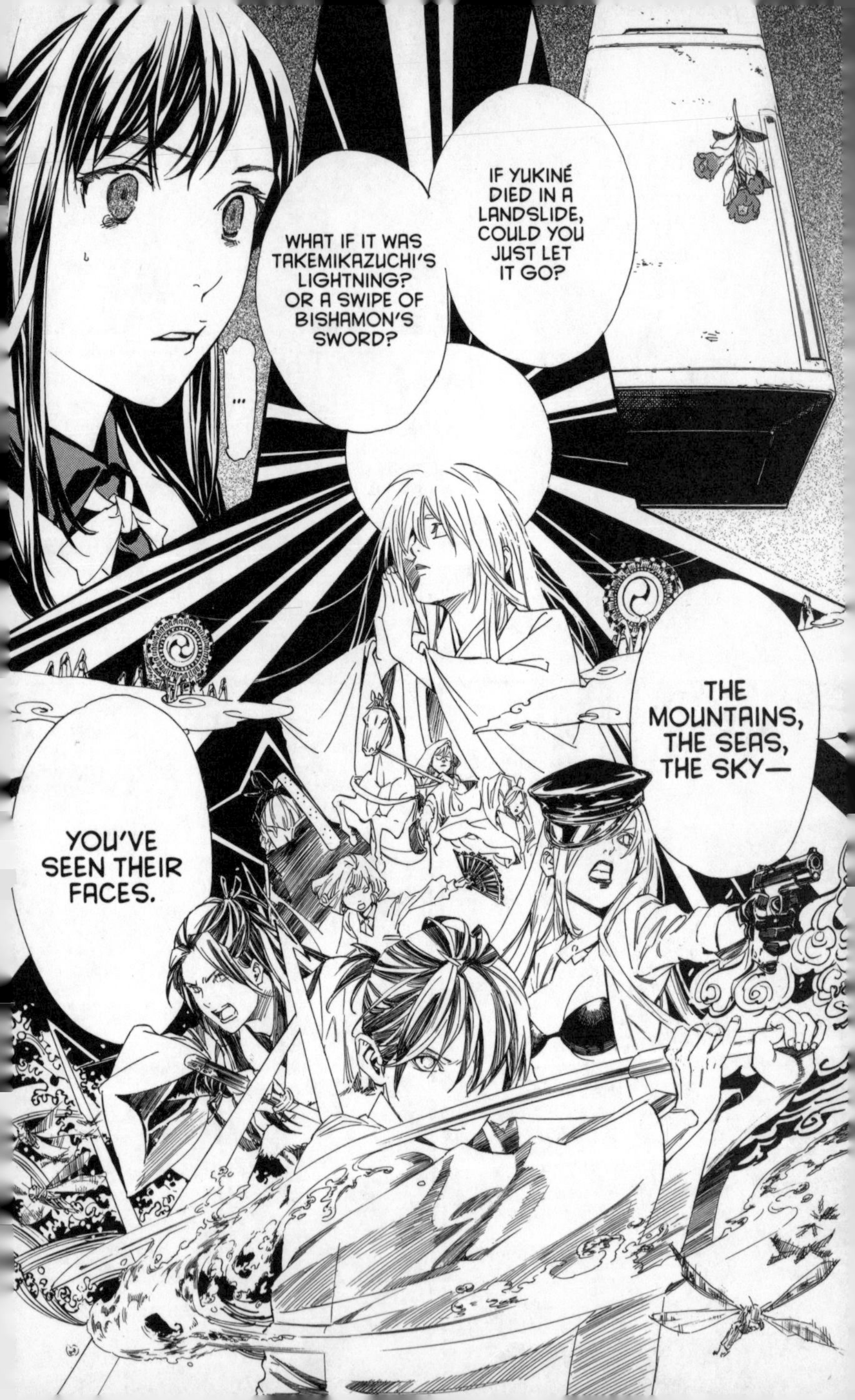
IF YUKINÉ DIED IN A LANDSLIDE, COULD YOU JUST LET IT GO?
WHAT IF IT WAS TAKEMIKAZUCHI'S LIGHTNING? OR A SWIPE OF BISHAMON'S SWORD?
...
THE MOUNTAINS, THE SEAS, THE SKY—
YOU'VE SEEN THEIR FACES.

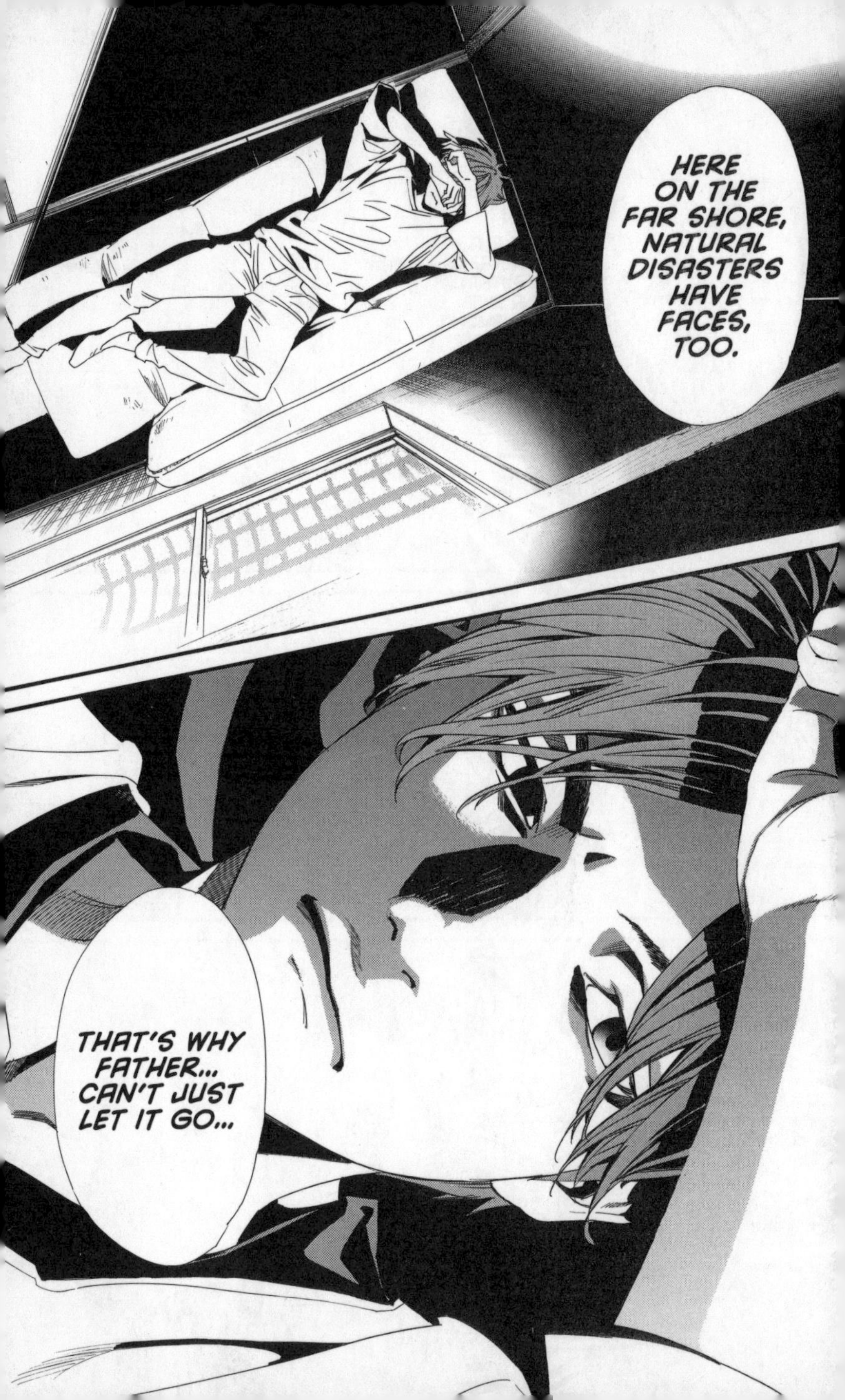
HERE ON THE FAR SHORE, NATURAL DISASTERS HAVE FACES, TOO.
THAT'S WHY FATHER... CAN'T JUST LET IT GO...

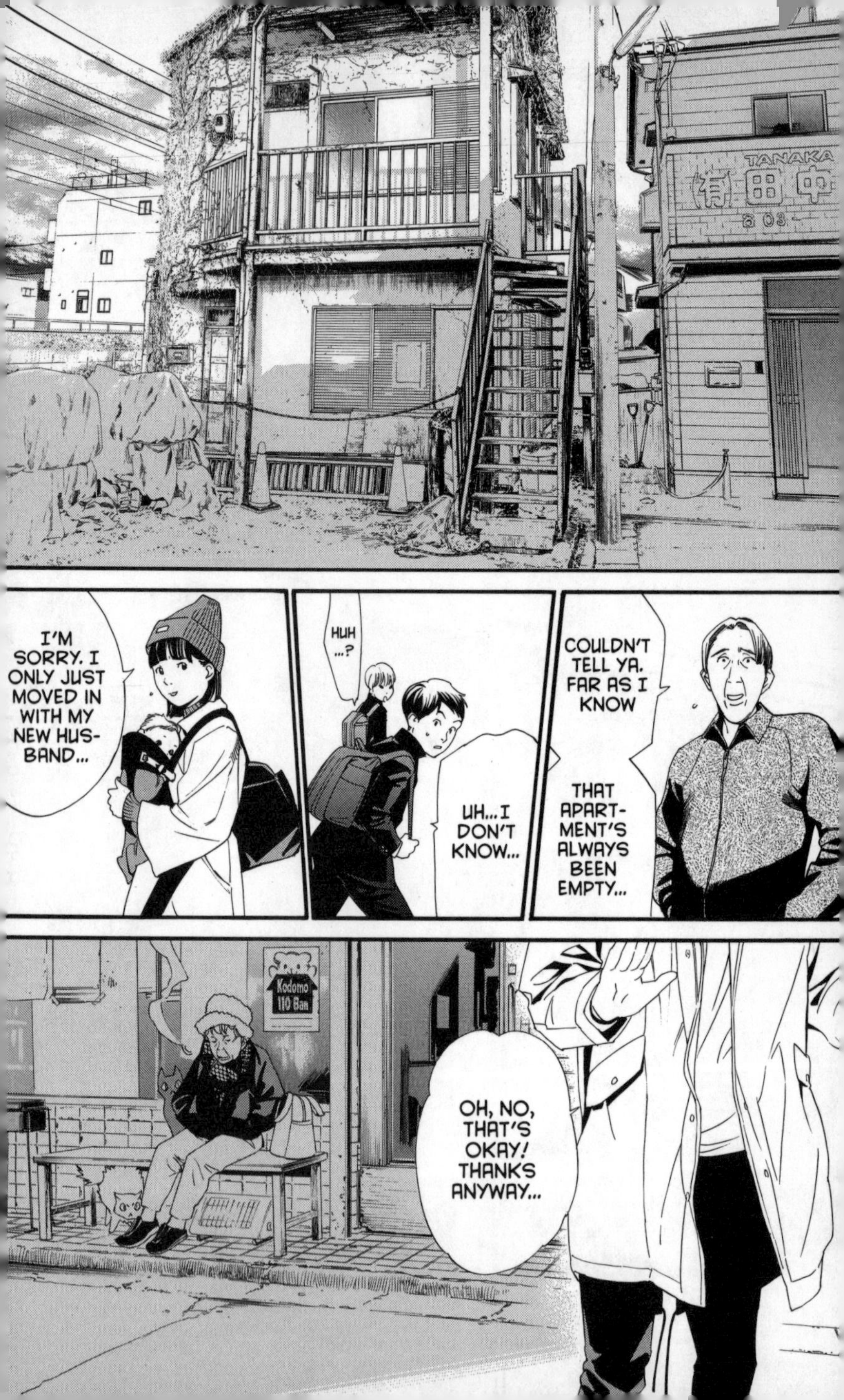
TANAKA
COULDN'T TELL YA. FAR AS I KNOW
THAT APARTMENT'S ALWAYS BEEN EMPTY...
HUH ...?
UH...I DON'T KNOW...
I'M SORRY. I ONLY JUST MOVED IN WITH MY NEW HUSBAND...
OH, NO, THAT'S OKAY! THANKS ANYWAY...
Kodomo 110 Ban

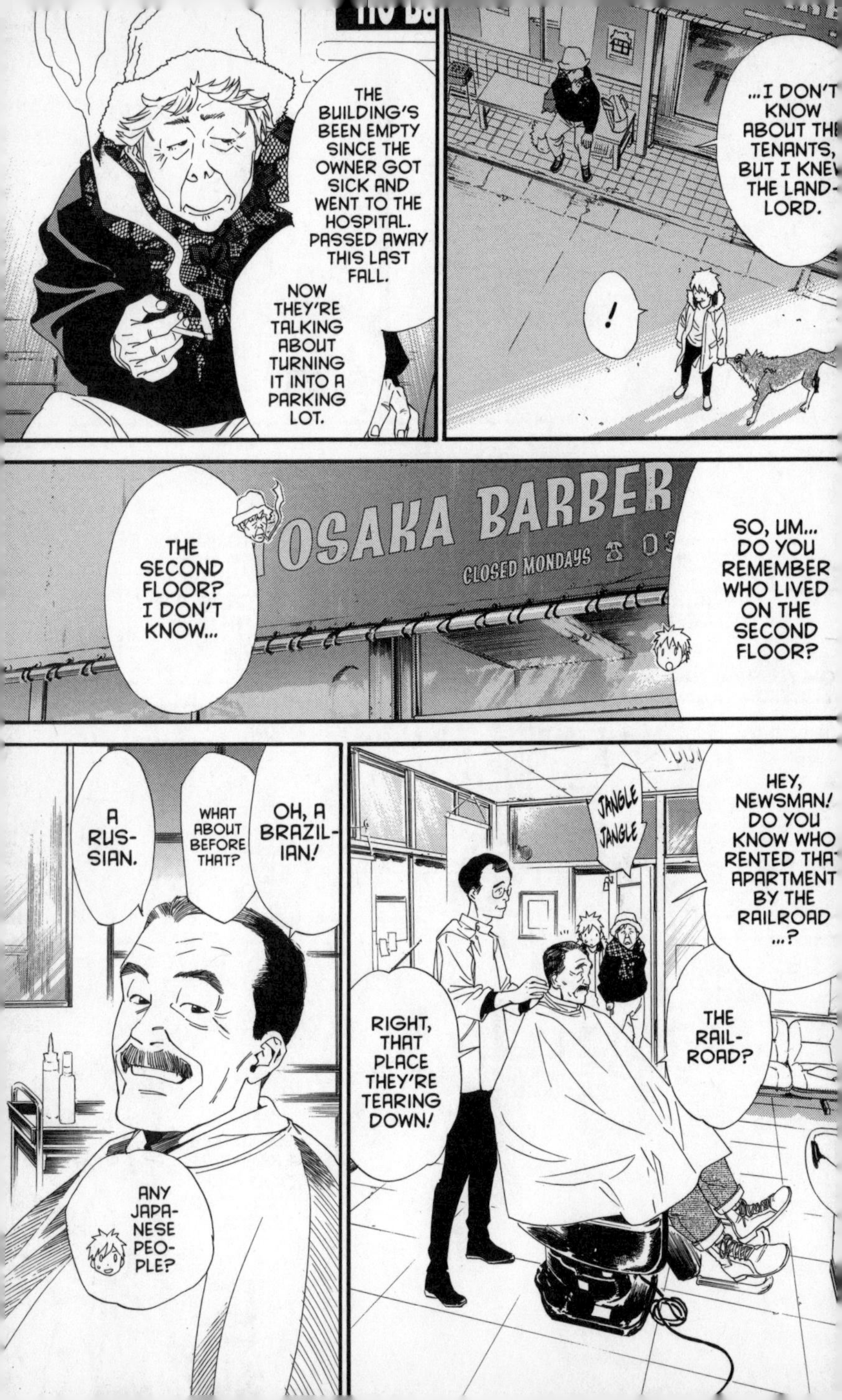
...I DON'T KNOW ABOUT THE TENANTS, BUT I KNEW THE LAND-LORD.
!
THE BUILDING'S BEEN EMPTY SINCE THE OWNER GOT SICK AND WENT TO THE HOSPITAL. PASSED AWAY THIS LAST FALL.
NOW THEY'RE TALKING ABOUT TURNING IT INTO A PARKING LOT.
SO, UM... DO YOU REMEMBER WHO LIVED ON THE SECOND FLOOR?
OSAKA BARBER
CLOSED MONDAYS ☎ 03
THE SECOND FLOOR? I DON'T KNOW...
JANGLE JANGLE
HEY, NEWSMAN! DO YOU KNOW WHO RENTED THAT APARTMENT BY THE RAILROAD ...?
THE RAIL-ROAD?
RIGHT, THAT PLACE THEY'RE TEARING DOWN!
OH, A BRAZIL-IAN!
WHAT ABOUT BEFORE THAT?
A RUS-SIAN.
ANY JAPA-NESE PEO-PLE?

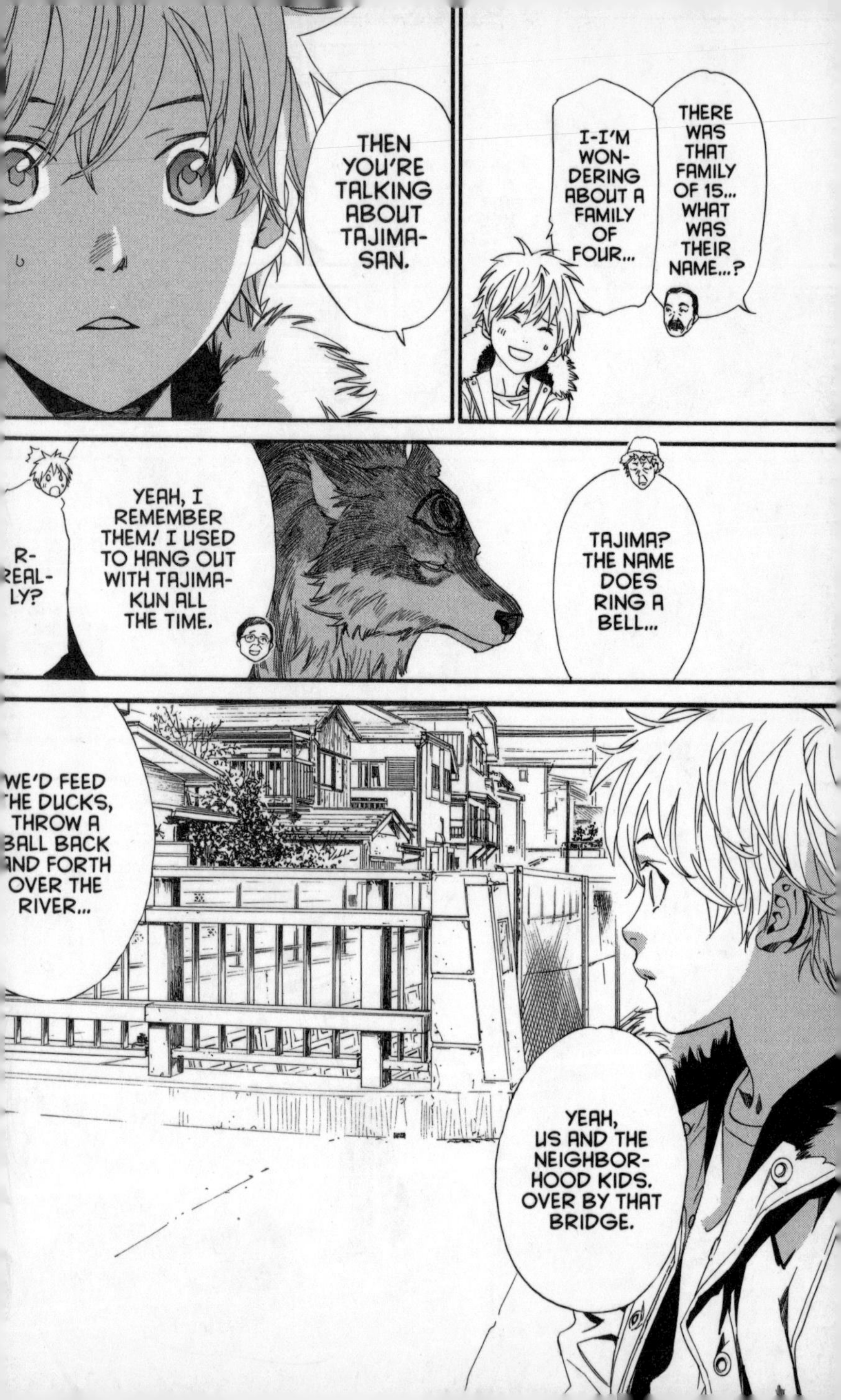
THERE WAS THAT FAMILY OF 15... WHAT WAS THEIR NAME...?
I-I'M WONDERING ABOUT A FAMILY OF FOUR...
THEN YOU'RE TALKING ABOUT TAJIMA-SAN.
TAJIMA? THE NAME DOES RING A BELL...
YEAH, I REMEMBER THEM! I USED TO HANG OUT WITH TAJIMA-KUN ALL THE TIME.
R-REALLY?
YEAH, US AND THE NEIGHBORHOOD KIDS. OVER BY THAT BRIDGE.
WE'D FEED HE DUCKS, THROW A ALL BACK ND FORTH OVER THE RIVER...

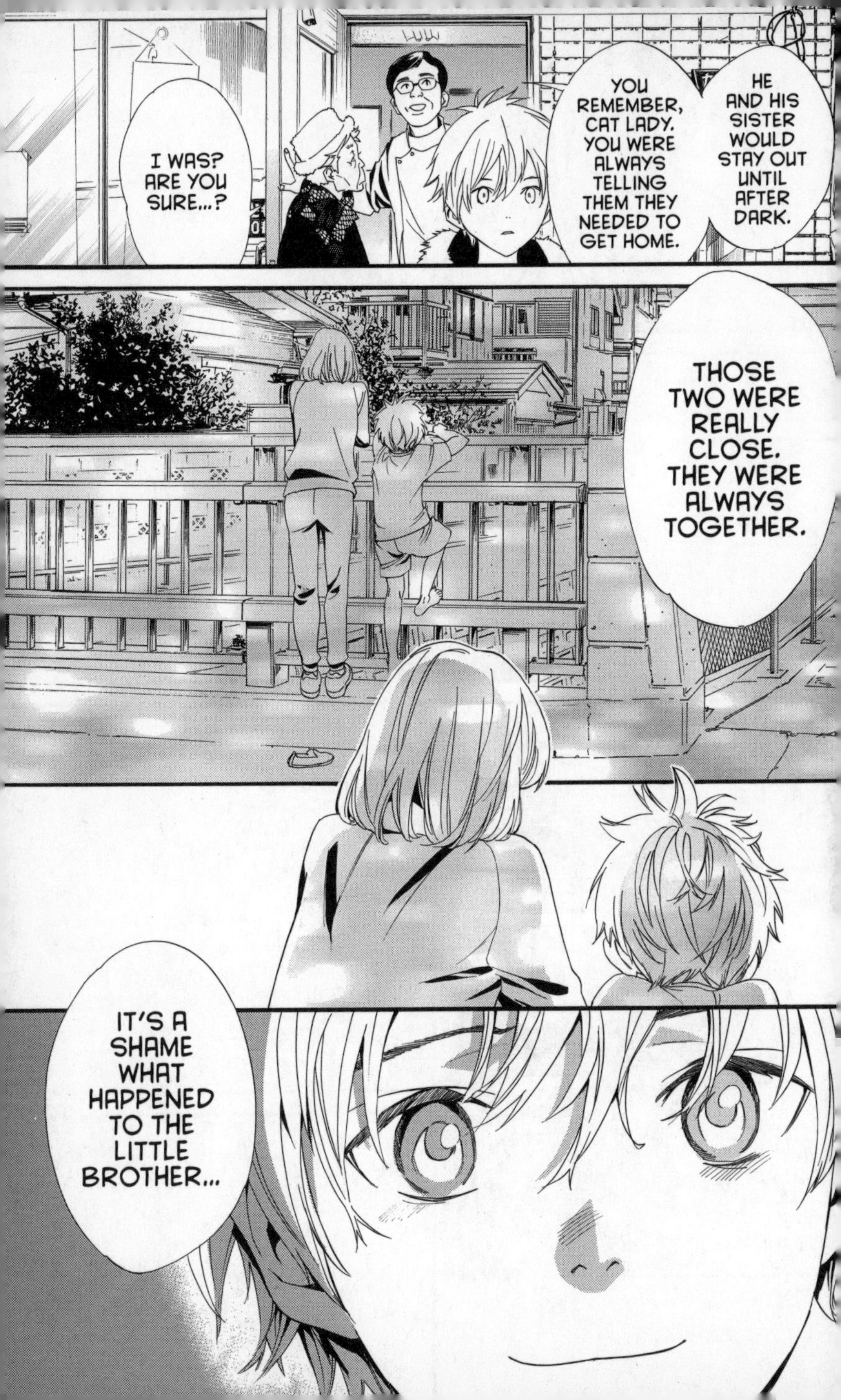
HE AND HIS SISTER WOULD STAY OUT UNTIL AFTER DARK.
YOU REMEMBER, CAT LADY. YOU WERE ALWAYS TELLING THEM THEY NEEDED TO GET HOME.
I WAS? ARE YOU SURE...?
THOSE TWO WERE REALLY CLOSE. THEY WERE ALWAYS TOGETHER.
IT'S A SHAME WHAT HAPPENED TO THE LITTLE BROTHER...

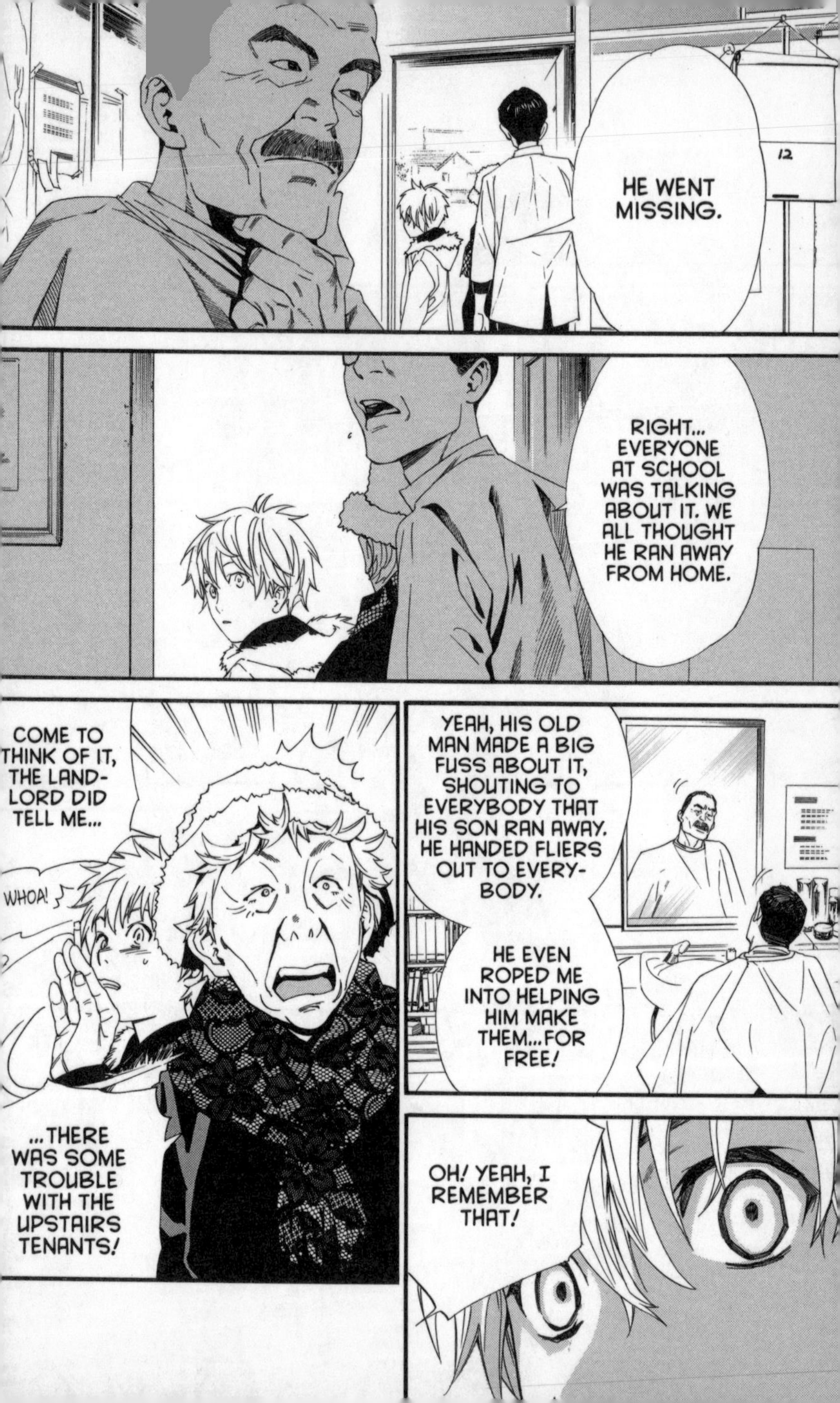
12
HE WENT MISSING.
RIGHT... EVERYONE AT SCHOOL WAS TALKING ABOUT IT. WE ALL THOUGHT HE RAN AWAY FROM HOME.
YEAH, HIS OLD MAN MADE A BIG FUSS ABOUT IT, SHOUTING TO EVERYBODY THAT HIS SON RAN AWAY. HE HANDED FLIERS OUT TO EVERY-BODY.
HE EVEN ROPED ME INTO HELPING HIM MAKE THEM...FOR FREE!
OH! YEAH, I REMEMBER THAT!
COME TO THINK OF IT, THE LAND-LORD DID TELL ME...
WHOA!
...THERE WAS SOME TROUBLE WITH THE UPSTAIRS TENANTS!

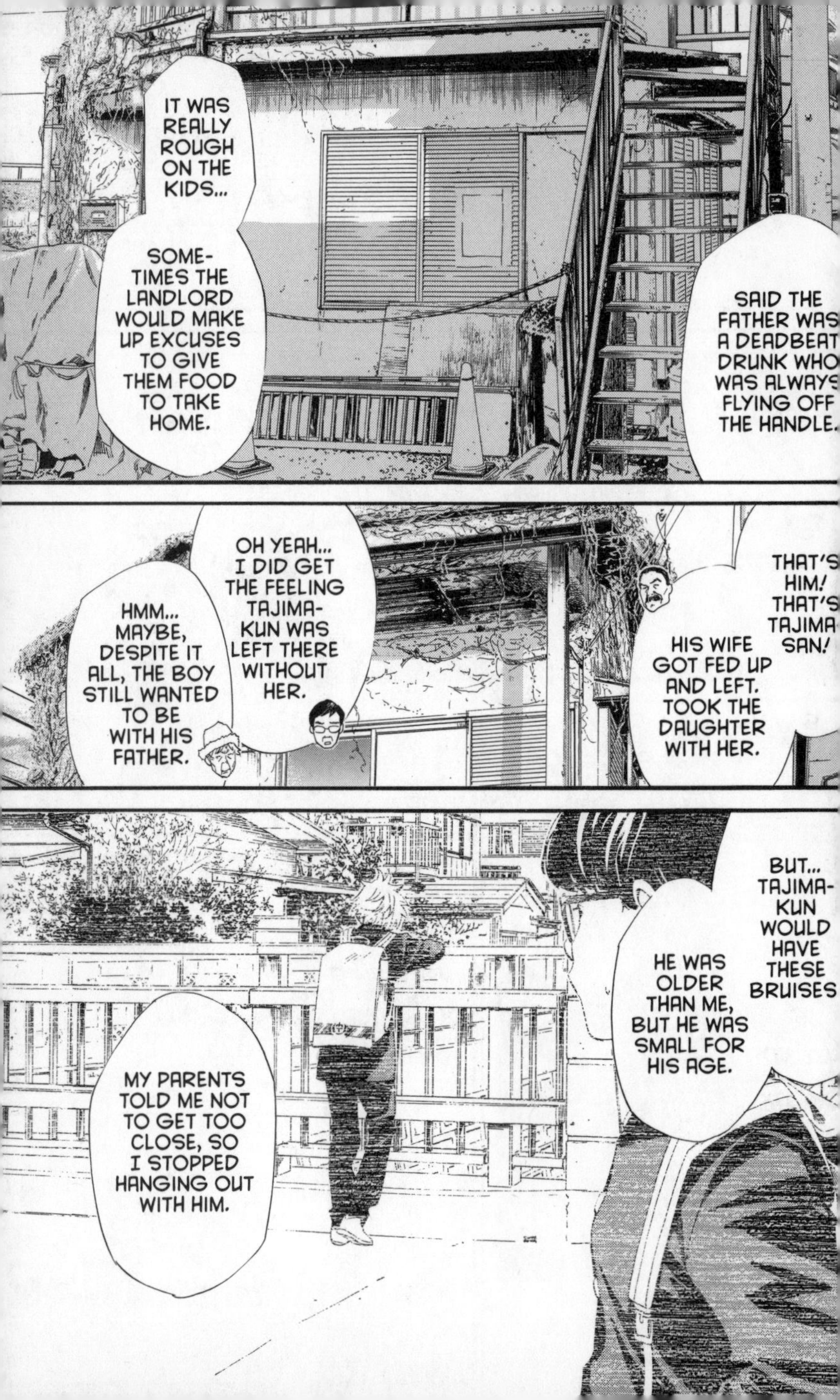
SAID THE FATHER WAS A DEADBEAT DRUNK WHO WAS ALWAYS FLYING OFF THE HANDLE.
IT WAS REALLY ROUGH ON THE KIDS...
SOME-TIMES THE LANDLORD WOULD MAKE UP EXCUSES TO GIVE THEM FOOD TO TAKE HOME.
THAT'S HIM! THAT'S TAJIMA SAN!
HIS WIFE GOT FED UP AND LEFT. TOOK THE DAUGHTER WITH HER.
OH YEAH... I DID GET THE FEELING TAJIMA-KUN WAS LEFT THERE WITHOUT HER.
HMM... MAYBE, DESPITE IT ALL, THE BOY STILL WANTED TO BE WITH HIS FATHER.
BUT... TAJIMA-KUN WOULD HAVE THESE BRUISES
HE WAS OLDER THAN ME, BUT HE WAS SMALL FOR HIS AGE.
MY PARENTS TOLD ME NOT TO GET TOO CLOSE, SO I STOPPED HANGING OUT WITH HIM.

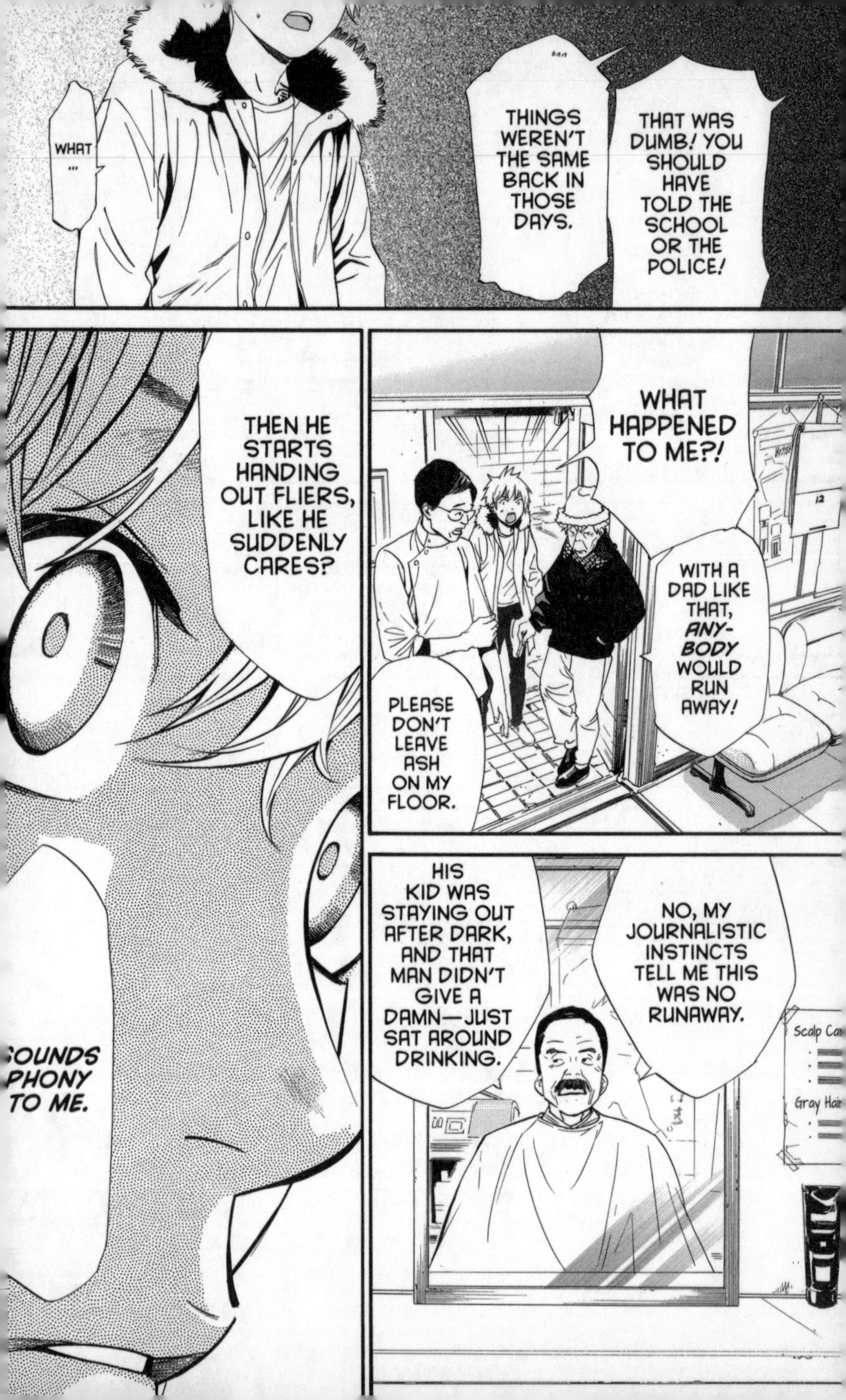
THAT WAS DUMB! YOU SHOULD HAVE TOLD THE SCHOOL OR THE POLICE!
THINGS WEREN'T THE SAME BACK IN THOSE DAYS.
WHAT ...
WHAT HAPPENED TO ME?!
WITH A DAD LIKE THAT, *ANYBODY* WOULD RUN AWAY!
PLEASE DON'T LEAVE ASH ON MY FLOOR.
NO, MY JOURNALISTIC INSTINCTS TELL ME THIS WAS NO RUNAWAY.
HIS KID WAS STAYING OUT AFTER DARK, AND THAT MAN DIDN'T GIVE A DAMN—JUST SAT AROUND DRINKING.
THEN HE STARTS HANDING OUT FLIERS, LIKE HE SUDDENLY CARES?
SOUNDS PHONY TO ME.

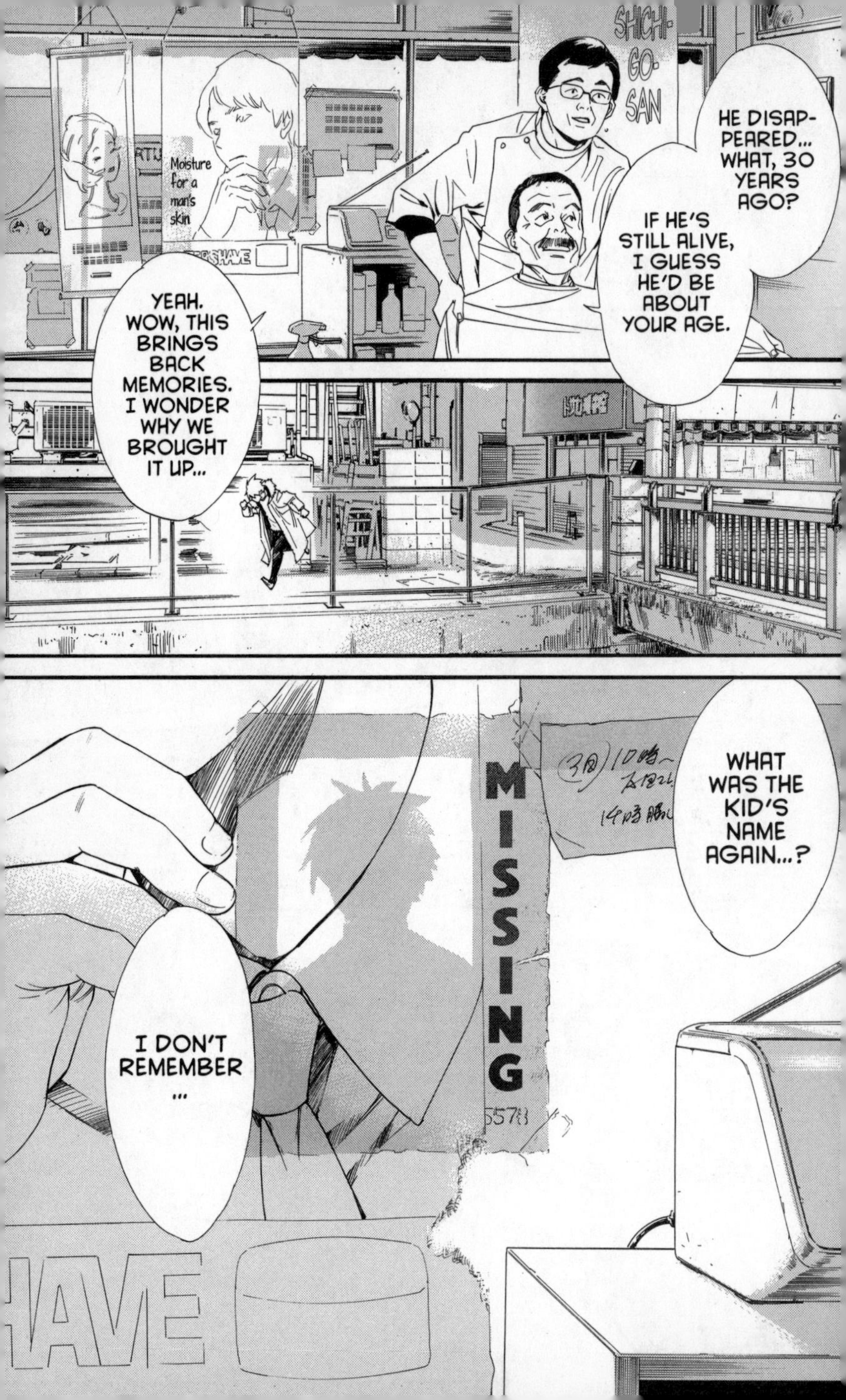
SHICHI-GO-SAN
HE DISAPPEARED... WHAT, 30 YEARS AGO?
IF HE'S STILL ALIVE, I GUESS HE'D BE ABOUT YOUR AGE.
Moisture for a man's skin
YEAH. WOW, THIS BRINGS BACK MEMORIES. I WONDER WHY WE BROUGHT IT UP...
WHAT WAS THE KID'S NAME AGAIN...?
MISSING
I DON'T REMEMBER...

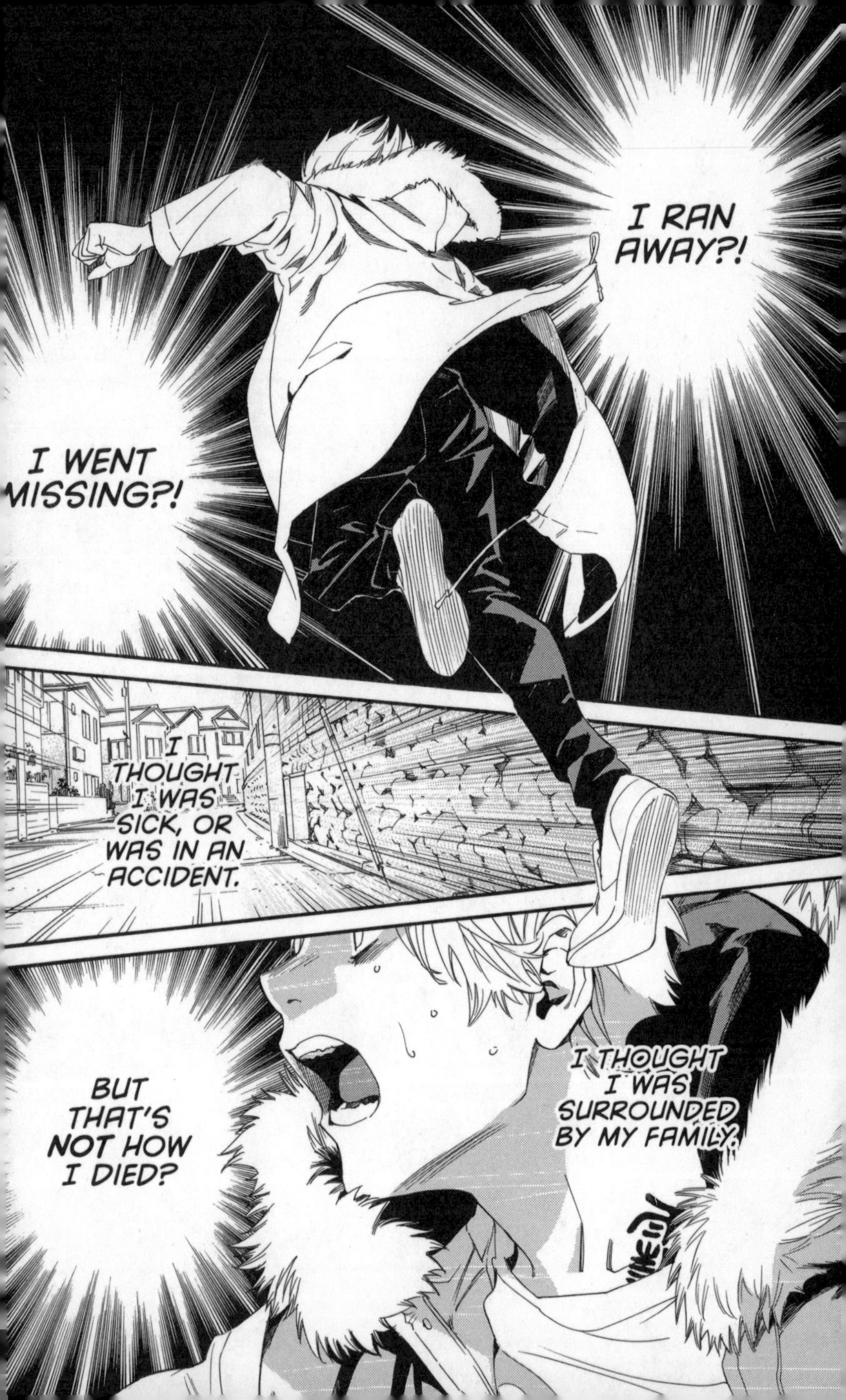
I RAN AWAY?!
I WENT MISSING?!
I THOUGHT I WAS SICK, OR WAS IN AN ACCIDENT.
I THOUGHT I WAS SURROUNDED BY MY FAMILY.
BUT THAT'S NOT HOW I DIED?

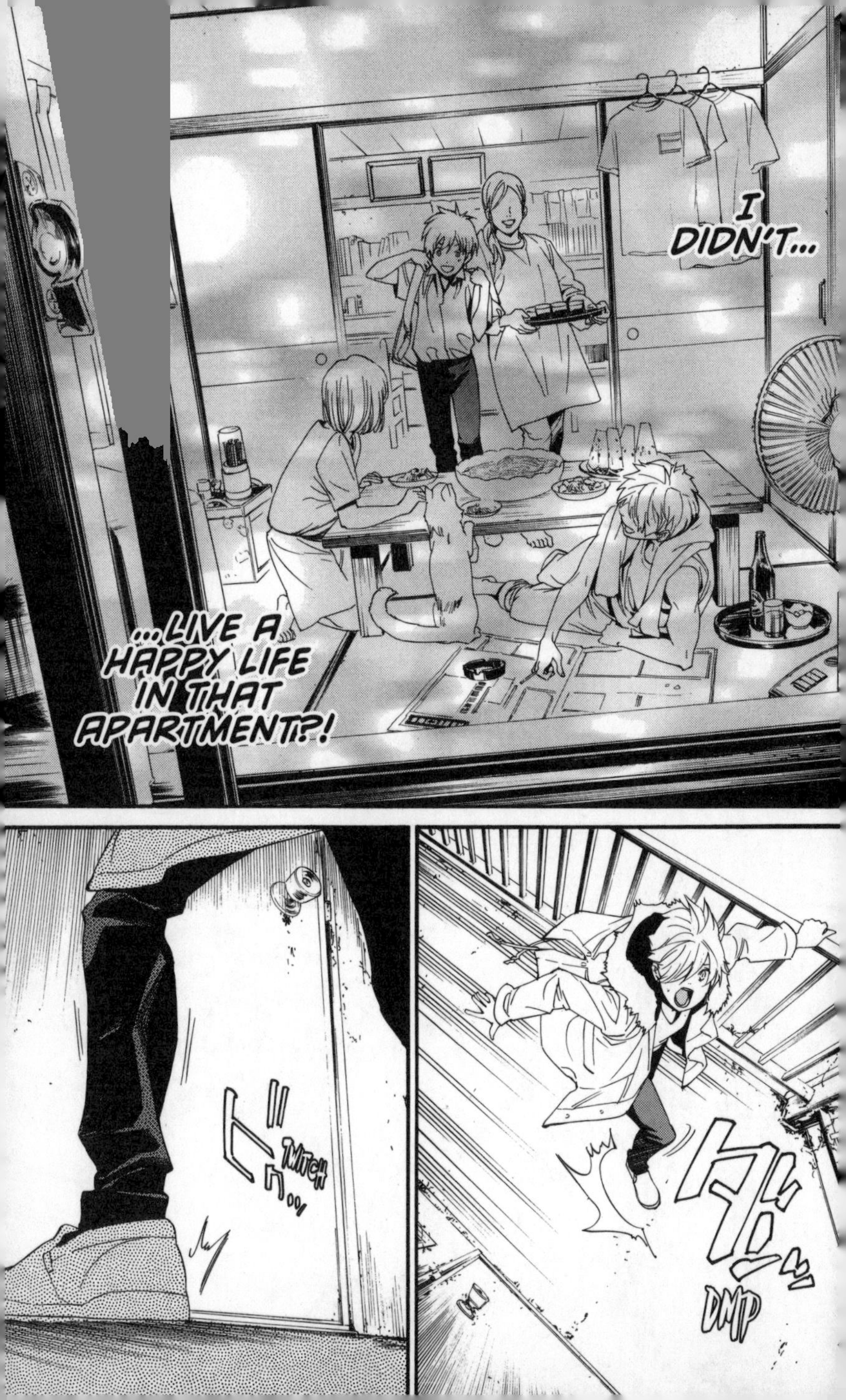
I DIDN'T...
...LIVE A HAPPY LIFE IN THAT APARTMENT?!
DMP
TWITCH

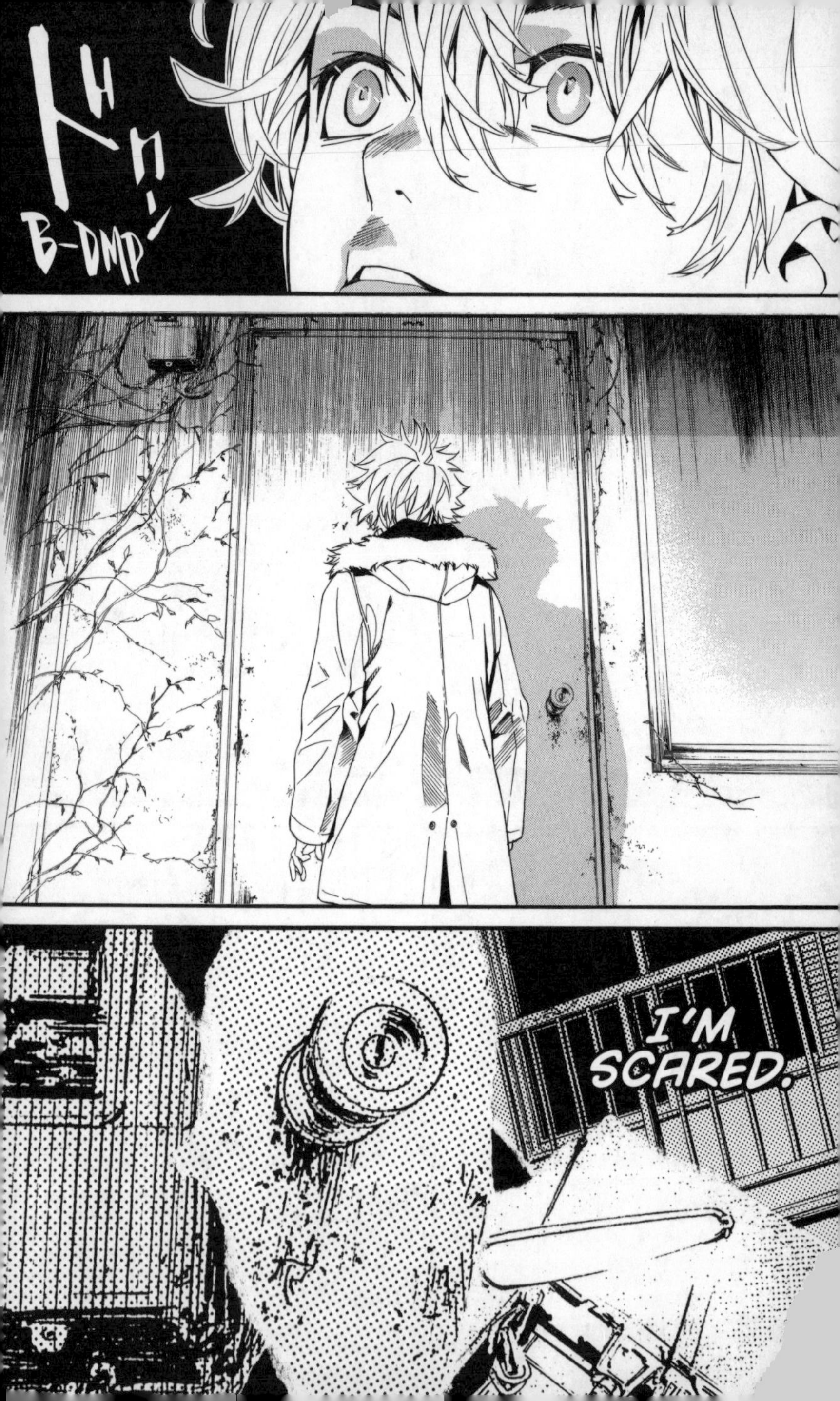
ドクン
B-DMP
I'M SCARED.

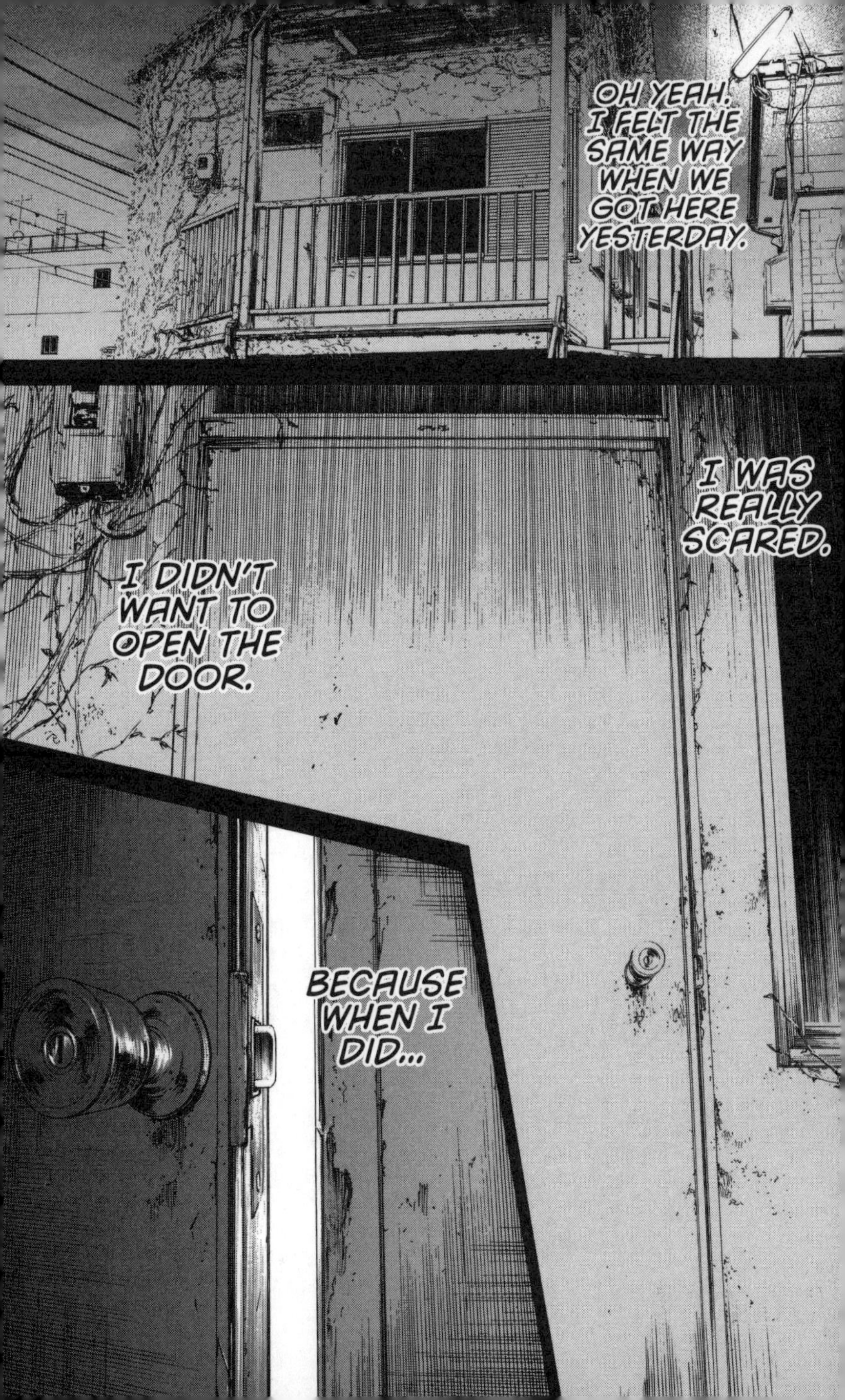
OH YEAH. I FELT THE SAME WAY WHEN WE GOT HERE YESTERDAY.
I WAS REALLY SCARED.
I DIDN'T WANT TO OPEN THE DOOR.
BECAUSE WHEN I DID...

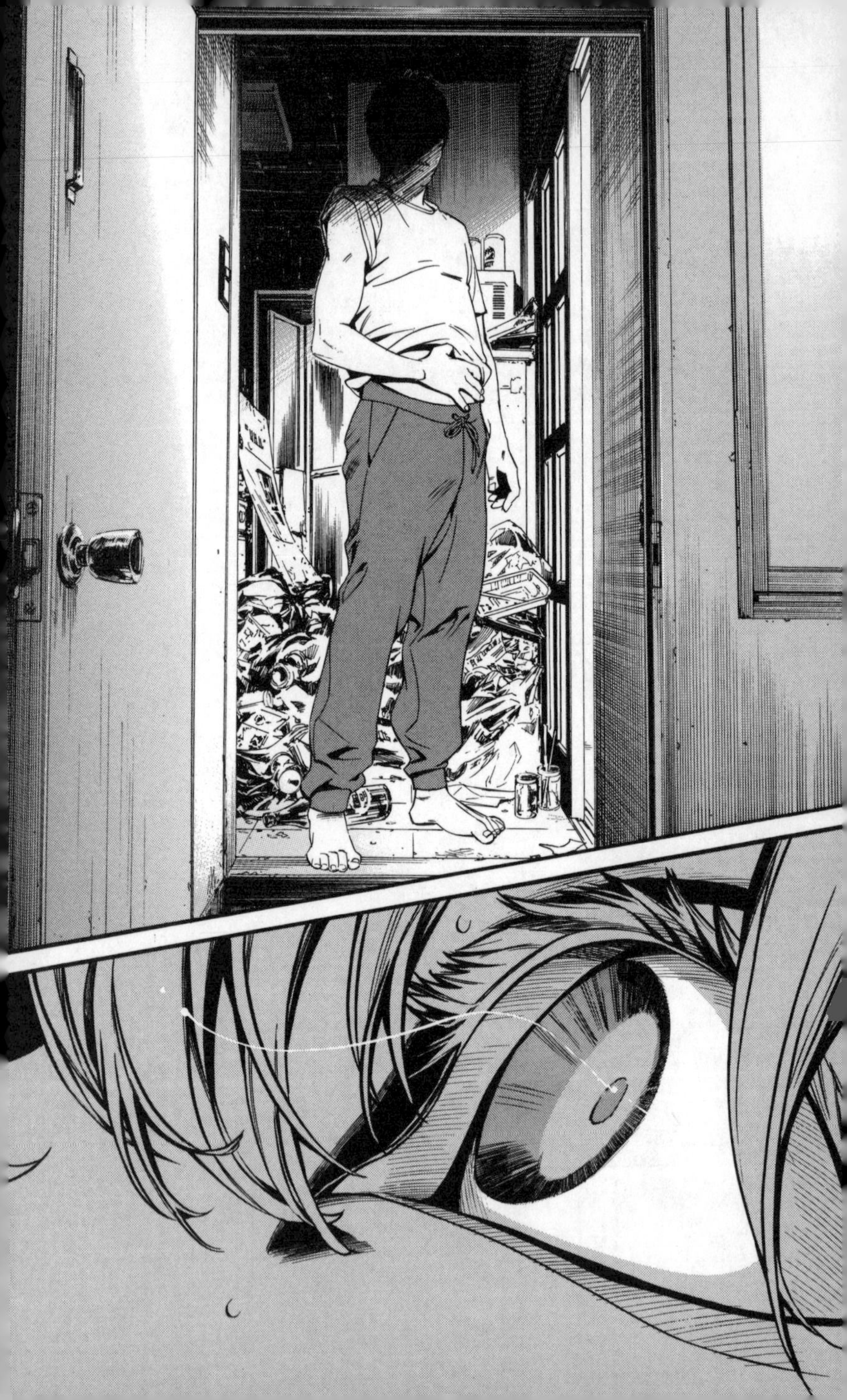

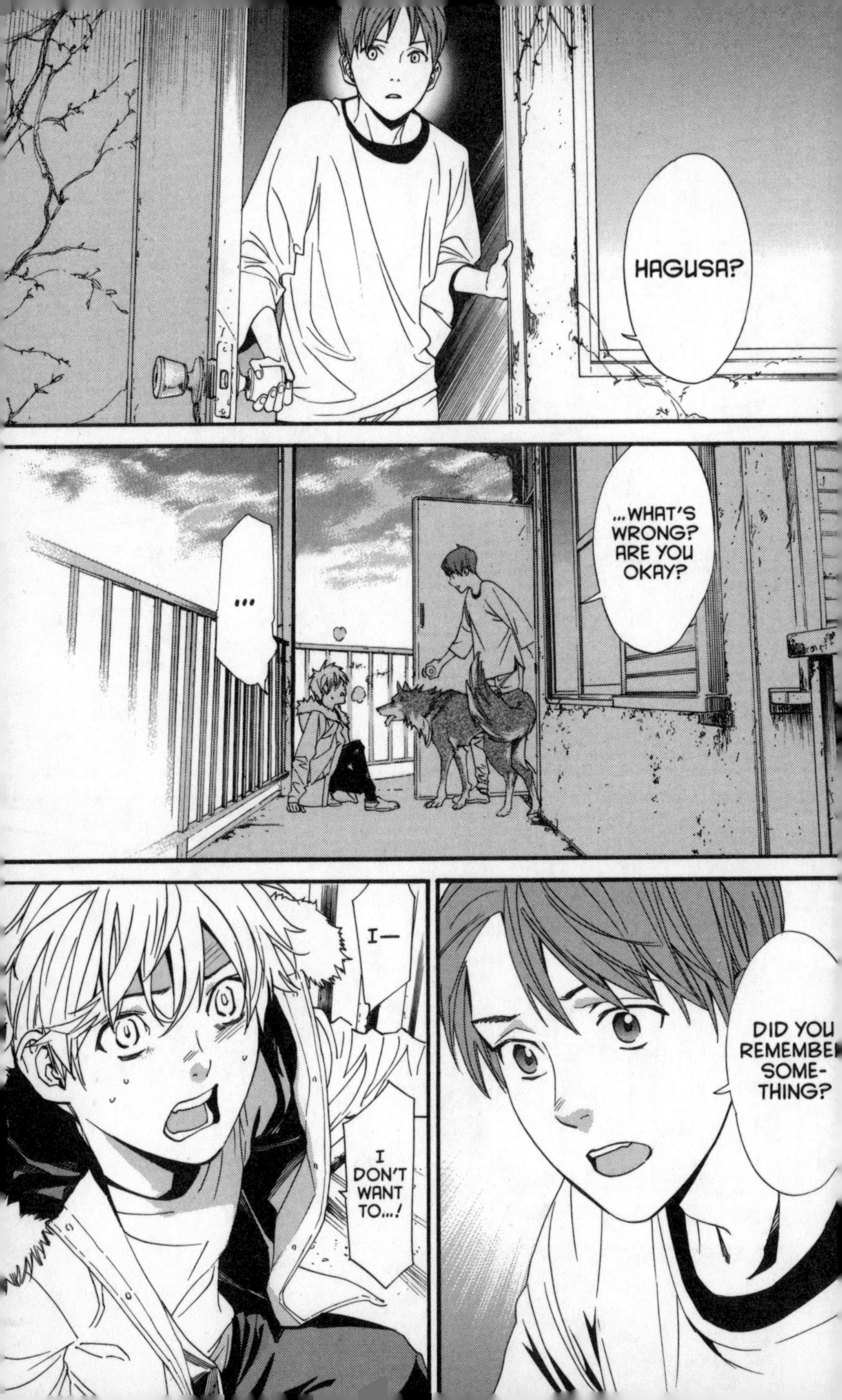
HAGUSA?
...WHAT'S WRONG? ARE YOU OKAY?
...
DID YOU REMEMBE SOME-THING?
I—
I DON'T WANT TO...!

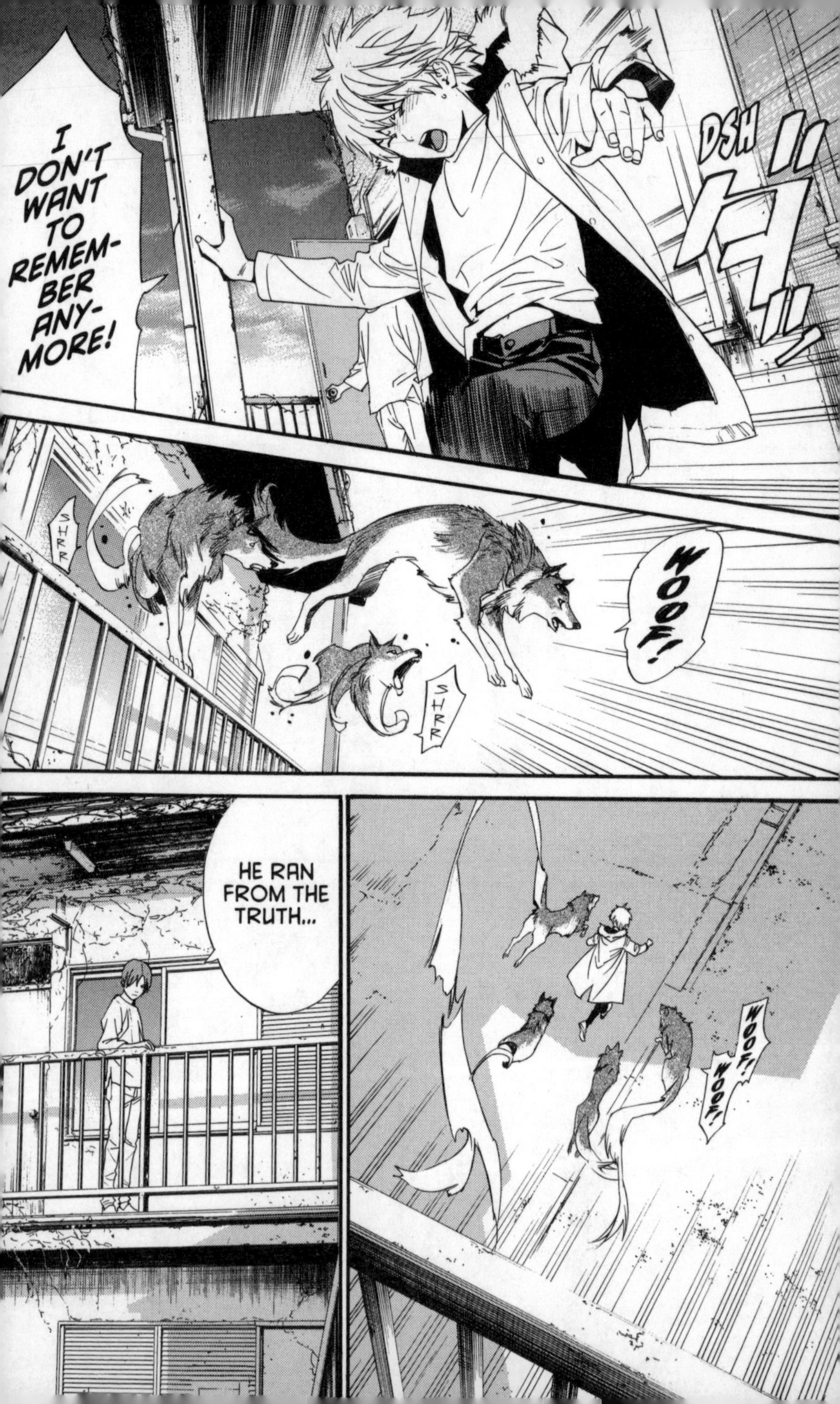
DSH
I DON'T WANT TO REMEMBER ANYMORE!
WOOF!
SHRR
SHRR
WOOF! WOOF!
HE RAN FROM THE TRUTH...

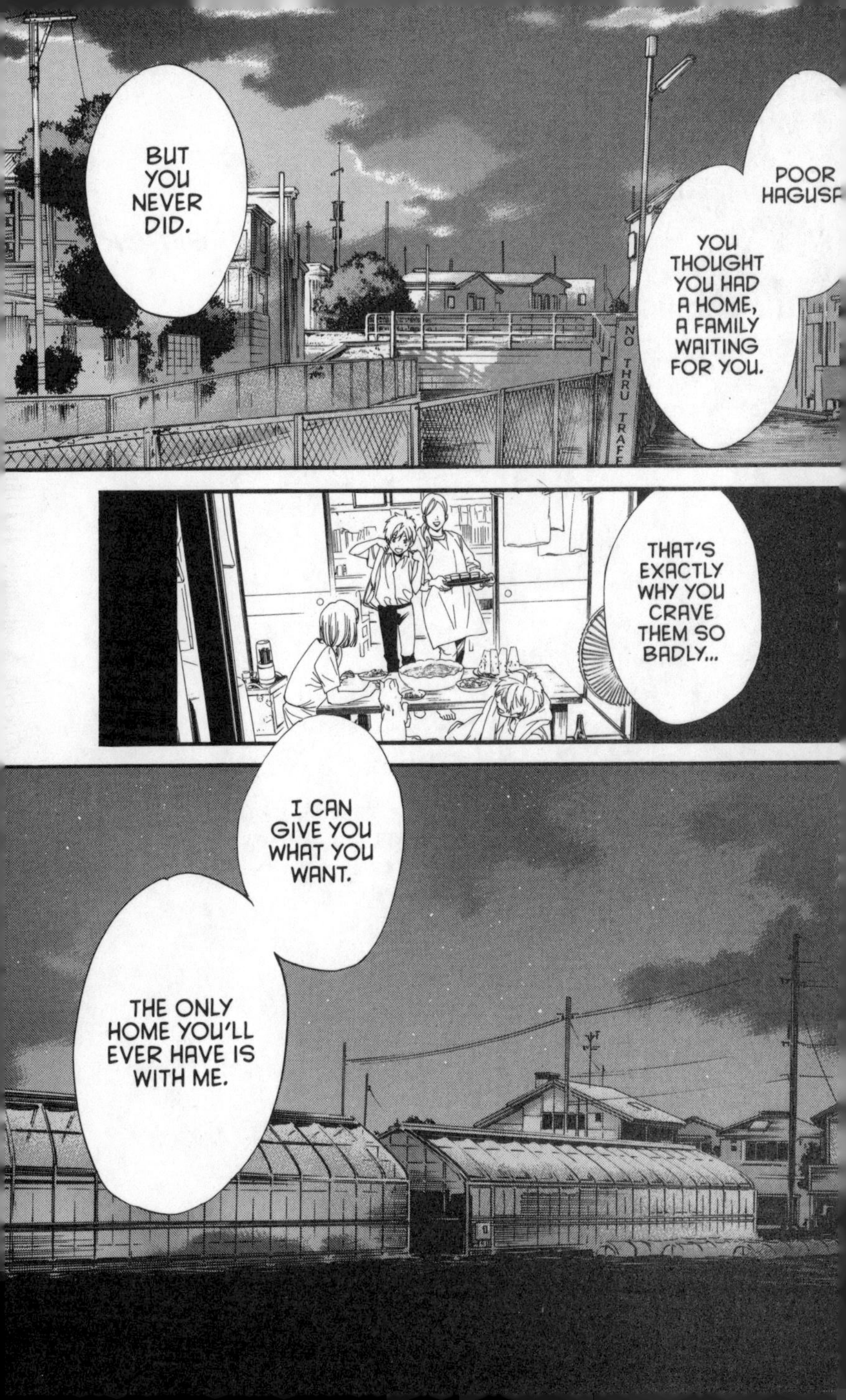
POOR HAGUSA
YOU THOUGHT YOU HAD A HOME, A FAMILY WAITING FOR YOU.
NO THRU TRAFF
BUT YOU NEVER DID.
THAT'S EXACTLY WHY YOU CRAVE THEM SO BADLY...
I CAN GIVE YOU WHAT YOU WANT.
THE ONLY HOME YOU'LL EVER HAVE IS WITH ME.

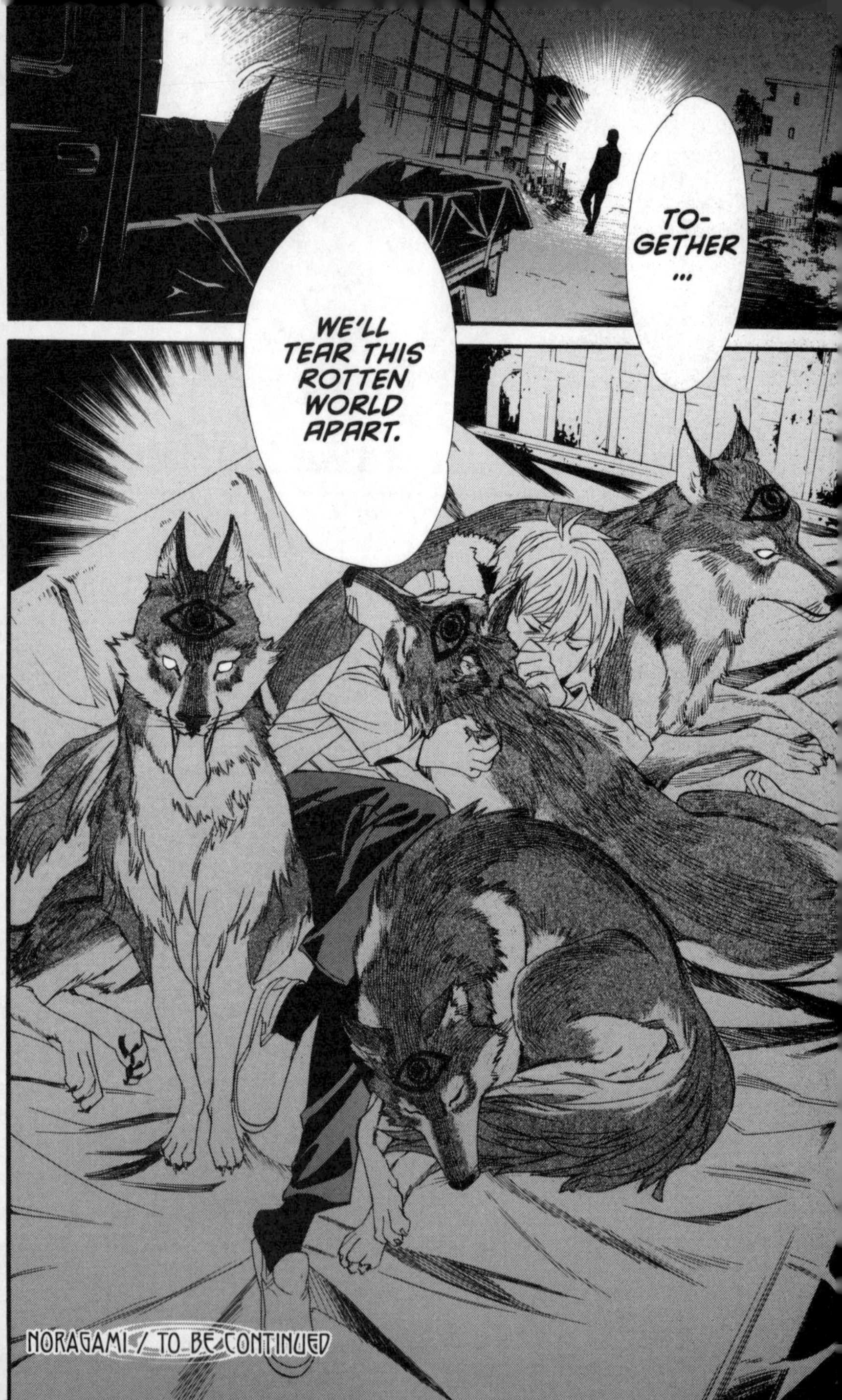
TO-GETHER...
WE'LL TEAR THIS ROTTEN WORLD APART.
NORAGAMI / TO BE CONTINUED

野

貴

神

ATROCIOUS MANGA

BIGGER, STRONGER, TOUGHER

W-WAIT. IS MY NAME...
H...
VHAT'S RONG? YOUR KIN IS REEN.

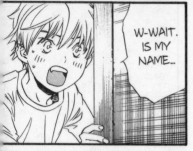

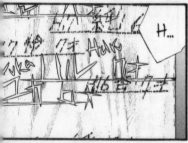

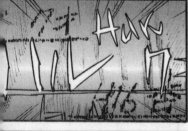

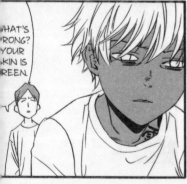

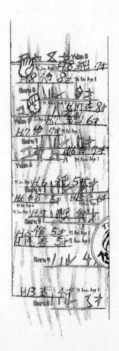

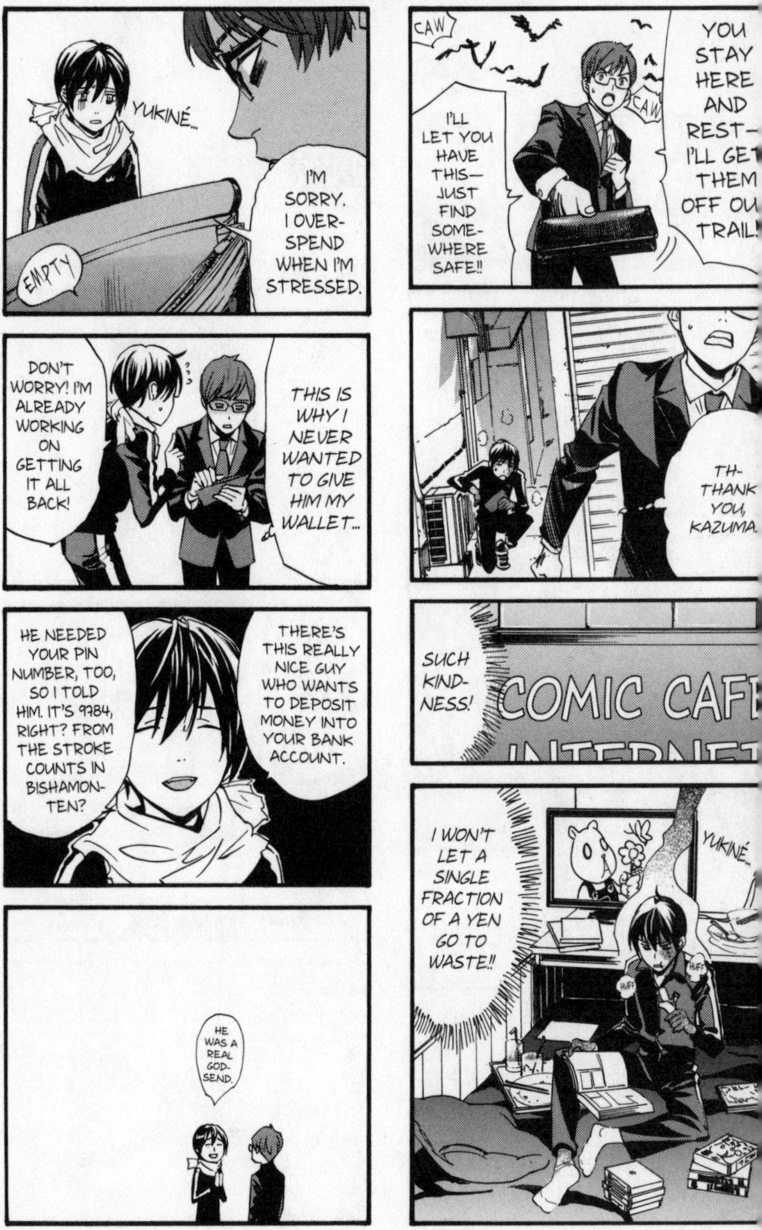
YOU STAY HERE AND REST— I'LL GET THEM OFF OU TRAIL!
CAW
CAW
I'LL LET YOU HAVE THIS— JUST FIND SOME-WHERE SAFE!!
TH- THANK YOU, KAZUMA.
SUCH KIND-NESS!
COMIC CAFE
YUKINÉ...
I WON'T LET A SINGLE FRACTION OF A YEN GO TO WASTE!!
HUFF
HUFF
YUKINÉ...
I'M SORRY. I OVER-SPEND WHEN I'M STRESSED.
EMPTY
THIS IS WHY I NEVER WANTED TO GIVE HIM MY WALLET...
DON'T WORRY! I'M ALREADY WORKING ON GETTING IT ALL BACK!
THERE'S THIS REALLY NICE GUY WHO WANTS TO DEPOSIT MONEY INTO YOUR BANK ACCOUNT.
HE NEEDED YOUR PIN NUMBER, TOO, SO I TOLD HIM. IT'S 9784, RIGHT? FROM THE STROKE COUNTS IN BISHAMON-TEN?
HE WAS A REAL GOD-SEND.

WORRIES

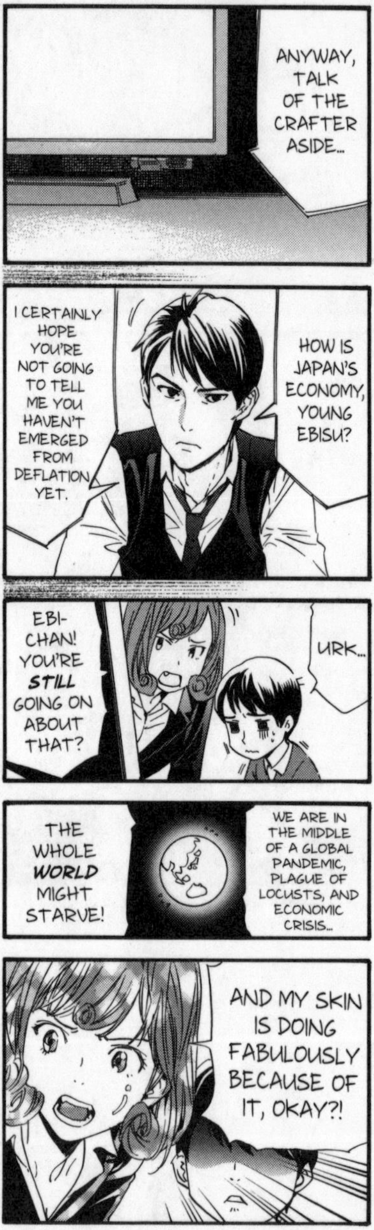
ANYWAY, TALK OF THE CRAFTER ASIDE...
HOW IS JAPAN'S ECONOMY, YOUNG EBISU?
I CERTAINLY HOPE YOU'RE NOT GOING TO TELL ME YOU HAVEN'T EMERGED FROM DEFLATION YET.
URK...
EBI-CHAN! YOU'RE STILL GOING ON ABOUT THAT?
WE ARE IN THE MIDDLE OF A GLOBAL PANDEMIC, PLAGUE OF LOCUSTS, AND ECONOMIC CRISIS...
THE WHOLE WORLD MIGHT STARVE!
AND MY SKIN IS DOING FABULOUSLY BECAUSE OF IT, OKAY?!

FUN FACT

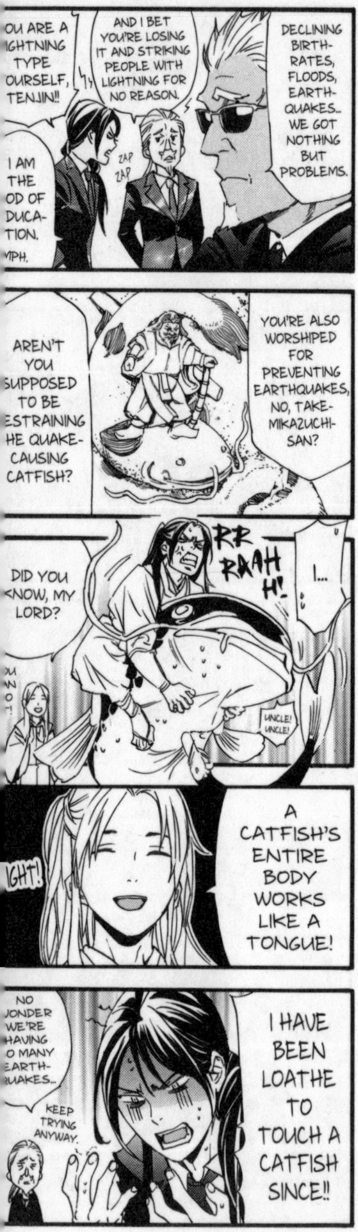
DECLINING BIRTH-RATES, FLOODS, EARTH-QUAKES... WE GOT NOTHING BUT PROBLEMS.
AND I BET YOU'RE LOSING IT AND STRIKING PEOPLE WITH LIGHTNING FOR NO REASON.
OU ARE A IGHTNING TYPE OURSELF, TENJIN!!
ZAP ZAP
I AM THE OD OF DUCA-TION.
MPH.
YOU'RE ALSO WORSHIPED FOR PREVENTING EARTHQUAKES, NO, TAKE-MIKAZUCHI-SAN?
AREN'T YOU UPPOSED TO BE ESTRAINING HE QUAKE-CAUSING CATFISH?
I...
RR RAAH H!
UNCLE! UNCLE!
DID YOU NOW, MY LORD?
A CATFISH'S ENTIRE BODY WORKS LIKE A TONGUE!
IGHT!
I HAVE BEEN LOATHE TO TOUCH A CATFISH SINCE!!
KEEP TRYING ANYWAY.
NO ONDER WE'RE HAVING O MANY ARTH-UAKES...

ECONOMIC STRATEGY

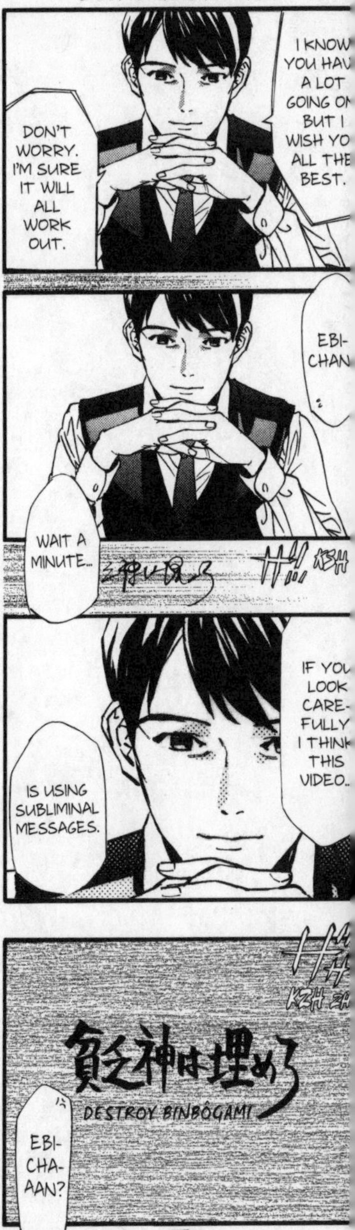
I KNOW YOU HAV A LOT GOING ON BUT I WISH YO ALL THE BEST.
DON'T WORRY. I'M SURE IT WILL ALL WORK OUT.
EBI-CHAN
WAIT A MINUTE...
KZH
IF YOU LOOK CARE-FULLY I THINK THIS VIDEO...
IS USING SUBLIMINAL MESSAGES.
KZH
貧乏神は埋めろ
DESTROY BINBÔGAMI
EBI-CHA-AAN?

OLDER GENERATIONS

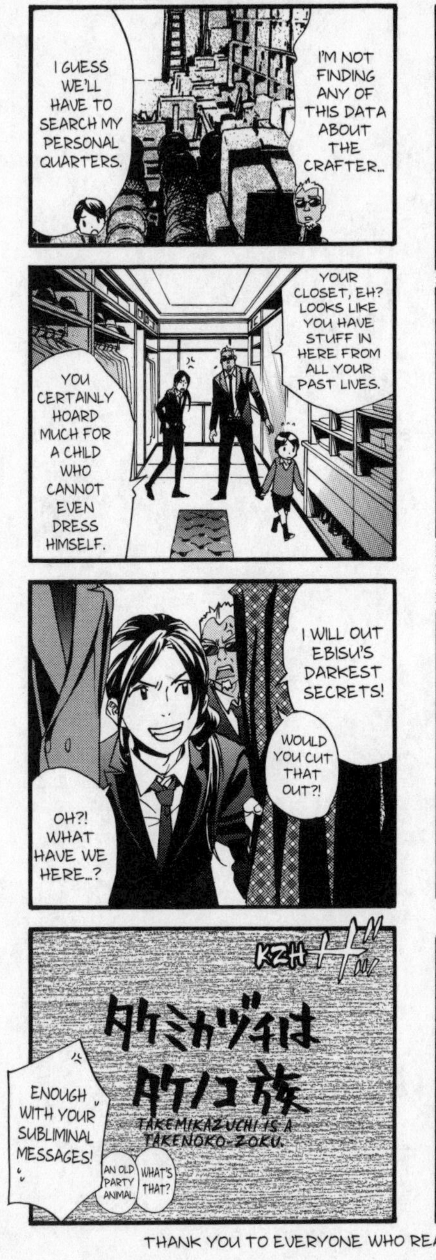
I'M NOT FINDING ANY OF THIS DATA ABOUT THE CRAFTER...
I GUESS WE'LL HAVE TO SEARCH MY PERSONAL QUARTERS.
YOUR CLOSET, EH? LOOKS LIKE YOU HAVE STUFF IN HERE FROM ALL YOUR PAST LIVES.
YOU CERTAINLY HOARD MUCH FOR A CHILD WHO CANNOT EVEN DRESS HIMSELF.
I WILL OUT EBISU'S DARKEST SECRETS!
WOULD YOU CUT THAT OUT?!
OH?! WHAT HAVE WE HERE...?
KZH
タケミカヅチはタケノコ族
TAKEMIKAZUCHI IS A TAKENOKO-ZOKU.
ENOUGH WITH YOUR SUBLIMINAL MESSAGES!
WHAT'S THAT?
AN OLD PARTY ANIMAL

THANK YOU TO EVERYONE WHO READ THIS FAR!!

野

[illegible]

師

TRANSLATION NOTES

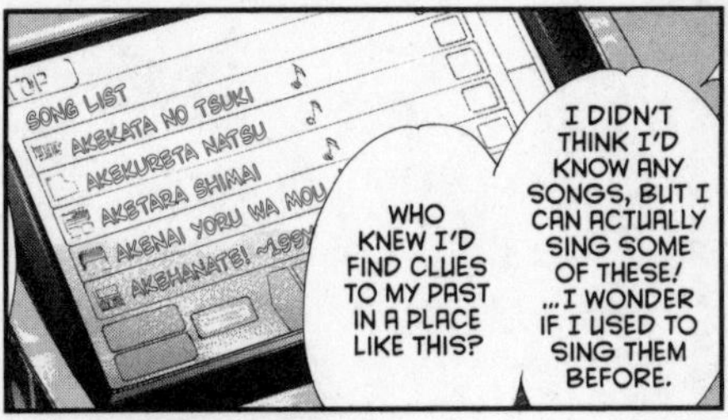
I DIDN'T THINK I'D KNOW ANY SONGS, BUT I CAN ACTUALLY SING SOME OF THESE! ...I WONDER IF I USED TO SING THEM BEFORE.
WHO KNEW I'D FIND CLUES TO MY PAST IN A PLACE LIKE THIS?
SONG LIST
AKEKATA NO TSUKI
AKEKURETA NATSU
AKETARA SHIMAI
AKENAI YORU WA MOU
AKEHANATE!

Karaoke options, page 12
While these songs have similar titles to real world songs, they are not exactly the same. Note also that they are not in alphabetical order, but in Japanese syllabary order. They translate very roughly to "The Moon at Dawn," "Summer All the Time," "Open and Shut," "There Is No Night Without a Dawn," and "Open Wide!"

Seahorses are dragon spawn, page 33
One Japanese word for seahorse is *tatsu-no-otoshigo*, which roughly translates to "illegitimate dragon baby." Ebisu uses that word association to find a name for his new marine friend while at the same time calling Takemikazuchi, the god whose lightning form also resembles the mythical reptile, an illegitimate dragon baby.

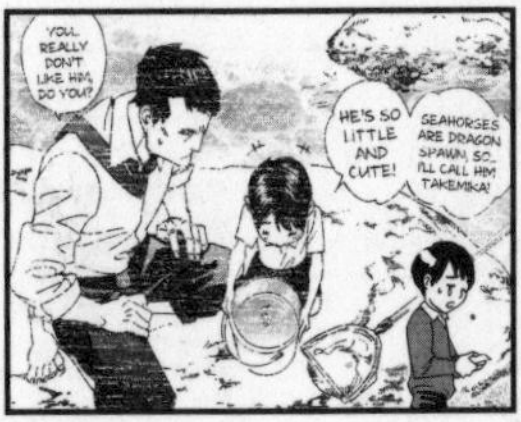
SEAHORSES ARE DRAGON SPAWN, SO... I'LL CALL HIM TAKEMIKA!
HE'S SO LITTLE AND CUTE!
YOU... REALLY DON'T LIKE HIM, DO YOU?

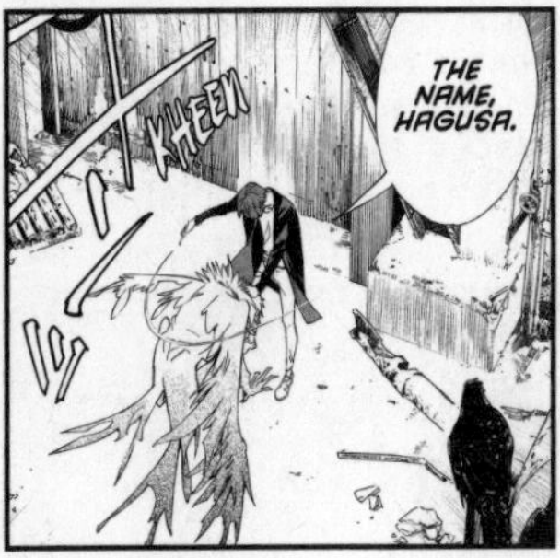
THE NAME, HAGUSA.
KHEEN

Hagusa, page 46
The name Kôto gives his new shinki can mean "ugly" or "bad." It can also refer to a hardy type of grass known in English as green foxtail, among other names. While this plant can be considered an unwanted weed, it also has a structure that makes it a perfect wand-like toy that may attract cats.

No, page 71
In English, Hiyori has just repeated the word "no" three times with varying punctuation to show the progression of her feelings. But it bears pointing out that in the original Japanese, she used two different words. The first two expressions were *masaka*, which is an expression of disbelief or a strong hope that something is not true. It is often translated as, "No," "It can't be," or "Don't tell me..." The final, and more emphatic expression is *iya*, which means "no" in the sense of rejection, as in, "No, that is something I do not want."

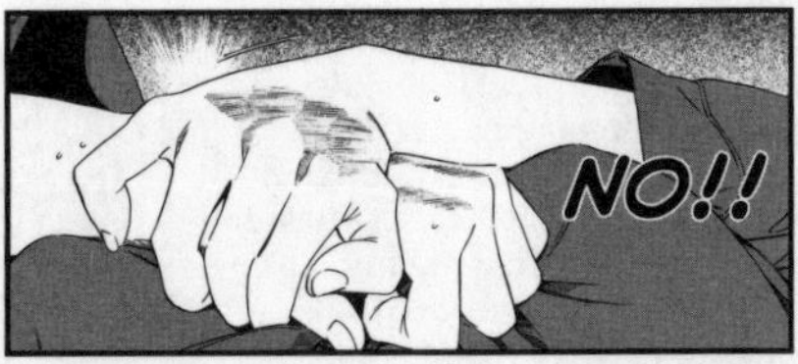
NO!!

He became a part of the family, page 84

More specifically, Hiyori's grandfather became a part of the family known as a *muko*. It can just be translated as "husband," but often it refers more particularly to a man who takes his wife's surname, and may take over her family's business when her parents retire.

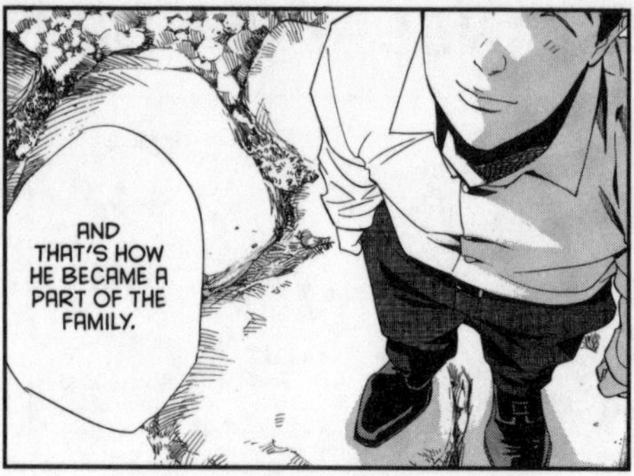
AND THAT'S HOW HE BECAME A PART OF THE FAMILY.

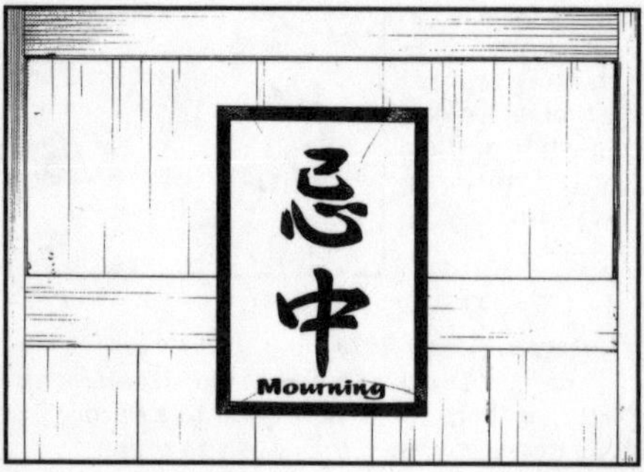
忌中
Mourning

Mourning, page 97

The sign posted at the Iki home indicates not only that there has been a death in the family, but that they are in the period of mourning called *kichû-fuda*, or "mourning sign." This period is one day of intense mourning. The family and friends of the deceased visit to express their condolences, and the immediate family dresses in black or formal wear (such as Hiyori's school uniform).

Ebisusha, page 110

Ebisu's organization is called Ebisusha, where *-sha* is a suffix usually applied to companies, such as the publishing company Kodansha. (In fact, the Ebisusha building does bear a striking resemblance to said publishing company's main office.) The *kanji* used for *-sha* also means "shrine," so the main Ebisusha office building is also his main shrine.

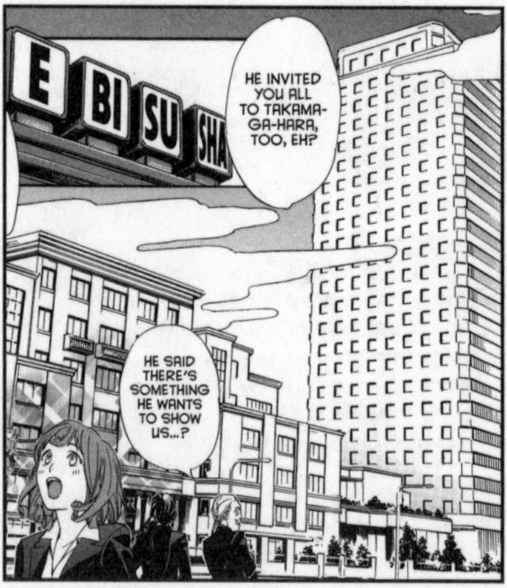
E BI SU SHA
HE INVITED YOU ALL TO TAKAMA-GA-HARA, TOO, EH?
HE SAID THERE'S SOMETHING HE WANTS TO SHOW US...?

Thank you for protecting me, Ebisu, page 125

In English, when speaking to oneself, someone will often use their own name. In Japanese, when speaking to oneself, they will use the first-person pronoun. When little Ebisu addresses his past self, he uses the first-person pronoun *boku*, thus making it very clear to the reader that he still considers his predecessor to be a part of himself.

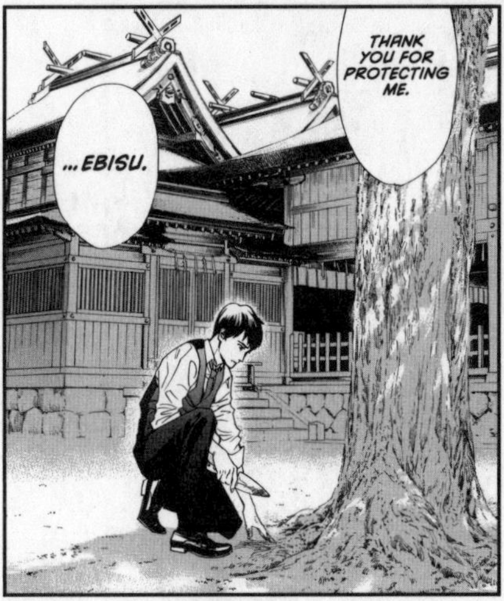
THANK YOU FOR PROTECTING ME.
...EBISU.

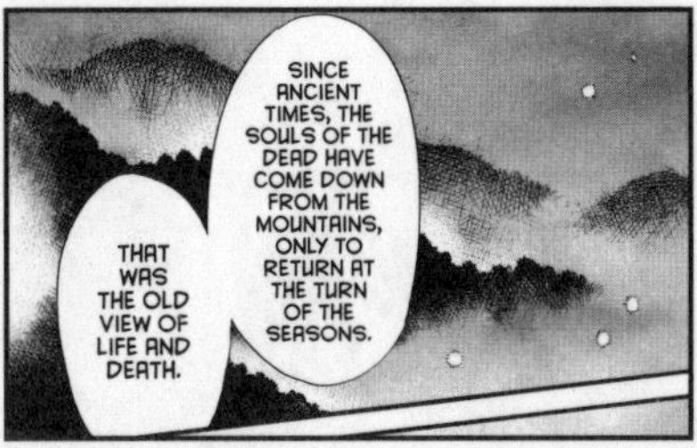
SINCE ANCIENT TIMES, THE SOULS OF THE DEAD HAVE COME DOWN FROM THE MOUNTAINS, ONLY TO RETURN AT THE TURN OF THE SEASONS.
THAT WAS THE OLD VIEW OF LIFE AND DEATH.

The old view of life and death, page 131

Before the Shinto religion was born in Japan, there was a faith known as *sangaku shinkô*, or "mountain worship." As the name suggests, mountains were considered sacred, as the dwelling places of divine spirits (*kami*) and ancestral spirits (*sorei*). As the stray explains, these spirits will come down from the mountains to live with the villagers during certain times of the year, such as to help with the farming before autumn harvest. The term *sorei* is often used to refer to a soul that has lost its individuality and joined a collective of ancestral spirits. This happens after the mourning period with all its memorial services (over a span of at least 33 years in Japan) is officially over.

Kodomo 110 Ban, page 168

110 is the Japanese emergency number for calling the police. This sign, meaning roughly "child 110," indicates that the store displaying it is a refuge for children. If they ever find themselves in trouble and need help, they can wait there safely until the police arrive.

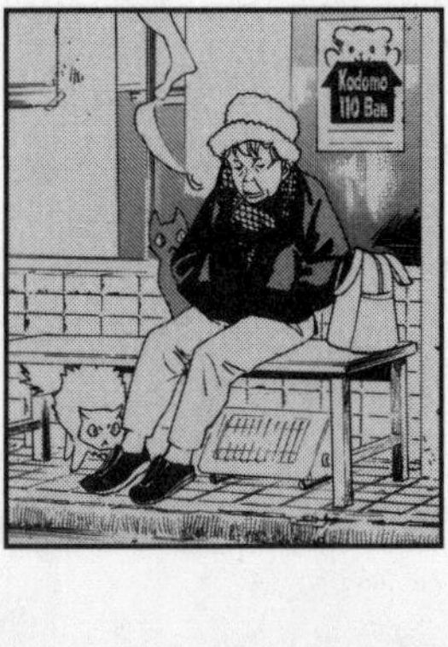
Kodomo 110 Ban

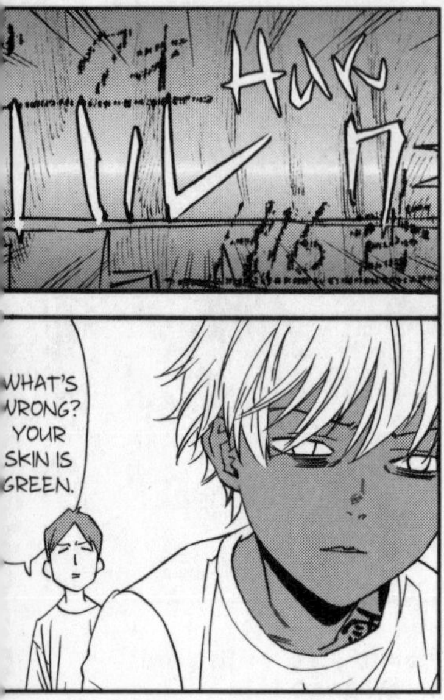
Hulk
WHAT'S RONG? YOUR SKIN IS GREEN.

Haru the Hulk, page 186
Whoever carved these names into the wall for this height chart used *katakana*, which is the Japanese syllabary used for foreign words, and they put a serif on the number 7, making it resemble the *katakana letter* "*ku*." Thus, instead of Haru 7, the engraving looks like it might read "Haruku," which is the Japanese pronunciation of Hulk.

784, page 187
he *kanji* characters used to write the name f Kazuma's most beloved deity are 毘沙門 ₹. Kazuma thought up his PIN by using the umber of brush strokes it takes to write ach symbol.

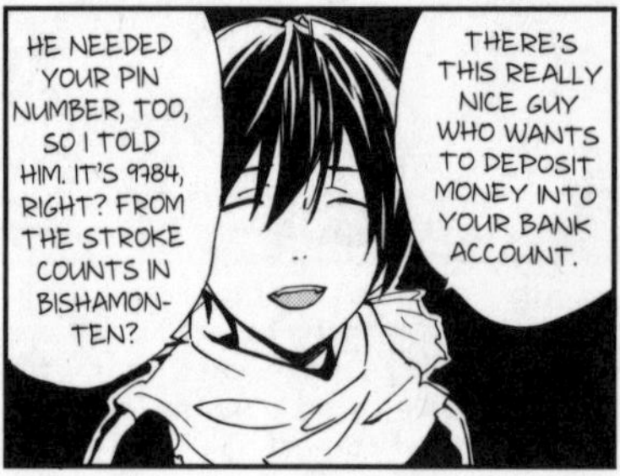
THERE'S THIS REALLY NICE GUY WHO WANTS TO DEPOSIT MONEY INTO YOUR BANK ACCOUNT.
HE NEEDED YOUR PIN NUMBER, TOO, SO I TOLD HIM. IT'S 9784, RIGHT? FROM THE STROKE COUNTS IN BISHAMON-TEN?

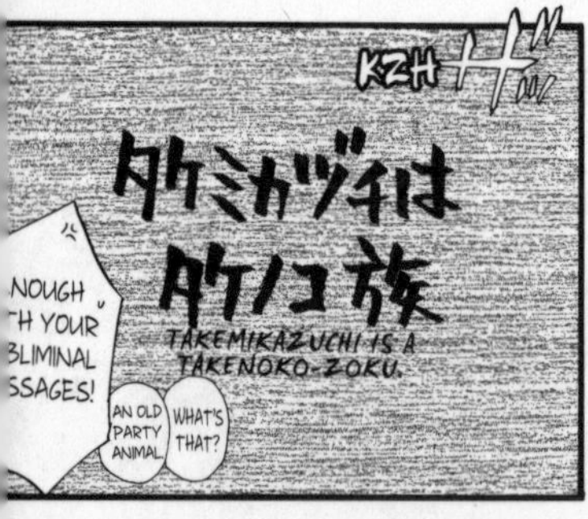
KZH
タケミカヅチは
タケノコ族
TAKEMIKAZUCHI IS A TAKENOKO-ZOKU.
WHAT'S THAT?
AN OLD PARTY ANIMAL
NOUGH TH YOUR BLIMINAL SSAGES!

Takenoko-Zoku, page 189
To add to Ôkuninushi's explanation, Takenoko-Zoku, meaning "bamboo shoot tribe," refers to groups of kids who would dress up in brightly colored clothing (usually loose-fitting jumpsuits) and dance in the streets of Tokyo.

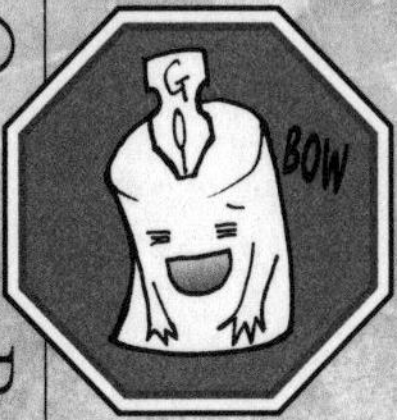
BOW

As it is important to learn of offerings for our rabbit, we have come to know weedy greens quite well. However, the plots with grass are run amok with children playing capture the flag constantly, and it's hot outside. Shocking news this year: The veteran field horsetails are growing over the newly introduced long-headed poppies.
Ah, rhizomes...

Adachitoka

SAINT ☆ YOUNG MEN

A LONG AWAITED ARRIVAL IN PREMIUM 2-IN-1 HARDCOVER

After centuries of hard work, Jesus and Buddha take a break from their
heavenly duties to relax among the people of Japan, and their adventures in this
lighthearted buddy comedy are sure to bring mirth and merriment to all!

"Brilliant…the physical comedy
and facial expressions will
make you literally LOL."
—Sam Humphries
(host of *DC Daily*;
writer, *Green Lanterns*,
Legendary Star-Lord)

THE WORLD OF CLAMP!

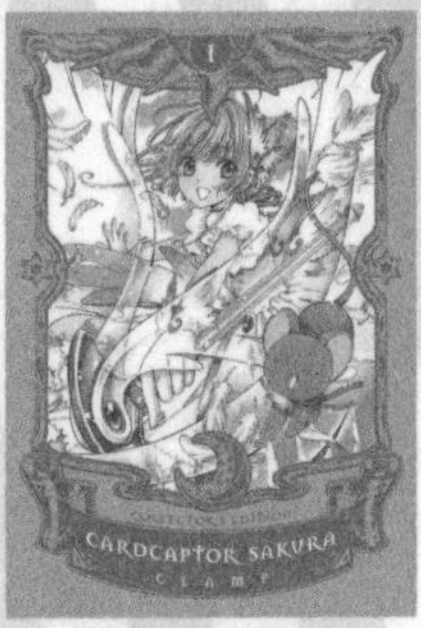
CARDCAPTOR SAKURA
CLAMP
Cardcaptor Sakura Collector's Edition

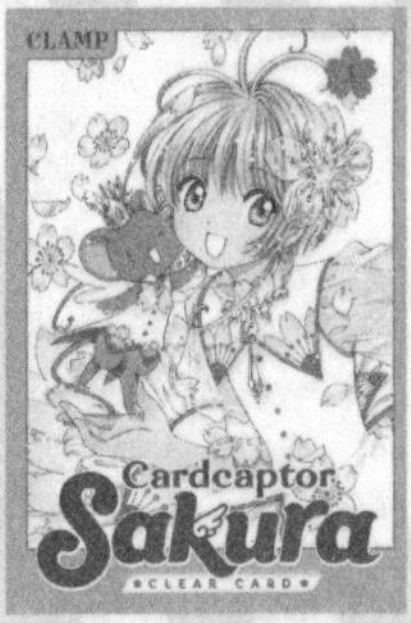
CLAMP
Cardcaptor Sakura
CLEAR CARD
Cardcaptor Sakura: Clear Card

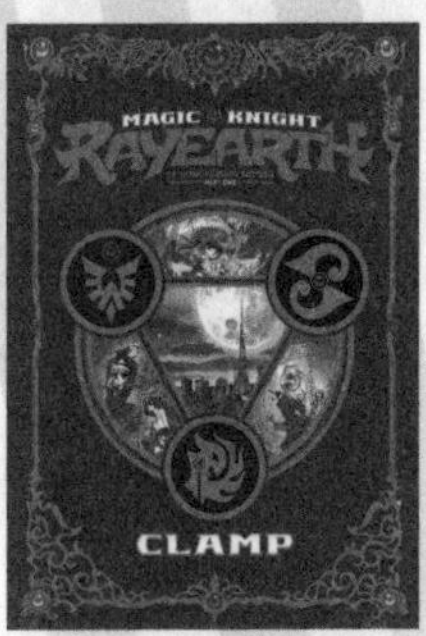
MAGIC KNIGHT
RAYEARTH
CLAMP
Magic Knight Rayearth 25th Anniversary Box Set

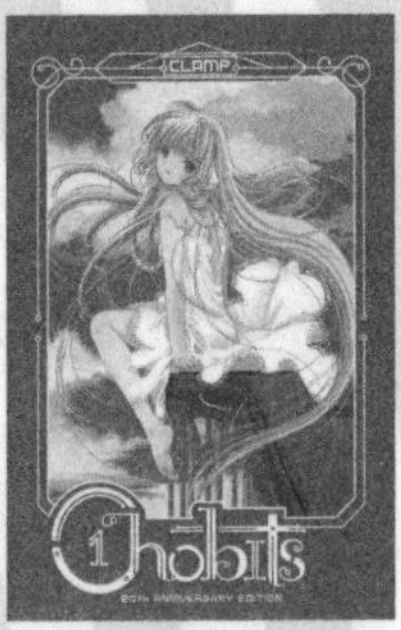
CLAMP
Chobits
Chobits

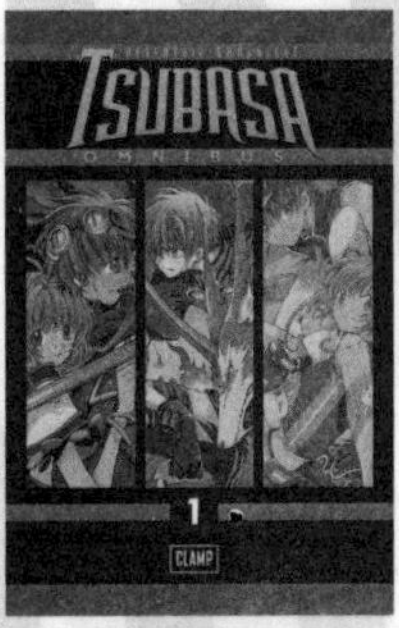
TSUBASA
OMNIBUS
1
CLAMP
TSUBASA Omnibus

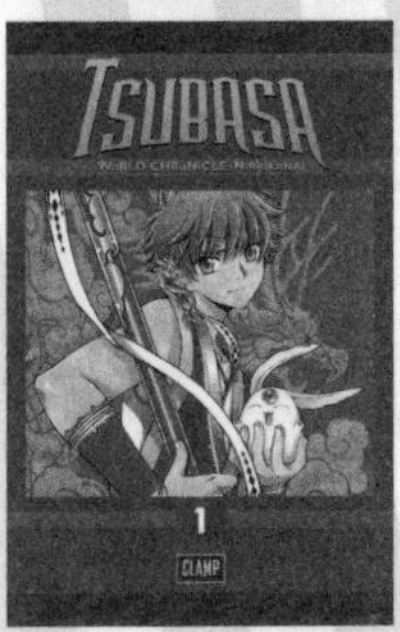
TSUBASA
1
CLAMP
TSUBASA WoRLD CHRoNiCLE

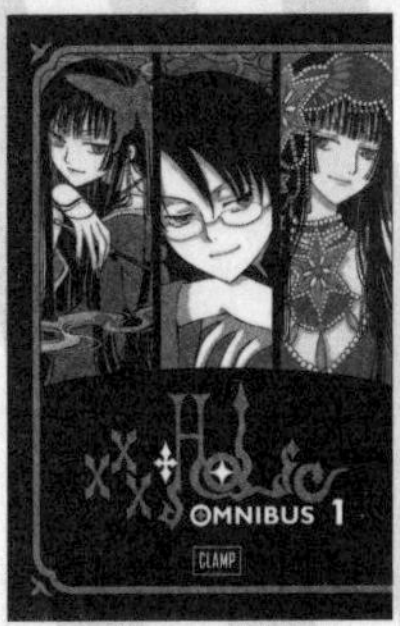
xxxHOLiC
OMNIBUS 1
CLAMP
xxxHOLiC Omnibus

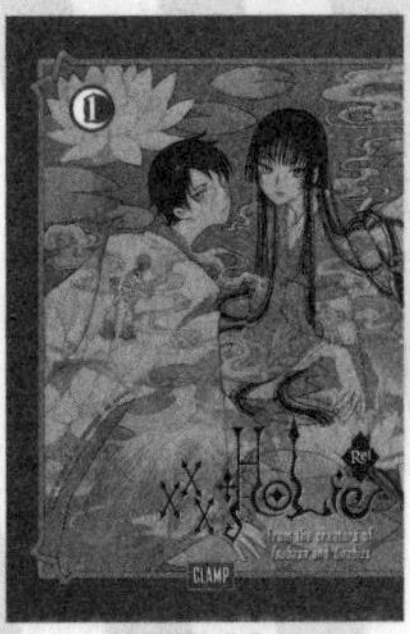
xxxHOLiC
Rei
CLAMP
xxxHOLiC Rei

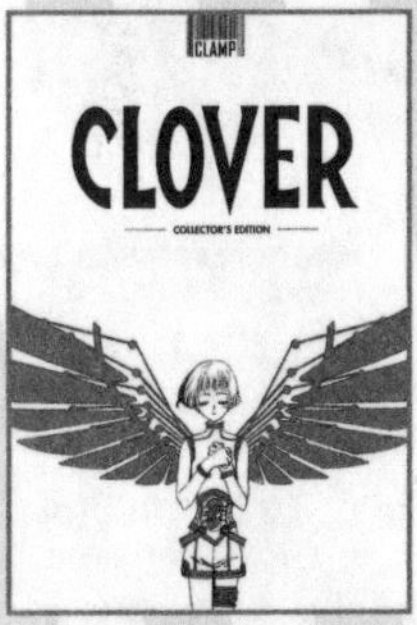
CLAMP
CLOVER
COLLECTOR'S EDITION
CLOVER Collector's Edition

KC KODANSHA COMICS

Kodansha Comics welcomes you to explore the expansive world of CLAMP, the all-female artist collective that has produced some of the most acclaimed manga of the century. Our growing catalog includes icons like *Cardcaptor Sakura* and *Magic Knight Rayearth*, each crafted with CLAMP's one-of-a-kind style and characters!

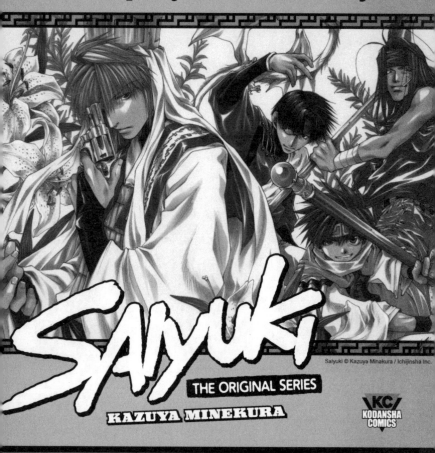

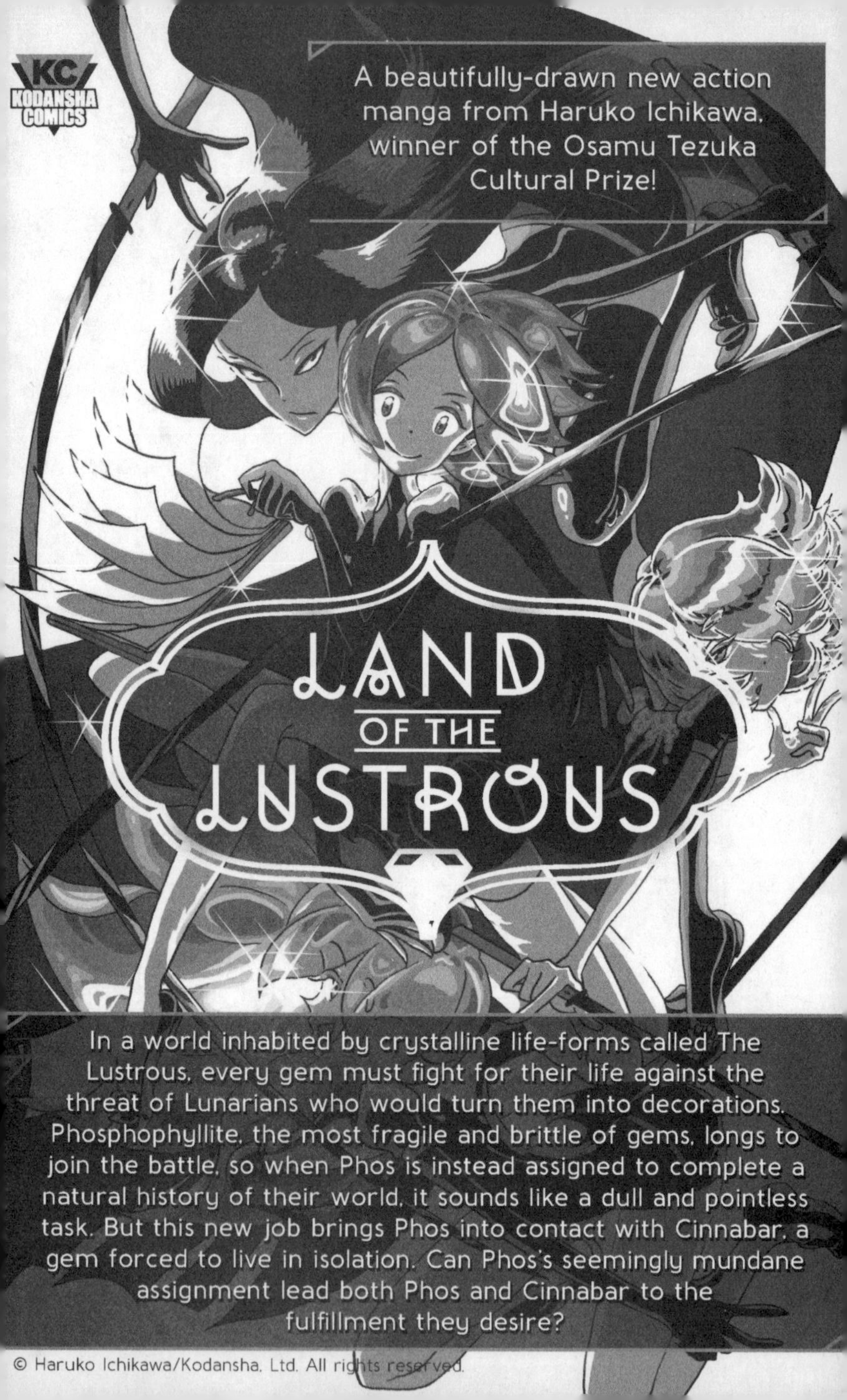
KC KODANSHA COMICS
A beautifully-drawn new action manga from Haruko Ichikawa, winner of the Osamu Tezuka Cultural Prize!
LAND OF THE LUSTROUS
In a world inhabited by crystalline life-forms called The Lustrous, every gem must fight for their life against the threat of Lunarians who would turn them into decorations. Phosphophyllite, the most fragile and brittle of gems, longs to join the battle, so when Phos is instead assigned to complete a natural history of their world, it sounds like a dull and pointless task. But this new job brings Phos into contact with Cinnabar, a gem forced to live in isolation. Can Phos's seemingly mundane assignment lead both Phos and Cinnabar to the fulfillment they desire?
© Haruko Ichikawa/Kodansha, Ltd. All rights reserved.

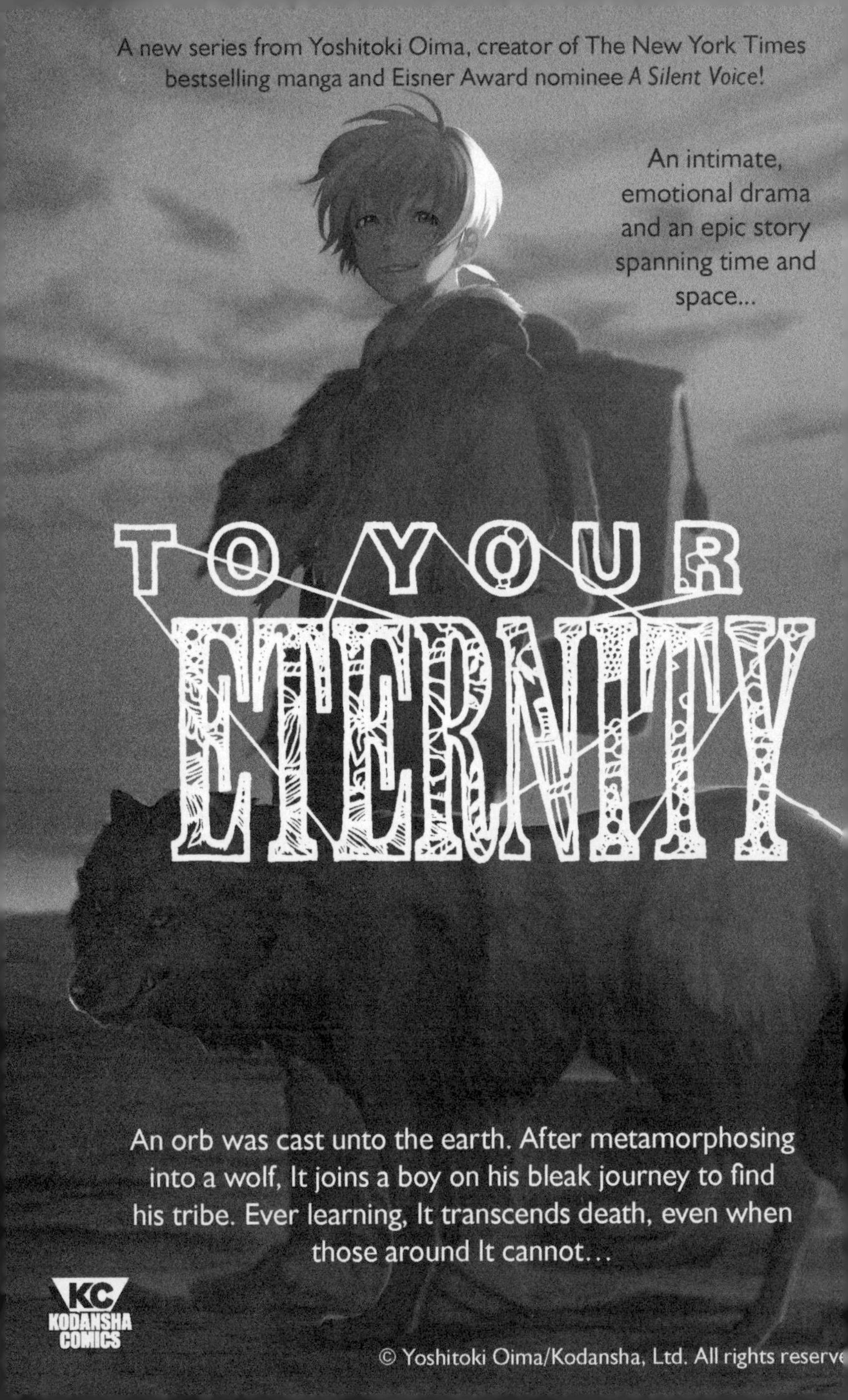
A new series from Yoshitoki Oima, creator of The New York Times bestselling manga and Eisner Award nominee *A Silent Voice*!
An intimate, emotional drama and an epic story spanning time and space...
TO YOUR ETERNITY
An orb was cast unto the earth. After metamorphosing into a wolf, It joins a boy on his bleak journey to find his tribe. Ever learning, It transcends death, even when those around It cannot…
KC KODANSHA COMICS
© Yoshitoki Oima/Kodansha, Ltd. All rights reserve

Magus of the Library

Mitsu Izumi

MITSU IZUMI'S STUNNING ARTWORK BRINGS A FANTASTICAL LITERARY ADVENTURE TO LUSH, THRILLING LIFE!

Young Theo adores books, but the prejudice and hatred of his village keeps them ever out of his reach. Then one day, he chances to meet Sedona, a traveling librarian who works for the great library of Aftzaak, City of Books, and his life changes forever...

◄ KAMOME ►
SHIRAHAMA

Witch Hat Atelier

A magical manga adventure for fans of Disney and Studio Ghibli!

Witch Hat Atelier © Kamome Shirahama / Kodansha

The magical adventure that took Japan by storm is finally here, from acclaimed DC and Marvel cover artist Kamome Shirahama!

In a world where everyone takes wonders like magic spells and dragons for granted, Coco is a girl with a simple dream: She wants to be a witch. But everybody knows magicians are born, not made, and Coco was not born with a gift for magic. Resigned to her un-magical life, Coco is about to give up on her dream to become a witch...until the day she meets Qifrey, a mysterious, traveling magician. After secretly seeing Qifrey perform magic in a way she's never seen before, Coco soon learns what everybody "knows" might not be the truth, and discovers that her magical dream may not be as far away as it may seem...

KC
KODANSHA
COMICS

From the creator of *The Ancient Magus' Bride* comes a supernatural action manga in the vein of *Fullmetal Alchemist*!

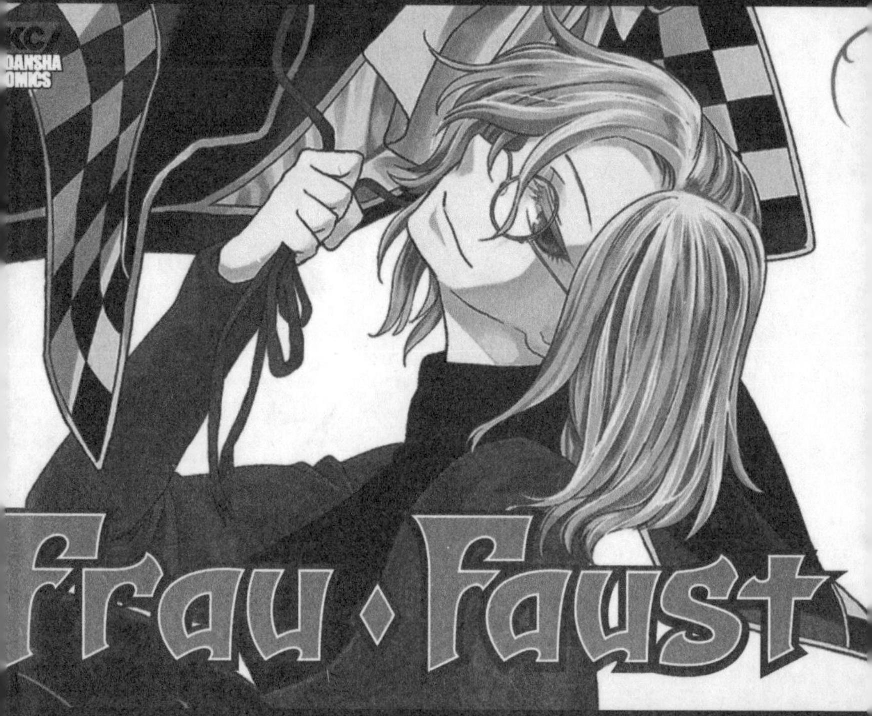
Frau · Faust

More than a century after an eccentric scholar made an infamous deal with a devil, the story of Faust has passed into legend. However, the true Faust is not the stuffy, professorial man known in fairy tales, but a charismatic, bespectacled woman named Johanna Faust, who happens to still be alive. Searching for pieces of her long-lost demon, Johanna passes through a provincial town, where she saves a young boy named Marion from a criminal's fate. In exchange, she asks a simple favor of Marion, but Marion soon finds himself intrigued by the peculiar Doctor Faust and joins her on her journey. Thus begins the strange and wonderful adventures of *Frau Faust*!

Young characters and steampunk setting, like *Howl's Moving Castle* and *Battle Angel Alita*

Beyond the Clouds © 2018 Nicke / Ki-oon

A boy with a talent for machines and a mysterious girl whose wings he's fixed will take you beyond the clouds! In the tradition of the high-flying, resonant adventure stories of Studio Ghibli comes a gorgeous tale about the longing of young hearts for adventure and friendship!

EDENS ZERO
エデンズゼロ

HIRO MASHIMA IS BACK! JOIN THE CREATOR OF *FAIRY TAIL*
AS HE TAKES TO THE STARS FOR ANOTHER THRILLING SAGA!

A high-flying space adventure! All the steadfast friendship and
wild fighting you've been waiting for...IN SPACE!

At Granbell Kingdom, an abandoned amusement park, Shiki has lived his
entire life among machines. But one day, Rebecca and her cat companion
Happy appear at the park's front gates. Little do these newcomers know
that this is the first human contact Granbell has had in a hundred years! As
Shiki stumbles his way into making new friends, his former neighbors stir at
an opportunity for a robo-rebellion... And when his old homeland becomes
too dangerous, Shiki must join Rebecca and Happy on their spaceship and
escape into the boundless cosmos.

A new series from the creator of *Soul Eater*, the megahit manga and anime seen on Toonami!

"Fun and lively... a great start!"
-Adventures in Poor Taste

FIRE FORCE

By Atsushi Ohkubo

The city of Tokyo is plagued by a deadly phenomenon: spontaneous human combustion! Luckily, a special team is there to quench the inferno: The Fire Force! The fire soldiers at Special Fire Cathedral are about to get a unique addition. Enter Shinra, a boy who possesses the power to run at the speed of a rocket, leaving behind the famous "devil's footprints" (and destroying his shoes in the process). Can Shinra and his colleagues discover the source of this strange epidemic before the city burns to ashes?

Noragami: Stray God 22 is a work of fiction. Names, characters, places, and incidents are the products of the author's imagination or are used fictitiously. Any resemblance to actual events, locales, or persons, living or dead, is entirely coincidental.

A Kodansha Comics Trade Paperback Original

Published in the United States by Kodansha Comics, an imprint of Kodansha USA Publishing, LLC, New York.

Publication rights for this English edition arranged through Kodansha Ltd., Tokyo.

First published in Japan in 2020 by Kodansha Ltd., Tokyo.

ISBN 978-1-63236-991-8

Printed in the United States of America.

www.kodanshacomics.com

9 8 7 6 5 4 3 2 1
Translation: Alethea Nibley & Athena Nibley
Lettering: Lys Blakeslee
Editing: Haruko Hashimoto
Kodansha Comics edition cover design by Phil Balsman

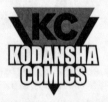

Publisher: Kiichiro Sugawara

Director of publishing services: Ben Applegate
Associate director of operations: Stephen Pakula
Publishing services managing editor: Noelle Webster
Assistant production manager: Emi Lotto, Angela Zurlo